John Ross Browne

Yusef: or, The Journey of the Frangi. A Crusade in the East

John Ross Browne

Yusef: or, The Journey of the Frangi. A Crusade in the East

ISBN/EAN: 9783744746274

Printed in Europe, USA, Canada, Australia, Japan

Cover: Foto ©Andreas Hilbeck / pixelio.de

More available books at **www.hansebooks.com**

YUSEF;

OR,

THE JOURNEY OF THE FRANGI.

A

CRUSADE IN THE EAST.

BY

J. ROSS BROWNE,

AUTHOR OF "ETCHINGS OF A WHALING-CRUISE," "REPORT OF THE DEBATES IN THE CONVENTION OF CALIFORNIA," AND "CRUSOE LIFE: A NARRATIVE OF ADVENTURES IN JUAN FERNANDEZ."

With Illustrations.

NEW YORK:

HARPER & BROTHERS, PUBLISHERS,
329 & 331 PEARL STREET,
FRANKLIN SQUARE.
1872.

TO THE

HON. ROBERT J. WALKER,

AS A TOKEN OF ADMIRATION FOR HIS GENIUS AS A STATESMAN,
ESTEEM FOR HIS VIRTUES IN PRIVATE LIFE, AND GRAT-
ITUDE FOR HIS MANY ACTS OF KINDNESS
TO THE AUTHOR,

THIS VOLUME

Is respectfully Inscribed.

PREFACE.

An essayist in the Reflector tells us that "Columbus can not be more famous than a man who describes the Temple of Jerusalem." Now, although I have a great desire to be as famous as Columbus, it is due to the reader to state at the outset that he will find very little about temples in this volume. The only ground upon which I can aspire to such a distinction is, in having avoided, as far as practicable, every thing that has given fame to those who have preceded me. If there be any important fact, therefore, in scriptural or classical history, that the reader is disappointed in not finding in these pages, I beg that he will adopt the suggestion of my friend and fellow-traveler, Dr. Mendoza, and "remain tranquil for the present." There is no telling what the future may bring forth, or to what extremes of research a man may be driven by the force of circumstances.

Part of this narrative was originally written in the form of letters to the "National Intelligencer," chiefly for the amusement of my friends in Washington. The style was rather more familiar than the usual contributions to that journal, and certainly more so than I would have chosen to adopt, had I thought seriously at the time of publishing the letters in book form. That I considered it probable I might make use of the material at some future period, I frankly admit; but in looking over my notes and the mass of sketches thus brought together, the task of re-writing, and making any thing of them in the way of a serious work on Palestine, seemed too formidable to be undertaken by one who has scarcely yet commenced his travels.

Such as the sketches are, I have chosen to put them together in the form of a connected narrative; and they are now presented to the public, with such illustrations from my own portfolio, drawn on wood by competent artists, as I thought would give them any additional value.

It will be seen that I have not felt it to be my duty to make a desponding pilgrimage through the Holy Land; for upon a careful perusal of the Scriptures, I can find nothing said against a cheerful frame of mind. If there be any person, however, who may think that a traveler has no right to be lively in that part of the world, I beg that he will suspend his judgment till I visit Jerusalem again; in which event he may depend upon it I shall use every exertion to be depressed in spirits, and produce something uncommonly heavy and substantial.

In regard to the apparent egotism of writing so much about one's self, I can not do better than quote the words of Thomas de Quincey: " It is not offered as deriving any part of what interest it may have from myself as the person concerned in it. If the particular experience selected is really interesting, in virtue of its own circumstances, then it matters not to *whom* it happened. Let him [the reader] read the sketch as belonging to one who wishes to be profoundly anonymous." In this view, should there be any thing that strikes the reader as very good in the volume, he can not do better than to look at the title-page, and give credit accordingly; but where it appears to him that there is any thing very bad in it, he will greatly oblige me by regarding it as the production of the gentleman who figures in the conversations with Yusef.

Written without any other purpose than that of describing faithfully what fell under my own observation, it may be that the design is not sufficiently apparent; yet if, on the whole, from the general tenor, a more liberal feeling should be encouraged respecting the customs and prejudices of the uncivilized world, and a clearer sense of our own weaknesses, the book will not have been written in vain. There may be a moral also in the circumstances under which the journey was performed.

Ten years ago, after having rambled all over the United States—six hundred miles of the distance on foot, and sixteen hundred in a flat-boat—I set out from Washington with fifteen dollars, to make a tour of the East. I got as far east as New York, where the last dollar and the prospect of reaching Jerusalem came to a conclusion at the same time. Sooner than return home, after having made so good a beginning, I shipped before the mast in a whaler, and did some service, during a voyage to the Indian Ocean, in the way of scrubbing decks and catching whales. A mutiny occurred at the island of Zanzibar, where I sold myself out of the vessel for thirty dollars and a chest of old clothes; and spent three months very pleasantly at the consular residence, in the vicinity of his Highness the Imaum of Muscat. On my return to Washington, I labored hard for four years on Bank statistics and Treasury reports, by which time, in order to take the new administration by the fore-lock, I determined to start for the East again. The only chance I had of getting there was, to accept of an appointment as third lieutenant in the Revenue service, and go to California, and thence to Oregon, where I was to report for duty. On the voyage to Rio, a difficulty occurred between the captain and the passengers of the vessel, and we were detained there nearly a month. I took part with the rebels, because I believed them to be right. The captain was deposed by the American consul, and the command of the vessel was offered to me; but having taken an active part against the late captain, I could not with propriety accept the offer. A whaling captain, who had lost his vessel near Buenos Ayres, was placed in the command, and we proceeded on our voyage round Cape Horn. After a long and dreary passage we made the island of Juan Fernandez. In company with ten of the passengers, I left the ship seventy miles out at sea, and went ashore in a small boat, for the purpose of gathering up some tidings in regard to my old friend Robinson Crusoe. What befell us on that memorable expedition is fully set forth in a narrative recently published in "Harper's Magazine." Subsequently we spent some time in Lima, "the City of the Kings." It was my fortune to arrive penniless in California, and to find, by way of consolation, that a reduction had been made by Congress in the number of revenue vessels, and that my services in that branch of public business were no longer required. While thinking seriously of taking in washing at six dollars a dozen, or devoting the remainder of my days to mule-driving as a profession, I was unexpectedly elevated to the position of post-office agent; and went about the country for the purpose of making postmasters. I only made one—the post-master of San Jose. After that, the Convention called by General Riley met at Monterey, and I was appointed to report the debates on the formation of the State Constitution. For this I received a sum that enabled me to return to Washington, and start for the East again. There was luck in the third attempt, for, as may be seen, I got there at last, having thus visited the four continents, and traveled by sea and land a distance of a hundred thousand miles, or more than four times round the world, on the scanty earnings of my own head and hands.

If there be any moral in the book, therefore, it is this: that there is no great difficulty in traveling all over the world, when one sets about it with a determination to do it, and keeps trying till he succeeds; that there is no position in life disreputable or degrading while self-respect remains; and nothing impossible that has ever been done by man. Let him who thirsts for knowledge go out upon the broad face of the earth, and he will find that it is not out of books alone that he can get it; let him make use of the eyes that God has given him, and he will see more in the world's unwritten revelations than the mind of man hath conceived.

"Our doubts are traitors,
And make us lose the good we oft might win
By fearing to attempt."

J. R. B.

WASHINGTON, D.C., *February*, 1853.

EASTERN RUINS.

CONTENTS.

A GIRA THROUGH SICILY.

	PAGE
CHAPTER I.—Palermo	13
CHAPTER II.—Catacombs of Palermo	20
CHAPTER III.—Journey to Catania	28
CHAPTER IV.—Ascent of Mount Etna	35
CHAPTER V.—The Crater	41
CHAPTER VI.—A Quarrel with the Ancients	53
CHAPTER VII.—On the Road to Syracuse	58
CHAPTER VIII.—Syracuse	66
CHAPTER IX.—Taormina	73

A CRUSADE IN THE EAST.

CHAPTER X.—The Breach	80
CHAPTER XI.—Athens	85
CHAPTER XII.—Syra	101
CHAPTER XIII.—Smyrna	107
CHAPTER XIV.—Constantinople	114
CHAPTER XV.—A Visit to the Bazaars	129
CHAPTER XVI.—Turkish Beauties	141
CHAPTER XVII.—Manners and Customs	149
CHAPTER XVIII.—Babel Revived	164
CHAPTER XIX.—The English Tourist	167
CHAPTER XX.—The Syrian Dragoman	174
CHAPTER XXI.—My Horse Saladin	182
CHAPTER XXII.—The Arab Story Teller	192
CHAPTER XXIII.—The Cedars of Lebanon	197

CONTENTS.

	PAGE
CHAPTER XXIV.—BAALBEK	206
CHAPTER XXV.—YUSEF DANCES THE RAAS	218
CHAPTER XXVI.—A SOCIAL CHAT WITH YUSEF	227
CHAPTER XXVII.—THE GREEK BISHOP	232
CHAPTER XXVIII.—THE ARAB MULETEER	240
CHAPTER XXIX.—FROM BAALBEK TO DAMASCUS	244
CHAPTER XXX.—DAMASCUS	254
CHAPTER XXXI.—BATHS OF DAMASCUS	263
CHAPTER XXXII.—THE AMERICAN MISSIONARIES	272
CHAPTER XXXIII.—THE BATTLE OF THE MULETEERS	276
CHAPTER XXXIV.—GRAND SECRET OF HUMAN HAPPINESS	285
CHAPTER XXXV.—THE MILL OF MALAHA	296
CHAPTER XXXVI.—THE REBEL SHEIK	306
CHAPTER XXXVII.—THE SYRIAN HORSES	310
CHAPTER XXXVIII.—THE SEA OF GALILEE	319
CHAPTER XXXIX.—JOURNEY TO NAZARETH	326
CHAPTER XL.—NAZARETH	330
CHAPTER XLI.—A GAZELLE HUNT	335
CHAPTER XLII.—DJENIN	343
CHAPTER XLIII.—ADVENTURE WITH THE SAMARITANS	348
CHAPTER XLIV.—NABLOUS	352
CHAPTER XLV.—A STRIKING SCENE	354
CHAPTER XLVI.—JERUSALEM	359
CHAPTER XLVII.—ARAB GUARD TO THE DEAD SEA	366
CHAPTER XLVIII.—THE DEAD SEA AND THE JORDAN	371
CHAPTER XLIX.—THRILLING ALARM IN JERICHO	378
CHAPTER L.—CHRISTMAS NIGHT IN BETHLEHEM	387
CHAPTER LI.—CROSSING THE RIVERS	391
CHAPTER LII.—THE DESOLATE CITY	394
CHAPTER LIII.—A SERIOUS CHARGE	398
CHAPTER LIV.—AN EXTRAORDINARY AFFAIR	404
CHAPTER LV.—RISE, DECLINE, AND FALL OF YUSEF BADRA	410

LIST OF ILLUSTRATIONS.

[FROM SKETCHES BY THE AUTHOR.]

EASTERN RUINS. *Frontispiece.*

	PAGE
THE MUMMIES	21
CATACOMBS OF PALERMO	24
SICILIAN MONK	33
CASA DEGL' INGLESA	44
DESCENT OF MOUNT ETNA	51
SICILIAN POSTILLION	62
SICILIAN GENDARMES	64
SICILIAN BEGGARS	68
COUNSEL FOR THE ACCUSED	75
AMPHITHEATRE OF TAORMINA	78
CONVENT NEAR ATHENS	97
SMYRNA FROM THE ANCHORAGE	107
PILGRIMS ON SHIPBOARD	116
A BUSINESS TRANSACTION	127
THE HAMIL	131
SHOPKEEPERS	138
TURKISH BEAUTY	143
GENERAL VIEW OF CONSTANTINOPLE	152
THE DANCING DERVISHES	155
THE HOWLING DERVISHES	158
ENGLISH TRAVELER RECOGNIZING A VENUS AND HERCULES	168
TOWN OF RHODES	171
VIEW IN LARNICA	172
YUSEF	178
SALADIN	185
SALADIN IN ACTION	188
BEN-HOZAIN	192
CASTLE OF DJBEL	201
COLUMN IN THE DESERT	210
YUSEF DANCING THE RAAS	223

LIST OF ILLUSTRATIONS.

	PAGE
THE ARAB MULETEER	240
A GENTLEMAN OF ELEGANT LEISURE	243
ANCIENT ARCH IN DAMASCUS	260
IBRAHIM	261
BATHS OF DAMASCUS	268
TAKING IT EASY	285
THE MILL OF MALAHA	303
TOKINA	318
BATHS OF TIBERIAS	325
JERUSALEM	359
MOHAMMEDAN SEPULCHRE	363
PILGRIMS TO JERUSALEM	367
THE ARAB GUARD	370
CROSSING A RIVER	391
GREEK BISHOP	39
VILLAGE OF EL MUKHALID	394
KAISABIYEH	397
RUINS NEAR TANTURA	403
THE END OF YUSEF	421

YUSEF.

A GIRA THROUGH SICILY.

CHAPTER I.

PALERMO.

It was rather early in the season to start for the East September was not yet over. I had thoroughly explored Naples and the neighborhood; and the only question was, how to dispose of the fine weather. Lounging about the quay one afternoon it occurred to me that a trip to Pàlermo would be just the thing. There were signs pasted up every where of an immense steamer, of wonderful horse-power, bound for that very port. I walked into the first Bureau (in Naples, every office is a Bureau): the same large steamer was over the door under full way, with a heavy head of steam, for Palermo. The name of the steamer was printed on the paddle-box in big golden letters; it was the Ercolano. When I told the gentleman, who was waxing the points of his mustache behind the counter, that I wanted a passage in the Ercolano, he shook his head despondingly, and applied some more wax to one of the points. This induced me to go out again and look at the sign. There certainly was no mistake about the name, and I endeavored to make him understand that it was a ticket I wanted for a passage in the steamer represented upon that sign. He applied some additional wax to the other point of his mustache, shook his head despondingly again, and, as well as I could understand him, said he was very sorry; that he didn't know any thing about such a steamer; perhaps it was at number seventy-one, two doors above. I went into number seventy-one, two doors above, and was told by a small but very imposing gentleman, with a brass band on his cap, that seventy-one was the bureau of the French steamer; it didn't go to Palermo; it went to Marseilles, and he would be very happy to have me landed there; perhaps the Bureau of the Neapolitan steamer was number seventy-six, which I would find somewhere on the same street, about eight or ten doors above—or below. I walked up and down a long time, till I was fortunate enough to find number seventy-six. The gentleman in that Bureau was smoking a cigar, which he continued to smoke in silence for two minutes; at the expiration of which time he calmly removed it, and said in reply to my question concerning the Ercolano, that there *was* such a steamer; it was called the Ercolano; it was a Neapolitan steamer; it was bound for Palermo; the proper place to apply for passage was at the Neapolitan Bureau. He was not exactly certain where the Neapolitan Bureau was, but thought it was number sixty-nine; that was his impression—sixty-nine. I told him that I had already applied at sixty-nine; to which he responded by a shrug of the shoulders, a pinch of snuff, and some strange contortions of the face, as if he had accidentally swallowed the snuff-box. It may have been that my manner of speaking the Italian was not clear, or that my understanding of the Neapolitan was less so; at all events I could make nothing of these signs, so I returned to Bureau sixty-nine. There were some other officers in sixty-nine this time; and, after some consultation, they arrived at the conclusion that it was the Bureau of the Neapolitan steamer for Palermo. I offered money for my passage; but they refused to take it, or to give me a ticket without it; they said something else was necessary, my passport and certain *visés* and *cartes*. Next morning I got my passport and the *visés* and *cartes*, and they still refused to give me a ticket. Certain other *visés* and *cartes* from the Polizia were necessary. I went to the Polizia and got certain other *visés* and *cartes*, and they still refused to let me have a ticket; a certain word was omitted in one of the *vises.* I went all over the city of Naples in search of all the authorities that were concerned in the insertion of that word, and eventually got it written down in black and white, with all the additional stamps that were necessary to give it validity. This time they reluctantly conceded that the passport was *viséd* in due form; that all the documents were correct; that I could get a ticket by waiting a while until the officers were served. The Bureau was quite filled with Neapolitan officers, who were all very much covered up with red cloth epaulets, tin buttons, brass sword-cases, and general embroidery. I waited at least an hour, and then, by the sheer force of perseverance, prevailed upon the gentleman who was engaged in making porcupine quills of his mustache, to cease his labors one moment, and give me a ticket. All the harm I wish that man is, that these quills may be broken off before his personal beauty produces such an effect as to cause any unfortunate lady to marry him; for I am certain if ever he gets a wife, they will run her through the eyes in less than a week.

On the 30th day of September, 1851, in virtue of all these proceedings, I left Naples, in the Neapolitan steamer, for Palermo. The Ercolano was a good specimen of the Italian steam service. It had nothing like the amount of horse-power that I expected from the bills; nor was it in any respect a good steamer; but it afforded an excellent example of what a nation already distinguished in ancient art, may attain in the way of modern art by intercourse with less classical countries. Without any exception it was the smallest, and dirtiest, and worst-contrived craft, to be moved by steam and paddles, that it was ever my fortune to behold. There were on board two hundred and fifty Neapolitan soldiers and officers, on their way to Sicily, for the better protection of that remote portion of the Neapolitan kingdom. After we got well out to sea, there came on a gale, and every one of these soldiers, and every officer who commanded them, fell dreadfully sea-sick; and thus two hundred and fifty fighting characters, armed to the teeth, were in the brief space of a few hours cast down and mixed together upon the decks, at the mercy of any body who chose to attack them. I verily believe that had I been a person of blood-thirsty disposition I could have slain them all with a bodkin. Such, however, was not my nature. The poor little fellows looked so forlorn, so small and dirty, so sorry they were going to an unknown country, twenty hours distant from their native land; so unlike men who would ever kill any body, that I was exceedingly moved, and took occasion, when the captain of the boat was not looking, to give one of them a pinch of snuff. My natural impulse was to give them snuff all round, but they were so piled up over the decks, the heads, and heels, and mustaches, and arms, and legs in such a state of confusion that it was utterly impossible to move without stumbling over a misplaced limb, and falling upon a sick man.

Thank heaven, the hills of Bagheria at last hove in sight. I was glad enough to see land, as well on my own account as that of the soldiers, who certainly could not have survived the horrors of the sea another night. The voyage from Naples to Palermo is usually performed in twenty hours. Owing to the rough weather, and the want of additional horse-power, it took us twenty-four. We were six hours more getting ashore, which made it thirty. The reason of this delay was, that the soldiers had to be landed first. Then the captain had to go ashore and have a talk with the officers of the port; then he had to come on board again and walk up and down the deck and smoke his cigar; then the passengers had to get certain *cartes*, and some of them, who were going beyond Palermo, their passports under certain restrictions; then the officer of the customs had to come on board and have a talk with the captain; then he had to go on shore again, and the health officer had to come on board; then, after all the officers were done going on shore and coming on board, the baggage had to be properly distributed; and, after the baggage was distributed, and every thing apparently all right, there was an additional delay of two hours for the purpose of showing the passengers that they were in the hands of persons high in authority, who would permit them to land, as a matter of favor, whenever it became apparent that the public interests would allow such a course to be pursued.

Next to Naples, the harbor of Palermo is perhaps the most beautiful in the Mediterranean. Indeed, many consider it quite equal in picturesque effect to Naples; for, although it has not Mount Vesuvius, or the breadth and extent of shore line, yet the eye comprehends more at a glance, and a nearer approach is permitted without destroying the scenic beauty of the mountains and villas. At a sufficient distance to embrace a complete view of Naples and its environs, the city is almost lost; but the finest view of Palermo is just opposite the town, within a mile or two. The harbor forms a beautiful crescent, surrounded by hills covered with verdure throughout the greater part of the year; villas and orange groves adorn every prominent point; rich gardens lie along the shores; vessels of many nations float sleepily on the smooth waters of the bay; fishing-boats, crowded with sunburnt crews, ply merrily through the flashing brine; and along the wharves groups of swarthy sailors, quite like the piratical-looking fellows you see in the French prints, are constantly lounging, smoking, chatting in strange tongues, and casting sly glances at the Sicilian belles, who look like operatic chorus-singers; and then there are pale Italians without number, and occasional Greeks; with a sprinkling of American and fresh-looking English captains, to give variety and animation to the scene. There is an aspect of business activity about the streets and shops of Palermo, not a little cheering after one has been mouldering for some time among old ruins and cities of by-gone prosperity. Yet Palermo is not what it might be under a judicious system of government. I hold myself in readiness to apologize for the remark, when called upon, to his Majesty the King of the two Sicilies, and to declare, if required, that the Neapolitan States are well governed; that the people are well governed; that I never saw so many soldiers and so much governing in all my life. Every man seems to be individually governed, and so careful is his Majesty of the faithful administration of the laws and the personal security of his subjects, that the ramifications of government extend into every family circle, and wind every body up as in a cobweb. The stranger who lands at Palermo, and succeeds in getting through the Polizia, will respect good government all the rest of his life. I have a very pleasing impression of the officer in attendance there. He opened my knapsack when he heard me speak English, because he knew I must be an Englishman to address him in that language; he opened my letters one by one and carefully read them, commencing at the signatures and ending at the dates; and when he saw that I was not Mr. Gladstone, and had no printed documents for private circulation among the people of Sicily, he gave me a kindly nod and let me pass. Now, I depend upon that officer, as a man of honor, never to divulge the contents of my letters—especially one that was written in German and some private memoranda in shorthand.

The streets of Palermo are wider than those of the principal cities in Italy, and at night the shops present a very cheerful appearance. Cafés abound in all the public places, but there are none equal to the cafés in Florence. I visited during my stay the magnificent villa of the Marquis Fourche, which is embellished in the style of a Pompeiian palace, with fountains and interior decorations designed strictly according to the antique models found in the ruins of Pompeii. The mosaic marble saloons, frescoes, and general arrangement of the chambers, as also the style of the furniture, afford a very good idea of Pompeii in its days of splendor. It was a festa day in Palermo, so I went to all the churches worth seeing, and heard some good music at the Santa Catherina. Coming from Italy, I was surfeited with sight-seeing of this kind, but I still found much to interest me in Palermo, where something of a different architectural order may be seen.

With respect to the fine arts in Palermo, of which the Marquis of Artala, in his Guide to Sicily, speaks in enthusiastic terms, I must confess I saw nothing of a high order of excellence. He dwells with particular admiration on the magnificent statuary which he says adorns the public promenades. I believe I thoroughly explored Palermo and its

environs, but I saw no magnificent statuary; and was at
length obliged to come to the conclusion that great allowance
must be made for the florid imagination of gentlemen who
write guide-books. Often have I walked for miles through
the dusty streets of an Italian city, baking myself into an
Egyptian mummy under a burning sun, to see some exquisite
gem of art, and when I reached the place found a stick or a
stone, or an old daub of a painting, that I am free to confess
I would never have recognized as the work of a master-hand
had I not been told so. The statuary in the churches of
Palermo is generally exceedingly bad; the paintings are of
very little merit, most of them being disgusting illustrations
of scenes that never existed in the Scriptures or any where
else, badly drawn, badly painted, and in the worst possible
taste. In one of the churches I was introduced with great
solemnity to a picture of the Madonna, which was carefully
covered to preserve it from the vulgar gaze. I paid two
carlini for the privilege of seeing it. Judge of my astonishment when the grave old sexton drew back the curtain and
revealed to my wondering eyes the dingy features of an old
black woman, with a silver crown on her forehead, that
made her skin look a good deal like darkness visible. The
pupils of her eyes were gilt with gold, and her eyebrows were
radiant with precious stones. Her dress was of tawdry lace,
glowing with little patchwork of silver paper; and altogether
she was the most extraordinary object I ever saw; yet the
old sexton bowed to her reverentially and said she was a
great work of art.

CHAPTER II.

CATACOMBS OF PALERMO.

Chief among the wonders of Palermo are the Catacombs of the Capuchin Convent, near the Porta d'Ossuna. It is said to be a place of great antiquity; many of the bodies have been preserved in it for centuries, and still retain much of their original freshness. Entering the ancient and ruinous court of the convent, distant about a mile from the city, I was conducted by a ghostly-looking monk through some dark passages to the subterranean apartments of the dead. It was not my first visit to a place of this kind, but I must confess the sight was rather startling. It was like a revel of the dead—a horrible, grinning, ghastly exhibition of skeleton forms, sightless eyes, and shining teeth, jaws distended, and bony hands outstretched ; heads without bodies, and bodies without heads—the young, the old, the brave, the once beautiful and gay, all mingled in the ghastly throng. I walked through long subterranean passages, lined with the dead on both sides ; with a stealthy and measured tread I stepped, for they seemed to stare at the intrusion, and their skeleton fingers vibrated as if yearning to grasp the living in their embrace. Long rows of upright niches are cut into the walls on each side ; in every niche a skeleton form stands erect as in life, habited in a robe of black ; the face, hands, and feet naked, withered, and of an ashy hue; the grizzled beards still hanging in tufts from the jaws, and in the recent cases the hair still clinging to the skull, but matted and dry. To each corpse is attached a label upon which is written the name and the date of decease, and a cross or the image of the Saviour.

Soon recovering from the shock of the first impression, I

was struck with the wonderful variety and marked expression of character in the faces and forms around me. There were progressive dates of death, extending from remote centuries up to the present period, the niches being so arranged as to admit of a regular order of deposit. Many of the bodies stood erect, as if just lifted from the death-bed; the faces colorless, and the horrible agonies of dissolution stamped upon the features; the lower jaws hanging upon the breast; the teeth grinning and glistening between the parched lips, and the black hue of sickness about the mouth and around the sunken sockets of the eyes; and in some the sightless orbs were open and staring with a wild glare of affright, as if peering into the awful mysteries of the future; while others wore a grotesque laugh of derision still more appalling, with the muscles of the mouth drawn up, the eyebrows lifted, the head tilted knowingly on one side, the hair matted in horny tufts, the bare spots on the skulls, like the piebald wig of a harlequin; the skeleton arms outstretched, and the bony fingers spread as if to clutch the relentless destroyer, and wrestle with him to the last. These I fancied were lively fellows, who were carried off suddenly after a midnight carouse. I sat down on a box containing a dead child, and looked up at a row of bodies opposite that attracted my notice in a particular degree. In the middle stood a rolicking fellow, about two years dead, whose sunken eyes appeared still to burn with the fire of life and humor. His hands were lifted in a deprecating manner over a congregation of corpses sitting on a shelf below. Some appeared to be listening; some grinning at his humorous harangue; others, with their heads together, seemed to question the propriety of his anecdotes; old gentlemen, with knitted brows and lantern jaws; ranges of bodies stood on each side of him as if laughing, talking, praying, dying, suffering, listening, rejoicing, and feasting at the banquet of death. One little man, in a dingy suit of black, sat in a corner; the end of his nose was eaten off by the worms; his mouth was compressed, and had a pinched expression; his hands grasped eagerly at something. I thought that little man was a miser, whose death was caused by starvation. Another figure, a large portly body, stood in a conspicuous part of the vault; it was the corpse of a fat old bishop, whose jaws were still rotund and smooth with good living, and his sleek hair was patted down to his head as with the oil of bygone roast beefs and macaroni soups, and his jolly cast of countenance betokened a system liberally supplied with the juices of life, and a conscience rendered easy by attention to the creature comforts. That man lived an easy life, and died of good feeding. He was carefully labeled, and carried on his wrists a jeweled cross. There stood in another part of the vault a fiery orator, with open mouth and distended arms. The head was thrown back, the breast partially bare, a few tufts of black hair fell from his piebald skull; his round staring eyes were stretched wide open, and his brows arched high on his wrinkled forehead; he looked toward heaven for inspiration. I fancied I could hear the flaming torrent, as it blazed and crackled and scintillated from his thin ashy lips. It was the glowing eloquence of an ardent soul that left its parting impress upon the clay; the form yet spoke, but the sound was not there. Passing on from vault to vault, I saw here and there a dead baby thrown upon a shelf—its innocent little face sleeping calmly among the mouldering skulls; a leg, or an arm, or an old skull, from which the lower jaw had fallen; now a lively corpse, jumping with a startling throe from its niche, or a grim skeleton in its dark corner chuckling at the ravages of the destroyer. Who was the prince here? Who was the great man, or the proud man, or the rich man? The musty, grinning, ghastly skeleton in the corner seemed to chuckle at the thought, and say to himself, "Was it you, there on the right, you ugly, noseless, sightless, disgusting thing? Was it you that rode in your fine carriage, about a year ago, and thought yourself so great when you ordered your coachman to drive over the beggar? Don't you see he is as handsome as you are now, and as great a man; you can't cut him down now, my fine fellow! And you, there on the left. What a nice figure you are, with your fleshless shanks and your worm-eaten lips! It was you that betrayed youth and beauty and innocence, and brought yourself here at last to keep company with such wretches as I am. Why, there is not a living thing now, save the maggots, that wouldn't turn away in disgust from you. And you, sir, on the opposite side, how proud you were when I last saw you; an officer of state, a great man in power, who could crush all below you, and make the happy wife a widowed mourner, and bring her little babes to starvation; it was you that had innocent men seized and cast into prison. What can you do now? The meanest wretch that mocks you in this vault of death is as good as you, as strong, as great, as tall, as broad, as pretty a piece of mortality, and a great deal nearer to heaven. Oh, you are a nice set of fellows, all mixing together without ceremony! Where are your rules of etiquette now; your fashionable ranks, and your plebeian ranks; your thousands of admiring friends, your throngs of jeweled visitors? Why, the lowliest of us has as many visitors here, and as many honest tears shed as you. Ha! ha!. This is a jolly place, after all; we are all a jolly set of republicans, and old DEATH is our President!"

Turning away from this strange exhibition of death's doings, I followed the old monk into the vaults allotted to the women. Here the spectacle was still more shocking and impressive. The bodies were not placed in an upright position like those of the men, but were laid out at full length in glass cases; the walls on both sides were covered.

The young, the gay, the beautiful, were all here, laid lowly in the relentless embrace of death; decked out in silken dresses, laces, and jewelry, as in mockery of the past. Each corpse had its sad history. I saw a young bride who was stricken down in a few brief months after her marriage. She was dressed in her bridal costume; the bonnet and vail still on, the white gloves drawn over her skeleton fingers; a few withered flowers laid upon her breast by the mourning one she had left behind. Through the thin vail could be seen a blanched, grinning, bony face; the sunken sockets of the eyes marked around with the dark lines of decay; the long hair drawn in luxuriant masses over her withered bosom. Another held in her arms a skeleton babe. Some were habited in walking dresses; others in all the finery of ball-room costume, with gay silks, slippers, silk stockings, and tawdry lace. It was a ghastly sight to look under the bonnets, and gaze upon the sunken ashy features, decked around with artificial flowers; to trace in those withered lineaments no lingering line of beauty, no flickering ray of the immortal spirit, but a dreary history of mortal agony, decay, and corruption. Yet here the husband comes to hold communion with the beloved soul that once dwelt in that mouldering corpse; to look upon those blanched features, that were once animate with life and affection; to kiss the cold lips, and feel no returning warmth. And here, too, the father, brother, sister, and wife come to gaze upon the dead; and here the mother comes to weep over the withered corpse of her babe. Once a year, as I learnt from the old monk, the relatives of the deceased come to pray for the salvation of their souls, and deck the bodies with flowers.

Many a night had that old monk spent down in these dark vaults, among the dead; not as a penance for evil-doing, though he confessed that he was weak and sinful, but to pray for the soul of some brother, who had been his companion in years past. It was not gloomy to him, he said; it made him hopeful if not happy; for he felt, when surrounded by these mortal remains, that he was nearer to God. There were friends here, whom he had loved in youth and manhood; whose hands he had grasped in fellowship, whose eyes had beamed kindly upon him when his heart was sad: now grim and motionless in the dark recesses around him. He liked to gaze upon them, and think of a re-union with the immortal spirits that had left them tenantless.

Surely that old man was sincere. What more was the world to him than to the dead with whom he mingled. What pleasures could life have to one whose capacity for earthly happiness had long since been destroyed by continued self-denial, by the tearing out from his heart of every unbidden hope, by fasting and penance, and by all the sacrifices of light and sunshine that could turn inward the tide of thought?

B

What save the contemplation of the future? Yet it seemed as if in his midnight watches he must sometimes feel undefined terrors check the flow of his blood; that the rustling of the night air among the folds of the shrouds, and the dropping asunder of skeleton forms; the sudden grating of the doors, when moaning gusts of wind swung them open upon their hinges; the dry rattling of fleshless jaws, the gnawing of bones by the vermin, the sepulchral gloom, must sometimes startle him from his reveries like a coming solution of the dread mystery. Who can tell—not even himself—of all the strange thoughts that flit through his brain in the dreary watches of the night;—what weird visions he sees of life brought back again into those ghastly corpses; what faint moans rise from out the darkness—moans for lives misspent, and never more to return upon earth; wild bursts of anguish for errors that can never be retrieved, prayers for one drop of mercy before the day of eternal doom! In these dread, dark hours, I thought how the cold sweat must gather upon his brow, and the strength forsake him, and the clammy grasp of the unseen hand—the skeleton hand that never relents for youth or beauty, for fame or virtue—draw tight around his throat, and make his breath come thick and short, and his eyes stare affrighted, like the sightless orbs of the dead along the walls.

From the conversation of the monk, I learnt that these catacombs are supported by contributions from the relatives of the deceased, who pay annually a certain sum for the preservation of the bodies. Each new-comer is placed in a temporary niche, and afterward removed to a permanent place, where he is permitted to remain as long as the contributions continue; but when the customary fees are not forthcoming the corpses are thrown aside on a shelf, where they lie till the relatives think proper to have them set up again. Whole shelves are filled with skulls and bodies of the dead, put out of the way to make room for others of a more profitable character.

It might be supposed that the air of the catacombs is in some degree affected by the fresh bodies; but this is not the case. There is no offensive odor, and the visitor would scarcely know, if he did not see them, that he was surrounded by the dead. I could perceive no difference in the atmosphere of these vaults from that of any other subterranean places, except a slight smell of mould, not altogether disagreeable. The fresh air is admitted from the top, and it is to its extreme dryness that the preservation of the bodies may be attributed.

CHAPTER III.

JOURNEY TO CATANIA.

AMONG the many curiosities of the city is an establishment for foundlings. The institution is designed to prevent infanticide. It is a large gloomy old building, in an obscure part of the town, and must be approached with circumspection lest the inhabitants of the neighborhood should indulge in erroneous suspicions. I threw all the responsibility on my guide, however, and went to see it in open daylight. There is a hole in the wall large enough to admit a good-sized bundle, inside of which is a revolving machine, such as they use in post-offices for the delivery of letters, with four compartments, each large enough to hold a *bambino*. The unfortunate mother, who is either unable or unwilling to support her offspring, rolls it up in a small package, which she carries to the pigeon-hole at night, thrusts it in, gives the revolving baby-holder a turn, and departs with all possible speed. A bell is so connected with the machine as to arouse the nurses on the floor above. By pulling a string the whole establishment is whirled up aloft, and the *piccola bambina* tumbled out of the package into the arms of the matron, who duly inspects it, labels it Angelo, or Francisco, or Antonio, as her taste may dictate, records the date of its admission in a register, its sex, &c.; and so commences the foundling life of the *débutante*. The mother is permitted to take it away whenever she chooses, but it is seldom the little unfortunate is called for. What the moral effect of this institution is, it is not for an inexperienced person like myself to determine.

During my sojourn in Palermo I visited Morreale, a village situated on a hill, about three miles distant. The chief object

JOURNEY TO CATANIA.

of attraction here is a very ancient church, in which may be seen some of the finest mosaic in Sicily, and a court containing two hundred double columns, each different from the other. Among the pictures in mosaic is a representation of St. Paul in the act of pulling the devil out of somebody's mouth; to which one of the reverend padres pointed with a grim smile of triumph. I believe he suspected that I had something of the kind in me that could be extracted by hard pulling; but I gave him a couple of carlini, which seemed to afford him as much satisfaction as if he had extracted an entire nest of devils.

After a stay of four days, I took my post in a rumbling old diligence for Catania, on the southeastern side of the island. The distance is a hundred and seventy Sicilian miles from Palermo. It was late at night when we started; for you must know that diligences in Sicily always make it a point to start at the most unseasonable hours. The pleasure of the trip was in no degree enhanced by the information, confidentially conveyed to us by the conductor, when we asked him why we had a guard, that on the trip from Catania, just three days before, the diligence had been robbed; that the mountains were infested with banditti, and we might consider ourselves fortunate if we reached Catania without broken heads. I had heard so much of the robbers in Italy, who were always somewhere else, that I had no great faith in those of Sicily; but, inasmuch as all parties united in terrible stories of the bad character of the Sicilians, I thought there might be sufficient truth in it to be a little cautious; so, having a very slim purse, I put it in my boots, and slept comfortably for the night—as much so at least as a person can when he has to hang on outside on the driver's seat, for want of one in the interior. It was a bright moonlight night, and we jogged on pleasantly enough, up hill and down hill, and over rugged roads, and through dark, low, dirty-looking villages, till daylight broke, and the sun rose over the barren mountains with a refreshing warmth. That sun was welcomed most heartily by the whole company, for the mountain air had chilled us throughout; and I am not sure but it would have found us frozen stiff, had it not been that at each post we were roused into a fit of honest indignation at the inordinate demands of the postillions, hostlers, and guards. The postillions charged us half a carlin for driving us; the hostlers charged half a carlin for putting the horses in; the guards robbed us of half a carlin for preventing us from being robbed; and the beggars begged the loose change from us, because they were in want of money, and thought they had a legitimate right to be paid for wanting it. Little boys begged as a matter of amusement and education; old women and old men begged, whether they were in need of funds or not, as a matter of example to the rising generation; and after one party of beggars had chased us from the bottom of a hill up to the top, and done their very best in the way of hopping on crutches (which they only made use of for the occasion), there was another party ready to begin the moment we stopped, without the slightest reference to the labors of the first party, and when they were done we were chased to the bottom of the hill by a third party, and so on to the end of our journey.

But the real beggars are tame and reasonable in their demands compared with the soldiers, postillions, and conductors who have charge of the diligence. With them it is a matter of right to fleece every unfortunate gentleman who places himself in their power. They live on him. He is meat and drink to them. His pockets are their pockets. He is a sort of gold mine into which they are continually digging. They explore him; they find out how many precious veins he has; and they insert their picks and shovels wherever the dust glimmers, and root it out with surprising perseverance. By the time he reaches the end of his journey he is dug clean out, and they turn their attention to other mines.

Let me warn the traveler who thinks of making the tour of Sicily, not to delude himself with the idea that when he pays for a seat in the diligence, or a seat outside of it, that he is done paying—that the owners thereof consider themselves under the slightest obligation to take him to his place of destination. You simply pay for the use of a foot or a foot and a half of cushion (according to your breadth of beam), and the contract is concluded. You may be left, as I was on the road to Syracuse, in the middle of the public highway, without horses or driver, an object of mingled wonder and derision to the inhabitants of a populous village—stared at as the man who wouldn't pay; ridiculed as the man who couldn't go without horses; abused in an unknown and abominable tongue, for refusing to be legitimately swindled; and compelled, in the end, to give an additional *buono mano* for creating the difficulty and losing temper. Good humor and small change are the only locomotive powers by which you can get on in Sicily. The one keeps you in a state of self-satisfaction; the other greases the wheels, makes the whip crack, and the horses go. Depend upon it, you will never gain an inch by a rebellious spirit against customs which you can not change.

Of the character of the country in the interior of Sicily, I can only speak as it appeared to me in the month of October, after the parching heats of summer. The brilliancy of the skies and the salubrity of the climate at this season of the year can not be surpassed in any part of the world; but I am not sure that it is the best season to enjoy the scenery. Certainly the parched and barren aspect of the whole country gave me a very unfavorable opinion of the fertility of the soil, or the beauties of Sicilian scenery. Nearly the entire tract of a hundred and fifty miles lying between Palermo and Catania is a perfect desert of rocky mountains and barren valleys, without water or trees, and nothing to indicate any means by which the inhabitants subsist, save here and there a miserable-looking spot of terraced ground, scratched over, and dotted with the stumps of grape-vines. Yet they do live, and apparently without labor; for, during my whole journey to Catania, I do not think I saw a dozen men at work. An intelligent Italian, however, informed me that the land, though apparently so sterile, yields abundant crops when cultivated, and requires very little plowing. The villages throughout the interior are the dirtiest and most wretched-looking places imaginable; filled with beggars and ragged idlers, and dilapidated to the last habitable degree. Syria, or the Holy Land.

can scarcely furnish a more deplorable example of the decay of civilization in the old world than one meets with at every turn of the road throughout the interior of Sicily. It is almost impossible for the American traveler, accustomed as he is to progress and enterprise, and all their concomitant results, to comprehend the barbarous condition in which these poor people live. Passing through the villages at night, I saw many of them asleep on the road-side, without covering or shelter; and the squalor and destitution of those who lived in houses surpass belief. Whole families are huddled together in one wretched apartment, without beds or furniture, living in common with mules, goats, and swine, and about as cultivated as the brutes around them. Few that I conversed with had ever heard of America, and even those who knew there was such a country, had no idea whether it was in China or in England. That such a state of things should exist in the nineteenth century, in a country once so highly civilized, and still boasting antiquities that excite the admiration of the world, is almost incredible.

The implements of agriculture, the rude and half-savage appearance of the people, the entire absence of the comforts of civilization, all bore evidence of the depressing effects of military rule. "What object is there in these poor wretches endeavoring to benefit their condition?" said my friend, the Italian, to me. "What good will it do them to increase their crops, or build better houses, or educate their children? The more they have, the heavier they are taxed; they naturally think they might as well remain idle as labor for the support of a horde of brutal soldiers to keep them in a state of slavery; and there is no incitement to education, for it only makes them the more sensible of their degraded condition. Yet it is not to be contended that they are fit for self-government; all they need is a judicious and humane system of laws, which will afford them adequate protection against the errors and follies of despotic rulers. They are not deficient in capacity or industry, where they have any object in making use of their natural gifts. You see them now in a state of hopeless degradation and bondage."

JOURNEY TO CATANIA.

While the Italian was talking, a Capuchin friar came to the door of the diligence to beg for the church. I thought my friend might have added some reflections on this branch of the subject, that would have shown more clearly the root of the evils under which the Sicilians labor; but being a good Catholic he was silent. I contented myself by giving the poor friar a baiocco, and making a sketch of his face as he stood waiting for the Italian to give him another. There was plenty of time to get a good likeness.

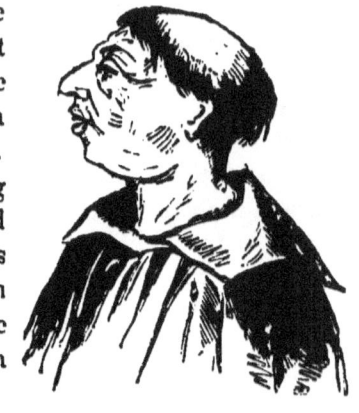

I said we started from Palermo at night. It is a journey of thirty-six hours to Catania, making just two nights and one day on the road. One would naturally suppose it would be quite as well to set out in the morning, and make two days and one night of it; but these are among the unaccountable peculiarities of Sicilian travel.

Catania is a large town, containing a population of fifty thousand, many fine buildings, many soldiers, many churches and some of the finest convents in Sicily. The monastery of San Benedetto is the most extensive establishment of the kind I have yet seen. Here the monks, who are chiefly of noble families, live in royal style. If I had money enough, nothing would please me better than to adopt the cowl and sack, and become a brother in the monastery of San Benedetto. The building is a magnificent palace, ornamented with courts and fountains, gardens, pleasure-grounds, bowers for devotional exercises, splendid marble halls in the interior, suites of elegant apartments, pictures of all the saints, organs that fill the spacious chapels with a flood of solemn music; statuary, mosaic, and voluptuous frescoes—all that can charm the senses and make glad the heart of monks. The wines are the choicest selections of the Marsala and San Nicoloso brands; the macaroni is the purest and richest; the fish are the best that can be fished out of the bay of Catania; the chickens and capons, the salmis, the salads, the roast-beef and mutton are unexceptionable. They have their separate apartments; their servants, their private wines, their—but it won't do to be too particular. You know the brotherhood do not use these things—they are for the use of visitors. Perhaps with all their failings they are as good as most men; and it must be admitted that no traveler can visit the convent of Monte Sanario or Val Ombrosa, in Tuscany, or indeed any of the convents throughout Italy or Sicily, without a grateful sense of their genuine good-nature and hospitality. They are not soured by an ascetic mode of life, or misanthropic from their seclusion; the world is open to them, and they enjoy it in a quiet way.

Close by the convent of San Benedetto is a female convent. I was not permitted to enter, having no friends there.

Six miles from Catania, on the road along the coast to Messina, is the group of rocks where it is said the Cyclopes were born. They are called the Cyclopean Isles. I went up one forenoon to make a sketch of them. The weather was unpropitious; and, after a glance at the rocks and a thorough drenching, I was compelled to return without the usual boat excursion to the grotto.

CHAPTER IV.

ASCENT OF MOUNT ETNA.

It is a good forenoon's work to prepare for the ascent of Mount Etna. There are horses to be hired, bargains to be made, warm clothing to be put in readiness, provisions to be laid in, brandy and cigars to be stowed away for the night; and sundry other little matters to be attended to, if the adventurer designs spending the night on the mountain. My companion on the occasion was a young Englishman attached to the army at Malta, a very pleasant and gentlemanly traveling acquaintance; he was anxious to see the sun rise from the summit of the mountain. To this arrangement I was opposed for several reasons: first, I had often seen the sun rise from the top of a mountain; secondly, the season was late, and it is no pleasant journey over the beds of lava to the crater of Mount Etna in the middle of the night. But, inasmuch as my friend had no recollection of ever having seen the sun rise from a mountain, I gave up, and agreed to be victimized.

The distance from Catania to the crater of Mount Etna is twenty-three miles; the area of the base covers an extent of more than a hundred miles; and the height, according to the most authentic French measurement, is eleven thousand four hundred feet above the level of the sea. It is generally covered with snow from October to June; but, owing to an unusually fine autumn, we were fortunate in finding it entirely free from snow on the 10th of October, and we afterward learned that it remained so until the beginning of November. On the road from Palermo we made repeated inquiries as to the practicability of the ascent at this season;

but it was not till we came in sight of it at a distance of forty miles that we could ascertain any thing satisfactory. In fact, nobody that we asked knew any thing about Mount Etna, or had ever heard of such a mountain—at least under that name. Some thought it must be in Italy, and others declared there was no such mountain. Our conductor knew it when he saw it, but he could not tell us two hours before when we would see it.

At two o'clock we sallied forth, duly mounted and caparisoned. The animal upon which I rode was intended for a horse, I believe, but it bore very little resemblance to that noble animal. Had any body offered to bet me ten dollars that it wouldn't drop before I got half way to San Nicolosi, I would have taken him up. Rosinante was nothing to compare with the bony, shaggy, sway-backed old charger that bore me out of the gates of Catania.

Immediately after leaving the suburbs of the town, the ascent commences, and it continues, more or less, the entire distance of twenty-three miles to the summit of the mountain. The road as far as San Nicolosi is tolerably good—the first part of it, to the fountain, being a public highway to the principal villages back of Catania. The devastating effects of the volcanic eruptions are visible every where on the roadside, and even below Catania the face of the country is blackened with masses of the lava. The foundations of the villages along the sea shore for miles, the walls around the fields, the lanes and terraced grounds, are all formed of volcanic deposits, and give a dreary aspect to the whole country; hundreds of villages lie buried beneath the desolating streams that have poured from the crater in times past; vineyards and olive groves, castles, villas, works of art, thousands of men, women, and children, lie mouldering under those fierce floods of ashes and lava. Other towns and villages have sprung up on the ruins; thousands of living beings dwell in the same places, and look up every day with careless indifference at the smoking crater; vineyards and olive groves are nourished from the bones of the dead. What matters it? Nobody believes there will be another eruption in his lifetime;

and, if it comes, then it will be time enough to think of escape. So they live on in a happy sense of security; and, if the climate permitted, no doubt the crater itself would be inhabited. Does any body refrain from traveling by railway because cars have run off the track? Do the people of the West go in keel-boats because steamboats blow up? Does a man abstain from going to the mines of California because his brother or friend has "shuffled off the mortal coil" in a gold pit?

Vineyards thrive in the lava of Mount Etna. The whole district of San Nicolosi, which has been covered a dozen times, and which will most likely be covered again the very first time old Etna rouses from his long *siesta*, and belches forth his fiery floods, is thickly inhabited, and doubtless would, if practicable, go on increasing and extending up toward the summit till it got into the regions of fire and brimstone.

The village of San Nicolosi is about two hours from Catania. We reached the *locanda*, or inn, an hour or so before sunset; and having nothing there to interest us, we cast about us for some means of passing the rest of the afternoon. The padrona, a good-natured, talkative fellow, informed us that there lived not far off one Senor Gemmellaro, who was a sort of conspicuous character in the neighborhood, and who spoke good English, and was always glad to see Englishmen and Americans—in short, that he could tell us a good deal about Mount Etna that would be of use to us. Encouraged by this piece of information, we set out, under the padrona's guidance, to pay a visit to Senor Gemmellaro, who was at his villa outside the village.

A pleasant walk of half a mile through the narrow lanes that separate the vineyards of Nicolosi brought us to the gate of Senor Gemmellaro's villa. Here we found collected forty or fifty merry damsels, with baskets on their heads filled with the grapes of the vineyard. It did our hearts good to see the merry sunburnt faces of these damsels, and hear their jovial voices as they sang their songs of gleesome labor. A happier looking set of beings I never saw, in their ragged dresses and broad-brimmed hats; and I venture to say they were as happy as they looked. These were the peasant girls of the country.

Senor Gemmellaro met us at the gate in the true spirit of a fine old country gentleman. "I am very glad to see you," said he, "though I have but little to offer you here. You see my country house there—a mere straw cabin, but good enough for an old bachelor." The cottage was indeed a curiosity. Robinson Crusoe never designed or inhabited any thing more picturesque. Pleasantly shaded by trees stood this rustic little wigwam, with its peaked straw roof and single door, and the inviting aroma of grape vines and flowers around it, and in front a laughing, dancing, buxom gang of country girls, full of life and fun, and apparently not at all disposed to work. "They are a very troublesome set," said Senor Gemmellaro; "I can't do any thing with them." Then the old gentleman would laugh and shake his head at the girls: "Ah, you young imps; you think because I am a bachelor you can do as you please with me. Never mind, I'll pay you up; I'll get a wife to keep you all in order." Here the old gentleman would laugh again, until his eyes seemed ready to pop out of his head; and the girls would laugh, and we laughed as a matter of politeness.

We went into the cottage, where we found the roof ornamented with choice selections of grapes and various productions of the villa. The old gentleman prides himself on a particular wine, which he makes with his own hands, to which he gallantly gives the name of "Vino del Donna." It is a wine peculiarly for the ladies; and I must say it is the very best that could be devised for the delicate palate of the fair sex. Any lady who could drink two glasses of the Vino del Donna without experiencing an immediate inclination to accept of the first offer, must be possessed of an adamantine heart. The grapes are perfectly delicious—far superior to any we had tasted down in the lower country.

We learned from Senor Gemmellaro that the climate and soil of San Nicolosi are peculiarly adapted to the cultivation of the grape. Black and parched as the whole face of the country appears, it produces most abundant crops, and the quality of the wine very far surpasses that of the Marsala region in richness and delicacy. Wealthy families often come up to spend the summer here, in order to enjoy the pure air and the delicious grapes and wines of the neighborhood.

The view from San Nicolosi over the valley of Catania is one of the finest in Sicily. Vineyards, white shining villas, groves of olive and almond trees, meadows, and ruins of half-buried villages are spread out below in all the variegated hues of a living panorama, bounded by the glistening sea and the far-off hills of Syracuse. From the rustic observatory of our host we had a sunset view of this magnificent region that made an impression never to be effaced. Senor Gemmellaro was delighted at the effect of his skill in rustic architecture, and I have no doubt attributed the admirable manner in which the sun went down to the remarkable construction of his observatory.

We walked back with him, after feasting ourselves on figs, grapes, wine, and scenery, to the village, where he took us into his old *palazzo* and showed us all the curiosities of the establishment. There were dogs innumerable in the yard, white rabbits and gray rabbits, squirrels, and cats, and rats, pea-fowl, and guinea-fowl, and all manner of fowl; strange-looking things creeping on the ground and up the grape-vines; old guns, and horns, and shot-pouches hanging under the piazza; old vases to catch the rain, and antique columns starting up out of the ground in all directions. It was a strange, bachelor-like old place, with no sign of life about it save that of the strange animals that kept company with their old master. Yet he seemed to be happy, and to take a quiet pleasure in feeding his pets; perhaps as much as most people do in feeding their wives.

The cabinet of Senor Gemmellaro contains a rich and wonderful collection of volcanic specimens; lava in all possible forms; some in the shape of snakes, lizards, and pigs; others not unlike old castles, statuary, columns, and antique vases; also coins of rare value, relics of Sicilian history, old papers and old books, and a thousand curious things impossible to describe.

In his register of visitors were the names of some distinguished travelers. I saw some few names of Americans of a recent date. Chief among those were Mr. E. Joy Morris and family, and Mr. Alexander Clements, of Washington, who made the ascent in company last spring a year ago; and of a later date, I believe in May last, those of Professor Silliman and a party of friends, who had spent several days in a scientific tour in the neighborhood of San Nicolosi. The ascent of Mount Etna has been rendered much less difficult of late years than it formerly was, by the laudable exertions of Senor Gemmellaro in opening better mule paths, and removing many obstacles that formerly existed. All travelers unite in speaking highly of his hospitality and intelligence, and none will be disappointed in visiting his cabinet of volcanic curiosities.

Naturalists make four divisions of soil and production between the base of the mountain, commencing at Catania, and the summit; the *piedmonte*, covering an extent of about eight miles, embracing villages, country residences or villas, vineyards and meadows; the *sebrosa*, or *nemorosa*, five miles, producing pine trees and ilex, oaks, coarse grass, and wild flowers, but destitute of springs; the *scoperta*, three miles in extent, mostly of sand and patches of wild plants, and the *deserta*, three miles farther, extending to the summit, consisting almost entirely of lava, scoria, and ashes.

Down to the present period there have been seventy-five eruptions, twelve of which were prior to the Christian era. That of 1669 destroyed a great number of villages, and did great damage to Catania; but in 1693 occurred the great eruption, accompanied by earthquakes, which destroyed sixty towns, including Catania. The latest eruptions were those of 1831, '32, '38, and '42. It is not my province, however, to go into a history of these convulsions of nature, and their causes and effects. They have been described at great length in the works of many learned travelers who have visited this region, though much yet remains to be written.

CHAPTER V.

THE CRATER.

AT eight o'clock, after a good supper at the *locanda*, we set out for the crater of Mount Etna. It was a mild, clear night; the moon was in her prime, and the stars shone out like gems of crystallized light, without a single cloud to obscure their glorious radiance. Our horses being no longer available, I was reluctantly compelled to leave my favorite old charger and take a mule.

Oh, ye stars, which are the poetry of heaven, what omnipotent works ye revealed to us that night! What still, shadowy forests of gnarled old oaks, and yawning precipices of darkness unfathomable, opened to us as we toiled upward; what ghostly mountains, and cities, and temples of blackened lava loomed through the shadowy distance; what boundless valleys of mystic light lay outspread beneath us; what a solemn stillness reigned over the slumbering earth! Up, high over all, with its bare and grizzled cone, towered the smouldering crater, lonely and desolate, but mighty in its desolation. Where are the castles and palaces that once decorated the dim valleys in the depths below? where are the boasted deeds of Roman and Saracen heroes? where are the victors and the vanquished now? where is all that the vaunted ambition of man has accomplished? Not for human ken is it to penetrate the dim vista of centuries, and tell of all that lies buried beneath those dark floods; not for all the records of the past to reveal the millionth part of their sad mysteries.

But I think I hear my friend, the Englishman, say, "Sad nonsense all this; Etna is a stunning place, to be sure; devilish high, devilish cold, and all that; throws out an amazing quantity of smoke now and then—didn't do a bad job when it buried all those beggars of Romans and Saracens, to say nothing of the number of rascally Sicilians it has since covered up. Nonsense—all fudge!"

In about three hours and a half from San Nicolosi we reached an old tree lying in a sheltered ravine, where the guides lit a fire and fed the mules. A very marked difference was perceptible in the atmosphere at this elevation; the cold was penetrating, though not apparently of great intensity. It was with difficulty we could keep our feet and hands warm, and maintain a healthy circulation of the blood; but, after resting an hour or two, we pushed on.

From the oak forest we emerged into a region of scoria and lava, abounding in narrow and difficult passes, and of the wildest and most desolate aspect. The moon, which had thus far befriended us, now disappeared, and left us in almost utter darkness. It was surprising how the guides adhered to the path over the rough beds of lava; often, as we thought, depending altogether upon instinct; in many places there appeared to be not the slightest trace of a path. Huge masses of lava, over which we stumbled, deep gulches, and yawning precipices, all enveloped in gloom, threatened each moment to bring us up with a sudden check; but we always contrived to keep on, winding round them, and into them, and through them, after the stalwart figure of old Pedro, who took the lead and never for an instant slackened his pace. How that man kept breath enough in his body to sustain life during so many years of hard climbing, I could never divine; for, accustomed as I was to exercise, I must say it made me puff not a little to keep pace with him for one night. The highest bluffs, the roughest passes, the deepest chasms were all the same to old Pedro; up he rose and down he went, sometimes looming against the sky like a gigantic wizard of the mountain in his shaggy capote, sometimes sinking with rapid and steady strides into unfathomable depths; now grasping the scraggy points of lava and lifting himself out of mysterious pits; now scrambling over precipices of scoria like a monstrous bear; a moment after, astride of his mule, on some lonely ledge of rock, ever toiling onward with the same noiseless, steady, unwearying tread. A weather-beaten, grizzled, manly fellow was Pedro, the guide; rough as the winds, and rains, and smoke of old Etna could make him; dirty and shaggy like his tattered capote; but, with a strong pair of legs and an unflinching will (in the way of climbing), he had a childlike nature and a heart that filled well his capacious breast. As we neared the summit of the mountain the air became so rarefied and the cold so piercing that I felt as if there was not an ounce of blood in me, and it was only by hard walking I could keep up any thing like a circulation "Pedro," said I, "it's getting mighty cold; don't you think so?" "*Si, signore, un poco—ma pilliare questa,*" pulling off his capote. "No, no, thank you, keep it on." Pedro said nothing, but casting his capote around me, fastened it on in such wise that it was no use to struggle against his kindness: a moment after he was striding up on a ridge of lava, far above, looking like a great black giant that had come suddenly out of the earth.

We reached the last station, or *Casa degl' Inglesa*, about three o'clock in the morning. The cold was not so intense as I had often experienced before, but much more penetrating from the decreased power of resistance in the blood. My friend, the Englishman, who had ridden nearly all the way, was as stiff as a piece of buckram when he dismounted, though not disposed to admit that he felt at all "uncomfortable." There was not much in the *Casa Inglesa* to cheer us, save the shelter afforded by its dilapidated walls. Originally the house consisted of three rooms, a kitchen, and stable, but now the stable is in ruins, and we found but one of the rooms at all habitable. Into this we betook ourselves, with a couple of the mules that were half famished by cold and hunger; and, thus quartered, awaited the proper time to commence our ascent to the crater. Pedro, taking pity upon us, broke off a piece of the door, which, together with a small contribution from the window-frame, and the remains of an old bench, made a very tolerable fire; and if there had been a chimney we might have been rather comfortable. Wrapped in the shaggy capote, I stretched myself on a piece of plank, and looking into the crackling pile, around which sat the guides and muleteers, moralized on the vaulting ambition of man which induces him to cross stormy seas and climb volcanic mountains. Said I to myself (for the Englishman was lost in a cloud of smoke on the other side), Here you are, at three o'clock in the morning, ten thousand feet above the level of the sea, cold as a lump of ice, choking with smoke, with scarce a shoe on your feet or a coat on your back; tossed and tumbled about till you hardly know what language you talk or where you belong; now up on the top of Mount Etna to see the sun rise, and next to take a peep into the valley of Jehosaphat. And all for what? *Quein sabe*, as the Spaniards say.

The *Casa degl' Inglesa* is a small stone building, constructed in the rudest manner, for the temporary accommodation of travelers on the way to the crater. It is ten thousand feet above the level of the sea, and is of course uninhabited, being merely a place of shelter, without water or other accommodations by which life could be sustained in that remote

CASA DEGL' INGLESA.

region. According to Senor Gemmellaro, it was built by his father, the distinguished naturalist, in 1810, when the English army occupied Sicily. It was originally intended that it should have attached to it an observatory, with all the instruments necessary for determining the temperature and observing the volcanic phenomena of Mount Etna; but, owing to the want of suitable encouragement, this design was abandoned. For many years past it has been repaired from time to time by Senor Gemmellaro entirely at his own expense.

The dawn of day began to lighten up the eastern horizon as we sallied forth, with our staffs and guide, from the solitary walls of the old Casa. All was black and craggy under foot, and the sharp gusts of wind moaned gloomily against the rugged masses of lava as we wound our way among them. Neither path nor trace was perceptible to us now, for the earth was covered with beds of dark lava; yet onward strode Pedro, with the same sure and steady tread, looking neither to the right nor the left, and never for a moment stopping to search for the path. How many times he had gone up that mountain, by day and by night, when it was covered with snow and when it was wrapt in darkness, in sunshine and storm, from youth to the sere of manhood, not even himself could tell. A hard life it was at best; up and down those dreary heights for more than twenty years; a crust of bread or a bone now and then from some tender-hearted tourist to keep his spirits up, and a good many sunrises and sunsets to feed his imagination. That Pedro was a man of imagination was attested by the number of charms he wore to keep away the evil spirits that infest these lonely mountains, and if he had thoughts at all, what strange thoughts they must have been! His whole world lay between San Nicolosi and the crater—a very strange world in itself; a world of burnt earth, of ashes, and lava, and sulphur, and smoke, of wondrous fires and earthquakes past, and eternal ruin and desolation in the future. What to others was the great event of a life was an every-day affair to Pedro; in his heels he carried more practical knowledge of Etna than all the learned men of Europe carried in their heads. God speed that grim and stalwart mountaineer; may his last smell of brimstone be in this world, and his last ascension be into that better one where there is everlasting rest for the weary!

From the *Casa Inglesa* to the highest crater occupies about an hour. The direct elevation is about fourteen hundred feet, but the winding of the path more than doubles the distance.

As daylight broke clear and broad over the still earth, and the eastern sky gleamed with the first rays of the rising sun, we reached the highest peak, and turned to look down into the vast depths below. The whole island was wrapt in an impenetrable mass of sleeping clouds; covering mountain, and valley, and ocean as a mantle of mist, while not a shadow dimmed the bright sky above. It was thus upon the solitary cone of Etna, with the broad lucid firmament arched over us, and the vast sea of floating clouds outspread below, that there uprose before us a sublime picture of the shattered ark, as it rested of old amid the subsiding floods on the heights of Ararat, when the fountains of the deep and the windows of heaven were stopped and the rain from heaven was restrained.

On the right and on the left yawned a vast crater, lined with banks of sulphur and ashes; and from out the bowels of the earth came clouds of hot smoke, rolling upward till they vanished in the thin air; and a thousand fissures around sent out jets of scalding steam, and smouldering fires seemed ready to burst forth and spread ruin and death under their seething floods of lava. And now, from the bed of clouds that rested on the deep, up rose the sun, scattering away the thin vapors that hung around his couch, and filling the air with his glorious radiance; and the slumbering ocean of mist that lay upon the valleys upheaved under his piercing rays of heat and light, and gathered in around the mountain tops; and green valleys, and villages, and vineyards, and gleams of bright waters lay outspread in the calm of the morning, as it opened upon the shores and vales of Sicily. One gigantic shadow, the shadow of the mighty Etna, stretched across the lesser mountains below as far as the eye could reach; and the valleys beneath it were still covered with clouds and the darkness within the shadow. Up rose the sun higher and still higher; and now the floating vapors that rested upon the earth disappeared, and there was nothing left but the bright glowing abyss of mountain and valley, bathed in his effulgent rays; for "his going forth is from the end of the heaven, and his circuit unto the ends of it: and there is nothing hid from the heat thereof." There was not a breath of air to disturb the glittering sea; ships lay motionless on its unruffled surface; and on the shores glistened, like flakes of snow, the villages that were washed by its waters. Far in the distance the towering mountains of Calabria reared their rugged peaks, bounding the view toward the east; to the north lay Messina and the rocks of Scylla and Charybdis; and stretching southward the coast swept under the base of the mountain; its shores lined with villas and towns, and indented by the bays of Catania, Agosta, and Syracuse. Back toward the west lay the interior of Sicily, a desert of parched and barren hills, with scarce a tree or spot of verdure to relieve the sterility of the vast wilderness. And now, as we gazed entranced upon this scene of awful sublimity, the smoke rose up in heavy masses from the crater, and whirling around us with a sudden gust, shut out sea and earth, and filled the air with noxious gases; and the sun had a lurid and ghastly glare through the gloom, and we thought the earth trembled. But soon the gust passed away, and left us unharmed amid the smouldering masses of ashes and sulphur.

My friend, the Englishman, considered the whole thing "excessively fine;" in which sentiment I heartily agreed with him, with the understanding, however, that it would require the simultaneous rising of the sun, and moon, and all the stars to get me up there again in the middle of the night; a sentiment in which we both agreed, and thus compromising all previous diversity of tastes, we sat down in a comfortable bed of sulphur, and, warming our hands in a jet of steam, lit a couple of cigars, and smoked cosily with old Etna.

It is difficult, without any means of measurement, to give a correct idea of the extent and depth of the craters; and, unfortunately, I have no books at hand from which to derive the required data. The extent of the rim of the upper crater must be about three miles and a half; the depth, as far down as the neck or narrowest part, perhaps three or four hundred yards. The nearest estimate we could make of the depth was by rolling down large pieces of lava, and listening to the reverberation made as they struck for the last time. We went down a short distance within the rim of the great crater to collect some volcanic specimens, but were soon driven back by the smoke. The sides are so precipitous that, to make any extended descent with safety, it would be necessary to be provided with ropes; and then it could only be done in very calm weather, when there is but little smoke. I am not sure whether this feat has ever been accomplished; but, so far as I could judge, there is no reason why it should not. The crater of Mount Vesuvius has been explored by several daring adventurers, and there does not seem to be any greater difficulty in effecting the descent into that of Mount Etna. For that matter, indeed, it requires neither ropes nor ladders to get down; start at the top and you are sure to get to the bottom; but it might be found agreeable, after reaching the bottom, to have some means of getting up again.

Standing on the ridge between the two craters, where there is barely a foothold, I could not help thinking how short a time it would take to reach an entirely new and unexplored region. A little step, just a foot, would give a sufficient start; and then what a sliding, and rolling, and skipping there would be! what a whizzing through smoke and brimstone! what visions of devils and fiery furnaces within the bowels of the earth! The whole scene was worthy of Dante. It was terribly infernal; indeed I may say it was infernally so. Even old Pedro, as he stood wrapt in his shaggy capote, looming through the smoke, and peering over into the seething abyss, looked diabolical; black and grim of visage he stood, as good a looking devil as ever walked upon brimstone. Now, I do not mean to speak lightly of a serious subject; but I do think no person can visit the crater of Mount Etna without entertaining a much more vivid idea of the lower regions than he ever had before. For my own part, I dreamt of nothing but flames of sulphur, huge figures with cloven feet, and little dancing blue fellows with pitchforks all the next night, which I assure you, on my honor, was not the effect of a bad conscience, but altogether the result of the vivid impression created in viewing the crater.

We remained on the summit about two hours, enjoying all the changes of light and shade produced by the rising of the sun and the dispersing of the light clouds that rested in the lower strata of air. An entirely clear sunrise might have afforded us a more extended prospect, but we were satisfied it could not have presented such a magnificent combination of atmospheric phenomena. Some traveler speaks of having seen the Island of Malta with the naked eye from this point; but, although the weather was tolerably clear before we commenced our descent, we saw nothing of it. It is quite possible, however, and not at all improbable. The distance can not be more than a hundred and twenty miles—the nearest point of Sicily from Malta being about eighty miles; and it is a common thing in Malta on any clear day to have a distinct view of Mount Etna. I have myself seen the Andes, in approaching Callao, at the distance of a hundred and twenty miles. It is perhaps easier to see a great distance, looking upward through an atmosphere decreasing in density, where there is a distinct outline, than downward through a less transparent medium, where there may be no outline. I have often seen land from the deck of a vessel when it could not be seen from the masthead. The Peak of Pico has been seen at the distance of a hundred and twenty miles, and the Peak of Teneriffe at a still greater distance.

Our descent to San Nicolosi was of course a good deal easier and rather more pleasant than the night's journey up. With the mules it occupied very nearly the same time; but I had become quite convinced that there was a prejudice against me on the part of the whole mule species. I had turned involuntary somersets from divers mules; I had been bitten at and kicked at by mules; I had endeavored to befriend mules by leading them up steep hills instead of riding them, and they were always sure to pull back and try to go down,

C

I had attempted to lead them down hill, and they invariably insisted upon going up; I had bought mules at three hundred dollars, that looked well on the morning of the purchase, but found they could not go by night, in consequence of being foundered; in sober truth, my talent did not lie in the navigation or management of mules; so I walked. A walk down Mount Etna includes a slide of about a mile from the edge of the crater, which I must tell you about.

Commencing near the crater is a steep bank of ashes and cinders, extending nearly to the Casa Inglesa, by which the trip is made with a locomotive speed quite delightful. Peeping over the brink of the precipice, you enter into a calculation as to the probability of having your limbs dislocated, in case you should strike some unseen rock; and about the time you become satisfied that a leg or an arm must be sacrificed, there rises a dust some hundred yards below, and you see a large dark body bouncing down like a man of India rubber, scattering cinders and ashes before it, and yelling like a demon Away it goes, rising and jumping and tossing, till it looks like a great black bird hopping down into the gulf of lava below, dwindling as it goes, till you see nothing but a dark speck. Then down dashes another and another, and you see that it must be old Pedro leading the way, and the stragglers following. Committing yourself to Providence, you draw a long breath and jump over too; and then, *Per Baccho*, how you go; up to your ankles in cinders, ten feet every jump! The wind whistles through your hair; you half shut your eyes to keep out the dust that has been raised by the guides; you shout like a drunken man, without knowing why, Hurra! glorious! splendid traveling this! hold me somebody! stop me, Pedro! by Jupiter there goes my hat! I knew it couldn't stay on! for heaven's sake belay me! It is no use, nobody will belay you! There you go, faster and faster at every jump, till you don't know which end will come out first. Now you bet ten to one that your feet will win the race; now a hidden mass of lava brings them up with a sudden jerk, and you'd lay heavy odds on the end of your nose—yes, the nose must win; you feel the premonitory jar as it nears the end of the track; terror seizes your soul; you jump desperately ten, twenty, thirty feet at every bound, twisting yourself back in the air like a cat; you vow in your agony of mind that you will never drop poor puss over the bannisters again in order to see her land on her feet: another leap, another twist does it; your feet are in the air, and you go sailing down gallantly on the seat of your breeches. Hurra! clear the track, there! don't stop me! glorious! splendid! Here we are, Pedro, all right; keep a look out for my hat, it'll be down here presently! Bless my soul, what a slide that was!

Emerging from the oak forest, three hours below, the view in the noon-day sun is beautiful beyond description. The whole semi-circle of valleys and mountains, villages and vineyards, as seen through the vistas of dark foliage, seems hung in the golden atmosphere like some magnificent scenic illusion; bright and glowing, and full of rich coloring. The tinkling of the goat-bells from the rocks below, the songs of the shepherds, and the mellowed sounds of life from the distant valleys, rise upon the still air like the murmuring of dreamy music; and around about us the earth was fragrant with wild flowers; and the gnarled old oaks made a pleasant shade.

In due time we reached the *locanda*, at San Nicolosi, where we enjoyed a good wash and a dinner that did great honor to the padrone. We called again upon Senor Gemmellero, to give in our experience; and, having satisfactorily acquitted ourselves in the way of *buono manos* to the guides and domestics, we set out toward evening for Catania. This time my old charger acquitted himself to the admiration of the entire community, local and migratory, between San Nicolosi and Catania. Falling asleep at the very first step, he dropped his head between his fore legs and his tail between his hind legs, and, thus comfortably indifferent to public opinion, jogged on at so sleepy a pace that it was a miracle how we ever reached Catania. Such indeed was the force of example, and the striking pictorial effect of both horse and rider, that the venerable muleteer—a fat old gentleman of fifty, who rode behind—fell into a fit of musing, from which he gradually fell into a pleasant doze, and from the doze he fell into a profound sleep; then he swayed from one side to the other, and bobbed down in front and bobbed back again, and then started out of horrible dreams; and nodded again, and fell asleep again as hard as ever; and at last, as I had prophesied from the beginning, fell off his mule. Down in the dust he lay for as much as two minutes in a state of mute astonishment. "*Sacramento!*" said he, getting up and shaking the dust off, as soon as he found that no bones were broken, "*Accidenta, Donna Maria, Santa Sophia!*" And, climbing up again on the mule, he belabored the unfortunate animal with such vigor and good will that it danced Sicilian waltzes all the rest of the way into Catania.

CHAPTER VI.

A QUARREL WITH THE ANCIENTS.

THERE is not much to be said of Catania in addition to what is said in the guide-books. It is a dirty, shambling old place, a good deal like all other towns in Sicily, and owes any interest that it may now possess to its history. Here it was that Polyphemus and his Cyclopes had their local habitation; here was the port of Ulysses; and Thalia and her sons, the Palici, were of Catanian memory; and here dwelt successively the Egyptian shepherds, the Sicanians, and the Romans, and the Saracens, and the Normans, and heaven knows how many other useless and quarrelsome people, who did nothing but build temples and churches and kill each other. Mount Etna was not half so cruel as these cut-throat races, whose deeds are blazoned forth in history for the admiration of mankind. Not all the burning lava that ever desolated the plains of Sicily has done a hundredth part of the killing so gloriously done by the blood-thirsty hordes that slew their fellow-creatures on these very plains. Every ruin, every column, every moss-covered stone is a history of ferocious wars. The cathedrals and crucifixes are baptized in blood, and the tombs of the slayers of men are worshiped.

The flames of Etna were not enough; famine and pestilence were too slow; so the great warriors of old swept whole tribes from the face of the earth, and built grand cathedrals, and temples, and amphitheatres, and aqueducts, and public baths, and reigned in triumph till greater warriors slew them, and razed their churches, and temples, and fine edifices; and history glorified them in turn, and they did great deeds in turn, and were slain.

It was civilization, all this. We know it, because we see the broken statuary and the ruins of palaces and war-battered castles that tell us of their deeds; and we are told that such things could not be done in the present benighted state of art and architectural knowledge. There was Homer, and Virgil, too, to sing the glories of war; and there was Thucydides and a thousand others to make killing mighty in the world's history; and even the mist of centuries has not obscured the deeds therein described. And those heroes are still worshiped. The precious years of youth are spent in the study of these dark histories; thousands who scarce can write their mother tongue are taught to chant the glories of war in the dead languages, that they may be versed in the bloody lore of classic times. Oh, wondrous people! Oh, mighty kings and chieftains! Listen to a few plain facts. I am going to address you solemnly in your tombs, and post you up concerning the nineteenth century. Tourists have so long sung your praises that I mean to make a martyr of myself by telling you the truth.

It is quite true, as enthusiastic travelers say, that your temples, and castles, and palaces are splendid specimens of architecture; that your baths are on the grandest scale; that your statuary is wonderfully beautiful; that you lived in a style of magnificence unknown to the people of the present day, except through your poets and historians; that all the relics of antiquity you have left us bear evidence of great power and extraordinary skill. But you were a barbarous people at best. The very splendor of your works is an evidence of your barbarism. What oceans of money you spent on palaces, and tombs, and mausoleums! What an amount of human labor you lavished in doing nothing! If the Pyramids of Egypt were ten miles high instead of a few hundred feet, would the world be any the better for it—would the mass of mankind be more enlightened, or more virtuous, or more happy? If the Coliseum at Rome had accommodated fifty millions of people instead of fifty thousand, would it have taught them the blessings of peace and good government, or disseminated useful knowledge among them? If all your palaces were built of pure gold instead of marble, would it have caused the thousands of human beings that you were continually embroiling in war to entertain a more fraternal spirit toward each other ? True, we go to war now and then ourselves in this the nineteenth century ; but it is not the chief business of our lives ; we do something else that is better. We don't build pyramids and coliseums, but we build railroads. The smallest steamboat that paddles its way up the Hudson is greater than the greatest monument of antiquity, and does more to promote the civilization and happiness of mankind ; the wires of our electric telegraphs carry more power in them than all the armies you ever brought into battle. And, for the matter of magnificent temples, if we had the time and money to waste, we could erect, for the amusement of kings, and women, and children, toys a great deal bigger and quite as useless. Your literature, your poetry and arts, only show how much the gifts of God may be perverted to bad purposes. War, and murder, and rapine, lust and bestiality, are the chief subjects of inspiration in what has been handed down to us ; yet we are asked to bow down to you with a blind adoration ! You had your merits and your weaknesses, just as we have ; the greatest of you had as much littleness as the greatest of us now ; you were just as weak, just as mortal, and a great deal more ignorant. Feasting, and fighting, and toy-making made you distinguished. We will profit by your follies, and endeavor to earn a name in ages to come by encompassing the earth with the blessings of freedom and civilization.

It is very unkind, I admit, to talk to dead people in this way ; but the fact is, one must let off a little indignation now and then. Of late I have been traveling with a friend so overcharged with admiration for the antique, and so deeply imbued with classical literature, that it is quite a relief to be revenged by an explosion. I have patiently endured broiling in the burning sun that he might enjoy an old stone with an illegible inscription on it, and walked for miles in search of tombs under which were buried men whose names I had never heard before ; I have listened for hours to learned discourses on the wars of the Greeks and Romans, in which, to be candid, I felt no interest whatever; for what consequence was it to a peaceful wayfarer like myself—simply an honorary General in the Bobtail Militia—how many were killed on certain occasions, or who were the best cut-throats of ancient times? All this I have done from the purest good-nature. But now the remembrance of roasting suns, and long walks for nothing, and longer discourses, and lost dinners, comes upon me with such force that I must have some satisfaction Yea, have I not seen men prate learnedly about Titian, and Rubens, and Guercino, who scarce knew red from blue; and young ladies go into ecstasies over a splendid Corinthian column, which was Doric, or an antique fresco which was painted about a dozen years ago?

We were overtaken at Catania by a Portuguese gentleman and his wife, fellow-passengers in the Neapolitan steamer from Naples to Palermo. Doctor Mendoza was a man of the world and a philosopher, and we were very glad to join him in an extra diligence to Syracuse. He was rich in worldly possessions, and, like a good many tourists whom we had met, traveled chiefly to kill time and hunt up the best hotels. There was no good hotel on the top of Mount Etna, so he staid at the "Corunna," in Catania; "because," said he, "I can see Mount Etna from my window." Having ascertained that there was a good hotel at Syracuse, he concluded to go; and he kindly entertained us on the road with a detailed account of the hotels through Germany, Switzerland, Poland, and Russia, dwelling with particular enthusiasm upon the style in which they get up hotels in St. Petersburg. He had been traveling constantly for three years in search of good hotels; if he had any guarantee that there were hotels in Athens and Jerusalem he would go there, but had not yet made up his mind to run so great a risk. The interest of a country depended altogether upon the excellence of its hotels. It was a matter of surprise to me how a man should go to so much expense to find comfortable accommodations in uncomfortable countries, when he could have found them so much better and so much cheaper at home or in Paris. Nor was my Portuguese friend alone in this mania for good hotels. I have seen English tourists, and I am sorry to say some American, made perfectly miserable by being compelled to pass the night in a respectable country inn, where the accommodations were not so good as those of the Parisian hotels.

CHAPTER VII.

ADVENTURES ON THE ROAD TO SYRACUSE.

THE morning was bright and bracing as our diligence rattled out of the streets of Catania, our little postillion as sparky as a red-bird in his jacket and feathers; our conductor as sleepy as conductors usually are, and our horses as long and lean and full of latent fire as the diligence horses of Sicily are in general. The road for seven or eight miles was along the shores of the bay over a low plain, passing a few scattering farm-houses and some of the battle-fields famous in the history of the early Sicilian wars. About seven miles from Catania we crossed the river Simeto, the largest, I believe, in Sicily. The plain through which the Simeto runs is of great extent, and abounds in fine meadow lands. Numbers of thatched cottages, of conical shape like hay-stacks, are scattered along the banks of the river, having a very peculiar and picturesque effect. We all dismounted at the ferry, and were ferried across in a dilapidated boat, which miraculously reached the opposite bank without sinking. The road now turned slightly inland, over rough barren hills, passing near Lake Beviero, or the Lake of Lentino, a pretty little fish-pond, till we reached the town of Lentini, where the horses are changed. Lentini is the modern name of Leontinum, once ranked among the most powerful cities of Sicily. It possessed in olden times handsome temples, rich public edifices, a palestra, and various works of art, but was laid waste during the wars; and now scarcely a trace remains of its ancient grandeur. It is a wretched collection of dirty dilapidated houses, with a population of filthy and half-barbarous peasantry.

Here commenced that series of calamities to which I have already incidentally referred. Eighteen miles in the bracing morning air had given us a ravenous appetite. The *Hôtel de Parigi* was recommended by our driver as the best in the place, and although it bore very little resemblance to any thing we had ever seen in Paris, being about as black and dirty a looking *locanda* as could well be found in Sicily, we ascended through the hostlery to a large bare room, with a table in the middle, and half a dozen wooden chairs ranged round the walls, and called for *qualche cosa mangera*—in plain English, something to eat. The padrona, a sour-looking woman, eyed us with a speculative glance, having reference to the size of our purses, and said: " We have nothing but eggs and bread, signores; the meat has been devoured by a party that have just gone ahead." " Very well, then," said we, " let us have the eggs and bread as soon as possible." In about half an hour we had a scanty *collazione* of fried eggs, to which we did as much justice as the subject permitted. " Now, padrona, what is to pay?" " What you wish, signores." " No, no; you must fix your own price." " Then, as you have had nothing but eggs and bread, we will only charge you two dollars." " Two dollars! why that is impossible. We have only had a dozen eggs and a little bread!" " Well then, say a dollar and a half; that is very little for four persons, signores." We paid the dollar and a half, and considered ourselves very cleverly done. As we were about to leave, our hostess reminded us of another small charge—three carlins for the room. " What!" said we, in an honest fit of indignation, " do you mean to say we are to pay for the privilege of eating your miserable *collazione* in this barn of a place?" " Of course, signores, you have had the use of the room." " Very true, but did you think we were going to eat out of doors?" " By no means, and that is the reason why I charge you for the accommodation of the room." It was no use to argue against a system of reasoning so cogent as this; the postillion was calling to us to come on; so we paid the three carlins for the use of the room. Passing out, we were attacked by a dirty *cuisine*, who demanded a trifling remuneration for her services. "Please your excellencies, I cooked breakfast for you!" "The deuce you did! how do you suppose we could eat it unless it was cooked? Are people in the habit of eating breakfast raw at the *Hôtel de Parigi*?" "No, signores, I cook it for them, and they always give me something for my trouble." It was no use to rebel; the cook hung to us like a leech, and it was only by paying her three carlins that we could extricate ourselves from her clutches. "Thank Heaven, we are done now!" was our involuntary exclamation, as we made our exit. "*Aspetto*, signores," said a voice behind, "you have forgotten the *facchino*." "The what?" "The porter, gentlemen." "And pray what have you done for us?" "I attend to the baggage, signores." "But we have no baggage here; it is all in the diligence." "Ah, that makes no difference; I could have carried it for you: I must live, you know, and this is all the pay I get to support a large family." The claim was irresistible; we rebelled at first, but it was no use, the *facchino* followed us till we had to give him a few baiocci to get rid of him. "Well, this beats Italy all hollow," was our unanimous conclusion, as we took our respective seats in the diligence, and began to enjoy the luxuries of sunshine and cigars, after the storm through which we had passed. "*Buono mano*," said our small postillion. "For what, you rascal?" "For driving you." "But you did not drive us; you were asleep all the time; we won't pay you!" However, we did pay him, after a great deal of talking. "Drive on now," shouted the Englishman. "*Andate!*" roared the Portuguese. "Go ahead," said I. "*Aspetta*, senores," cried the hostler; "*buono mano* for the hostler." We threw the hostler a few carlins, and shouted, "Drive on, *andate!* go ahead again!" "*Aspetta!*" cried the hostler, "this is an extra diligence; extra diligences are always double price. Besides, it is two posts from Catania, and you have only paid for one change of horses." "*Diabolo*," roared the Portuguese, "we have only had one change, and that has just been put in now." "Stunning business this," said the Englishman. "Done brown!" said I. "True, senores, but you must pay for the half-way post." "There is no post there, you scoundrel—no horses—nothing at all!" "*Da verro*, signores, but these horses have done double duty; so they must be paid for, or they can't go on!' This was too bad. "*Cospetto!*" shrieked the Portuguese. "Excessively annoying!" said the Englishman. "Great country!" said I—"great country, gentlemen!" We unanimously determined that we would not pay for changing horses, when no such change was made. "Go to the devil with your horses, then; we won't pay a cent more." "*Va bene*, senores!" replied the hostler, very coolly unhitching the horses, and leading them off to the stable. "I'll go to the devil to oblige you, signores; but I can't go to Syracuse till the halfway post is paid for. You will have to go on without horses, that's all."

Here was a predicament! The inhabitants of the classical city of Lentini were pouring down from all the neighboring streets to see the diligence that was bound to Syracuse without horses. Matrons with children in their arms held up their precious babes to see the sight; piratical-looking fellows gathered around and examined us with a deliberate and speculative stare; the little boys shouted merrily, and called the attention of all straggling acquaintances to the pole of the diligence that pointed toward Syracuse, but wouldn't pull for want of horses! What was to be done? Go to the Mayor? Perhaps there was none, and if there was, who knew the way? "Senores," said the hostler, in a soothing tone, perceiving our distress of mind, "you had better pay me, and allow me the pleasure of putting the horses in." We considered the advice, and took it. It was rather humiliating to our feelings; but we were hemmed in with difficulties on all sides; in vain we looked round upon the crowd; not a sympathizing face was there; not a soul to pity us in our misfortunes. The pervading sentiment seemed to be—" Hit 'em again! they've got no friends!" There was one universal shout of laughter as the postillion cracked his whip, and drove us rattling out of Lentini. I turned to look back as we ascended the hill, and caught a glimpse of the hostler, who was still bowing to us with the utmost **gravity** and politeness. If ever I meet that man on Pennsylvania avenue, it is my settled intention to do him personal violence.

As to the sparky little postillion who drove us so furiously out of Catania, and who afterwards fell asleep when there was nobody on the roadside to admire his driving, I have him safe enough. Here he is. Public indignation is respectfully solicited:

The individual mounted upon that horse, swindled us out of two carlins. What he did with so much money it would be impossible to say; he may have put it in his boots for safe keeping; but he certainly could not have deposited his ill-gotten gains in his coat-pockets. I only know that we paid him the sum above specified for doing certain duties that he never performed; and that implicit confidence is not to be placed in a man simply because he wears a feather in his hat, a jacket with red cloth embroidery and small tails, and a pair of top-boots, big enough to bury him in when he dies.

From Lentini to Syracuse the distance by the public road is twenty-four miles, making the entire distance from Catania forty-four miles. After leaving the valley of the Simeto, the country becomes barren and rugged, and there is very little to attract the attention of the traveler. What the appearance of the country may be in spring I had no means of ascertaining; but certainly a more desolate picture of poverty and barrenness I never saw than it presents in the month of October. Naked hills of parched earth and bleak rocks; a few miserable vineyards, either entirely without fencing, or surrounded by ragged hedges of prickly pear; villages rudely built of stone, without shade or comfort, and in a wretched state of ruin; an occasional mule with a load, driven by a man of beard and rags; a gang of beggars, as voracious as a pack of wild beasts; here and there a half-naked and withered woman, with the rough features of a man, scratching the ground with a hoe, or tottering under a heavy burden, while her husband lies basking in the sun; litters of dirty children rooting in the mud, without covering of any kind—these are the sights that one sees on the road to the ancient City of the Sun, the abode of gods whose shrines no longer burn.

In a few hours from Lentini we had a good view of the Cape St. Croce and the town of Agosta. Giovanni Power, whose "Guida di Sicilia" I have now before me, says of Agosta that it is supposed to have risen out of the ruins of Megara, and Megara from those of the little Keybla. It was there, according to Herodotus, that the people were sold at auction, in the time of Gelon.

From an eminence, as we approached Syracuse, we had a very pretty view of Ortigia, the only inhabited part of the ancient city. It is built on an island connected to the main land by a long pier and a bridge, and strongly fortified by high walls, forts, and castles.

The number of gates, bridges, fortified arches, and vaulted passages through which one is driven before he can fairly consider himself within the walls of Ortigia quite surpasses all powers of computation. When the diligence stopped at one of the outer gates, we were carefully inspected by a couple of officers, in flashy uniforms and feathers, who politely requested us to allow them the pleasure of looking at our passports. One stood a little in the background, with pens, ink, and paper in his hand : he was evidently a subordinate character, notwithstanding the brilliancy of his plumage, which, from a hasty estimate, I calculated to consist of the tails of three game-cocks ; the other was a portly man, of grave and dignified demeanor, rich in tin buttons and red cloth epaulets, and with a mustache that would have done credit to the Governor himself; in fact, I thought at first that he was the Governor, so imposing was his personal appearance. The

passports he opened slowly and cautiously, either from habitual contempt of the value of time, or a latent suspicion that they contained squibs of gunpowder ; and at last, when he had fairly spread them out, with the signatures inverted, he carefully scanned the contents for five minutes, and then calmly addressed us, in bad Italian ; "Your names, Signores, if you please." Our friend the Portuguese, being the oldest, was accorded the privilege of speaking first. "My name,

Signor, is Mendoza, and this lady is my wife." "Grazia, Signor." Then, turning to the subordinate. "Put that down—Men-z-z-a. *Va bene.*" After some other questions as to profession, place of nativity, &c., he turned to the Englishman, "Your name, Signor?" "Mine? My name is Norval : on the Grampian hills my father feeds his flocks, a frugal swain"—— "Excuse, Signor, what did you say? "Smith, John Smith, if you like it better !" " *Va bene*, Signor; put that down: Giovanni Smiz; no, Semmit—Giovanni Semmit." The man with the tails of the game-cocks in his hat put it down. "And your name, Signor?" turning to your humble servant. "Sir," said I, with a dash of honest pride in the thought that I was giving a name known in the remotest corners of the globe, "My name is Brown—John Brown, Americano, General in the Bobtail Militia." "Grazia! Signor," said the officer, bowing, as I flattered myself, even more profoundly than he had bowed to my friend John Smith. "Put that down—Giovanni Brovvenni." "BROWN !" said I; for I had no idea of having an honest name so barbarously Italianized. "Si, Signor, *Bruvven*." "No !" said I, sternly, " not Bruvven—BROWN, Sir." "Si, Signor—BRUIN." "No, Sir !" said I, indignantly, "do you take me for a bear, Sir ? My name's BROWN, Sir." "Certo, Signore, BRUIN !" And Bruin was written down by the feathered man; and so stands my name to this day in the official archives of Syracuse—GIOVANNI BRUIN, or JOHN BEAR.

After this pleasant little passage of official dignity and governmental wisdom, we rattled on over a drawbridge, and under an arch, and through half a dozen gates, and up a long pier, and through some more gates, and finally into Ortigia, or modern Syracuse, where we rattled through an interminable labyrinth of narrow and dirty streets, our postillion alternately cracking polkas with his whip, and blowing his brains through his horn, scattering the astonished inhabitants in all directions, and running over lazy dogs in his mad career. At last we brought up near the *Hotel del Sole*, where we were dragged out of the diligence by a whole regiment of ragged *facchini*, and piloted into the dark recesses of the *Sole* by the bald-headed Padrone.

CHAPTER VIII.

SYRACUSE.

At this hotel (the *Sole*) we were so fortunate as to secure the services of a guide, who was not only an accomplished cicerone, but an artist of considerable merit, and the author of a work on the antiquities of Syracuse. I have forgotten his name, but any body who visits Ortigia can not fail to recognize him in the elegant person of a young man, a little *blasé* in his manners, who lounges gracefully about the *Sole*, and does things up as *valet de place* with the resigned air of a gentleman of broken fortune, who has been reduced to the necessity of bartering his classical knowledge and personal services for the contemptible sum of one dollar per diem. He will converse with you on art and history, point out to you all the antiquities of Syracuse, sell you his pictures, attend to your passport, carry your umbrella, see that your boots are blacked, and go of messages—all for the miserable pittance of a dollar a day; and if you like he will go with you to the opera, and tell you the history of the prima donna and of each of the chorus-singers individually. For my part, I took it as rather a compliment that so fashionable a looking man should be seen in my company, and, notwithstanding the horror and disgust of my young English friend, always invited him to join us in a cigar or a glass of wine, and felt quite happy when he sate with us in a public café, sipping the *nero* with a languid air, or dallying elegantly over a glass of ice-cream at my expense.

In America one would be ashamed to exact menial services of so accomplished a gentleman; but in the old world it is so common as not to attract attention, except from strangers. Indeed, we republicans are much more stiff and haughty toward our subordinates than the Germans or French, and quite as much so as the English. Sometimes it is such a relief to be natural and kind that I try it for variety. The other day, up in Austria, I was caught by a party of friends in the act of drinking beer with our hack-driver, a very jolly, respectable old Dutchman; but, from the disdainful manner in which they refused to join us, I felt exceedingly mortified about it, and resolved never to be good-natured again. The very same evening, walking in one of the public gardens, I met a former guide, with whom I thoughtlessly sat down to have a cup of coffee, and was in the act of being perfectly happy when my friends discovered me again, and this time they showed such decided symptoms of disapprobation that I vowed never to be sociable any more. Shortness of funds compelled me soon after to take passage in the third-class cars, where I was terribly afraid some one would see me—some American or Englishman, I mean, because I knew nobody else would be distressed about it. There was a respectable-looking man on the next seat who spoke English. He was very chatty and agreeable, and it was quite a consolation to find so intelligent a man in the same reduced circumstances. We talked very pleasantly for some time, when he informed me that his master was in the first-class; that the said master was a countryman of mine. I was terribly mortified, of course; there was that lonely and high-minded man in the first-class, and I, with the most ambitious aspirations, in the third-class with his courier. However, it was some comfort to think that I had passed my time pleasantly so far, and had received all the information for which the lonely man in the first-class was paying a dollar a day, besides the courier's expenses.

But this is a sad habit I have fallen into of rambling off from the main subject. I believe I was in Syracuse.

Now, if ever a man tried hard to get up some enthusiasm about a place that he had read of with wonder and admiration in early youth, I tried it in Syracuse. I went down into the ancient baths, and suffered damp and chilling airs without seeing any thing but subterranean passages and uncomfortable holes; through miles of ancient catacombs I roamed without one sentiment of admiration for the mighty dead who were no longer there; bones I picked up, but they looked so like common bones that I threw them down again: it was no use; the enthusiasm wouldn't come. As for the amphitheatre at Neapolis, it is just like any other amphitheatre, only less perfect than those of Italy. The ancient aqueduct is in so dilapidated a state that scarcely a vestige remains. The Ear of Dionysius is one of the few things worth seeing. It is a large excavation in solid rock, where it is said Dionysius the Second imprisoned his victims, and amused himself listening to their groans. The reverberation in this cavern is so great, owing to some peculiarity in the construction, that the tearing of a piece of paper produces a loud report. There are other excavations in the vicinity, of great size and extent, formerly used as prisons, but now occupied by rope-makers, which is much better. If Dionysius himself had turned his attention to the manufacture of ropes, he might have deserved hanging less, and have enjoyed a better reputation in history. The museum in Ortigia contains a very scanty collection of antiquities, dug out of the ruins of Syracuse. The chief attraction is the broken statue of Venus, which is a very beautiful work of art, and justly admired. Very little remains of ancient Syracuse except the excavations from which the stone was taken to build the city. Some of these are occupied by a miserable population of outcasts, who seem to have no

houses or means of living, and prey upon travelers for the wretched pittance by which they support life.

The whole region around Syracuse is rocky and desolate, and so little remains of its ancient grandeur that it requires a warm imagination to invest it with sufficient interest to repay a visit. It is difficult to conceive how a city that once contained a population of two millions should be reduced to such utter ruin: now a mere hill-side of quarries and a dirty little town with a population of seventeen or eighteen thousand. Where the land was to support such a population, or the port for such a commerce as they would have required, is a mystery that can not be solved by any evidences now existing; and the probability is that history in this instance, as in many others, has greatly exaggerated the facts.

Some distance from the gates of Ortigia, on an eminence, is an old convent, and near it the cemetery in which lie buried the remains of two Americans—one a young midshipman, killed in a duel, and the other a gunner. We visited their graves, and took copies of the inscriptions placed upon their tombs by some kind shipmates. It was sad, in a foreign land, amid the vestiges of ruin and decay, to stand by these lonely graves and think how died these two of kindred blood and language, so far away from home. The young midshipman was cut short in his bright career, not by wasting disease, but by the hand of a brother officer. A brief notice in the guide-book was all that told the story. He fell in a duel, near the place of his burial; and he sleeps his last sleep in a far-off land, with none to mourn over his lonely grave, none to feel a pang of pity, save the passing stranger. This was honor! Does the slayer of that youth, if he still lives, feel that he has done an honorable deed when he thinks of the lonely grave of his victim? Is there a charm in the thought to wash out the stain of blood? Has the admiration of the world made him feel in his secret heart that he is the braver for having risked his life and slain his fellow-man? Was forgiveness of an injury so base an act that it would have embittered his whole future? Oh, honor, honor! for what dark and bloody crimes hast thou to answer!

We paid a visit to the modern catacombs in the convent, but found them much inferior to those in Palermo, of which I have given some account. While strolling through among the bodies, accompanied by an old monk, one of the heads rolled off and fell on the ground. The monk quietly picked it up, thanked God for the accident, and placed it on the neck again, but in such an extraordinary position as to produce a most ludicrous effect. "*Non fa niente!*" said he, "it makes no difference now," and we walked on.

In the evening we went to an opera in Ortigia; rather an odd thing, you will admit, among the ruins of Syracuse. The piece was quite new to me, and abounded in terrible love scenes, murders, and thunderings of brass instruments. The prima donna created a great furore by her violent manner of dying; she died three times in succession by special request of the audience, and so great was the enthusiasm on the subject that I could not help joining in an attempt to get up a fourth death, in the faint hope that she might remain dead till the conclusion of the opera.

Now this, to be sure, is rather a scanty description of Syracuse—a mere budget of anecdotes, you will say. But what can I tell you without copying from the guide-book, which you will find in any public library. To be candid, I think there is more in the name of Syracuse than any thing else. The ruins are in such a state of dilapidation that one can scarcely recognize any thing, even with the assistance of a guide. Those of Agrigentum are considered much finer. After Rome, and the ruins of Pestum, near Naples, there is little worth seeing in Sicily in the way of ruins, except Sicily and its government, which may be considered a ruin on a large scale; one of the grandest ruins, if we are to believe its early history, in Southern Europe. War and rapine, and all the evils of military despotism; pestilence and famine, earthquakes and volcanic eruptions, have scourged that ill-fated island till its mountains are bare and its valleys are waste; and the spirit of desolation broods over its ruins even as the scourge of the Divine hand yet rests upon Jerusalem and the hills of Judea.

We spent a day and a half in Syracuse, and would have continued on to Noto and Girgenti but for the want of time. It was getting late in the season, and each of us had plans of Oriental travel for the coming month of November. It must be said in favor of Sicily, at this season of the year, that the climate is perfectly delicious; and the skies unsurpassed in any part of the world. The sunset scenes every evening were beautiful beyond description; and the soft tints of the distant mountains of Calabria, and the interior of Sicily, were such as Claude Lorraine delighted to paint, and which no other artist has ever given in such perfection. It is pleasant, after all the annoyances of passports and beggars, in a country like this, to get up in the morning at day-light, drink your coffee, pay all your bills, thank Heaven when you are through; jump into the open diligence; listen to the lively crack of the postillion's whip and the rattling of the wheels as you are whirled off out of the narrow streets; and then, when fairly beyond the gates, to snuff the fresh air as you fly along the smooth roads by the sea-shore, and watch the first glimmer of the sun as it lightens up the Eastern horizon, and trace out cities of gold among the light clouds that float over the mountains of Calabria; to draw in the fresh morning air again until you feel as if it would lift you up into the realms of pure spirits. A wild joy thrills through your blood at such a time—a gladness that you are born, and in the world, and capable of feeling its beauties; and you inwardly thank God for all the blessings that life still contains, even amid the ruin and desolation wrought by man's evil deeds. What if that sun has risen for centuries over battle-fields, and scorched with thirst the wounded and the dying; mingled its rays with the flames of Etna, and shed its softest evening glories over scenes of terror and death: through the unfathomable past, in the alternate phases of good and evil throughout all the wicked deeds that man has wrought against man, and all the fierce convulsions of nature, it has shed its healing glow upon the human heart; it has cheered the houseless and the homeless with its warmth; it has nourished and ripened the fruits of the earth for countless generations;

it has filled millions of souls with adoration of the Divine Creator; and in its light, and warmth, and sublime beauties, in all the joy and gladness that it sheds upon earth, there is still enough of heaven to make us feel that we are mortal here to be immortal hereafter.

Pardon these little bursts of enthusiasm, I pray you; the fact is, being unable to get up any inspiration on the subject of antiquities, I have to let out now and then on the sun, and moon, and stars by way of experiment; for when I see my fellow-travelers go into raptures over an old stone wall, or a musty picture, or broken column, which fails to produce the slightest effect upon me, I begin to imagine that there must be something lacking in head or heart, and it is only by soaring among the mountains and clouds that I can conjure up a particle of enthusiasm.

CHAPTER IX.

TAORMINA.

On our arrival in Catania, we proceeded at once to demand satisfaction of the proprietor of the diligence for the misconduct of the conductor in suffering us to be stopped at Lentini and other *postes* on the road to Syracuse. We had drawn up a bill against him for all the extra charges for horses, postillions and hostlers, over and above what were specified in the article of agreement. That article of agreement contained every item that we felt legally bound to pay; and we had carefully preserved it as a warning to the proprietor that we were not the kind of people to be imposed upon.

Our first measure, therefore, upon arriving at the door of the Corunna, was to send for the proprietor of the diligence. We had taken the names of all the conspirators who had fleeced us on the road—such names, at least, as they gave us; and thus prepared, we formed ourselves into a sort of tribunal on the pavement, for the vindication of our rights and the infliction of a severe reprimand upon all who dared to outrage the majesty of the law. Doctor Mendoza was appointed prosecuting attorney, as he was much the largest man in the party and rather the most fluent in Italian. The proprietor, or padrone, as he was called, when he approached and saw us formed into a high Court of Inquiry, turned very pale, and bowed a great many times before our honors. All the idlers about the Corunna began to gather round, and every body being an idler, the audience was soon of very imposing dimensions. Doctor Mendoza opened the case—rather violently as I thought—by thrusting the contract in the face of the trembling padrone, and calling him a sporka, a robber, a miserable poltroon! and a great many other names of the kind; which the padrone received with the most unbounded resignation. Indeed, had he been used to such charges all his life he could not have manifested a more forgiving spirit. His only answer was to demand meekly the cause of all this violence. Had he pulled Doctor Mendoza by the nose, he could not have offered him a greater insult than this question. For two minutes that gentleman was perfectly breathless with rage; he stormed, he stamped upon the pavement; he tore his hair; he spluttered and spat all about; and then, after this explosion, he shrieked in English, in Portuguese, in French, and in Italian; during which time the padrone took several pinches of snuff, and awaited the conclusion. At the conclusion he demanded again the cause of this extreme violence.

"*Sacr-r-r-r! Diablo!*" screamed the Portuguese, rushing at him, with his fingers bent as if to claw the eyes out of him—"*Calaboca! Per-r-r Baccho!* By dam! you rob! you dam rascal! *Perche questa?* (shaking the paper in his face) *Due baiocco!—due, tre, quatro, cinqua carlin! Sempra! Sempra! Per-r-r Deo! baiocci, carlini, scudi! Sacr-r-r!*"

The counsel for the accused, which consisted of the conductor, the driver, the postillion, and several of the ragged *facchini*, belonging to the hotel, broke in and protested that it was the custom of the country, that any other padrone would have charged double the price; they all talked at once, and their appeals in behalf of the padrone were so eloquent and moving that he evidently began to consider himself a much injured man, and this sense of outraged honesty so inspired him with courage, that he began to protest that he would have justice for such unmerited accusations; he couldn't stand it; he'd go to the police office.

The upshot of the whole business was, that we had to pay the full amount on the agreement, and suffer an additional loss of several carlins in fees to the counsel of the accused, who never ceased to persecute us till we showed symptoms of a disposition to pay the required amount. The ground upon which they based their claim was that they had helped us out of the difficulty! Such a course of conduct might well be considered as adding insult to injury; but having no alternative we paid the fees in order to get rid of the counsel, who were getting stronger every moment; and who had already enlisted the sympathies of every straggler in the street.

COUNSEL FOR THE ACCUSED.

Leaving Catania as soon as we could get a change of horses, we passed in sight of the Cyclopean isles, and about dark reached a town distant ten miles. Here we stopped for the night, much to the disgust of our Portuguese friend, who was rather sore in mind after the affair at Catania, and consequently could not tolerate an indifferent hotel. He was always particular about hotels; but this time he was uncommonly fastidious. The Posta, where we stopped, had rooms good enough if they were only clean. Doctor Mendoza was incensed at the filth of this establishment. He excited himself to such a degree on the subject of the bed-linen, that he ended by tearing his hair and rushing out in search of another hotel, and I was so fearful of some tragical act on his part, that I ran after him, imploring him to return. There were only two other hotels in the place, which he explored in the most violent manner; darting furiously into the bedrooms, lifting up the bed-linen, making horrible faces of contempt and disgust, calling every body in the town, sporka, and then darting out again. In the end he was forced to return to the Posta, where we contrived to survive the tortures of the vermin, and get something to eat.

The next day's travel along the sea-shore was the most pleasant we had enjoyed in Sicily. Good-humor was restored after all these trials of temper, and we laughed heartily at the incidents of our journey to Syracuse.

We now entered a fertile region along the base of Mount Etna, abounding in green valleys and luxuriant vineyards, and dotted over with pretty little towns and farms. The road on either side was lined with pleasant-looking and picturesque villas, and the population had a much more thrifty appearance than that of the southern portion of the island. At *Aci Reale*, a handsomely situated town about half-way between Catania and Messina, our party took mules to go up to the ruins of Taormina, about an hour distant up the mountain. My experience in mules was not such as to encourage another trial; so I walked. The town of Taormina is one of the most picturesque old places in Sicily. For variety of outline and wild scenic effect, I have seen nothing in Italy or any part of Europe to surpass the ruins of the Teatro di Taormina and surrounding mountains. On three sides are towering peaks of rock; Mount Etna is clear and blue in the distance; and the Straits of Messina and the mountains of Calabria lie outspread in front with all the rich coloring given by an autumnal sun. I stopped long enough to explore the ruins and make some sketches, rather to the annoyance of my traveling friends, who generally did their admiration up in broken exclamations, and left me to do the artistical part, while they pushed on in search of further antiquities.

Touching the history of Taormina, it belongs chiefly to classical times. Now, to tell the honest truth, I have no predilection for the classics. In my younger days that sort of reading was forced upon me as physic for the mind; and having no taste for extravagant scenes of bloodshed and disgusting exhibitions of sensuality and folly, the result was that I took to Don Quixote, Gil Blas, Robinson Crusoe, and other authentic histories in which I could believe, without doing violence to common sense. Fortunately, however, I have friends who are of a different way of thinking, and who consider that the best and most reliable sources of knowledge are to be found in classical history. I am indebted to Mr. Alexander Clements, United States Consul at Messina, who is a most esteemed fellow-townsman, for a sketch of Taormina, translated from the Italian, which I have taken the liberty to condense. I have since had the pleasure of seeing a fine view of the ruins, painted by Mr. Clements; and I am glad to learn that he contemplates a work illustrating the beauties of Sicilian scenery, with historical sketches from sources not usually accessible to persons unacquainted with the language.

Taormina was once a very rich and notable city; and was called *Taurominum*, because it was built upon the summit of Mount Taurus. It was founded by Andromaches, father of the historian Timeos, in concert with the inhabitants of Naxos, after the tyrant Dionysius had destroyed the latter city. Taormina has been so often exposed to the vicissitudes of war, and especially in the times of the Saracens, who in the year 893 razed it to the ground, that its population, once most numerous, is now reduced to about 3000 souls. Earthquakes, especially that of 1693, have likewise contributed to the fall of the city; and it is probable that this state of ruin and depopulation will continue in consequence of the town of Giardini being since founded in a much more advantageous position for all the relations of commerce. It is easy to comprehend why fugitives from slavery or death should found a city upon a rock, almost inaccessible; but it seems a marvel that in times of peace the inhabitants have not abandoned their aerial retreat, and descended to a more convenient place. The suburbs of Taormina contain many interesting antiquities, and the ruins of its theatre are in a position so picturesque that they are incomparably more striking than any in Sicily. Of less importance among the antiquities are the ruins of a cistern, of a gymnasium, a little temple and some tombs. The most notable of all the ruins, however, is that of the theatre. It is regarded by the best judges as one of the finest specimens of architecture for scenic effect in existence. From the position of the seats the spectators enjoyed a most imposing scene; such in fact that no description or painting can give a just idea of it.

It is a remarkable peculiarity in all the ancient theatres of Sicily that they conform entirely in their construction to the local circumstances by which they are surrounded, as at Segesta, Syracuse, Taormina and other places. This was done with a view to the sound of the voice, as well as to the scenic effect. The theatre of Taormina it is said was capable of accommodating twenty-five thousand persons. It was subjected to some changes after its primitive construction, under the Greeks whose work it was, as also under the Romans who repaired and embellished it. The entire edifice was surrounded by galleries of brick, and niches are still seen

in which statues were placed. Many columns of granite and marble, still remain upon the walls, but not in their original places. Some of the finest of the architectural ornaments, have been carried away in times of ignorance by the inhabitants, who used them as material for building.

The sketch on the preceding page hastily taken on the spot, represents the amphitheatre and a portion of the main edifice.

CHAPTER X.

THE BREACH.

On our arrival in Messina we lost no time in securing the best rooms at the Vittoria for Doctor Mendoza and lady; and it was a source of great pleasure to behold him when he came down to the dinner-table, with the Madam on his arm. He was shaved and oiled to the extremest point of nicety; his brows were unclouded for the first time within a week; he smiled pleasantly over his soup, and discoursed eloquently of the hotels at St. Petersburg over his salad and salmis. The Madam was charmed; she was radiant with smiles; she never stopped looking with admiration at her husband, and evidently thought he was rather the handsomest man in the world, when the dust of travel was rubbed off his face.

Next morning we set out, all bright and smiling, accompanied by Mr. Clements, to explore the city of Messina. There is not much in it to attract attention, but what there is we ferreted out with uncommon ingenuity.

The foundation of Messina (according to a translation from the Italian) extends to times so remote that the precise epoch is not known. It once boasted many precious monuments, among which mention is made of a splendid temple of Neptune, and another of Hercules. There was also the Palace of Cajo Ejo, from which was taken the celebrated statue of Cupid made by Praxiteles; but the many sieges sustained by this city and the frequent earthquakes by which it has been desolated, have not left any vestiges of its ancient edifices. The population of Messina was once very numerous; in 1575 the plague destroyed 65,000 persons, and civil wars and other calamities have since reduced it to a mere remnant.

At present the entire population, including the suburbs, amounts to about 90,000 souls. The greater part of the town is new, having been entirely rebuilt since the famous earthquake of 1783.

There is so little to be seen in Messina that we got through on the day after our arrival. A few churches, convents, and old walls are about the only sights in the way of antiquities that the traveler is called upon to endure; and, after seeing these, he may pass the time pleasantly enough rambling about the neighborhood, which is full of fine scenery, or lounging about the wharves, where he will enjoy something in the way of maritime life on shore. The position of the town is scarcely less picturesque than that of Palermo, and for all the evidences of progress and civilization I greatly preferred this neighborhood to any part of Sicily.

On the occasion of a second visit to Messina I was accompanied by an Irish major from India and an old English gentleman returning from the East, both fellow-passengers on the steamer from Malta, and very jovial and agreeable traveling acquaintances. We had but three hours on shore, the steamer having merely touched for passengers. It was, therefore, on landing, a matter of consideration in what way we could spend our time most profitably. The Englishman was in favor of seeing the breach at the risk of every thing else; the major of that happy and accommodating temperament which renders a man capable of enjoying all things equally; and I, having on a former occasion seen every thing in Messina except the breach, yielded, against an internal conviction that a hole in a wall is not an object of peculiar interest. But habitual martyrdom makes a man magnanimous, and the old gentleman was bent upon seeing the breach; he had set his heart upon it; he had enlightened us upon the historical points, and the breach we must see. Nor would he have a guide, for he spoke French, and could ask the way. The major, too, spoke a foreign language; it was Guzerat or Hindoo, and not likely to be very useful in the streets of Messina, but it might come in play; and I prided myself on speaking Italian; that is to say (between you and myself), a species of Italian formed chiefly of Arabic, French, Tuscan, Neapolitan, and English, but chiefly of English Italianized by copious additions of vowels at the end of every word. Yielding, however, to the superior zeal of our English friend, Mr. Pipkins, we kept modestly in the rear; while he took the middle of the main street, and kept a sharp lookout for any intelligent-looking man that had the appearance of understanding French. "*Parlez vous Français, monsieur,*" said Pipkins to the very first man he met. "*Nein!*" replied the man, "*sprechen Sie Deutsch?*" "Talk to him in Hindoo," said Mr. Pipkins. The major addressed him accordingly in Hindoo. "*Nicht,*" said the man. "Maybe he understands Italian," suggested the major. "*Parle Italiana?*" said I, "*Si, signor, un poco.*" "*Dove il breccha* in the *Muro,*" said I, going to the full extent of my Italian. The man looked puzzled, but, not wishing to appear ignorant, addressed me in such a complicated mixture of German and Sicilian that I had to stop him at length. "*Si, si, grazia.*" "What does he say?" inquired Mr. Pipkins. "I think he says the wall is somewhere outside the city; but he speaks abominable Italian." "Humph! never mind; here's a gentleman that speaks French, I'm certain. Monsieur! I say, monsieur!" (calling to a stiff-looking man just passing), "*Parlez vous Français, monsieur?*" "*No, signor; Italiana.*" Upon this hint I spake Italian, as before. The stiff man unbent himself, and politely conducted us round the corner, where he showed us the ancient CHURCH; and bidding us adieu, went his way with the same grave and studied aspect. I shall never forget the look of mingled doubt and disappointment with which my venerable English friend surveyed me. "Did you ask him for a church?" "No, I asked him for the wall with the breach in it." From that moment, I believe Mr. Pipkins suspected me of bad Italian. Disappointment, however, only added to his zeal. Pushing on with a determined step, he led the way through innumerable streets, till at length we reached an open piazza, where we halted close by a hack stand to gain breath and take an observation. Here we were soon surrounded by such an eager gang of vetturini, in consequence of an indiscreet question in Hindoo by the major, that we had to work ourselves out of the crowd by main force. "Leave it all to me," said our English friend, "I'll find somebody presently who speaks French. Ha! that man has a French look. I say, monsieur, monsieur!" The man stopped. "*Parlez vous Français, monsieur?*" "*Oui, monsieur.*" "I told you so," said our friend, turning to us triumphantly; "see what perseverance will do;" and then he propounded a series of questions to the strange gentleman concerning the location of the wall, interrupted at every pause by "*Oui, monsieur, oui, oui.*" "Now, sir, can you tell us where it is? (still in French). What language the individual addressed spoke in reply it would be impossible to say ; but it was brief and to the point, for he immediately conducted us round another corner and showed us the DILIGENCE OFFICE, after which he touched his hat politely, and walked on. Mr. Pipkins regarded the sign upon the diligence office with ineffable disgust, and then casting a ferocious look after the stranger, struck his stick heavily upon the pavement, and said : "Damme, if that's French! He doesn't understand the language!" For some time previously I had observed a suspicious-looking fellow dodging from corner to corner in our rear, who now came up touching his hat respectfully. "Gemmen," said he, "me speakee Inglees. What you want?" Our friend explained in full, evidently much relieved at this sudden accession to his cause. "Yes, yes, me know," replied the man. "Come on." We followed with a good will, certain that our troubles were at last at an end ; and really I began to feel quite interested in the wall from the sheer force of disappointment. We had proceeded some distance through a labyrinth of streets, when Mr. Pipkins, who was engaged in a hopeless attempt to extract additional information out of the guide concerning the wall, stopped short, and indignantly uttered these words : "You infernal rascal, that's not what we want!" Now, the full force of this violent language was of course lost upon the major and myself. The only words we overheard were—"just seventeen"—"arrived from Paris yesterday," which of course left us in a most painful state of mystery; nor could we prevail upon Mr. Pipkins to give us the least satisfaction on the subject. He merely turned back, muttering something about a deplorable state of morals; and upon consulting his watch found that it was about time to go on board the steamer.

A CRUSADE IN THE EAST.

CHAPTER XI.

ATHENS.

We left Messina on the afternoon of the 15th of October, and on the following morning were in sight of the Island of Malta. By noon we were at anchor in the harbor of Valetta. It was really refreshing to see something like cleanliness and civilization once more. The houses of Valetta, with their light cheerful coloring, their varieties of elevation, their pleasant verandas and balconies, are the neatest specimens imaginable of toy-work on a large scale; and the streets are the very queerest streets conceivable, with their uprisings and downfallings, their steps of stairs, their crowds of darkly hooded women and noisy men, and the strange mixture of races and languages, Europeanism, Orientalism, and Barbarism, scents and sounds, and all the varieties of life that abound in them. But British ascendency is apparent at the first glance. All one need do, after casting an eye upon the endless rows of cannon peeping from the fortifications, is to look at the banded and gilded officers strutting about every where, the red-coated guards armed to the teeth, and stationed at every gateway and public building, the never-ending drill of companies in the public squares, the bristling armories, the theatres, porter-houses, billiard saloons, club-houses, and army-tailor shops; and above all, at the places of worship, where the teachings of the Gospel are expounded, and peace and good will enjoined toward all mankind—to be convinced that he is once more among a progressive and enlightened people.

Doctor Mendoza and the Madam, who were on the same steamer from Messina, were charmed with the hotels of

Valetta. I saw nothing of this party in my rambles about the streets; but afterward was informed by the Doctor that they were fatigued by the voyage, and had spent the time in their hotel, which was very comfortable; the wines were excellent; the Madam was "indispose;" the mutton uncommonly fat and tender; and altogether they were *tres contents* to repose awhile after the perils and hardships of the voyage.

I took passage in the French steamer for the Piræus. The sea was rough and the weather very unpleasant. Compelled as I was, in all my traveling, to take the cheapest places, ranging from deck-passages up to the second cabin, I did not discover until we were in sight of Greece that my friends Dr. Mendoza and the Madam were on board the steamer with me again. They had eventually, upon consultation with the Portuguese Consul, as to the hotels, concluded to pursue their travels to the East. The purse of the Doctor was well lined, and of course he spared no pains in making himself and the Madam comfortable. Unlike most people with full purses, they were generous to a fault; indeed, I was often forced to interfere between the Doctor and his guides in order to prevent him from being cheated. If there was any one thing that troubled this amiable couple, it was the dreadful and unheard-of hardships which they supposed I must encounter in my second and third-class passages. Repeatedly melted by the pictures of starvation and desolation which they conjured up in my behalf (partly because I carried no baggage, and partly no doubt on account of my being naturally of a meagre habit) the Doctor offered me the use of a hundred pounds, payable at any convenient point in the world, or at any date however remote; and I never could make him understand the philosophy of traveling on the principle of Rough and Tumble; studying bodily deprivations, like Socrates and other renowned characters, as a practical science; enjoying the luxuries of hardship in European travel by comparison with past experience in flat-boats on the Mississippi, whalers off Madagascar, and bushing it in California; nor could he see how any reasonable man could take pride in such a way of traveling, even when that pride was based upon necessity.

ATHENS.

After a dreary passage of two days and a half from Malta we reached the Piræus, or sea-port town of Athens. The first thing that struck me upon landing was the absolute absurdity of being surrounded by a whole legion of boatmen, porters, and hack-drivers in petticoats. Their very earnestness in gesticulating for fees and baggage and a thousand other things, partly in Greek and partly broken English, while they sauntered about in all the pomp of mustaches, whips, and petticoats, was the most irresistibly ludicrous sight I had seen for many a day.

We took a large hack-man, with a splendid mustache, and an uncommonly fine pair of legs, petticoated in the most imposing style, who drove us through seas of dust, till we reached the half-way house. There we had to stop for sweetmeats, because it was the custom for all people of quality upon their first visit to Athens to stop at that place for that purpose. Why, I don't know; unless that a trifle of change might be divided between the hack-driver and his friend who keeps the establishment.

The distance from the Piræus is about seven miles; but the road being covered with a thick bed of dust which covered up the hack, we saw nothing of the Acropolis or other ruins till we were within a mile or two of the place.

On our arrival in Athens, my Portuguese friends went to the "Orient." It was a new hotel, and was recommended in the guide book as the best in the city. The "Angleterre" was very good; perhaps a little larger than the Orient, but it was not mentioned so favorably in Doctor Mendoza's book. Probably the author had fallen out with the proprietor on account of an indifferent beef-steak; for I rather incline to the opinion that the Angleterre is a better hotel than the Orient. However, neither of them suited my limited means; and I was reluctantly forced to leave my friends at the Orient, and go in search of the worst hotel in the place. Having no baggage except what I carried on my back in the shape of a knapsack principally filled with leaves and small pieces of various ruins for my friends at home, I was not troubled about porters. I soon found a very indifferent-looking hotel. It was the *Hôtel de Vienne*. If there be any worse in Athens, it must be very bad indeed. The price for a small room was three francs a day, and no reduction made for vermin. I had limited myself to four, all expenses of living included; and the consequence was that while I remained in Athens, being obliged to pay five cents out of the franc for domestic service, my means of support were reduced to fifteen cents a day. I breakfasted generally on bread and grapes, dined on grapes and bread, and supped on bread and grapes again. It agreed with me wonderfully. Never in my life did I feel stronger, or more capable of enduring fatigue. I had some letters of introduction to present on the day after our arrival; and it was not until the following morning that I had the pleasure of meeting my friend Doctor Mendoza. He shook hands with me very cordially, and said he liked Athens; he thought he would stay some time; the Orient was a very good hotel; he was very comfortable at the Orient; he had seen the Acropolis, the temple of Theseus, and some few other ruins, but the Orient was the best thing he had found in Athens; the dinners were excellent; he liked the way the dinners were cooked and served up; the Madam was "indispose;" and altogether he thought he would repose for a week or two at the Orient, as it was "imposs" to find such comfortable quarters on board a steamer.

Having studiously avoided, up to the present writing, all flights of fancy on the subject of the classics, I shall endeavor to suppress the inspiration derived from a ramble on the Acropolis. It is not for an unpretending General in the Bobtail Militia to attempt a description of the glorious old Parthenon, the ruined temples, the columns and cornices that lie broken and scattered upon that classic spot, the view of naked and desolate hills, with all their glowing associations, wherever the eye is cast; or to indulge in poetic reflections upon the fall of Greece from its Attic eminence to its present state of barbarism. A few practical facts, however, from recollection, may be of interest to the reader. The Acropolis is a rock or pile of rocks, some three or four hundred feet in height, crowned with the ruins of the principal temples of ancient Athens, which are encircled by a wall. It is situated at the edge of the modern town, toward the interior; is ascended by a good pathway to the principal entrance, where a guard receives tickets of admission, or pay, or something, and takes down the name of the visitor, in order that he (the visitor) may be found out in case he pockets a temple or a piece of one. On the whole, the Acropolis is a very respectable mass of ruins, besides being conveniently situated for a general view of the country. There are shops in Athens where French lithographs of the principal ruins throughout Greece may be had in every variety of size, so that the tourist, who has but little time to spare in Athens, may carry them all home secretly, and describe the details in full to his friends, as if he had carefully studied the original ruins. By a little tact and a glance now and then at the guide-book, aided by a good memory, the most ignorant person is enabled in that way to puzzle, confound, and completely triumph over the most learned professor in the universities—provided the professor has not acquired his fame in the same manner. I should be sorry to have it supposed that this is intended as irreverence toward the ancients, or contempt for the learning of the moderns; but if it be taken in that light, I can only say that one who attempts to think with his own brains and see with his own eyes (both of which may be defective) is apt, unintentionally, to run against the prejudices of his fellow-creatures, and should rather be pitied for his folly than censured for his presumption. Besides, the classical tourist and learned professor, who have striven so hard to enlighten the world in regard to ancient times, should console themselves with the reflection that—

"When with much pains their boasted learning's got,
'Tis an affront to those who have it not."

Modern Athens is a small town, composed chiefly of frame houses. The population is about seventeen thousand, principally degenerate Greeks. A considerable number of Italians, French, Germans, Russians, and some few English families, are included in this estimate. The streets are rambling and irregular, narrow and wide by turns, dusty or muddy according to the season, abounding in streams of filth from the house-doors, and over-run with miserable dogs, as in most of the cities of the East. In the poorer parts of the town, the houses are mere hovels of mud; the filth is such as to render it difficult even to pass through; and the inhabitants are in the most wretched condition. The bazaar or market-place is perhaps the most pleasant place of resort for the stranger who wishes to study the manners and costumes. Here all the country people come with their mules and packs of produce, and here are gayly-dressed idlers lounging about, in all the glory of silks, and sashes, and swinging petticoats. The "shaggy capote," referred to by Byron, is seen on all sides, and shaggy enough it is, being made of sheep-skins, and dirty enough too, in all conscience; for the country Greeks (town Greeks are above shaggy capotes) live in their sheep-skins as they do in their own skins, neither of which they are in the habit of washing more than once or twice in a life-time. In all their rags, however, and in all their filthiness, these degenerate sons of glory are fine-looking fellows, with bold, prominent features, eagle eyes, and commanding forms. Some of the handsomest men I ever saw were Greeks, dressed in the Albanian costume. The free, graceful bearing, the manly stride, the undaunted air of self-reliance, the expression of energy and intelligence in every feature, struck me as something admirable. It is a little remarkable that even the lowest classes of the men are handsome, yet not one in a thousand of the women even comely in form or feature—at least of such as are seen in ordinary places of public resort.

On a Sunday afternoon, during my stay in Athens, I went to see the king and queen—not to call upon them personally at their palace, because I had heard of a difficulty that had originated in a matter of etiquette between a party of Americans and the royal party, not long before, and I was resolved to keep clear of trouble by seeing them in public. There was an exhibition of rope-dancers in the open space near the Hôtel d'Angleterre. At an early hour the place was crowded with spectators—Greeks, Italians, French, Germans, English, and Americans. The Greek women did not seem to me at all remarkable for beauty. In the whole crowd of several hundreds, I saw but three or four passably pretty faces: and they owed more, perhaps, to fine suits of hair, dark eyes, and rich head-dresses, than to any thing really striking in their features. The ordinary classes of Greek women to be seen about the streets are about the most uncouth and miserable-looking beings one meets any where in this part of the world. I looked in vain for the Maid of Athens. She lives at the Piræus, and I thought it likely she might be in the crowd. Perhaps I saw her; if so, however, I did not recognize her from Byron's description. There was no Greek maiden present on that occasion, from whom any man of ordinary taste might not part without an application for the return of his heart. The young German girl who walked on the rope from the ground up to the fourth-story window of a house, took a much stronger hold upon my affections than any of the Maids of Athens. She was a beautiful little blonde, radiant with cheap jewelry and gauze: she waved her wand majestically; smiled triumphantly; twirled her pretty legs provokingly; and bowed to the unanimous applause of the spectators bewitchingly. Then there were splendid-looking fellows in flesh-colored hose, who came out and rode in a most extravagant manner upon the tight-rope; turning heels over head, and head over heels again; and shaking their locks when they bowed, in a way that must have won a great many hearts from the Greek maidens before they parted.

But my business is not with rope-dancers. Hang the rope-dancers! What did I care about such buffoonery! I could see rope-dancers enough at home; but it was not every day I could see a live king and queen.

There was a buzz in the crowd; a suppressed hum of voices; a rattling of swords and guns; a clattering of horses' hoofs; I knew by instinct that the king and queen were coming. By Jove! there they came sure enough, prancing along gallantly on a pair of spirited steeds, side-ways, and front-ways, and every possible way, right up between the two files of soldiers, opposite to where I stood, and there they halted, as if to enjoy the general sensation. I was perhaps the most enthusiastic person in the whole crowd. The probability is that I would have shouted, God save the King!—God save the Queen! had I not been apprehensive that the soldiers might mistake my meaning, and run me through the body for an attempt to create a revolution. As it was, I pressed my way through the crowd to the very first rank, and, in my zeal for royalty, displaced two officers who were standing before me, and who, upon seeing that I was a foreigner, looked daggers at me, in Greek.

King Otho was dressed in the Greek costume. The costume looked well enough, but the king looked rather insignificant for a king. I expected to see a man seven feet high at least, with a head as big as a five-gallon keg, crowned with diamonds, and the nose and eyes like those of an eagle; but King Otho is rather a small man, with a small head and face, and rather a small show of character in the expression of his countenance. He is a pale, ugly little man, with dark eyes, dark hair, a dark mustache, and a very meagre face. To me he looked uncommonly unwholesome in mind and body. His dress was rich, but not more striking than many of the Greek costumes in the crowd. I thought he wore it to show his subjects that he was Greek to the back-bone—at least to the outside of the back-bone. There is not much Greek inside of him, according to all I could glean from the people of Athens, or much love for the Greek people; and for this reason, perhaps, he puts on as much Greek outside as he conveniently can.

The queen was dressed in a plain riding-habit, with a plain black riding-cap, instead of a golden crown, as I expected to see. She is a buxom young woman, of about thirty, of light complexion, blue eyes, full face, rather plain in features, but lively and good-humored looking. In Washington City, which I have the honor to represent, she might pass for the daughter of a neighboring farmer, more accustomed to jumping fences and hunting up the cows than to the atmosphere of royalty. However, I like Queen Otho, and for this reason I feel disposed to compliment her by the comparison. God bless Queen Otho! She was born for better things; she might have been the life and soul of some happy family circle; she looks ready for a laugh or a romp even now, with all the cares of royalty upon her mind. Besides, how could I help liking her when she smiled at me? she, Queen Otho, of Greece, smiled at ME, reader; not that I hold myself at all cheap, but it is no every-day matter to be smiled at by a queen. I saw her do it; I smiled back again; she saw ME smile; then she stopped smiling, and I stopped smiling. When I stopped smiling, Queen Otho smiled. I liked that in her; it showed delicacy of feeling; it showed that she appreciated delicacy of feeling on my part; it was intended as a reward for my forbearance in not continuing to smile when she stopped smiling. Consequently, when she smiled again, I smiled likewise, to show her that I understood it; upon which she quickly stopped smiling again, and turned away her face; and I also stopped at the same time, and turned away my face; I turned it toward the king. The king frowned at me. Otho, King of Greece, had the audacity to frown at ME, a General in the Bobtail Militia! My republican blood was up in a moment. I frowned at Otho, King of Greece. He saw me frown; he saw the danger that might result from it; he stopped frowning; and when I perceived that I had frowned him down, I also stopped frowning. King Otho was so little pleased at being frowned down in this way that as soon as I had stopped frowning, he frowned again. Of course I returned the frown in the most emphatic manner. The queen, perceiving that King Otho and myself were frowning at each other, began to smile; in fact she fully smiled. I understood her; I returned her smile. We both smiled together. King Otho saw that we understood one another; that we did our smiling together; that consequences unpleasant to himself might ensue. Therefore he frowned more darkly than ever; and I, knowing that jealousy was the cause, was determined to show him that I was not the sort of person to be intimidated by a frown. Hence I frowned back again. King Otho quickly stopped frowning, the queen at the same time stopped smiling; and I, having no further cause either to smile or frown, turned away and looked at the rope-dancers.

Up to this date, I had always supposed that there was not in my nature the slightest leaning toward royalty; that I was republican to the heart's core. But I now began to doubt it. I felt a most unmistakable leaning toward royalty. To be noticed in this manner by a real king and queen, was flattering to my feelings. Had any President of the United States frowned at me, I should have simply asked him what he meant; had the lady of any President of the United States smiled at me, I should have thought nothing more of it than that she had mistaken me for some acquaintance; but to be smiled and frowned at by royal blood, was something calculated to produce novel and agreeable sensations. There were thoughts within, which I hardly dared to own even to myself—thoughts of high offices which might be had by proper influence, if we had a king and queen in America. It was natural to suppose that it must be gratifying to the ambition of any MAN to be made Prime Comptroller of the Kitchen; Chief Examiner of the Bed-chambers, Lord High Admiral of the Duck-ponds; Commander-in-chief of the Royal Nurses, or General Superintendent of the Cake Department, and Feeder-in-chief of Sugar-candy to the Royal Babies; with a salary of forty or fifty thousand dollars a year, and the privilege of occasionally beholding in private life the royal couple. In this train of thought I called to mind a great many of my lady-friends (some traveling on the Continent, and some at home), whose chief ambition I strongly suspect is, to be associated in some way with royalty. There might be some little difficulty at first in regard to providing titles sufficiently long and high-sounding, but I am certain there would be no difficulty in picking out of the first ranks in Boston, New York, and elsewhere, Ladies of the Royal Bed-chamber, Train-bearers to her Majesty, Holders of her Majesty's Combs and Brushes; High Powderers-in-chief of her Majesty's Face and Elbows; and Lady High-washers of her Majesty's Babies—especially when there would be brilliant prospects of matrimonial alliances with the Grand Comptroller of the Kitchen, Lord High Admirals of the Duck-ponds, Knights of the Bed-chamber, and other distinguished men of rank.

Men did I say? MEN? Pardon the slander! It was unintentional. I mean no disrespect to my fellow-creatures of the male sex; the word is used in a conventional sense. There is, however, in certain countries where royalty exists, a class of creatures who consider it no degradation to occupy positions of this kind; and there is in our own country a class so slavish in their devotion to rank and station, that they are ever ready to worship such creatures—to bend the knee before the titled minions of royalty. It may be said that these titles are nominal. Does that make them the less degrading? He who would suffer himself to be called the Prince of Flunkeys, or the High-chief of Sneaks, and deliberately accept the title as merely nominal, is a flunkey or a sneak at heart, whether he be paid in money for the indignity, or rewarded with imaginary honors; and he who would accept the title of a base-born menial, not from necessity but from choice, is more despicable than the basest of menials; he is one, who, in the language of Junius, could never aspire to hatred, never rise above contempt: to claim for such a creature any attribute of manliness, is to desecrate God's own image in which man is made.

But really, I had almost forgotten in the struggle between my growing passion for royalty and the prejudices of education in favor of democracy, the high hopes of preferment suggested by the attentions of King Otho and his amiable spouse. The fact is, my zeal on both sides has been productive of some slight discrepancy. I can only account for it in this way: that we tourists who visit the old world, have our share of that natural weakness which causes the mass of mankind to sacrifice principle where vanity and self-importance are concerned. We like to astonish our untraveled brethren at home by boasting of our intimacy with people of rank in Europe; we scorn titles as a matter of principle, and worship them as a matter of personal ambition. We fashionable people who travel, as well as some of us who don't travel, are just as prone to aspire to what we condemn in others, as the weakest; just as rabid in the improper use of power when we obtain it, as the most despotic. The frailties of human nature abound under every form of government; the principles of right exist every where, and are every where sustained or abused, according to the interests which they involve; hence we should be careful that the mote be not in our own eye, before we point to it in the eyes of others. There are principles of liberty and of right implanted in us by the Deity; the most enlightened of mankind have ever recognized them as the only true basis of government, the only enduring foundation of human happiness; let us, therefore, while we condemn the errors and follies of others, profit by the condition to which we see them reduced, and aspire to be the most consistent as well as the freest and most liberal of nations.

Doctor Mendoza and the Madam having seen all that was to be seen in Athens, invited me to join them in an excursion down to Eleusis, which I very gladly did, inasmuch as it enabled me to enjoy their society, and at the same time see something of country life in Greece. We hired the only guide that happened to be unemployed at the time—a lean ill-looking fellow, whose expression of countenance gave us but little promise of being enlightened by his intellectual researches. There was no help for it, however; and having employed the best carriage the place afforded, and moreover, provided ourselves with some cold chicken and bread from the Orient, we set out at an early hour, and were soon rolling along over the dusty road toward Eleusis. A short distance from Athens we came to the Academical Groves, where we descended to see the sights. The only sights we saw were an old villa, in a very dilapidated state; a few dust-covered trees and grape-vines of modern growth, some fine bunches of grapes; a ditch of water that one could jump over with ease, called the river Ilissus, and some ragged and dirty Greeks lying on their backs in the shade—descendants probably of the ancient philosophers.

Some miles farther on, we came to a sort of way-side inn, near the Convent of Daphne, where the Doctor thought it expedient to stop for refreshments; "because," said he, "de Madam is indispose: 'tis imposs to proceed without some wine."

While my friends were sipping their wine and "reposing" after the fatigues of the "voyage," I stepped into the adjoining yard and made a sketch of the old Convent, which may

CONVENT NEAR ATHENS.

be seen here on a small scale, just as it appeared to me on a large scale, except that it looks rather better in print, and leaves more room for exercise of the imagination. It is built upon the ruins of the temple of Apollo, which may account for the fact that it is really a very beautiful piece of Byzantine architecture. The priests were all asleep or dead. I neither saw nor heard any thing of them.

Not far beyond the old Convent we came to a pass with a rugged bluff on the right, upon which were some ancient inscriptions. Our dragoman stopped the carriage, and in a very imposing manner called our attention to the fact that we were now at a most interesting point in our journey. Doctor Mendoza never suffered any thing mentioned in the guide-book to escape his attention; but unfortunately he had forgotten his book in Athens, and was reduced to the necessity of depending solely upon the classical attainments of our dragoman.

"Wat you call dis place?" said he; for the dragoman spoke

E

nothing but English, in addition to his native language, and Doctor Mendoza was not very proficient in either tongue;
"Wat hiss de name of dis place?"

"Um call um-er-r-a—e-r-r-a ; wat you say, sare?"

"Wat hiss de name?"

"Oh, de name ; me know de name; me tell you by'm by. Dis great place, shentlemans; much great ting happen here in ancient time; grand ting happen here. Dey stop here; much grand feast; plenty people; Oh, great ting happen here."

"But wat *hiss* it? Wat gran ting—wat gran feast you call her?"

"She call 'um feast, wat de plenty people have wen dey come dis way ; Oh, much fine time! Dere's de mark, shentlemans; on de rock dere you see de mark."

Doctor Mendoza looked at the rock, but could make nothing of the mark. Evidently it was all Greek to him, for it perplexed and irritated him exceedingly.

"By dam! you no conosce nienta! Mal-a-detta! wat you call herself? heh? you call herself dragoman? One multo buono dragoman she be! Sacr-r-r-r diabolo!"

"Yes, shentlemans; me dragoman; me plenty recommendation; me know more all dragomans in Atens! All American shentlemans say me good dragoman ; all English shentlemans say me good dragoman; every body say me good dragoman."

"Den wat for you no conosce de name of dis place?"

"De name? Oh de name sare? yes sare: me know de name well as any body. De name's er-r-ra—er-r-ra ; you know dis de place, shentlemans, were de plenty peoples come for de gran ting; much grand feast. Dat's de name; same name wot you find in de book, yes sare. Me best dragoman in Atens ; all de shentlemans say me de best. Me know de name all de place."

"Andate!" roared the Portuguese, turning furiously to the driver; "Tis imposs to understan dat, she no speak Inglees!" and away we rolled over the road, as fast as two skeletons of horses could drag us. Presently the carriage stopped again.

and the dragoman informed us that we had arrived at another important point.

"Dere, shentlemans, you see de water; much sheep come dere in old time; two tousan sheep?"

"Wat?" cried the Portuguese, "dat de bay of Salamis? Dat de place were Xerxes come wid two million sheep."

"Yes sare; dat de same place, sare; de sheep all fight de Greek mans dere; de Greek mans kill all the sheep and sink 'em in de water. Greek very brave mans; kill two hundred sheep dere. Yes sare."

"Wat dey do wid all de dead mans?"

"Oh, dey bury all the dead mans down dere were you see de tombs. Yes sare. De Greek mans dere, and de oder mans wot come in the sheep be dere in that oder place wot you see. Yes sare. Oh, me know all de ting—me no tell lie; me good dragoman."

"Poh! 'Tis imposs to comprehen 'Twill be necess to to have de book," said the Doctor in great disgust; "de sheep be buried in de tombs, and de Greek mans be buried in de sheep—imposs! imposs! Andate, diabolo!"

So the carriage rolled on again, not exactly in the direction indicated by the Doctor, but certainly to a place that appeared to have no great local advantages over the residence of the dark gentleman referred to. It was the far-famed city of Eleusis—a most abominable collection of pigsties, inhabited by filthy Greeks. From the time of our departure from Athens, I had seen no inhabitants on the roadside at all superior in point of civilization, either in their way of living or general appearance, to the Indians of California—certainly none that were not in an absolute state of barbarism.

We ascended the hill of Eleusis, and stood upon the Acropolis. The utter desolation of the scene all around presented a striking and melancholy picture of the fall of Greece. Nothing could exceed the weird and impressive grandeur of the scenery. All was ruin, barrenness and decay, wherever we looked; not a spot of verdure within the vast amphitheatre of mountains; the whole face of the country arid and blasted; all still, dreary, and deathlike—all wrapt in hopeless desolation.

Our return to Athens was devoid of incident. Doctor Mendoza and the Madam were delighted to get back to the Orient. The Madam was "indispose;" and the doctor declared that without dinner it was "imposs to exiss."

I spent the evening at the residence of Mr. Hill the American Missionary. No American who has visited Athens and enjoyed the acquaintance of this gentleman, can feel other than the highest sentiments of esteem and admiration for his character and talents, and a national pride in his successful dissemination of knowledge and of the true principles of Christianity among the rising generation of Greeks. His school is well attended by the most intelligent classes of Greek children; who by the admirable manner in which it is conducted soon become capable of teaching what they have learned themselves; and in this way the cause of education and Christianity is making rapid progress. Some of my most agreeable recollections of Athens are associated with the few brief hours spent in the society of Mr. Hill and his accomplished family.

Bidding good-by to my Portuguese friends, who had made up their minds to "repose" a while at the Orient after the fatigues of the "voyage" to Eleusis, I looked for the last time at the glorious Acropolis, shook from my feet the dust of Greece, which is living Greece no more, and departed on my journey eastward.

CHAPTER XII.

SYRA.

I TOOK passage in the Austrian steamer from the Piræus to Syra. The decks were crowded with Greek, Italian, and French merchants, and a fair show of English tourists, on their way to the various ports of the Levant. I was a good deal surprised upon getting into conversation with a Greek to hear him quote the "Isles of Greece" from beginning to end; and still more surprised to find that he was the redoubtable Professor Castanis of rhetorical memory, whom I had heard lecture fifteen years before in Louisville, Kentucky. He carried a book in his hand, written by himself, containing his portrait in full Greek costume; so being both in the scribbling line, and somewhat known to each other, and moreover in the same reduced circumstances, we were very good friends and went to a very bad hotel in Syra, kept by a Greek, where we got exceedingly small and rather cheap accommodations. I did not remain long there, however; for having a letter of introduction from Mr. Hill to Evangelides, the American Vice Consul, he provided me with much better quarters in his own house, contrary to every assurance on my part that I was very comfortable at the Greek hotel. Evangelides is not only the most hospitable, enthusiastic, and obliging consul imaginable, but the very perfection of a Greek gentleman; dashing, off-hand, and intelligent, with a touch of wild romance in his character that renders it a real pleasure to become acquainted with him. He speaks English uncommonly well, and is thoroughly versed in all the Oriental languages. The history of Evangelides is a romance. His father was a *Klepht*, or mountain robber, of which he is rather proud; for it is considered no disgrace to be a robber in Greece; indeed, it is looked upon as a token of a daring and chivalrous spirit. The old gentleman carried on his operations by land and sea, much after the fashion of Conrad. Falling in love with the daughter of a rich Greek merchant in one of the neighboring islands, he contrived to get her on board one of his feluccas, and carry her off to his own island, and secrete her in his rendezvous in the mountains. Of course she was moved by this extreme devotion and became his Medora; but unlike Medora she bore him a son, and that son was Evangelides. During the massacre of the Greeks by the Turks in 1822, they were both slain; and Evangelides was left an orphan. He was taken to the United States in some American ship, where his history excited much interest, and he was educated at one of the first colleges of Massachusetts. After fifteen years of collegiate life, he returned to Syra, where he established a school for the education of Greek children; and soon after, finding his business prosperous, he got married to a lady of Syra. He now has a flourishing institution, filled with pupils from nearly every port in the Levant, is well off, and holds the position of Vice Consul of the United States.

Hermopolis, the sea-port town of Syra, is the principal commercial depot of Greece. Within the past ten years it has acquired considerable importance as a stopping-place for the various lines of steamers bound to and from the Levant; and its trade and population have enjoyed a proportionate increase. The harbor is safe and convenient; the situation of the island central, and the inhabitants generally enterprising and intelligent, for this part of the world. One of the first things that strikes the attention of the traveler is the romantic position of the town, especially the Catholic portion of it back on the hill, which rises in the form of an immense pyramid. All around the environs, are seen innumerable windmills; the houses along the wharves are remarkable for their fanciful shapes and gay coloring. The population of the entire island is about twenty-five thousand.

To the classical tourist the fountain of the Nymphæ, back of the town, is the most interesting relic of antiquity. I walked out there on the afternoon of my arrival, in company with two English gentlemen. Nothing remains of the fountain, except the water, which it is but reasonable to suppose is of modern formation. The location perhaps is the same as it was in the time of the Nymphæ, who, according to the Greek historians, were in the habit of bathing there. It is more than the Greeks themselves, who live in the vicinity, are in the habit of doing at the present date—if one may judge by their appearance. While we were looking for some more portable relic of antiquity than the water, and enjoying the pleasure of being stared at by some scores of ragged women and children, who were waiting for their pitchers to get filled, a very little old man, with a thin and withered face, and a very sharp pair of eyes, came out through a doorway in the wall near the fountain; and making a profound bow to us all, said in English, or something intended for English, that he was the proprietor of that establishment; it was his own property, and he hoped we would make ourselves at home, and look at it as long as we pleased. He was always happy to meet the countrymen of Mélor Beeron, because Mélor Beeron and himself were intimate friends. They had traveled together through Greece; had fought together in the wars against the Turks; had sailed together among the Greek islands; had lived and loved together in Athens; in short for many years they were inseparable. He was Mélor Beeron's friend. Mélor Beeron was his friend. He was Mélor Beeron's dragoman, guide, interpreter, courier, and valet, as occasion required; and Mélor Beeron was his master—a very kind master too; sat up rather late, but good pay. He remembered Mélor Beeron's personal appearance as if he had only seen him yesterday; very tall, very large man; red hair, blue eyes, raw-boned figure; great man to fight; very fine-looking man; wrote poetry about Greece and was author of a book called the History of England. He had read them in the Greek language, and considered them very fine. Hoped our honors would excuse him, but thought we would like to see a friend of Mélor Beeron, who was acquainted with him personally and could tell us all about him. Was in very roduced circumstances now; lived by means of the fountain; gentlemen who came to see it always gave him a trifle of change.

Of course after receiving all this information we could not do less than give the old man a trifle of change. He bowed very low again, expressed his devotion to the English, his undying attachment to Mélor Beeron, and gradually disappeared through the doorway in the wall.

Our walk back from the fountain was over rugged and precipitous rocks. The distance to the town is about two miles.

I chanced next day to be passing the *Hôtel de Commerce*, rather a dirty establishment kept by an Italian, but the best in Hermopolis, when it occurred to me that it would be well to look in and see if there were any late arrivals. I did so; I looked in, and saw some late arrivals that astonished me not a little. Seated at a table, in all the glory of omelette, coffee, bread, and wine, were my friends, Doctor Mendoza and the Madam, who had arrived that morning in the French steamer. "Oh, mon Dieu!" cried the Madam, "Voila le General!" "Very bad Hotel dis," said the Doctor; "come sit down; no much for mange here. I no like Hermopolis. Sacr-r-r! Diabolo! One miserable Sporkeria dis hotel! Eh, bien! I shall be tres contents to leave Hermopolis! 'Tis imposs to remain here!"

The coffee was muddy to an excess; it choked the Doctor; and this excited him to such a degree that the Madam was forced to interfere in order to prevent him from chastising the waiter for not making better coffee. However, we made the best of what there was, exclusive of the coffee, which indeed was no worse than any I had tasted in Syra; and then the Doctor informed me that he had concluded to go on as far as Constantinople, having heard that there was an excellent hotel in Pera, kept by one Missêri, a celebrated oriental dragoman.

I was very glad to meet my friends again; and we spent the rest of the afternoon rambling about the suburbs of the town in search of novelties, and enjoying such conversation as we could carry on in a mixture of French, English, and Italian. The Madam was quite enthusiastic on the Acropolis of Athens; but the Doctor could not rid his mind of the vast difference that existed between the *Orient* of Athens and the *Commerce* of Hermopolis—especially in the matter of coffee, which he declared was one of the necessaries of life. He hoped, however, to get some clear coffee on the French steamer to Constantinople, by means of which he anticipated being enabled to wash the grounds of the Hermopolis coffee down his throat by the time he arrived at the *Hôtel de Missêri*.

The Island of Syra, described by Homer as one of the most beautiful and fertile in the Grecian Archipelago, must have suffered a considerable change in its aspect since the days of the great poet. Certainly there is no beauty about it now, save that of a pleasant climate and richly-colored atmosphere; and its fertility seemed to me to consist chiefly in rocks, which grow all over it with wonderful luxuriance. The green spots, if there be any, are few and far between I saw nothing that looked at all green there except the green spectacles of Doctor Mendoza, and an English tourist, with a red guide-book. The fact is, I have always been of opinion that Homer drew largely upon his imagination. His battles are rather tough, to say the least o them; his heroes somewhat given to marvelous deeds of courage; and his poetry and facts a little on the blood-and-thunder order. Besides what could he tell about the beauty or fertility of Syra, except from hearsay? He was perfectly blind, according to all historical accounts, and if he saw the island at all when he wrote about it, he probably saw it in imagination, which every body knows is a very delusive way of seeing. Now plain facts, upon being distilled through the brain of a poet, often become highly charged with the colors of fancy. Homer distilled largely; his brain was an extensive establishment; he worked up facts and fictions with equal facility; a thirsty public swallowed with avidity; and thirsty publics have swallowed ever since as a matter of fashion. The fashion is kept up chiefly by other distillers of facts. Byron did a large business in that way; he did it well; his brain was on a grand scale ; nothing passed through it without acquiring an intoxicating power. Who is there, with a soul in his body, that has not been glorious on draughts of Byron? Lamartine distills also; I recommend him as an antidote; he produces soda-water that allays the thirst; he sobers people who have been made drunk by all the poets, from the days of Homer down to the days of Lamartine. No man, however intoxicated by the powers of genius, can read Lamartine's experience in Greece without becoming instantly sobered. The dying request of this great poet, when attacked by a slight indisposition, that he should be buried under a certain classical tree ; that on the bark of that tree but a single word should be inscribed to mark his grave—no other word than the name of his Maker, so that the world might know where Lamartine lay—is the most intensely affecting piece of bathos, to say nothing of its blasphemy, in the whole range of sentimental literature. If that fails to make the tourist weep who follows, he should be condemned to read Raffaelle the remainder of his days.

CHAPTER XIII.

SMYRNA.

Our passage from Syra to Smyrna was very pleasant, notwithstanding a stiff breeze which compelled us to lie close in under the lee of Chio. The weather was clear and bracing; and upon entering the Gulf of Smyrna nothing could surpass the rich glow of the atmosphere, and the variety and beauty of the scenery. By the time we reached the anchorage, every passenger was ready to go on shore and enjoy a day's ramble on terra firma. While we were waiting for the officers of the port to come alongside, and give the required permission, I made a hasty sketch of the town including the neighboring hills and the old Genoese castle, which I have since filled up

SMYRNA FROM THE ANCHORAGE.

more in detail from a drawing kindly presented to me in Florence by my esteemed friend Kellogg, the artist. It will give a better idea of Smyrna, perhaps, than pages of description.

In the course of two hours, during which we were forced to restrain our impatience and listen to the most barbarous jargon of tongues on board and all around the steamer, it was formally announced to us by the Captain that Smyrna was in quarantine, and that any body who went ashore would have to remain there until the quarantine had expired. We were at liberty to go ashore if we pleased, because the steamer was not in quarantine, but we were not at liberty to come on board again because Smyrna was in quarantine, and the steamer required *pratique* for the next port. Smyrna and every body in it had been laboring under the influence of quarantine for the past five days, and would continue to labor under it for three days to come, by which period he (the Captain) hoped to be safely at anchor in Constantinople

This piece of information enabled me to comprehend certain proceedings which had occasioned me much anxiety of mind for some time previous. I saw now that the dark-looking men in the boats, with flashy uniforms, who were taking little slips of paper from the officers and passengers of the steamer, in wire tongs and strange-looking boxes with long handles; and shouting fiercely to all the boatmen who dared to approach us—sometimes giving them a thrust with the boat-hooks—were *not* really convinced that we had the plague on board; but that they were simply doing their duty in the usual form. It was my first experience in the mysteries of quarantine; and I was much interested in all the forms and ceremonies. The wrath of the chief officer in the boat, when there was any danger of contact; the excessive caution of the men with the little tongs; the intense fear under which all parties seemed to labor, that the smallest scrap of paper, or the slightest touch of human flesh, even in its most healthy condition, would carry death and destruction somewhere, either into Smyrna or out of it, was a very curious and striking exhibition of the power of fancy. It was enough to fill the soul of any timid man with such dreadful visions of cholera, plague, fevers and other diseases, as could scarcely fail in the end to result in a serious fit of illness, if not in plague itself. The cause of the present quarantine was equally as absurd as the ceremonies. It appeared that some vessel under quarantine, was taking in a supply of water, which is permitted under certain rigid rules, in regard to the handling of the hose. One of the men in the waterboat lost his balance and touched the hose with his hand, by which means he brought himself and Smyrna with its hundred and fifty thousand inhabitants, under the restrictions of quarantine for eight days.

I had no great desire to go ashore, previous to this unpleasant piece of intelligence, simply because there appeared to be no difficulty in the way; but I now became inspired with an irresistible desire to take a ramble through Smyrna; and although it was my intention to stop here on my return from Constantinople, it was impossible to wait that length of time under existing circumstances. Such a *taboo* as this, in a country professing to have some intercourse with civilized nations, was not to be borne; it was an outrage upon the rights of man. My ticket was for Constantinople; it was good for the next steamer—if the next steamer should not be laid up in quarantine by a similar misfortune to its hose-pipe. But I was not going to sacrifice the rights of man for a miserable piece of leather. The water-boat was going ashore, and so was one individual from the steamer, if he was destined never again to leave the precincts of Smyrna. Taking my knapsack upon my shoulder, I bade an affectionate farewell to Doctor Mendoza and the Madam, who looked exceedingly concerned for my future fate; and jumping into the boat was soon under way for the wharf. It was quite probable, from the uncertain contingencies upon which the liberty of locomotion depends in this part of the world, that I should never see my worthy friends again; so I turned to take a last look at them before the boat reached the landing. The Doctor was shaking his head gravely, as if he thought it "imposs" that all could be right in a certain quarter; and the Madam was talking with rapid gestures as if she fully concurred in that opinion, and was enabled from observation on various occasions to confirm it by the most ample testimony.

One Salvo, the son of a ship-chandler, took possession of me, and led me off victoriously to a small hotel, kept near the wharf by his father, Salvo the elder. There I was fed on ham and eggs, in the most sumptuous manner by the whole Salvo family, who were not only proud, but extremely happy in being enabled to claim acquaintance with so distinguished a guest. Salvo Junior had spent three years in America, where he was certain he had seen me hundreds of times, and Salvo Senior was the father of Salvo Junior, and had furnished American ships with articles of chandlery for thirty years past, and, consequently, on both grounds had a perfect right to know me; and Mrs. Salvo, although she spoke nothing but Greek and Italian, and had never seen me either in America or elsewhere, up to the date of my arrival at the Salvo Hotel, yet being the wife of Salvo Senior, and the mother of Salvo Junior, and, moreover, a very fat and good-natured old lady, I was forced to acknowledge that I had seen either herself, or somebody a good deal like her, before. It was really a luxury to receive so much kindness in a strange land, accompanied as it was by ham and eggs and several cups of excellent black tea; and I was altogether too happy to analyze the motives. That it was all genuine kindness, I found to my great satisfaction before leaving Smyrna, for the bill was unusually moderate, and it required some persuasion to induce that worthy family to accept any thing for service, which is rather a rare occurrence at the best establishment in Europe or Asia Minor.

Salvo Junior gave himself up wholly to my pleasure during my sojourn in Smyrna. We rambled about the bazaars, explored the ruins of the old Genoese fort, rode out to all the neighboring villages, and smoked the chibouck and sipped caffé in every respectable establishment throughout the city.

A few days may be spent very pleasantly in Smyrna. The costumes of the inhabitants are remarkable for richness and variety; and the bazaars and different places of public resort, both for business and pleasure, afford an excellent idea of Oriental life. The beauty of the Smyrniote women (some travelers call them ladies) is proverbial; nor has it, like most accounts of the refined state of society in Smyrna, been exaggerated. They certainly deserve their reputation for dark flashing eyes and classical features; and that being the only flattering reputation they do deserve, from all I could learn on reliable authority, as well as from my own limited observation, it affords me great pleasure to accord it to them.

Lounging about the bazaars a day or two after my arrival in Smyrna, I thought I recognized a familiar voice. A fashionable-looking tourist was making a bargain for a fez. His dress was new to me; but there could be no mistake in the voice. I went up cautiously and looked at his face. It was the face of an American gentleman whom I had met in various parts of Europe. Bimby was his name. He was in the most exquisite distress in regard to the texture of the fez. The fact is, poor Bimby was the victim of want; not that he was in want of money; he had plenty of that—too much for his own happiness; but he always wanted something that it was very difficult, if not quite impossible, to find in this world. Every morning he got up oppressed with wants; every night he went to bed overwhelmed and broken down with wants. I never saw a man in comfortable circumstances in such a dreadful state of destitution in all my life. When I first saw him, he was on the way from Florence to Milan, in quest of a pair of pantaloons of a particular style. No man in Europe understood cutting except Pantaletti. There was a sit in Pantaletti that made him indispensable. He (Bimby) had tried the Parisian tailors, but they were deficient in the knees. It was his intention to proceed at once from Milan to Leipsic for boots; the Germans were the only people who brought boots to perfection, and decidedly the best were to be had at Leipsic. He expected to be obliged to return to Paris for shirts; there was a sit in the collar of the Parisian shirt that suited him. His medicines he always purchased in London; his cigars he was forced to import from Havana; his Latakia tobacco he was compelled to purchase himself in Smyrna, and this was partly the occasion of his present visit. As to wines, it was nonsense to undertake to drink any but the pure Johannisberg; which he generally saw bottled on the Rhine every summer, in order to avoid imposition. His winters he spent chiefly in Spain; it was the only country where good cream was to be had; but the coffee was inferior, and he sometimes had to cross the Pyrenees for want of a good cup of coffee. No mode of traveling suited him exactly—in fact, he disliked traveling. Riding he hated, because it jolted him; walking, because it tired him; the snow, because it was cold; the sun, because it was warm; Rome, because it was damp; Nice, because it was dry; Athens, because it was dusty. (By the way, I disliked Athens myself, chiefly on that account; Bimby was right there.) But it was impossible for him to live in America again. What could any man of taste do there? No pictures, no ruins, no society, no opera, no classical associations—nothing at all, except business; and all sorts of business he despised. It was a ridiculous as well as a vulgar way of spending life. In fact, the only decent people he had met with were the French; a man might contrive to exist a while in Paris. Not that he approved altogether of the French language; it wanted depth and richness; the only language worthy a man of sense was the Sanscrit. As soon as he had suited himself in boots at Leipsic, he was going to perfect himself in Sanscrit at the University of Berlin; after which he hoped to recover the effects of hard study by a tour through Bavaria, which was the only country on the face of the earth where the beer was fit to drink.

Unhappy Bimby! miserable Bimby! Man wants but little here below, as a general rule; but there are exceptions. Bimby will be the victim of want to the last day of his life. If not born in him, it was bred in him by bad training, or no training at all.

But enough of human frailties. Bimby has a kind heart, and really wants nothing to make him a very good fellow, except ten hours a day of useful employment.

The next steamer for Constantinople was fortunate enough to escape the vexations of quarantine. I got my ticket duly *viséd* at the Bureau; and, having taken leave of my unhappy friend, who was bound to Athens in search of a Greek capote, and of Salvo Senior, and Mrs. Salvo, and Salvo Junior, I bade good-by to Smyrna, and departed for the City of the Sultan

CHAPTER XIV.

CONSTANTINOPLE.

There is no longer the charm of romance in Mediterranean travel; steam has swallowed up every thing—even in great part the beautiful turbans and flowing robes of the Turks, which are fast disappearing in all the traveled routes, and it seems likely to swallow up their prejudices and beards at last. Now one is whirled along at such a rate that he has to keep a book in one hand and a map in the other to know where he is. Tourists are even known and cheated according to the color of their books; red indicating Anglo-Saxon origin, full purses, and abundant credulity; black denoting cunning, and all other colors the poverty and insignificance of mongrel nations. It is a mere summer excursion all over the Mediterranean. Starting from Marseilles, you are steamed all round Spain in a few days; or if you like you take a glance at Africa from Algiers to Tunis, or a peep at Italy, commencing at Nice and ending at Naples; and then you have Neapolitan lines all around Sicily, and the French lines again to Malta; and from Malta English and French lines to Alexandria, or to Constantinople, touching at Athens and the Greek islands, and Austrian lines all over the Levant, and Russian and Austrian lines throughout the Black Sea and up through Eastern Europe. It is nothing now to be steamed from New York to Vienna, all the way by water, or from California into the interior of Russia. Even the Nile is done by steam from Alexandria to Thebes, and the old temples of Egypt reverberate with the thunders of the escape-pipe, while the Arabs of the Libyan Desert look down in wonder from their camels on the thing of life that plows its way against the rushing waters. And as for railways, I will not undertake to say with what facility one can become a traveled gentleman in Europe, lest you should deem me guilty of raillery, or at how cheap a rate a man may become classical, with the aid of Murray and steam, lest I should be suspected of puffing.

Near the Dardanelles we had a fine view of the plains of Troy, upon which stood in ancient times the famous city of that name, now the site of a small town called Taos. There stands in bold relief to this day the tomb of Achilles at Sigœum, where Homer says the hero was buried. It was here that most of the battles between the Greeks and Trojans were fought; and on this tomb Polyxena was sacrificed, and Alexander, in after ages, paid tribute to the "bravest of all the Greeks"—for which see Homer, Lempriere, and Murray, especially the latter, who gives the particulars neatly done up in a hand-book.

On entering the Dardanelles, we looked out for the place where Leander was drowned in swimming to his lady-love, and where the beautiful Hero threw herself from the tower in despair; also the precise spot where Byron caught a cold in swimming for fame, and where Xerxes built his bridge of boats, and made a fool of himself a long time before by beating the sea because it swamped his ships and destroyed his labors—all of which we probably saw, but I can not assert it as a positive fact.

We entered the Sea of Marmora by sundown, and became poetical over its sleeping isles. It was a night for romantic thoughts; the moon was so minutely visible through the clear atmosphere that its seas and mountains lay outspread upon it like a chart of silver, the sky glittered with stars, the waters of Marmora were as smooth as glass, and the isles softly steeped in a mellow light, and the dim outlines of the mountains of Europe and of Asia loomed up like sleeping giants in the mystic background.

About the decks lie bearded Turks, smoking their chiboucks, and Greeks in petticoats, and pale Armenians in tall turbans and long robes, sipping their coffee and talking of the money-market; and dirty Arabs, in their brown capotes, doing nothing at all, and not likely to do any thing for some time; and Jewish peddlers and pilgrims, nodding and reading aloud from the Talmud, or praying in dark corners; and Mohammedans of all castes, spreading their mats in the most inconvenient places, and bowing down toward Mecca, regardless of the world and all its prejudices. Some hundreds of stupid

Turkish soldiers, with heavy faces, half sea-sick, are gathered in huge piles on the forecastle deck, or gamble in groups about the gangways; and abaft the break of the quarter-deck is a large cross-barred cage, covered over like a tent, filled with masked, and black-eyed, laughing, romping Turkish women and squalling babies, belonging to the Harems of those old gray-bearded Mussulmans close by smoking their chiboucks or bobbing at Mecca; and now and then there emerges from the cage an ugly African, who draws her mask over her thick lips if you look toward her, with as much coquetry as if she thought it would not do to let too much beauty be seen at once. Officers without number, mustached, gilded, brass-banded, and buttoned to excess, go up stairs and down stairs, and smoke cigars about the decks, and never seem to be doing any thing but passing the time as pleasantly as possible: sometimes you see a gold-banded cap, with a gentleman in uniform under it, parading itself on a high plank amidships, and if you watch him carefully you will see him raise his right hand or his left, point mysteriously to either side, keep it so a few moments, and then drop it with graceful air, greatly exhausted by the effort. That man has done his duty; he has indicated to the helmsman that it would be advisable to port or starboard a little; and then he comes down, with a proud consciousness of knowledge which the generality of mankind does not share, and resigns himself to cigars and conversation. Stewards and waiters are continually going forward to and returning from the head-quarters of the *cuisinier*, where important consultations are held on diet, and matters prepared for the table, as in the German Diets. Grim, black-looking firemen, besmeared with coal and soot, come up so unexpectedly out of little round holes in the deck that the passengers standing near are startled out of a week's growth—if passengers in this part of the world can be startled. And we who walk the quarter-deck, speculating upon all these things, and the rise and probable destiny of Mohammedanism; priding ourselves upon our superiority over all other nations in piety, morals, and railroads; discoursing on the progress of civilization under the mighty influence of steam; damning Turks, Arabs, and Greeks when they get in our way; and apostrophizing the heavenly bodies, the scenery, and Latakia tobacco; we are gentlemen of elegant leisure, traveling for our own amusement and the benefit of mankind. We carry red books in our hands, and astonish our friends at home with our proficiency in the classics; we are the men who have seen the world, and are just popping in on Constantinople for pastime.

A wonderful sight is this city of the Sultan, after all; one of the few things the traveler enjoys on this side of the world that approach the enthusiastic anticipations formed by reading works of imagination. I know of nothing to compare with the first view of Constantinople. Any thing like description seems tame and out of place in attempting to give an idea of such a scene. It is purely a matter of feeling;

there is no analyzing the sensations experienced by the beholder; he may be perfectly conscious of the nature of his own impressions, yet entirely unable to convey any adequate idea of them to others. To me it seems a renewal of the unalloyed pleasures of youth; a return after mingling with the world and its realities, to the first pure, joyous sense of the beautiful. All that I had ever read of the East and its romance was here a gorgeous dream realized; yet not all a reality, for there was no dividing mark between the strictly real and what so imperceptibly merged into realms of fancy.

We reached the anchorage on the outside a few hours before daylight. The grating jar of the chain as it ran out aroused us from our pleasant dreams of home; and soon we heard the Arabs and Turks on deck echo in guttural tones the words Stamboul! Stamboul! There was a charm in the name that drove away from me every vestige of sleep. I was wide awake in a moment. My more experienced fellow-travelers, however, turned over to enjoy another nap, with the philosophical remark that "it's a great bore to be waked up when one can't see any thing in the dark." There was truth as well as philosophy in this, but all my efforts to sleep again were in vain. From the open sky-light came down now and then the magic words Stamboul! Stamboul! bringing before me, as I strove to keep down my eyelids, visions of gilded palaces and seraglios, and Sultans in turbans and flowing robes, and the spray of fountains, and caiques sweeping over the flashing waters, and the countless things of beauty that are involuntarily associated with the first thoughts of Constantinople. It was useless to try any longer—an invisible something lifted me up bodily and tumbled me out on the cabin floor, where I contrived, after slipping on two or three pairs of boots that were much too short or too long, and some trowsers that bagged in the legs with a very Turkish effect, to grope out what belonged to me, and rushing up on deck I just succeeded in not carrying away the roof of the companion-way.

The gleam of approaching day was spread over the eastern sky; low on the water were a few pale lights flickering with a faint glimmer, while overhead all was deep in night, but clear and soft, and spangled with countless brilliant stars. There was a loom of darkness visible in the distance, shapeless and shadowy as a cloud resting on the horizon; all eyes were turned toward it; that is to say, all eyes that were open, for the mass of the deck passengers were snoring away in perfect indifference to the Sublime Sultan and all his dominions. The women in the cage, however, were chattering like so many magpies, as usual whether by day or night; and about the bulwarks were lounging some of the more enthusiastic Turks and Arabs, who were awakened probably by the chattering, or unable to sleep, like myself, from a fevered state of the imagination; the very men whose conversation about Stamboul had so charmed me.

"Where is it?" said I to an old Turk, who reminded me of the pictures of Mahomet, "is that it where the lights are?" "Stamboul!" replied the old man, nodding. "There is nothing in sight but that dark hill, is there?" "Stamboul!" rejoined the Turk. "I can't see it," said I. "Stamboul!" cried the old man pettishly. "You don't speak English, do you, sir?" "Stamboul!" he bawled at the top of his voice, "Stamboul! Stamboul!" It was quite evident that the old gentleman was touched on the subject of Stamboul, so I said no more. To the best of my knowledge he never uttered a word but Stamboul while he remained on the steamer; and even long after sunrise, when every body with eyes could see the well-known mosques and minarets within gunshot, he continued to point at them and repeat to every passenger, "Stamboul! Stamboul!"

As the day opened fair and clear, the outlines of the higher points broke out through the morning atmosphere and stood in bold relief against the sky, and soon the whole magnificent view was revealed with the startling effect of an optical illusion. Mosques and minarets there were in profusion, palaces with all the architectural ornament of oriental taste, rising from within the walls of the city, hemmed around with green shrubbery; round white domes, glittering like globes of snow; strangely-colored houses, with projecting roofs and grated windows; the Turkish flags waving on the towers; sails gliding noiselessly out from under the shadow of the ramparts; vistas of valleys and hills steeped in a soft glow of purple, through which gleamed villages and pointed minarets, and the moist foliage of groves, the heights beyond tipped with golden rays of sunshine, and the sleeping waters of the Bosphorus, lost in the glitter of palaces and the shadows of mountains. With such a sky, such glowing lights and mystic shades, such soft distances, such strange and fanciful fabrics, looming up in a perfect maze of beauty, it is difficult to reconcile any idea of reality. It is an enchantment beyond all the dreams of fancy; the very soul is rapt in an ideal world, and for a moment reality itself becomes a dream too bright and beautiful for comprehension.

But the anchor is up; the hissing steam sends us dashingly into the Golden Horn, where, amid all the strange sights and confusing sounds possible to be conscious of in so short a time, the chain runs crashing out again, and we are permitted to land wherever the prophet wills, which is any where at all. Here let me solemnly pause, while six hotel commissioners from Pera are endeavoring to tear me to pieces, and relieve my mind of this moral truth; it has troubled me for three weeks, night and day; it has twisted itself into every imaginable shape for the sake of originality, but the truth remains the same—a truth involuntarily spoken by every traveler who has put foot ashore here. He who would fill his soul with a thing of beauty, that he would cherish as a joy forever, let him never go beyond the first full view of Constantinople. To see, is bliss; to smell, is reality; to touch, is misery in the last degree.

A very stylish gentleman in petticoats carried my knapsack, and conducted me to the Hotel de Byzant, a clean airy establishment, in view of Stamboul and the Bosphorus. The proprietor is a Hungarian, his wife an Italian, and his daughter a full-blown beauty of sixteen.

I took advantage of my first leisure hour to call at the Misseri for the purpose of seeing my Portuguese friends, Doctor Mendoza and the Madam; having learned from Carlo the guide that they had arrived several days before. The Misseri is a very handsome and fashionable hotel, situated in one of the principal streets of Pera. I recommend it at a glance to all traveling gentlemen who desire to get rid of their money in the most expeditious manner. The ante-rooms and passages are crowded from morning till night with stylish dragomans, guides, domestics and lackeys, who seem always ready and willing to show inexperienced tourists how such a thing can be accomplished without loss of time.

I was ushered up a flight of stairs into a grand saloon, and from the grand saloon out again and up several more flights of stairs, till a door was knocked at, and my name was announced. "Ah, mon Dieu!" cried the Madam, "encore Monsieur Général!"—"Very good hotel dis!" said the Doctor, coming forward to meet me, "walk in; sit down; take some wine! very good wine dis! De Madam is a little indispose, but to-morrow he shall be better."

We had a very pleasant time of it, in relating our adventures from the day of parting at Smyrna; and having made an engagement to visit the Giant's Mountain on the following day, we shook hands again and parted with a profusion of friendly bows on both sides.

After all the romance of oriental life, as described in books, and the charm of laziness so beautifully depicted by poetical writers, there is a want of real comfort and enjoyment painfully apparent throughout Constantinople. A person of energetic temperament would soon desire a change. The novelty of picturesque costumes and strange languages and customs soon wears away, and one begins to feel the want of more exciting scenes to keep up the interest. During the day it is pleasant enough to ramble about the bazaars, or take a stroll over the hills; but when night comes there is a dreary void, which nothing but the remembrance of more exciting scenes can fill. A miserable opera or a tawdry theatre in Pera may serve to kill time for one or two evenings, but after that you might as well be in the midst of a desert—better, in fact, for then you would not be disturbed by howling dogs or the everlasting cries of "*Yang far! Yang far!*"—the fire in Stamboul that can never be seen. The streets are of inky darkness; not a step can you venture out without a guide and a lantern; and even then it is problematical whether you will return without broken ankles in crossing the grave-yards, or the loss of a coat-tail in a battle with the dogs. In the register of the Hotel de Byzant there is a melancholy statement of an English traveler who complains of having been seized by some Turkish soldiers for throwing stones at what he supposed, in the darkness of night, to be dogs, but which turned out to be the soldiers themselves, who immediately seized him and put him in prison; and it was not until next day that he was liberated. The insecurity of life in the suburbs, and the total absence of every thing like law, are sufficient in themselves to keep the stranger within narrow limits; and, although there is more security now than there was some years past, it is still quite bad enough. Cases of assassination are frequent, and robbery is so common an occurrence as to excite but little attention. The police regulations are so inefficient, if any exist at all, that they have no influence whatever in the prevention of crime. There is no public press, except one or two small papers published in the Frank quarter, and of course very little is known of these occurrences, except what finds its way into other countries through private correspondence. It is but just, however, to state that most of these crimes are committed by persons residing in the Frank quarters—either Greeks, Italians, or the refuse population of other countries. The Turks themselves are too indolent to engage in any thing requiring energy and personal activity, and would sooner smoke the pipe of content on five piasters a day, than run any great risk to gain money or expend their time in useless exertion. They find it much easier to cheat in a quiet way, and enjoy the profits of others, than to incur the labor and inconvenience of open robbery; and for the shedding of blood in a small way they have no taste. It is only when thoroughly aroused by some great cause, as in the war with the Greeks, that they cast off their habitual lethargy, and go earnestly into the business of general massacre, and then there are few nations that can surpass them in deeds of cruelty and wholesale bloodshed.

The Turks are in many respects a most singular and incomprehensible people. Effeminate in their habits; dallying half their lives in the *harem*, or frittering away their time in trifling conversation; sipping their coffee from morning till night, and never without the chibouck, which must have a stupefying and enervating effect; yet they seem to be capable of enduring extraordinary fatigue; and when once roused into action no race of people exhibit greater physical courage or more ferocious determination. The toils of travel; the torments of hunger and thirst; the extremes of heat and cold; all the privations of military life, and all the terrors of death, fail to swerve them from their bloody career of revenge or rapine. This wonderful power of endurance may be attributed, in some measure, to their simple mode of living, and the frequent use of cold water in their daily ablutions. What would be considered extreme privation in America, in the matter of food and clothing, is habitual with the Turk. A crust of dry bread, with a bunch of grapes, or a dish of soup, is his ordinary meal; and his clothing, in winter or summer, consists of a few simple robes thrown loosely around him. Flesh of all kinds is sparingly used, and strong liquors are almost unknown in Oriental climates; and even here in Constantinople, where the winters are often as severe as in New York, the native population sit whole days in their shops without fire, and never think of destroying themselves by the use of hot-air stoves or the death-dealing salamander. It is a matter of surprise how they exist through the inclemency of the season, without those ordinary comforts which we are apt to regard as essential to life. Their houses are built without fire-places or chimneys, and no provision is made for heating them; so that all who are accustomed to these luxuries find it almost impossible to endure, even for a few weeks, what the Turks endure all their lives. For this reason, perhaps, they know little of those fireside enjoyments which tend so much in other countries to refine and socialize the human family, and cultivate the better feelings of our nature; for, whatever may be the sanitary evils of an atmosphere vitiated by an excessive use of fire, it may be set down as an axiom that in no country where the thermometer ranges for three months near the freezing point can a community of people enjoy the pleasures of domestic life, or the refining influence of social intercourse, without creating a comfortable temperature in their houses. A man must have more than Turkish stoicism, or Turkish philosophy, to retain for any length of time a kindly feeling toward his fellow-man, or a love of the genial pleasures of life, where he is subject to continual physical discomfort, or, what is equally as bad, reduced to a state of torpor, like a caterpillar, or compelled to make a smoking chimney of his mouth and nostrils, like a Turk. This custom, however, of living without fires, whether from taste or necessity, sometimes has an effect similar to that of the five straws a day upon which the horse was fed till he died—it kills a good many every winter. The sufferings of the poorer classes in Constantinople are very great when the winter is unusually severe or protracted; for, unlike the wealthier classes, who can cover themselves up in a cloak, and sit the season through in a state of lethargy, they are exposed to all the inclemencies of the weather, and almost without food or raiment. These facts I state to show that, although people may exist for months without fire, and sustain life on bread and cheese and an occasional scrap of meat, and become hardy animals, yet to be frozen or starved are extremes not calculated to prolong life.

The tearing down of a portion of the bridge extending from Galata to the opposite side of the Golden Horn, and certain repairs thereto, which have been in progress for some days past, have given me some idea of the manner in which work is done in this country. I expected to see laziness in its perfection, and am not disappointed. Several hundred workmen are engaged upon this extraordinary job. The bridge is constructed of wood, and a very creditable piece of work it is—quite as good as most bridges of the kind—built, I believe, under the auspices of the present Sultan, Abd-ul-Mejid, by native workmen; but I have forgotten my information on that point. It is a remarkable sight, this tearing down and putting up of the bridge by men in turbans and loose breeches—worth sitting down on the pile of lumber near the toll-house to enjoy for an hour or so. There is a gang not far off engaged in pulling some large beams out of the water. A small windlass would pull the whole raft up in ten minutes; but they work by hand in preference, or because their ancestors did it. Twenty able-bodied men are doing the labor which could be done in half the time by two, with proper machinery. See them tug at that beam! Not one putting a fourth of his weight on the rope. It moves two inches, after a tremendous amount of yelling and tugging, and an incessant confusion of tongues. There seems to be no master, unless the sleepy fellow sitting on the bridge, with a chibouck in his mouth, be the master, of which there is no evidence. Another fit of tugging and yelling ensues; all hands now give up work, and betake themselves to their respective pipes—the chattering of voices never flagging for a single moment, except when momentarily arrested by the chibouck. The smoking lasts a good deal longer than the other part of the work; but it is over at length, and they go at the beam again with renewed energy. Each man tugs on his own responsibility, without reference to the exertions of the others, and only at such long intervals as suit his peculiar views of the subject. By accident a general pull takes place, in the course of time; and the beam comes up two inches further. All hands are again exhausted, and find, by reference to the sun, that it is the hour of prayer; so to prayer they go—first, however, carefully making their ablutions. It is a picturesque and impressive sight, after all, to see these rude barbarians, in the midst of the busy turmoil of life, cast off all thought of worldly affairs, and bow down their heads toward Mecca, the sacred city of their Prophet. Absorbed in devotion, they seem unconscious of all the petty cares of humanity, and, for the time at least, are elevated above the mere animal man. Even Christians might profit by their earnest sincerity. Unmoved by the prejudices of other races; regardless of the busy world around them; forgetting that there is aught upon earth to claim a moment's time, save the salvation of the soul, they give their whole being up to the worship of God and the Prophet. Is it for vain and self-constituted judges to say. that these people, taught from infancy to regard their peculiar belief as the only true means of salvation, shall be rewarded for their sincerity by everlasting torture ? Oh, ye who are wrapt in the selfishness of a single idea! ye who bode destruction to others! look out upon the broad universe, and learn that there are millions of human hearts as sincere and devoted as yours, and that there is a Divine power, great and good and merciful enough to save all, even to the weakest and the most benighted.

At last the prayers are ended, and now the toils of the world commence again. But first, a general smoke is necessary to refresh the system for another tug. The chiboucks being emptied in due time, a few skirmishing attempts are made at the log again—mere individual trials of strength. The whole gang finally prepare to begin work in earnest; but just as you imagine they are going to run the log out of the water with a general rush, a casual remark, dropped in conversation, arouses the attention of the whole party. This has to be discussed in all its bearings, controverted, illustrated by anecdotes, sustained and repeated, till the subject is sufficiently exhausted for the present; and then the ropes are stretched, the shouting commences, and the beam, after many back-slides, is fairly landed on terra firma. You feel a sense of relief, an inward thankfulness, when this victory of human force over inert matter has been achieved ; and, leaving the turbaned gang to smoke the pipe of triumph, and talk over the struggle past and prepare for the struggle to come, walk on in search of further novelties. All the workmen, those who wield the adze, the hatchet, and the saw, the master mechanics, as well as the common laborers, are so much like our friends of the beam, in their various branches of industry, that it is unnecessary to call your attention to them ; and we leave them now, chatting, smoking, and praying, in the hope that, by the threats and promises of his Highness Abd-ul-Mejid, and the spiritual aid of the Prophet, the bridge will be completed some time during the present month—or century.

The difficulty of introducing any thing having a tendency

A BUSINESS TRANSACTION.

to improve the condition of the Turks, except where the effect is immediate and palpable, as in the use of steamers, is exemplified in all their implements of husbandry, which are of the rudest and most primitive kind. An effort was made some years ago, under the auspices of the Sultan, who seems to have been persuaded into the experiment rather by a paltry ambition to be considered a patron of public improvement, than by any real desire on his own part that it should succeed, to get up a model farm, so that all who had eyes to see might witness the superiority of a judicious system of agriculture. An American gentleman, from one of the Southern States, of known capacity and intelligence, was placed at the head of it, and great promises were made, should the result prove satisfactory. Plows of the most approved pattern, and all the best implements of husbandry, were brought over from the United States and put in operation; but, notwithstanding the most flattering progress, it failed from want of encouragement. The result was not sufficiently magical to arouse the Turks from their habitual lethargy; the productions of the earth did not spring up in a single night, like some of their fabled temples; and money began to grow scarce, or, at least, was found to be more satisfactorily invested in purchasing good faith from bad ministers, or replenishing the *harem* with fresh supplies of fat cattle from the mountains of Caucasus. The director and his family, after undergoing all the toils and privations of a long sojourn among a besotted and barbarous people, and suffering in health and purse, were finally compelled to give up all hope of success, and return to their native land; where, it is to be hoped, they are by this time surrounded by the comforts of home and the blessings of civilization.

CHAPTER XV.

A VISIT TO THE BAZAARS.

It is a strange life here—half-civilized, half-savage. One lives in such an atmosphere of Orientalism that he unconsciously becomes Oriental in his habits, and smokes chiboucks and drinks muddy coffee as a matter of course. If it were not for the civilizing influence of hotels, I believe we Frangi should soon be Turks, even in our dress and the luxury of laziness. No traveler considers himself completely initiated into the mysteries of Oriental life till he has suffered scalding and strangulation in a Turkish bath, purchased a fez, and smoked himself sick at a narguilla. When he has done all this, and learned to go about the bazaars alone, and say *Kats grosh?* or, What does it cost? he may congratulate himself upon having mastered the rudiments of Turkism. If he can double up his legs and squat like a tailor, it will be all the better, as he will be invited to sit on the floor whenever he visits a native house. Some of the pashaws, indeed, are getting Frankified in their notions, and keep two or three chairs for their guests; but this is an exception to the general rule. For three weeks I have labored hard to surmount these difficulties, and now I pride myself on being a very respectable Turk—in outward show at least, for I should be sorry to say any thing about morals. I have been thoroughly boiled out of my skin in a public bath; have suffered my beard to grow till I can swear by it; smoked narguillas till I came within an ace of getting the delirium tremens; and purchased a fez, which I wear two hours every night before going to bed, in the hope of conquering a certain bashfulness which yet prevents me from appearing with it in public. Sitting cross-legged on the floor was the great trouble at first; but that difficulty I have also surmounted by hard practice and some risk of dislocating my limbs, which required an immense deal of twisting and stretching before they would come into the proper position; and now I would defy any Turk in Stamboul to squat more gracefully. In the matter of chiboucks, great caution and judgment are necessary. No person pretending to have the slightest claims to Orientalism will disgrace himself by smoking with a glass mouthpiece. Amber is the only true indication of quality. None but the *hamil*, or burden-carriers, smoke glass. This fact I state for the benefit of all travelers who have an ambition to be truly Turkish—the glass mouthpieces being so dextrously colored that it requires an adept to distinguish them from amber. When a person pays three dollars for a very pretty one, which he supposes to be the purest amber, and, after discoursing to all his friends upon its superior softness and delicacy of temperature, is quietly told by some kind resident, whose opinion he can not dispute, that it is common glass, worth about twenty-five cents, he has a right to speak feelingly on the subject. The stems must be six feet long, and of the best cherry. Jasmine, for short smoking, makes an admirable stem, and rosewood is not bad. All these can be had and bored to order in the pipe bazaars.

The perpetual risk of life and limb to which the unwary traveler is subjected in rambling about the streets of Constantinople may be regarded as another test of Orientalism. I consider that any man who spends three weeks here and employs his time usefully in lounging about the bazaars and streets of Stamboul, and hanging around the quays and public bridges of the Golden Horn, without losing an eye, suffering dislocation of an ankle, or complete bodily crushing under a bale of merchandise, deserves ever after to be regarded as a shrewd and accomplished traveler. Running a *muck* among the Malays is agreeable pastime compared with the running of gauntlets through the streets of Galata or Stamboul. Take as an example a morning walk from the Hotel de Byzant to the bazaars on the other side of the bridge.

Confident in your ability to find the way without Carlo

THE HAMIL.

who has already made a small fortune out of you; rather hoping at the same time to meet with an adventure which you can relate on your return without a witness, you sally forth, stick in hand, and steer your way through the graveyard to a tower on the left with a green top. This you fix upon as a sort of landmark. So far, very well. Now you enter a gateway near the tower, where you are beset by a whole legion of beggars. There is a general clamor for alms —a whining and beseeching that Italian begging in all its variety never attained. *Effendi! Effendi!* is all you can understand; it means gentleman; most noble, exalted, and honorable sir, in the present case. Of course you must pay a few piasters for the pleasure of hearing yourself called Effendi; it sounds so Oriental, and makes one feel so Turkish. But this is only the first gang; you have only fought your way through it with small change to start up a still more determined gang a little below. Whole platoons of old women and young, ragged boys and decrepit men, on either side of the narrow street, attack you with Effendi! Effendi! and sublimest Effendi, ranging from the most dulcet soprano to the most importunate falsetto. You walk on, under the conviction that it would be impossible to relieve all this misery. Suddenly a voice of thrilling remonstrance reaches your ear; it is so desperate in its appeals, so irresistibly imploring, and seems to say so plainly, For God's sake, Effendi, don't see a fellow-creature starve; do save a human life by dropping half a piaster here—just what would buy you one cigar; give it and make a poor wretch happy for a day—that your conscience smites you, and you feel that it would be a sin to purchase a momentary pleasure with what would give a day's relief to a fellow-creature—so down goes the half piaster. Alas, this is only a drop in the ocean; you are instantly beset by the whole legion; the purse of Fortunatus would be ineffectual in appeasing the voracity of these poor wretches; arms are outstretched toward you, and hands thrown up in all the agonies of hunger; and the gaunt, leaden faces of the aged as they sit mute and motionless against the wall haunt you, and appeal to you with the terrible eloquence of despair. What can you do? It is impossible to give aid to all. In the utter hopelessness of the case, you rush on, thanking God that such misery does not exist at home. Supposing you now to have reached the vicinity of the wharves in Galata without spraining an ankle over the huge round stones that are designated paving-stones, it is here that the difficulties of locomotion begin in earnest. The streets are not more than eight or ten feet wide, and every possible means of obstruction seems to be resorted to in order to make the inconvenience still greater. Shop stands and tables that work on hinges; sharp pieces of wood upon which are hung all sorts of dangerous wares; boxes, and benches, and heaps of rubbish threaten instant destruction. Huge paving-stones, with conical tops, smooth and slippery with the slime of fish and other slimes, compose the groundwork of these thoroughfares, upon which people are expected to walk; and not only people, but horses, mules, asses, and sometimes camels. Now, walking is a simple operation in itself, and requires no great skill, but, coupled with these slippery stones and unexpected holes, these long wooden spikes, shop-stands, and bales of merchandise, it becomes an operation of great intricacy, and requires much study; it is, in fact, an art; one of the fine arts of Constantinople. Many an unlucky wight has been sacrificed in the pursuit, under the vain impression that ordinary proficiency would answer. You are now supposed to be looking up at a Greek capote, quite unconscious of harm. *Guarda! guarda!* yells a hoarse voice; it is the voice of a *hamil*. These lusty fellows, that you see trotting along through the crowd, four at each end of a long pole, with a hogshead slung in the middle, are the burden-carriers, the draymen of Stamboul and Galata, who carry hogsheads, boxes, stones, and burdens of all kinds on their poles; each pole acting as a powerful battering-ram on the human head. *Guarda! guarda* roars the *hamil*, dexterously aiming the pole at the corner of your eye. By a lucky instinct you start and dodge it; that time he has missed his aim. Scarcely have you escaped this danger when a clattering of hoofs startles you again. It is a fine horse, mounted by a Turkish officer. You admire the embroidery on the officer's uniform, while he coolly endeavors to ride over you— it would be so amusing to see a Christian under the horse's feet! You jump across the street at a single bound, flushed with indignation, but before you can say *Bosh!* a man with a heavy burden on his back, and his head bowed down so low that he can only see six inches before him, runs into you, depriving you effectually of all powers of articulation; without breath a man can not even swear by the beard of the Prophet. About the time you recover from the effects of this attack, a mule laden with kegs of water, which operate as outriggers on each side, bears down upon you so unexpectedly that you are scraped up and turned around by the main force of headway, and precipitated backward over a door-sill into the lap of an industrious artisan, who is at that moment refreshing himself with a narguilla and a cup of coffee—both of which as a matter of course, are sacrificed. Starting out anew, as soon as you have made suitable reparation for the damage, you work your way through the crowd very much as an eel might be supposed to wind through a stubble-field; and, by dint of perseverance and renewed caution, you eventually reach the bridge. Here you stop to draw a long breath, wipe the perspiration off your forehead, and enjoy the view. It is refreshing and Oriental, the whole thing—just like the beautiful engravings in the annuals, only a good deal larger and better done. There are the same Turks with turbans on, the flowing robes and long beards, and peaked slippers; the Persians with their tall shaggy hats, the Greeks and Albanians in petticoats, the palefaced Armenians, the bearded and turbaned Jews, the dusky Egyptian slaves—just as you have seen them in prints of the bridge a thousand times, all walking about like any other live people. But, on second thought, the whole scene is a good deal better than any thing in the line of art. It is absolutely splendid, you exclaim unconsciously; by Jove, sir, it is gorgeous! What a magnificent effect these mosques and minarets of Stamboul have—the domes looming up in the golden haze of the morning, high above the house-tops; the minarets piercing the heavens, clear and white, like gigantic ornamented needles wrought out of pure ivory; the quays lined with strangely-shaped houses, and forests of masts rising from the flashing waters of the harbor, with bright colors flaunting in the air; the steamers from Therapia and Bayukdere sweeping in gallantly, leaving long trails of smoke behind them; innumerable craft with flowing canvas, from the tiny felucca to the towering merchantman of the Black Sea, gliding about over the glorious Bosphorus; and far and near the very waters are alive with caiques, the most graceful and Oriental of little boats, with their smooth sides and pointed bows, darting hither and thither with the velocity of birds, skimming over the lucid deep as lightly as the swallows that sport around them—a picture of Oriental life that art has never attained. Half the population of Stamboul seem to be afloat; turbans of every color, brilliant robes, sashes, and uniforms glitter in the sunbeams; the oars of the caiques flashing as if tipped with silver, and the busy hum of life rising over all with a mellow cheerfulness. Along over the bridge, from end to end, flows another tide of life—the everlasting throng that crowd it from the dawn of morning to the darkness of night, and seem never to be done; the Frank merchants from Pera and Galata, the Armenians from the bazaars of Stamboul, the Turks, Jews, and Copts, the Greeks, the Italians, the French, the English —all the nations of the globe appear to be passing over the bridge, speaking all the languages that can distort the tongue of man, wearing all the varieties of costume that can disfigure or give dignity to the form, and engaged in all the different pursuits that occupy the human brain; the very vision, brought into glorious reality, that has haunted you from early youth in your dreams of the East. A voluptuous softness, an odor of strange incenses fills the glowing atmosphere, a harmony of lights and shadows and vistas of golden haze and soft purple distances, that never so charmed the senses before, save in the earliest glimpses of the beautiful, when the heart was warm with youth and the spirit looked up in its freshness through the realms of fancy. Now turn inward the stream of thought, and upon its surface arise a thousand happy memories of the past, gliding back with it as it flows, till the soul wanders again in mystic worlds, where dwell inhabitants with crowns of diamonds and robes of precious fabrics worked in gold, and white wands; and fairy castles are seen, and mountains of amber and pearl rise up and change into strange forms and vanish, as the clouds of a summer's eve. But this is all romance, aroused by outward show. There is as much sad reality in the City of the Sultan as any where else—a good deal more than you are prepared for after reading Miss Pardoe or Lady Montague. Don't give way to any weakness of this kind any more if you can help it. It makes one feel miserable when he wakes up—just like a nice mint-julep about bed-time and a bad headache the next morning.

Close by the bridge is a boat station, where some hundreds

of caiques are always in readiness to take passengers. For a quarter of a cent you can walk over on the bridge; but let us suppose that you have never been in a caique, and are tempted by its swallow-like bows, as also by the solicitations of a sturdy fellow, turbaned and breeched in genuine Oriental style, who beckons you to jump in. A very pretty one is that, of which he appears to be the chief ornament. It is a perfect little fairy boat, trim and elegant in form, with a very sharp bow, low in the water, and raking up at the stern, which is also sharp; smooth as glass outside, and decorated inside with carving in the true Turkish style; a beautiful model for swiftness and the very perfection of gracefulness. You jump in. *Mashalla!* what a dainty little duck of a thing it is! An inch more of headway would have tilted you overboard. Down you plump yourself on the carpet that covers the bottom and hold on nervously to the gunwales, your head peeping up and your eyes agog at all the strange faces around you, and the violent motions of the boatmen. Caiques are shearing in and skimming out all around. *Guarda! guarda!* is bawled in your ears, till, like the cry of wolf, it ceases to attract notice; and just then the long sharp bow of a rival caique, coming suddenly up, grazes your hand and bears off triumphantly with the skin of your knuckles. *Guarda! guarda!* again. This time you dodge; no damage is done. Soon you are fairly out of the thickest part of the crowd. Away darts the caique, scarcely throwing a ripple from her bows; turbans, fezzes, white robes, red cloaks and blue, flit by in other caiques; away you go! sweeping with a snake-like trail through a mist of confusing sights and din of sounds, darting in and out under the dark arches of the bridge, wheeled miraculously under chain cables and outstretched ropes, under the sterns of huge ships, across the bows of foaming barges, through whole fleets of racing small craft, till you are suddenly whirled around as upon a pivot and backed dexterously into the wharf at Stamboul, where the sum of two cents, deposited upon the bottom of the caique, affords the boatman an idea of your exalted rank in society. From this point of debarkation it is a perfect Babel till you can extricate yourself from the crowd. Boatmen are bawling madly for passengers, the *hamil* are running to and fro with heavy burdens, shouting *guarda!* as a matter of habit; crowds of bare-legged laborers are tugging at big timbers, and deafening one another with loud conversation; Greek sailors, piratical-looking Italians, Russian, French, and English men-of-war crews are lounging about the *cafés*, smoking, drinking, and quarreling; Turks and Arabs are bowing down to Mecca in the midst of the confusion; Jewish merchants are bartering their wares; native peddlers are crying the merits of their glittering trinkets; bakers are shouting from their bread stands; hucksters from their tables of figs, cheese, and sausages; fruiterers from out of baskets of grapes; coffee-carriers running about madly with large tin urns, heated by red-hot coals, shrieking the charms of muddy coffee; grave Persians and pale Armenians gliding silently and with ghostly solemnity through the crowd—all touched, you would say, on some point—a little cracked about the affairs of life, just like the rest of us.

At last, after getting lost a dozen times in the narrow streets, you enter a dark arched way, much as you would enter a cavern, with a lurking suspicion of an attack from a horde of banditti. This is the beginning of the famous bazaars of Stamboul. What a strange place it is, and how utterly impossible to give any adequate description of it on paper! All the pages that have ever been written on the subject fail to give a correct notion of these bazaars; either too much is expected or too little—any thing but the strange reality. A single glance at such a scene is worth all the pictures that pen or pencil has ever drawn; it dwells forever in the memory, with the vividness of a first impression; it is beyond the ornament of language or the glowing colors of art; it is fixed indelibly upon the brain, and rises unbidden before the eye throughout the future, in all its wondrous variety of lights, shadows, costumes, and glittering wares; in every thought of the glorious East it is the embodiment of the East itself. It must not be supposed, however, that there is any thing very magnificent about these bazaars—any thing to compete in splendor with the shops of the Palais Royal or the Arcades of Paris—it is their peculiar novelty, the semi-barbarous profusion of rich colors displayed at every point; the theatrical effect of the costumes and manners; the confusion of strange languages; the scents of musk and attar of roses that flit through the air, mingled with odd currents of smoke from the chiboucks and narguillas; the streams of light pouring down through holes in the roof relieving the darkness; the endless variety of Oriental curiosities; these it is that render the bazaars unique and wonderful, not to be compared to any thing except other bazaars, of which there are few in the East so interesting as those of Stamboul.

We must come over again and look more into the details. At present we have only time to make a small purchase, as a sort of evidence to our friends at the Byzant that this tour has really been achieved before breakfast. It is a pretty trifle, an embroidered something manufactured of silk, which will be very acceptable to a certain fair person—a nice little present from the bazaars of Stamboul.

SHOP KEEPERS.

A grave old man, with a tremendous turban on his head, and a long chibouk in his mouth, sits bundled up among his precious fabrics, totally indifferent to the matter of customers, in fact rather averse to any interruption, for he happens to be listening to a story about some ghouls and genii, which a neighbor is relating at the time. In the next bazaar every body seems to be asleep; though they are all bright enough when they hear the voice of a traveling gentleman; so bright indeed, that in a few moments half a dozen sharp-witted youths are after you from the immediate vicinity, telling you to "Come dis way; no good bazaar dat; bess bazaar dis way; plenty nice ting sheep." This eventually arouses the old gentleman, and he looks up, with a patronizing air; perhaps he might be prevailed upon to sell you something. You are determined not to trust yourself to the sharp-witted fellows who are pulling at your elbow. The indifference of the venerable gentleman piques you; besides you know he must be honest.—"*Kats grosh?*" you ask, taking up the article carelessly. Something in the shape of an answer is grunted by the old man; of course you can't have the faintest idea of the meaning, the language being Turkish, or Arabic, or some other barbarous compound of guttural sounds. "*Kats grosh?*" you say again, a little louder. The old man takes a puff of his chibouck, and raises up ten fingers, and shakes them at you four times. It must be forty piasters, or forty dollars. You draw out a piaster, and demand in plain English if he means to say that it requires forty of these to purchase the article? The old gentleman nods assent. Two dollars seems high for such a trifle. You shake your ten fingers at him three times, which means thirty piasters. "*Bosh!*" says the merchant, with a contemptuous toss of the head, and he coolly resumes his chibouck. As you turn to walk off he beckons you back, takes up the silk, points out all its beauties, grows eloquent upon its peculiar merits, enlarges in the most barbarous tissue of exclamations upon its cost, all of which you have to suppose, not understanding a single word he says. Eventually he concludes by shaking his ten fingers at you three times and five fingers once, signifying thirty-five. You shake back at him three fingers less, upon which you are determined to stand. No, it will not do; the old Turk stands on two, and the purchase can't be made for the sixteenth part of a little finger less. Off you start again, and this time you don't turn to look back. "*Hallo! come back here!*" shouts the old man, as plainly as possible in Turkish; and now he goes through an imaginary process of cutting his fore-finger in two. No, sir, you exclaim; not the first knuckle of a fore-finger more! The half of the fore-finger is resigned at last! the article is yours; and with a proud consciousness of shrewdness and self-dependence, you pocket it, and set out for Pera. Experience aids you greatly this time in wending your way through the narrow streets; a few knocks on the head and the loss of a little bark from the knee are trifles not to be thought of. By patience, perseverance, and the sweet oil of a good temper, you at length reach the Hotel de Byzant. Breakfast has just commenced, the purchase is duly exhibited, and extravagantly admired by the ladies; the price is miraculously low; it must have required extraordinary jewing to get it so cheap. It is passed round for the final judgment of a grave gentleman who understands these things thoroughly. Heavens! what a grim smile of pity and contempt; your beautiful specimen of Turkish skill is worth just ten piasters, and has been manufactured in Paris, where such things can be bought for little or nothing!

CHAPTER XVI.

TURKISH BEAUTIES.

There has been such a halo of romance thrown around the whole East by a certain class of writers who see every thing through highly-colored spectacles, with bubbles in the centre, that the idea of a Harem is enough to set one off in ecstasies. Who is there with a spark of enthusiasm that can approach Constantinople for the first time without a palpitating heart, and a thrilling anticipation of something extraordinary, something to lift up the soul above this earth to a realm of houris? The essence of all that one has ever read on the subject comes bubbling up through the memory, and gives rise to the most visionary aspirations for the beautiful. All the fervid imagery of Lalla Rookh; the fascinating splendor of Anastasius; the glowing eloquence of Eōthen, fill the mind somehow or other with extraordinary anticipations; a glimmering of something unearthly; a foreshadowing of Paradise. The Harem becomes a chief ornament in this Paradise, and the perfumes of flowers, and the cooling spray of fountains, and all the witchery of beauty and innocence reclining on soft Persian rugs, involuntary crowd upon the senses. Every *yashmack* is supposed to cover the features of a Gulbeyez or a Dudu; every grated window to shed light upon an inner world of beauty, the living and breathing realization of that voluptuous picture in Don Juan, of the sleeping beauties of the Harem, where innocent maidens dream of apples, and bees, and butterflies, and such things. Never was an unfortunate admirer of the sex worked up to such a pitch of enthusiastic expectation as your friend of the present writing. It was a purely Platonic devotion to beauty, of course. The first thought upon touching the romantic soil of Stamboul was of *yashmacks*, and dark flashing eyes, and forms of angelic contour. For a while I thought seriously of shutting my eyes the very first petticoat I should descry fluttering in the breeze; but eyes are indispensable where the *hamil* are continually bringing their battering rams to bear on one's head. At last a bevy of chattering damsels loomed up in the distance bearing down toward me. Good gracious, what voices! The croaking of ravens would have been music to the coarse masculine sounds that distracted my ear. It was the most barbarous gobbling of gutturals I have ever heard. Black eyes there were, to be sure, black enough all round, even underneath; which was rather a dirty sort of blackness. The *yashmacks* dropped accidentally, as they generally do when the observer is a Frank, and there are no Turks near. Every vestige of enchantment vanished in a moment. There was not a single passable face in the crowd. The features were coarse and sensual; the teeth disgustingly dark; the costume slovenly and unbecoming. As if conscience-smitten, after having exposed so much beauty to infidel eyes, they hastily drew the covering over their mouths, leaving the upper part of the face partially visible, and altogether denuding the breast. After they had passed I turned to enjoy a different view, in the faint hope of discovering some compensating attraction. The case was now still worse. As they drew up their loose cloaks, and gathered around them sundry highly-colored and tawdry rags of drapery, the names of which it is impossible to remember, their bare legs glistened underneath, buried over the ankle in yellow slip-shod boots and slippers; and they waddled over the rough stones very much like a parcel of ducks, making such awkward attempts at progress that it was quite distressing to see them. Surely the Turkish boots for females must have been devised by some clever fellow, who had in view the impossibility of their running away in them.

It would be unfair, perhaps, to judge of the whole sex from these specimens; so I reserved my final judgment until I should see something more of Turkish beauty. Since then I have seen every variety that can be seen beyond the sacred precincts of the Harem, from the highest to the lowest, and I must confess that I have seen very little to change my original impression. What there may be concealed in cages and fed on cakes and rose water, and never suffered to be rudely kissed by the air that common mortals breathe, I do not know from personal experience, having never been in the domestic circle of a Turk in my life, when the ladies were present; nor do I anticipate that pleasure soon, unless my friend, Abd-ul-Mejid, should take it into his head to invite me to a family tea-party, which is not likely. Let it not be supposed, however, that I entertain any hostile feeling toward the ladies of Constantinople. There is occasionally a pretty face to be seen, a young, round, doll-baby thing, that is very much admired by the Turks; nice plump little toys, with black eyebrows and thick lashes, soft peachy cheeks, and the softest possible expression. I saw one on the bridge near Galata that quite struck a tenderness through me. She was about fifteen, and as prettily costumed as a Turkish lady can be without a change of fashion. Dropping the white vail that covered her mouth as I passed, she gave me a good opportunity of admiring her bewitching features, and to be candid, they were very bewitching. The form of her face was round, like a full moon; her complexion of the purest transparency, just tinged with the roseate hue of health; her nose small and round, making a very beautiful natural di-

TURKISH BEAUTY.

vision between her cheeks; her eyes—but here was the killing attraction—they were so large and wide open, so deeply, beautifully black, so gazelle-like in their innocence of expression, or lack of expression; so indicative of a repose of soul, or unconsciousness of soul; so hedged around with black lashes and eyebrows, or black paint, that made the very darkness there more beautiful than light elsewhere ; so liquid with natural tear-drops, or the glare of the sun ; these, these it was that brought on the tenderness; these, and the lips which were parted with a smile of triumph, and looked as if they had just been kissed by the breath of a frosty morning, or bathed in twilight dews, or sweetened with a stick of candy, which she happened to be sucking at the moment ; and her form ! it was so round and soft, and shook so like jelly at every step! But it is entirely useless to undertake a description of her undulating walk: it was the very poetry of motion ; rolling in her yellow boots as gracefully as ever rolled a Dutch galliot in the trades. Mashalla ! I saw no more that day.

The Armenian women are very much superior in personal beauty to any I have seen in Constantinople ; indeed, to any of the Oriental castes, not excepting the far-famed Circassians. The best specimens of the latter that I had the fortune to see were gross and expressionless in feature, and without that compactness and elasticity of form which the more civilized world has assumed to be essential in female beauty. A certain obesity, very attractive to semi-barbarous people, is cultivated to perfection in the Circassians, and the most highly admired seemed to be those who bear the greatest resemblance to a balloon, and who are least capable of exercising the powers of locomotion. The Armenians, however, are tall and graceful, and of much greater delicacy of feature, and in form they approximate more nearly than any I have seen to what has been assumed by common consent as the standard of perfection. I saw many in my rambles about the heights of Chamlula who were really fine looking women ; their dark hair twisted loosely under their head-dress ; their complexion of the most delicate texture ; their eyes bright and not altogether expressionless, fringed with long black lashes ; and their forms showing to advantage in a costume resembling what certain of the fair sex at home have attempted to force into fashion in our matter-of-fact part of the world. And here, by way of parenthesis, let me hope that, should that costume prevail, it will never be followed by any attempt to introduce other Oriental fashions, such as smoking the chibouck and sharing in domestic circles the same husband.

The life of these inmates of the Harem has been delineated by writers who have had access to their society; but it has been done in such a way as to throw a halo of romance around them which has no foundation in reality. I have conversed with many intelligent Frank residents of Constantinople on the subject, and have been assured that these accounts of the innocent and luxurious seclusion in which they spend their lives are in the main a tissue of absurdities, gotten up by enthusiastic authors for the purpose of making readable books. Such books are sought with avidity, where the plain truth would make no impression. People are determined to feed the imagination upon something, and those who furnish them with the material are naturally disposed to make it as palatable as possible. The fact is, life in the Harem is one of absolute servitude and disgusting sensuality. Few, even in the highest ranks, understand how to read and write, and their conversation is only trifling inanity. They are purchased as slaves, treated as slaves, and valued according to their capacity to reach the most approved standard of degradation. Encouraged in all that is revolting to the better feeling of man's nature, is it to be wondered that they do not occupy the position of companions. It may be set down as an axiom, demonstrated by all past experience, that in no country where the position of woman is so utterly degraded can a people ever attain to a more exalted rank than that of a slavish and semi-barbarous nation. Abd-ul-Mejid may build frigates, encourage steam navigation and cotton factories, patronize model farms, surround his court with all the enlightening influences of foreign diplomacy; listen to disinterested plans for increasing the power and prosperity of the Turkish people; but until he learns the great secret that women must be companions, and not mere toys, his efforts, or the efforts of others, will be in vain; and the mass of the Turks will remain as they have ever been, an ignorant and slavish people.

It has been my fortune to travel in many foreign lands, and to mingle with many strange people as a spectator of passing events; and now, after years of wandering in almost every clime, I turn from the sad contemplation of their social condition with a grateful heart to our own free and happy country; where, amid all the turmoils of political strife, all the asperities of opinion upon matters of local import, all the differences of position that arise from the natural differences of our organization, there is a purity of sentiment in social life that has never obtained in any other country. It is refreshing, after inhaling the polluted atmosphere of the principal cities of Europe, to look back upon our own happy homes and firesides, and draw health, and vigor, and inspiration from a contemplation of the exalted condition of woman in America—subject to no restraints but the dictates of virtue, free in the exercise of all the rights that are claimed by the best and purest of the sex; respected because they command respect; beloved because they are womanly; admired because they are too modest to demand admiration. It is not of the giddy and the thoughtless, who parade their jeweled charms in the arena of fashion; not of the brawlers in public, who seek to overturn the whole fabric of society; not of them that are given to unseemly display, either of thought or person, that I would speak; but of the chaste keepers of home; of the gentle and the sympathizing, who rejoice with them that do rejoice, and weep with them that weep; these are the women of America, who, unknown to fame, are esteemed the highest; who, unadorned, are adorned the most.

During my rambles about Constantinople and the suburbs, my attention was frequently attracted by the strange and dilapidated appearance of the Mohammedan burial-grounds. Much of the beautiful effect of the view from the Bosphorus arises from the groves of tall green cypress that mingle their foliage with the mosques and minarets, and stand out in bold relief on every hill-side. Wherever they cover any considerable extent of ground, it is to afford shade and protection to a public cemetery. The largest, perhaps, of all the Mohammedan burial-grounds is that near Scutari, on the Asiatic side, which extends over a distance of three miles along the road. It is beautifully shaded by a thick forest of cypress, and forms, in the summer time, a favorite retreat for the idle and gossiping, who go over in great numbers from the city every afternoon. Here may be seen, in fine weather, groups of women of various castes sitting on the graves, smoking their chiboucks, and sipping their coffee; others, half-naked, chattering and lively, endeavoring to kill time; all unattended, except by female servants, for it is beneath the dignity of the male population ever to associate in public with women. It is a curious picture of gay, fluttering life, mingled with the mouldering tombs of the silent and ghastly dead. Often, when disposed to indulge in reflection, I come over here to read the history of Time's doings, past, present, and to come; Time, who has brought low alike the great and the little, the Pasha and the slave; who makes republics beneath the ground that factions can not destroy; Time, who opens the mysteries of the future, and "feeds oblivion with decay of things."

The Mohammedan tombstones are distinguished, for the most part, by a head or representation of the turban carved in stone. Many of these have been broken off or greatly defaced during the wars which have raged from time to time between the tribes of the East. The inscriptions are in the Arabic or Turkish characters, and in the more modern tombs are often covered with gilding. Of course, I could read none of these histories of human virtues and human sorrows, but it is not likely that I lost a great deal of reliable information. The whole aspect of these cemeteries is desolate and ruinous in the extreme. There is no order or arrangement, except in the direction of the heads, which are all toward Mecca; the head-stones seem to be scattered over the ground at random, pointed up in all directions, or lying prostrate in confusion. The earth is perfectly barren, and abounds in all sorts of abominations, too disgusting even for the gangs of voracious dogs that prowl among the abodes of the dead. It is a strange place, in every respect, to choose as a fashionable resort for pleasure and gossip; but, as the Turks say, in the name of the Prophet, may they enjoy themselves.

There are other places of amusement, chiefly resorted to in

the summer by the wealthier classes. Among these are the Sweet Waters of Europe, and the Sweet Waters of Asia, the villages of the Bosphorus, the Isles of the Princes, and various places in the country, within a few miles of the city. Steamers now ply all along the shores of the Bosphorus, to the Prince's Isles, to the seaport town nearest to Brusa, and other ports along the Sea of Marmora. There are also, for the poorer classes, large omnibus caiques, in which, for a few *paras*, they can be landed at any village on the Bosphorus, from the Golden Horn to Bayukdere.

CHAPTER XVII.

MANNERS AND CUSTOMS.

BEING depressed in spirits to-day, in consequence of a bad opera last night, I am going to be serious and give you a chapter on dogs. Doubtless you will think, after the essay I intend to give you on Parisian and Italian lap-dogs, that I am predisposed to hydrophobia, and labor under a prejudice against the canine species; but this is not so. The fact is, I was bitten in my younger days by a perfectly sane dog, without the slightest provocation; and ever since, I have taken a personal interest in the study of the entire race. Besides, the dogs of Constantinople are a legitimate part of the population. Without them it would be no longer Constantinople. They are as much a part of it as the mosques, or the Turks, the Armenians, or the bazaars. Dogs are here protected by public sentiment, or some superstition, or by law; so they swarm in immense numbers: they do not belong to any body, but roam in freedom, enjoying the fullest immunity from molestation. Travelers generally set them down as the great nuisances of the East, and heap unmeasured abuse upon every cur that dares to bark his sentiments. This is unjust; they might as well abuse the Turks for wearing beards and worshiping Mohammed, as denounce the poor dogs for showing hostility toward Christians. Now, for my part, I consider them an extraordinary race of animals, in spite of the prejudices of education, and especially those of Constantinople, and I intend to do them justice. Throughout the streets, and in all the grave-yards and public places, the attention of the stranger is attracted by the extraordinary number of wolfish-looking dogs that he sees prowling about or basking in the sun, and in some of the narrow passages he is often compelled to step over whole families of them. These animals abound in every quarter, Frank, Jewish, Armenian, and Turkish, and are formed into communities like their two-legged neighbors. Certain invisible lines determine the extent of territory belonging to each community, and so distinctly defined are these boundaries, that every member, down to the most illiterate cur, knows precisely how far he can venture, and what his inherent rights are. But let it not be supposed that dogs are more sensible than men; they have their territorial disputes as well as human beings, and very much on the same general principle. A strong community crowds over into the possessions of a weaker one; a quarrel ensues, and whichever cur can maintain the disputed territory by force of teeth and paws, holds it till some stronger one interferes and settles the difficulty by dispossessing both the others. There are various minor grades of difficulty between these canine communities, petty infringements upon the rights of others, such as cases of trespass, prowling beyond the lines in search of food, snatching up bones and the like, just as with us; but these infractions of the law are settled at once, which makes justice more terrible to evil-doers, and costs less in the way of fees to sheriffs, courts, and lawyers. The community fights its battles and defends its rights, punishes offenders within its own limits, and commits depredations upon others, very much after the fashion of the most respectable human communities; but I never knew an instance of one dog giving a bone to another for arguing a case, or of two dogs involved in a private quarrel drawing upon the resources of the community to compensate them, or pay the expenses of an appeal to a higher tribunal. I am not prepared to say what religious doctrines these dogs of Constantinople entertain, but they have a very pious hostility to all Franks, and bark or growl at Christians just as we do at the Mohammedans and other Oriental sects; and I have no doubt they are quite as firmly convinced that not one of us will reach heaven, as we are that the gates will be closed against all who disbelieve in our doctrines. We are good haters of other sects, and why should the dogs be condemned for trying to be human? If they hate with a bigoted cordiality, yet they love with a barbarous sincerity.

Opposite to the Hotel de Byzant is an open space, inhabited by one of these canine communities, whose operations of domestic and municipal economy afford me constant food for study. Near by is a Mohammedan grave-yard, inhabited by another tribe; and it is my chief employment, every afternoon, to sit on the portico, smoking a chibouck, and watching the movements of my four-legged neighbors. I have formed quite an attachment for the Byzantines, and a bitter prejudice against those sneaking fellows beyond, who skulk behind the tomb-stones. We of the Byzant region—for I have fought for them, and am now treated as a member of the community, and always received with a general wagging of tails—we, Byzantines, depend chiefly for our living upon the offal cast out from a range of houses just beyond the boundary. True, this is not strictly our property, but we consider that it ought to be; and so whenever a bone, or a mutilated cat, or defunct chicken, is thrown out, we are startled from our sunny corners and daily slumbers by the little curs that we keep to wake us; and, headed by the shaggy old veterans, who have fought their way to eminence, we sally forth in a body to seize our prey. Domestic difficulties ensue; hungry drones, who are the first to run, want more than their share, and scuffles take place, which arouse the scouts of the enemy. Now from every tomb-stone there springs a barking foe; the grave-yard re-echoes with the call to arms; big dogs and little dogs rush furiously into battle array; and down they thunder in terrible force upon the fighting Byzantines, in an avalanche of dust. One universal yell of rage and defiance rends the welkin; the smoke of battle rises on high, and for a while nothing is seen but a cloud of dust, and nothing heard but the gritting of teeth and the tug of strife at close quarters. It is a moment of awful suspense.. Shall it be victory and chicken, or defeat without chicken? The noble Byzantines or the skulking Tombers? Now there is a swaying to and fro of the struggling mass—tails begin to appear through the dust; the wounded rush out and skulk off, panting, to places of temporary safety. Individual foes, twisted up in motral strife, tumble out and roll together on the blood-stained field; cowards hover round in the outer circle, snapping at unguarded legs; and thieves sneak off with portions of the prey, and eat them behind the tomb-stones while the battle is raging. At last superior numbers prevail against desperate courage. Alas for the Byzantines! The Tombers drive them yelling beyond the lines. They rally and re-rally their exhausted forces, but it won't do; they are morally and physically vanquished—the chicken is gone, and the maimed and the dying skulk off, licking their wounds. Flushed with victory, the Tombers follow up to the very door-steps of the Byzant, and defile the sacred temple of the Byzantines. Do you suppose I can sit quietly, with a stick in my hand, and witness this crowning insult? Not I—to the rescue! to the rescue! On, Byzantines, on! Away we go! Down go the Tombers before a volley of sticks and stones, and we chase the flying foe into the very secret recesses of the grave-yard. Hurra for the Byzantines! Victory is ours at last; and for the rest of that day the Tombers are a crest-fallen set. Many a human battle has been decided in the same way, and why shouldn't we feel proud of our victories as well as others?

GENERAL VIEW OF CONSTANTINOPLE.

But enough of dogs. I am going to be terribly in earnest now, like Mr. Macready in Othello, and tell you about the dancing dervishes. Of the religious belief entertained by this singular sect I can give you no account. It is to their strange ceremonies that I wish to introduce you at present. Not far from the Hotel de Byzant is one of the temples or churches of the dancing dervishes; a low building without much ornament, situated back from the street in a court; and here once or twice a week strangers are permitted to witness the ceremonies. No entrance fee is required, and all sects are admitted without distinction of costume or nation; subject only to rules of good order and the customary prohibition of boots and shoes beyond the door. It was on a day of more than ordinary importance that I had the fortune to witness this curious exhibition. We had formed a large party of Frank travelers at the hotel, and all went together. At the door we took off our shoes, and those who had slippers were allowed to wear them, and those who had none were permitted to stand in their stockings. A servant in attendance showed us into the quarter allotted to the Franks: there were other quarters occupied by a miscellaneous crowd of natives. The hall, or place of worship is a large circular room, with an arched roof hung around with lamps, and the galleries for the spectators extend all around on the same floor, with a railing in front and a foot-board, as in a circus. All the decorations were of the plainest and cheapest kind, and the hall itself was entirely without furniture, the floor being of polished wood, quite bare of carpets. When we entered, a din of wild barbarous music, from some invisible place, reached us, and soon the priests of the order entered, walking slowly two by two, preceded by the patriarch, an old man with a long white beard. They were enveloped in plain brown cloaks, leaving nothing visible but their tall drab-colored hats without brims, and a small portion of the face and beard; their heads were bowed down, and they walked with a solemn and impressive air several times round the hall—the music waxing wilder and fiercer all the time.

At length the patriarch stopped; the priests or worshipers

G*

branched off, and, ranging themselves round the room, sat down and covered up their heads, leaving nothing but their hats visible, and, doubling themselves up into as small a space as possible, remained so for some time quite motionless. After this, at a signal from the patriarch, who was bowing down and praying all the time, they slowly arose, and while he stood at the head of the hall with folded hands and downcast head, each worshiper as he passed turned and bowed to the one in the rear, who bowed at the same time, bringing their heads almost to meet in front of the patriarch; and so they continued, each one bowing as he passed, till the whole party had bowed themselves through, three or four times in succession. They then ranged themselves round the hall again in their respective places, and, slowly casting off their cloaks, appeared in the dancing costume—a plain suit of white cotton, consisting of petticoats and a kind of roundabout, fastened at one side by the sash. No shoes were worn, and the tall strange hat still remained on the head; and now the music blew louder and wilder, and the dance commenced. Slowly and gracefully they merge into it, twirling around like the wooden figures on a hand-organ. The arms are extended, the hands thrown out, the feet together as if on a pivot, and round and round they go, with their long beards, and pale faces, and downcast eyes, whirling on their feet like men worked by machinery—all but the old patriarch, who stands at the head with folded hands, and prays during the ceremony of the waltz with his accustomed gravity. From the outer circle they whirl mysteriously into the centre, and from the centre back again; and soon the entire hall seems to be alive with the solemn waltzers. There is no noise but the blowing of the music and the low grinding of the feet. One almost wonders what powers of locomotion keep these men whirling around so long. They seem never to be tired; the spectator grows dizzy in following them. Round they go, with distended arms and sweeping petticoats, till you begin to think it must be all a strange vision, the grotesque dream of a distempered fancy. You rub your eyes and look again. Sure enough there they are, turning like tops—the very dancing dervishes that you have read about in books; and this is their temple—a wild, half-savage, Oriental place, full of novel sights and sounds. At last the waltz is concluded; the priests retire to their places, put on their cloaks, and double themselves up in little knots again; and, after another parade and the same profound ceremony of bowing before the patriarch they slowly retire; the audience follows their example; and thus ends the devout exhibition of the dancing dervishes.

There is another sect, called the howling dervishes, who hold their exhibitions over at Scutari, on the Asiatic side. On my return from the Mount of Chamlula one day, I stepped in to see them, in company with my Portuguese friends Dr. Mendoza and the Madam. The temple or house of worship is much the same as that of the dancing dervishes. Here we had to pay a small fee of a few piasters for admission, the ceremony being considered more attractive than that of the dancers. Nothing was said about our shoes, and we were ushered at once into the gallery allotted to Christian spectators. The exhibition had just commenced. Thirty or forty young howlers, from six years of age up to twenty-five, were ranged around the outer circle. At the head stood the chief priest, and in different parts of the hall the elders and common priests. The old patriarchs, who were unable to join in the violent exercises of the church, were seated in retired places, where they bowed their heads with a slow and clock-like motion, and chanted a kind of hum-drum song like the bass notes of an organ. In front of the chief priest stood a row of lusty fellows, with shaven heads and nearly naked, who bore the heaviest part in the performance. Commencing at a high key, rendered more piercing by the shrill voices of the little children, they screamed a sort of chant, so wild and unearthly that it was difficult to recognize them as human beings; and the whole fraternity started into motion as if struck with a palsy. Gracious heavens, what a sight! A menagerie of wild animals let loose would be tame to it. I can compare it to nothing but a bedlam of hopping and howling lunatics. First on one foot, then on the other, the shaven heads bobbing as a schoolboy bobs his head after a dive when he gets a bubble in his ear; all bobbing together, and nodding and jerking and jumping and hopping like gigantic puppets worked by secret wires; the high scream gradually lowering to a groan, and the groan jogging down by degrees into a grunt, and the grunt into a general howl, so deep and savage that the snarling of hyenas or the roaring of lions would be music to it. The lusty gang in front, work themselves into a phrensy; their shaven crowns jerk about at such a rate that one expects to see a head roll down on the floor every moment; their voices lose all semblance of human voices, and now it becomes a hoarse panting grunt from the pits of their stomachs, and streams of sweat roll down from their faces, and their scanty cotton robes hang dripping on their bodies. Through the wriggling, jerking mass you see a little howler who has hopped and howled himself out of breath; his head hangs on his shoulder, his eyes rolling, and his tongue hanging out while he gasps for breath; an old priest gives him a smart crack on the pate with his knuckles, and he starts into motion again as if suddenly galvanized, and the whole fraternity of little howlers are frightened into a fresh fit of hopping and bobbing and yelling. Now you detect a sly fellow in the crowd trying to cheat people with the idea that he is as zealous a worshiper as any of them;

but you can plainly see that he is an impostor or a backslider; he only hops once in a while, when he thinks he is noticed, and howls so faintly that nobody can hear him, and, as to the jerking of his head, it is the mere nodding of a head in the act of taking a private nap, and requires no exertion except to keep up a show of wakefulness. Old men with long grizzled beards sway to and fro, unable to hop, and too short of breath to howl; but they keep up a bass growl, and with their deep blood-shot eyes and the restless swaying of the head, look not unlike polar bears standing upright. Still older men, unable to stand at all, sit upon their mats and sway and growl in concert. At last the voices have been jogged out of the sturdiest worshipers; nothing is heard but the husky grating of the breath in the throat, and the hurried panting for air; and finally their chins fall loosely on their breasts, their tongues loll out, and all become motionless as statues. The chief priest thereupon makes a prayer, to which the most devout attention is paid. Not a whisper is heard till the prayer is concluded. For a moment a dead silence prevails. The whole congregation and all the worshipers are mute and motionless. It is a most impressive picture of rapt devotion. Barbarous the scene may be, but not devoid of solemnity. And now a low sobbing is heard around the hall of worship—so low at first that it seems to come from spirits in the air; gradually it swells and spreads around till the whole crowd of dervishes are sobbing, and the sobs deepen into a low crying, and the low crying into a wild burst of grief, swelling and winding around the hall like a funeral wail. From every eye the big tears roll down, and the faces and breasts of the sobbing crowd are wet with weeping. So strong, indeed, is the influence of the melting mood, that the wife of my Portuguese friend, who stood near me, covered her face with her handkerchief, and I verily believe cried as hard as any of them. It was the most earnest crying I ever witnessed—so like natural weeping that I began at length to feel moist about the eyes myself, and never in my life did I come so near bursting out into a regular cry. Five minutes more would have done it; for, however ridicu-

THE HOWLING DERVISHES.

lous such exhibitions may appear, there is always something in believing people to be in earnest when they pray, and especially when they cry, that touches one in a tender part. I am certain Alphonse de Lamartine would have opened the flood-gates of his tender heart, under a similar appeal to his sympathies, and deluged the whole place with tears.

"Come," said the Doctor, taking the weeping Madam by the arm, " de Madam is a little indispose; *he* are necess to proceed to de hotel. Dinner *shall* be ready. 'Tis imposs to remain longer."

Thus closed the ceremony of the howling dervishes—a strange Oriental sight, strikingly picturesque and impressive, from which some idea may be formed of the state of civilization in the East, and some reflections suggested upon the state of civilization in certain parts of our own country.

Learning that the Sultan was in the habit of making his exit once a week from some one of his palaces, and affording the public an opportunity of seeing his sublime person on horseback or in the royal caique, while escorted by the officers of his court to some mosque selected for the occasion, I walked down to Tophana yesterday to witness this grand ceremony. There was quite a respectable array of republicans in our party to enjoy the novelty of this Sultanic display of grandeur and condescension. On reaching the broad avenue between the palace and the gardens of the royal Harem we found it lined on both sides with officers and soldiers in all the pomp of court uniform, fezzed and brass-buttoned, sworded, tasseled, embroidered, and gilt, to the very climax of civilized Orientalism. The military uniform of the present day in Constantinople is a sad falling off from the magnificence of the native costume under the earlier Sultans. Copying the Frank nations of Europe in all the inconveniences and absurdities of dress, the Turks are quite as awkward, and as much out of their element in tight-laced coats, stiff collars, and scanty trowsers, as the stiffest Englishman or most vivacious Frenchman would be in their loose flowing robes and dignified turbans; and they have neither the smart elegance which results from good taste, even in what is objectionable, or the judgment to adopt only what is useful or convenient. The turban, which has been cast aside for the fez, had the double advantage of protecting the head and eyes from the glare of the sun, as also of forming a becoming termination to the figure; but nothing can be more ridiculous than the skimpy red night-cap, called a fez, which now supplies its place. What can be expected of a people who wear such things on their heads? How can they entertain any but mongrel notions, when their brains are subjected to the daily process of broiling? If they were semi-barbarous under the turban, they are more than semi-imbecile under the fez. It must be admitted, however that the present display of military costume and discipline was very much superior to what one ordinarily sees about the military stations of Stamboul. The guards and officers seem to be carefully chosen, and in general appearance are not inferior to those of more civilized nations.

Passing under the grated bridge which extends over the avenue connecting the gardens of the Harem with the palace, we entered a large open square in front of the mosque. The entire space was encircled by lines of soldiers, standing in readiness to receive the royal pageant. To the left, at a respectable distance, stood some few hundred native spectators, but owing to our dress, and perhaps a certain respect inspired for us by the daring manner in which our dragoman, Carlo, made room for us, we were permitted to stand behind a line of soldiers directly in front of the mosque. It wanted a quarter of twelve: the Sultan was to appear precisely at noon. During the interval four or five servants were busily engaged in sweeping down the steps upon which his Highness was to ascend, and spreading thereupon rich cloths to be pressed by his royal feet. These were also carefully swept down two or three times in succession, so that not a speck should be left. By the time all this was accomplished there was a general stir, a low murmur of awe and expectation. Nobody appeared to say any thing, or do any thing, or see any thing, but it was perfectly apparent that the great Abdul-Mejid was coming. There was an instinctive holding of breaths, and an anxious looking up the avenue toward the gates of the palace. And now the murmur of awe rises higher, the clatter of horses' feet is distinctly heard, the music strikes up, and out comes the sovereign Potentate of Turkey, mounted on a prancing steed, and surrounded by a legion of magnificent Pashas, likewise mounted on prancing steeds. Onward he comes, slowly and with solemn majesty. But his thoughts are on holy subjects, he looks neither to the right nor to the left, but straight toward the door of the mosque. A Sultan may condescend to bow before Allah and the Prophet, but he is too high a personage to bow to man; hats are pulled off and heads nodded in vain. He pays no attention to the homage; not even to us sovereigns, who have done him the honor to stand bare-headed before him these ten minutes for the sake of enjoying the show unmolested by his minions! The royal dress worn on this occasion was quite simple, consisting of ordinary European trowsers, an embroidered Turkish coat, and a fez, with a cloak thrown loosely over the shoulders. His face is pale and careworn, his person emaciated, and his appearance altogether *blasé*. People say that he is drugged and stupefied, for certain political purposes; and certainly, if ever a poor fellow bore the marks of premature decay and imbecility of mind resulting from excess, it is Abd-ul-Mejid.

Now, all hail to Allah and the Prophet! the Sultan has reached the door of the mosque. Bearded Pashas, glittering with buttons and gold lace, catch his bridle; and bearded Pashas again catch him as he painfully dismounts. Slowly he ascends the steps upon the well-swept cloths—that aged young man of twenty-eight—supported on each side by a Pasha. A shout of joy and devotion rises on high! Pashas, officers, soldiers and all shout glory and honor to the Sultan! Long life and happiness to Abd-ul-Mejid! All hail to Allah and the Prophet, the sovereign Potentate of the East has gone to prayers! Up goes the crier of the mosque on the highest minaret, and proclaims the important tidings to the world, "Allah akbar! the sublimest of Sultans is at his devotions. God is great, and Mohammed is his Prophet!"

For the space of half an hour there is silence in the outer world; then comes forth the Sultan again, purified in body and soul. Again the bearded Pashas catch him in their arms, and help him on his horse. He is seated once more on the favored steed, still regardless of the crowd, a melancholy picture of resigned misery. The music strikes up, the royal pageant moves on, and Abd-ul-Mejid is borne back to his palace to receive the congratulations of his devoted followers and the caresses of his loving wives.

Poor Abd-ul-Mejid! Miserable Abd-ul-Mejid! thou art an unhappy mouse, surrounded by cats! Sir Catford Scranning is an experienced old mouser; his eye is on you; his claws are sharp; his cunning surpasses your simple understanding. Don't believe in him because he purrs in the presence of the other cats. This very moment he would swallow you bodily if he dared; but Sir Catford knows very well that the great Russian Tom Cat has bigger claws and sharper teeth than himself; that when the swallowing commences he won't stand much chance in the scramble with Russian Tom. Sir Catford makes a great noise; threatens you very often; talks loudly about the prowess of British Cats: don't mind him Abdul; he won't do you much harm; he's getting old and likes to see himself in a rage; depend upon it "there's nothing in't." The Austrian and Russian party have you safe enough whenever they think proper to devour you; therefore take Sir Catford easy, and look well to the bigger cats.

I went away from this exhibition a thoughtful man. That very morning I had been reading in an American paper a tirade in favor of disunion, a series of resolutions passed at some sectional convention. Never before had the complete madness of the proposition occurred to me. What was it proposed to do? To annul the Confederacy of free States; to abandon all the blessings of liberty because of a single evil; to rush headlong from the highest eminence of prosperity and happiness that any nation upon earth has yet attained, into the dark abyss of anarchy and final despotism; to crush with sacrilegious hands the Constitution that has been bequeathed to us by the truest, and purest, and wisest of patriots that ever struggled for human rights and the perpetuity of human freedom and bury the glorious galaxy of stars too deep in degradation to excite the contempt of the pettiest despot that grovels beneath the ban of human hatred. It is not at home, surrounded by local influences, and blinded by the zeal of party, that we can appreciate the terrible immensity, the utter madness of this proposition. Go abroad, ye who would lightly cast away the priceless heritage of liberty, and study well the operation of other governments; feel but for a single day the crushing effects of religious intolerance and military despotism; mingle with the suffering masses that no longer breathe their woes, but hope against hope in the very darkness of despair; behold the misery that you would bring upon the heads of a happy and prosperous people, and ask yourselves, Is it well to talk of disunion? Roam from the North to the South; linger among the mouldering monuments of the past; ponder over the power and the weakness of man, what he has been, what he might be, and what he is; behold the fairest lands that ever breathed the charm of romance over the pages of history now waste and desolate; look back from out the gloom of human depravity upon your own free and happy country, rising to the zenith of its prosperity, spreading its genial influences over the whole face of the earth; and say, would you be no longer a nation of freemen? Would you aspire to a page in future history as that people who have fallen lower than ever yet man has fallen?

Whatever may be the evils under which we labor at home, let us hope that they are but temporary; they are dust in the balance compared with the evils that afflict the nations of Europe. Let us bear them patiently, and look to the healing influences of time for the remedy. Above all, let us never cease to cherish, in the deepest recesses of our hearts, the memory of those immortal men who have bequeathed to us the blessings of an enlightened and liberal system of government.

CHAPTER XVIII.

BABEL REVIVED.

The great variety of languages spoken throughout the East, but especially in Smyrna and Constantinople, is one of the first things that excites the astonishment of the stranger. Pera is a perfect Babel for languages. It is not uncommon to hear the same person speak in six different tongues, and I am told that there are some who speak as many as twelve. Our dragoman (Carlo, whose information, however, must be received with a grain of allowance) tells me that there are some sixty or seventy different castes in Constantinople and the suburbs. I have myself seen about the wharves of Galata, Turks, Persians, Armenians, Georgians, Circassians, Arabs, Egyptians, Algerines, Greeks, Italians, French, Germans, Poles, Austrians, Russians, Cossacks, English, and Americans, and I can not remember how many others. It is evident that the number of Oriental castes, leaving out the Franks of Eastern Europe, who can not properly be classed with them, must be very great. No person of any distinction in society here is considered ordinarily accomplished who does not speak at least four languages in addition to his own. A knowledge of the Turkish, Greek, Italian, and French is almost indispensable in all business transactions; and there are few merchants who do not speak in addition to these, tolerably good English. The business men of Pera and Galata display this extraordinary talent in the highest degree—the Greeks, perhaps, more than any. Of the relative facility with which the various languages of Southern Europe and the East are acquired, say by an American or Englishman, I am inclined, from all I could ascertain, to put them down as follows: French first; every body learns French, as a matter of course. The Italian is more difficult, because of the great variety of terminations to the same word, and the extraordinary number of conventional phrases; it is one of the easiest to acquire to a certain extent, so far as to answer the ordinary purposes of traveling; the pronunciation is simple; but it is one of the most difficult to become master of, so as to read Dante, Petrarch, and all the great poets. Many who speak it fluently in ordinary conversation, can not even translate a paragraph from a newspaper. The Spanish is of more difficult pronunciation, but less arbitrary in its construction. In two years, any person of ordinary capacity can, by study and constant practice in the society of the native population, speak these three languages fluently. The modern Greek is more difficult, and requires a much longer time to be acquired. The Turkish is not considered difficult, compared with other Oriental languages. To carry on an ordinary conversation requires no great study; but to speak and write it grammatically, and especially on any but common colloquial topics, is altogether another matter; it is then one of the most difficult. The Persian is considered the richest and most beautiful, and at the same time one of the most difficult. The Arabic is the study of a life-time. So many new sounds are necessary to be mastered, such a complexity of grammatical rules overcome, that none need hope to acquire even such proficiency as to read and speak it at all in less than five or six years; and it is seldom or never spoken by a foreigner with the fluency of the native Arabs, even the lowest castes, who roll it out with a rapidity and volume, and a violence of gesticulation and utterance quite astonishing to a civilized ear.

Among the most pleasant recollections of my three weeks' sojourn in Constantinople, is a ride from Therapia, on the Bosphorus, to the waterworks of Belgrade, in company with Mr. Marsh, our Minister. During my stay in Therapia, I had the pleasure also of forming the acquaintance and enjoying the kind hospitality of Mr. Brown, Secretary of the American legation. To both of these gentlemen I am indebted for many kind attentions; and the remembrance of the delightful hours spent in their society and that of their accomplished families, forms the most agreeable episode in my pilgrimage through the East.

Before my departure from Constantinople I was enabled, by joining a large party of tourists, who obtained a firman from the Sultan, to visit the Scraglio and all the mosques of Stamboul, including the far-famed Mosque of Santa Sophia. Lamartine calls this " a grand Caravanseri of God!" I looked in vain for something about it in the shape of camels or mules; but saw nothing of the kind to justify such a figure of speech. Probably when the great poet was there, he saw imaginary camels and mules; certainly there must have been an animal with very long ears about the premises.

Doctor Mendoza and the Madam having ascertained from the Portuguese Minister, that there was a good hotel in Jerusalem, and that it was quite practicable to make the tour of the Holy Land without starvation, made up their minds to encounter the risk. They departed in the first French steamer, intending to stop a few days in Smyrna. The doctor said it was not "imposs" that we should meet again in Beirut.

I was so fortunate during my stay at the Byzant, as to form the acquaintance of a most intelligent and agreeable young gentleman from North Carolina, who was traveling for pleasure and information. He readily joined me in my contemplated tour through Syria. On the 15th of November, having, through the kindness of Mr. Brown, Secretary of Legation, obtained a firman, signed by Abd-ul-Mejid, recommending us to all Pashas, Reis, and Sheiks throughout his dominions, as "prince-born gentlemen," we looked our last look at the glorious City of the Sultan, and departed for Beirut.

CHAPTER XIX.

THE ENGLISH TOURIST.

On our passage through the Sea of Marmora we were beset by a furious Levanter. The waters were lashed into a white foam, and floods of spray covered the decks fore and aft. The motion of the steamer in the short chopping seas produced the most unpleasant effects. Crowded as we were with deck-passengers, chiefly pilgrims on the way to Jerusalem, it was pitiable to behold their terror and the miserable condition to which they were reduced by sea-sickness and exposure to the weather. Some lay covered up in their dripping blankets, groaning piteously; others staggered about the decks, clinging to the rails, and looking vacantly toward the land; some prayed, some wept, some smoked, some did nothing at all, but it was evident there were not many aboard who would have objected to being put ashore again. In the midst of all the confusion, I noticed an English tourist on the quarter-deck, leaning against the companion-way, and contemplating the scene with a calmness that was really provoking. Hang it, man! I thought, have you no soul—no bowels of compassion? Why don't you look amused, or sorry, or interested, or sick, or miserable, or something? I went a little closer, to try if I could discover some trace of feeling in his stolid features. Surely I had seen that face before; that clean-shaved face; those well-trimmed, reddish whiskers; that starched shirt-collar of snowy whiteness; that portly figure. Certainly I had seen him. Every body has seen him. Bromley is his name—Mr. Bromley, an English gentleman of fortune, who travels to kill time. He is the Mephistophiles of Englishmen. I saw him every where—in Paris reading the newspapers in a *café*, on the top of the Righi criticising the rising of the sun, in Vienna wandering through the Paradei's Garten, in Berlin gazing calmly at the statue of Frederick the Great, on the Acropolis of Athens examining the Parthenon, in Constantinople lounging about the Bazaars, in Smyrna eating beefsteak at the Hotel of the Two Augustas —always reserved, serious, dogmatical, and English. When there were only Americans in the party he was a vast improvement upon Bromley. As a matter of principle and habit, he never makes acquaintances that may be troublesome hereafter. He is the embodiment of the non-committal. He never takes any thing on hearsay; he looks at nothing that is not designated in the guide-book; patronizes no hotel that is not favorably mentioned by Murray; admires no picture except by number and corresponding reference to the name of the artist; is only moved to enthusiasm when the thing is pronounced a *chef d'œuvre* by the standard authorities. He

shuts himself up in his shell of ice wherever he goes, and only suffers himself to be thawed out when he thinks, upon mature consideration, that there is no danger of coming in contact with somebody that may take advantage of the acquaintance. To his fellow-countrymen he is stiff and haughty, they may claim to know him on his return to England; to Americans he is generally polite and affable, and returns any advance with great courtesy; but seldom makes an advance himself. Bromley is a perfect gentleman in the negative sense. He does nothing that is ungentlemanly. He is too non-committal for that. Possibly he has a heart, and a soul, and just as much of the little weaknesses that spring from the heart and soul as any man—if you can only find it out. Touch his national pride, and you touch his weakest point. He is British from the crown of his head to the soles of his feet—looks British, feels British, talks British, carries with him the very atmosphere of Great Britain. In the course of five minutes' conversation he refers to our free institutions, and asks how can they be free when we tolerate slavery. One would think the question had never been discussed before. He starts it as a telling point, and refers to the glorious freedom of glorious old England! Can we, Brother Jonathan, stand that? Of course not; we are excited; we refer him for an answer to the coal-mines of Cornwall—to the report on that subject made by a Committee of Parliament. Ha! that makes him wince!—that hits him where he has no friends! He staggers—pauses—fires up again, and gives us a severe thrust back on repudiation! repudiation in Pennsylvania and Mississippi! disgraceful act! a stain upon the nation! That touches us; we writhe; we wince; we groan inwardly; we would give a quarter of a dollar at that very moment out of our own pocket toward paying the debts of the delinquent States; but we rally again; we put it to Bromley on the unholy wars with India; the tithe system in Ireland; the public debt of England, a most unrighteous institution for the purpose of sustaining a titled aristocracy—volley after volley we pour into him; till quite breathless we pause for a reply. Bromley is puzzled; the argument has assumed a variety

H

of forms; it has become a seven headed dragon; he doesn't know which head to attack; he retorts on the use of bowie-knives in America—the lawless state of things, where a man cuts another down for looking at him. True; we admit that; it's a habit we have—a short way of doing justice; but that's not the point—the point is this; has England ever produced any thing like the gold mines of California? Bromley smiles contemptuously, points his finger toward Australia, and says: "You only beat us in a yacht race—that's all." "Yes, sir, we beat you, sir, in steamers; in all sorts of sailing vessels; in machinery; in enterprise; in—by Jupiter, sir, what haven't we beaten you in? eh, sir, what?" The Englishman asks: "Where's your Shakspeare, your Milton, your Byron, your—dooce take it, where's your literature?" And so the battle rages, till both parties having exhausted all their ammunition, Bromley admits that America is a rising country; a great country; a country destined to be the most powerful in the world. Brother Jonathan is moved, and in the fullness of his heart protests that Great Britain is the only free government in the world besides the Republic of the United States. Bromley yields us the palm in the construction of steamers and sailing vessels; Jonathan cheerfully admits that England is ahead in literature; Bromley confesses that he always likes to meet Americans; Jonathan swears that he is devoted to Englishmen; finally both parties conclude that it is useless for people of the same race to quarrel; that all the difference between the two countries is merely the difference of latitude and longitude. So we journey on, as far as our roads lie together, very amicably, and find that with a little mutual concession to each other's vanity we can be very good friends. True, Bromley reminds us, now and then, that we chew tobacco; which we repel by an allusion to wine-bibbling; this reminds Bromley that we have a nasal accent, and use slang terms; that we say "I guess," when we mean "I fancy" or "I imagine;" but we make ourselves even with him on that score by telling him that John Bull speaks the worst English we ever heard; that he does it from pure affectation, which makes the case unpardonable; that for our life we can't understand an Englishman two steps off, his language is so minced and disguised by ridiculous effeminacy of pronunciation, by hemming and hawing, and all sorts of mannerisms—so shorn of its wholesome strength by the utter absence of simplicity and directness; to which he responds by asking us where we got our English from; which we answer by saying we got it from the people who first settled in America, but improved upon it a good deal after the Declaration of Independence. In this way we never want for subjects of conversation, and we find upon the whole that the English tourist is a very good sort of fellow at heart, with just about the same amount of folly that is incident to human nature generally, and not more than we might find in ourselves by looking inward. Bromley is but a single specimen—a man of many fine qualities, pleasant and companionable, when one becomes accustomed to his affectation. I have met others of a different stamp—but here we are in the Dardanelles; the chain runs out; the gale whistles madly against

TOWN OF RHODES.

the rigging and iron rods; the thing is fixed; we must stop for twelve hours.

A sorry twelve hours it was for second-class passengers. Time, however, stops for no class; it passed eventually; and we once more went foaming along on our way. At Mitylene we touched to land some passengers, and next morning we were in sight of Smyrna. From day to day, after our departure from Smyrna, we enjoyed a continual feast of scenery along the shores of Asia Minor; sweeping past islands, and towns, and towering mountains, in an atmosphere of Oriental richness, and out again upon a slumbering sea.

At Rhodes we spent a day not soon to be forgotten in our pilgrimage. The picturesque beauty of the island; the deserted and time-worn aspect of the town; the old houses ornamented with the armorial bearings of the Knights of Jerusalem; the strange, piratical appearance of the Greek population, afforded us ample material for enjoyment and observation during our brief stay.

On the following day we cast anchor opposite the town of Larneca in the Island of Cyprus. What time we had here

VIEW IN LARNECA.

was very pleasantly disposed of in rambling about the ruined old town, making sketches, wondering how such a beggarly and degenerate population could exist on the face of the earth, and musing upon the many changes in the condition of the Island since the birth-day of the Cyprian goddess who came out of the surf at Paphos.

CHAPTER XX.

THE SYRIAN DRAGOMAN.

ANY body stationed on the roof of Demetrie's hotel, near Beirut, might have seen, with a good spy-glass, early in the morning on the 23d of November, a steamer bearing the Austrian flag, paddling its way into the harbor. The decks of that steamer were crowded with pilgrims of all nations— Turks, Arabs, Russian and Polish Jews, and Greeks; but conspicuous on the quarter-deck were two Americans, who might also have been seen with the spy-glass above mentioned—one a tall slender gentleman, with a red book in his hand; and the other rather shorter, but not too short, habited in the unpretending garb of a backwoodsman. Any body might know in a moment that the first was a Southerner, and the last no other than your friend of the present writing.

The weather for nearly two months previously, during our wanderings in the Levant, had been unusually fine; and for the past month, in Constantinople and Smyrna, we had enjoyed cloudless skies and a climate of delightful temperature. Ah! if I could only give you a description of all the fine views of bare mountains, palm trees, and mosques that we saw along the shores of Asia Minor, or the glorious sunsets among the Greek Islands! Such scenes, however, are for artists and poets, not for practical men like us, who go about the world to study the realities of life, and dissipate the mists of fancy.

Scarcely had we cast anchor in the harbor of Beirut (which, by the way, like all the harbors on the coast of Syria, is a very bad one), when we were boarded by a whole legion of hotel-keepers and guides. Books of recommendation were thrust at us by lusty fellows in petticoats, who talked English,

French, Italian, and Arabic all in one breath; cards with views of splendid hotels that never have existed in Beirut and probably never will; private hints whispered in our ears by disinterested persons, and all sorts of strange things yelled at us by the boatmen, who crowded round the steamer. In five minutes I verily believe there was more talking done on that occasion, without a single movement being made toward disembarking the passengers, than one would hear during the whole process of clearing a California steamer. It is one of the peculiarities of Oriental travel that the moment a steamer drops her anchor the officers labor under the idea that the contract of transportation has been fulfilled; that there is nothing more to be done but obstruct as far as practicable all attempts at getting ashore. Even where there is no quarantine to perform, and no police or passport nuisance, they are so loth to part company with their passengers, that I have seen them turn in and go to sleep for the purpose of passing the time agreeably, leaving a man stationed at the gangway, who always says, "Excuse, senor, you can't go ashore yet." Can a person of nervous temperament, who has suffered all the horrors of confinement for two or three days, and who feels certain that the authorities on shore, who are expected every moment, will never come, in consequence of smoking the chibouck till they fall asleep, and sleeping till they are ready to smoke the chibouck again—can one, I say, be tried at the bar of public opinion and justly censured, under such circumstances, for saying *dammit?*

The season was late for a tour through Syria and Palestine. Already the rain was a month behind the time; it might come to-morrow or it might not; but that it would come before very long was regarded as a certainty. Travelers returning from the Nile usually cross the little desert to Gaza early in March, so as to take Palestine in the spring, or somewhat sooner, by Mount Sinai and Arabia Petræa. The season is then delightful; the country covered with verdure; and of course Palestine is seen in its most favorable aspect, before the earth has become parched by the scorching heat of summer. With us it was not a matter of choice. We had spent the time in rambling about the Levant, and had just a month or six weeks to spare, and it was Palestine now or never.

Demetrie, a fine looking Greek, who carried every thing before him by his splendid Albanian costume, pushed the babbling crowd aside, and took possession of us without opposition. His mustache was the blackest and thickest and most conspicuous I ever saw: it had killed half the Arab girls in Beirut, and well entitled the bearer to his distinguished reputation as Demetrie, the conqueror of the female sex. But Demetrie is also distinguished as a dragoman. He has been the guide of English lords and Russian counts without number; has made fortunes and spent them with a facility unknown to the cool-headed inhabitants of more temperate climes. He has gone through all the varieties of life; and is now proprietor of the principal hotel beyond the walls of Beirut; and I can conscientiously say to all travelers that he is a prince of a fellow, and that his hotel is the cleanest and most commodious in Syria.

Long before our arrival at the hotel we were beset by guides, all eagerly thrusting at us their certificates of character. Brief as our experience had been in Oriental life, we were discreet enough not to compromise ourselves by accepting the services of any of these ragamuffins, who, to say the least of them, were a very shabby-looking set. Besides, we were cautioned against them by a very distinguished personage who accompanied Demetrie to the steamer, and who seemed to be the bosom friend and confidant of Demetrie. That personage inspired me with profound sentiments of admiration for his character and genius from the moment I first saw him. There was a cool air of self-reliance about him; an off-hand, dashing style of address in the man; a contempt for all rivalry and opposition; an unmistakable superiority over all the other Arabs, that took both myself and friend captive at once. We belonged to him; we were his subjects from the very beginning. Demetrie held us by force of a fine mustache; but the great unknown held us by force of character. We were at once under mesmeric influence; he could have taken us to the public bazaars and sold us without the least opposition on our part, at almost any sacrifice, such was the mysterious nature of his power. What he was, or where he lived, or what he intended doing with us, it was impossible to say; all he did, so far, was to push aside the babbling crowd of guides, and utter contemptuous exclamations when they provoked him, such as, "Dirty blackguards! Poor devils! Never mind them, gentlemen; they don't know any better! Miserable dogs! Come on, gentlemen; come on; this is the way!"

On our arrival at Demetrie's, our friend and protector took us to the best room in the establishment, where he arranged us comfortably; told us we might rely upon Demetrie for good feeding; and then, drawing forth from his sash a small black book, addressed us substantially as follows:

"Gentlemen, I am YUSEF SIMON BADRA, the dragoman for Syria. This is my book of recommendations. I have taken a thousand American gentlemen through Syria. Yes, sir; the Americans like me; I like the Americans! I hate Englishmen; I won't take an Englishman; they don't suit me; can't get along together; I know too much for 'em. But the Americans suit me; always ready; up to every thing—fun, fight, or frolic. There are other dragomans here, gentlemen. Emanuel Balthos is my friend; I won't interfere, if you wish to take him. I don't say he's afraid of robbers; I don't say he hires guards in all the bad places on that account. I speak only of myself. The robbers know me. The name of Yusef Badra is guard enough in any part of Syria. Courage is a great thing in this country; courage will carry a man through where a thousand guards daren't show their faces. The last time I was out I killed six Bedouins. I sometimes kill such fellows for fun: They know me; they know it's a habit I have, and they always keep clear when they can. But you can choose for yourselves, gentlemen; there's my book; look over it. Of course you'll smoke some chiboucks. Ho! there—Hassin—chiboucks!"

The chiboucks were brought; and while we smoked, and looked over Yusef's book of recommendations, that renowned personage took our spare clothes, created a tremendous sensation down below by the manner in which he caused all the domestics to brush them, and made every Arab about the premises tremble by the ferocity of his looks.

Such an idea as that of entertaining any proposition from another dragoman never entered our heads. We felt that we belonged to Yusef from the beginning; that he had a right to us, which we could not resist; that he was just the man to take us through a dangerous country. Every recommendation in the book complimented him upon his indomitable perseverance and courage. It was enough; the thing was fixed.

YUSEF.

Yusef was already our dragoman. Here you have his portrait:

Face open and intelligent, eyes round and full of fire, mustache fierce, temperament nervous-sanguine, age twenty-eight, costume rich, careless, and dashing; figure well-knit and of medium height; manner frank, self-relying, and chivalrous; whole tone of character imposing, captivating, and Oriental.

Now I profess to be a judge of mankind. I claim some merit in knowing Yusef at a glance. I felt that we were perfectly safe in his hands; that he would fight for us; nay, wallow in blood for us, if necessary; that it would do us credit to travel with a dragoman so renowned and feared throughout Syria; that his lively energy would carry us through all difficulties; that there was nothing narrow or contracted in such a man, and he would feed us well, and provide us with good horses.

The duties of the Syrian dragoman are rather onerous, and require, perhaps, some explanation. He is interpreter of the party; he usually provides the provisions, horses, mules, tents, &c., and charges so much a day for the whole; he speaks various languages, seldom less than five or six; is expected to know all about the country, and something more. He is responsible for the name of every village and town on the route; he is responsible for every assertion made by Robinson and other authorities, and if there be any incongruity in the name or location, it is the dragoman who is compelled to answer for it; he is responsible for every moral and physical defect in the horses and mules; for every shower of rain that interrupts the journey; for every headache and fit of indigestion suffered by any member of the party; for the amount of fleas that infest every stopping-place; for the sterile and unsatisfactory character of the scenery in certain stages of the journey; for the roughness of the roads; for the uncivilized appearance of the Arabs throughout Syria; for the bad state of repair in which the bridges are kept; for every extreme of heat and cold; and all the discomforts of the climate and country; in short the dragoman is responsible for every thing. He must be a man of courage, of energy, of patience, of good temper, of intelligence, of learning, of every thing under the sun, moon, and stars. He must know all that the Howadji doesn't know, and all that the Howadji ought to know; his brains must act for himself and the Howadji, and for the muleteers, and for the horses, mules donkeys, and every living thing in the company; if they don't they are very poor brains indeed. He must be dragoman, tutor, lexicon, valet, cook, caterer, comforter, warrior—all in one; always ready for duty, night and day, never tired, never at fault in any emergency. In effect, the dragoman has a pretty busy life of it, and Yusuf is a good specimen of the best class. If he didn't know and do all these things, he was never at a loss to know and do something else equally satisfactory; and in the end we were forced to admit that his resources were unlimited. When he forgot the name of a village or important ruin, he invented a name that fully answered our purpose; when it rained he proved to us that rain was necessary in order to clear the atmosphere and make it healthy; when there were no robbers, he showed us what he would do if there were robbers; when we were dissatisfied in any way, he was more dissatisfied with the cause of our dissatisfaction than we were ourselves, which made us perfectly satisfied; he was, in all respects, a sagacious, ready-witted and obliging dragoman, highly qualified by nature for his arduous and responsible profession.

If he had any fault at all, it was an incorrigible hatred of the female sex. He never could refer to the subject, without strong expressions of contempt and disdain. He considered that all the misfortunes of life could be traced to woman; 'hat the whole female sex consisted of devils in the disguise of angels. As this singular prejudice concerned himself and not us, we paid but little attention to it in the beginning of our journey; though as we advanced we noticed some slight discrepancy between his practice and his preaching that struck us as somewhat remarkable. He had nieces at every stopping-place, and he never passed without calling to see them. Perhaps the relationship overcame his scruples—or it might be the pride of popularity.

In making a bargain with a dragoman it is considered safest to have a written contract, signed before the consul, specifying every thing to be furnished by the dragoman, the number of horses, mules, &c., and the compensation. The usual price, including tents, provisions, horses, and every thing necessary, is one pound sterling a day for each person; but, as the season was late, we agreed with Yusuf for ninety-six piastres, or about four dollars each. Having now made the tour and acquired some experience in bargain-making, I am very sure I could travel through Syria and Palestine for about half that; not of course in the luxurious style of fashionable tourists, who go merely for pleasure, but in quite good enough style for any person who wishes to acquire knowledge of the country on the most economical terms.

I was rejoiced, soon after we were installed at Demetrie's, to hear the well-known voice of Doctor Mendoza. He was making arrangements with Emanuel Balthos to take himself and the Madam through Syria. He said it would be necess to have a fine tent, to have chairs, tables, bedsteads and other conveniences, as the Madam was indispose; that without these it would be imposs to voyage.

My excellent friends were delighted to see me, and it was a mutual gratification to find that we would in all probability often meet during our tour; in fact that we would perform the greater part of it in company. They had stopped several days in Smyrna, and were much pleased with the *Hôtel des deux Augustes;* the Doctor had ascertained that there was an excellent hotel in Damask, and had caused Demetrie to write on to the proprietor and engage rooms, without which he said, it would be imposs to hazard the voyage. To-morrow morning they intended, if poss, to depart.

The same afternoon, it was an interesting and instructive spectacle to see the Doctor and the Madam in the front yard of Demetrie's hotel. Their tent was erected for inspection; it was of the most fanciful shape and coloring; there was a private chamber in it; and there was no end to the knick-knacks for comfort and convenience. The horses were brought up; the Doctor examined the saddles and the saddle-girths, mounted and got down again, and re-mounted and got down again a dozen times, before he was satisfied that the caparisons were safe. The Madam screamed, and endeavored to faint, when she saw the beautiful little mare upon which she was to ride cut a pigeon-wing by order of Emanuel Balthos; and it was only by great persuasion that she would consent to remain tranquil, in accordance with the advice of the Doctor, who said that the Madam was a little indispose; that he (the Madam) would be better after he had voyaged a few days on horseback.

On the following day we bade this excellent couple adieu and saw them proceed on their winding way toward Baalbek Here I may as well mention that we met them frequently during our tour, and sometimes traveled for days together; the greatest cordiality and friendship always existed on both sides; and it was only owing to the difference in our mode of traveling that we did rot permanently join the two parties

CHAPTER XXI.

THE HISTORY OF MY HORSE SALADIN.

IF there was any one thing in which I was resolved to be particular it was in the matter of horses. Our journey was to be a long one, and experience had taught me that much of the pleasure of traveling on horseback depends upon the qualities of the horse. For some reason unknown to me, and which I have never been able to discover even to this day, a sort of fatality has always attended my dealings in horseflesh. I had bought, hired, and borrowed the very finest-looking animals that could be found any where, and never failed to find out before long that they were blind, spavined, foundered, or troubled with some defect which invariably caused them to stumble and throw me over their heads. Not content with the entertaining spectacle thus afforded to public eyes, the very friends of my heart turned against me in the hour of misfortune, and said it was all my own fault; that any body of common sense could have foreseen the result; that the most honest men in the world, whose word would pass in bank for any amount, could not help lying when it came to horses; that a man's own father was not to be trusted in a transaction of this kind, or even a man's own mother, without looking into the horse's mouth and examining his hoofs. On this account I was resolved to study well the points of the animal that was to bear me through Syria.

Yusef had already given me some slight idea of the kind of horse I was to have. It was an animal of the purest Arabian blood, descended in a direct line from the famous steed of the desert Ashrik; its great-grand-dam was the beautiful Boo-hoo-la, for whose death the renowned Arab chieftain

Ballala, then a boy, grieved constantly until he was eighty-nine years of age, when, no longer able to endure life under so melancholy an affliction, he got married to a woman of bad temper, and was tormented to death in his hundred and twentieth year, and the last words he uttered were, *doghera! doghera! straight ahead!* All of Yusef Badra's horses were his own, bought with his own money, not broken down hacks like what other dragomans hired for their Howadji; though, praised be Allah, he (Yusef) was above professional jealousy. There was only one horse in Syria that could at all compare with this animal, and that was his own, Syed Sulemin; a horse that must be known even in America, for Syed had leaped a wall twenty feet high, and was trained to walk a hundred and fifty miles a day, and kill the most desperate robbers by catching them up in his teeth and tossing them over his head. I had not heard of this horse, but thought it best, by a slight nod, to let Yusef suppose that his story was not altogether unfamiliar to me. Being determined to examine in detail all the points of the animal destined for myself, I directed Yusef to bring them both up saddled and bridled, so that we might ride out and try their respective qualities before starting on our journey. This proposition seemed to confuse him a little, but he brightened up in a moment and went off, promising to have them at the door in half an hour.

Two hours elapsed; during which time I waited with great impatience to see the famous descendant of the beautiful Boo-boo-la. I looked up toward the road, and at length saw a dust, and then saw a perfect rabble of Arabs, and then Yusef, mounted on a tall, slabsided, crooked old horse, and then—could it be?—yes!—a living animal, lean and hollow, very old, saddled with an ancient saddle, bridled with the remnants of an ancient bridle, and led by a dozen ragged Arabs. At a distance it looked a little like a horse; when it came closer it looked more like the ghost of a mule; and closer still, it bore some resemblance to the skeleton of a small camel; and when I descended to the yard, it looked a little like a horse again.

"Tell me," said I, the indignant blood mounting to my cheeks, "tell me, Yusef, *is* that a horse?"

"A horse!" retorted he, smiling, as I took it, at the untutored simplicity of an American; "a horse, O General! it is nothing else but a horse; and such an animal, too, as, I'll venture to say, the richest pasha in Beirut can't match this very moment."

"*Tahib!*" Good—said one of the Arabs, patting him on the neck, and looking sideways at me in a confidential way.

"*Tahib!*" said another, and "*tahib!*" another, and "*tahib*" every Arab in the crowd, as if each one of them had ridden the horse five hundred miles, and knew all his merits by personal experience.

That there were points of some kind about him was not to be disputed. His back must have been broken at different periods of his life, in at least three places; for there were three distinct pyramids on it, like miniature pyramids of Gizeh; one just in front of the saddle, where his shoulder-blade ran up to a cone; another just back of the saddle; and the third, a kind of spur of the range, over his hips, where there was a sudden breaking off from the original line of the backbone, and a precipitous descent to his tail. The joints of his hips and the joints of his legs were also prominent, especially those of his forelegs, which he seemed to be always trying to straighten out, but never could, in consequence of the sinews being too short by several inches. His skin hung upon this remarkable piece of frame-work as if it had been purposely put there to dry in the sun, so as to be ready for leather at any moment after the extinction of the vital functions within. But, to judge from the eye (there was only one), there seemed to be no prospect of a suspension of vitality, for it burned with great brilliancy, showing that a horse, like a singed cat, may be a good deal better than he looks.

"A great horse that," said Yusef, patting him on the neck kindly; "no humbug about him, General. Fifty miles a day he'll travel fast asleep. He's a genuine Syrian."

"And do you tell me," said I sternly, "that this is the great-grandson of the beautiful Boo-boo-la? That I, a General in

THE HISTORY OF MY HORSE SALADIN.

SALADIN.

the Bob-tail Militia and representative in foreign parts of the glorious City of Magnificent Distances, am to make a public exhibition of myself throughout Syria mounted upon that miserable beast?"

"Nay, as for that," replied the fellow, rather crestfallen, "far be it from me, the faithfullest of dragomans, to palm off a bad horse on a Howadji of rank. The very best in Beirut are at my command. Only say the word, and you shall have black, white, or gray, heavy or light, tall or short; but this much I know, you'll not find such an animal as that any where in Syria. Ho, Saladin! (slapping him on the neck,) who's this, old boy? Yusef, eh? Ha, ha! see how he knows me! Who killed the six Bedouins single-handed, when we were out last, eh, Saladin? Ha, ha! you know it was Yusef, you cunning rascal, only you don't like to tell. A remarkable animal, you perceive; but, as I said before, perhaps your Excellency had better try another.

"No," said I, "no, Yusef; this horse will do very well. He's a little ugly, to be sure; a little broken-backed, and perhaps a little blind, lame, and spavined, but he *has* some extraordinary points of character. At all events, it will do no harm to try him. Come, away we go!" Saying which I undertook to vault into the saddle, but the girth being loose, it turned over and let me down on the other side. This little mishap was soon remedied, and we went off in a smart walk up the lane leading from Demetrie's toward the sand-hills. In a short time we were well out of the labyrinth of hedges formed by the prickly-pears, and were going along very quietly and pleasantly, when all of a sudden, without the slightest warning, Yusef, who had a heavy stick in his hand, held it up in the air like a lance, and darted off furiously, shouting as he went, "Badra, Badra!" Had an entire nest of hornets simultaneously lit upon my horse Saladin, and stung him to the quick, he could not have shown more decided symptoms of sudden and violent insanity. His tail stood straight up, each particular hair of his mane started into life, his very ears seemed to be torturing themselves out of his head, while he snorted and pawed the earth as if perfectly convulsed with fury. The next instant he made a bound, which brought my weight upon the bridle; and this brought Saladin upon his hind legs, and upon his hind legs he began to dance about in a circle; and then plunged forward again in the most extraordinary manner. The whole proceeding was so very unexpected that I would willingly have been sitting a short distance off, a mere spectator; it would have been so funny to see somebody else mounted upon Saladin. Both my feet came out of the stirrups in spite of every effort to keep them there; and the bit, being contrived in some ingenious manner, tortured the horse's mouth to such a degree every time I pulled the bridle, that he became perfectly frantic, and I had to let go at last and seize hold of his mane with both hands. This seemed to afford him immediate relief, for he bounded off at an amazing rate. My hat flew off at the same time, and the wind fairly whistled through my hair. I was so busy trying to hold on that I had no time to think how very singular the whole thing was; if there was any thought at all it was only as to the probable issue of the adventure. Away we dashed, through chapperals of prickly pear, over ditches and dikes, out upon the rolling sand plain! I looked, and beheld a cloud of dust approaching. The next moment a voice shouted "Badra, Badra!" the battle-cry of our dragoman, and then Yusef himself, whirling his stick over his head, passed like a shot. "Badra, Badra!" sounded again in the distance. Saladin wheeled and darted madly after him; while I, clutching the saddle with one hand, just saved my balance in time, "Badra, Badra!" shrieked Yusef, whirling again, and blinded by the fury of battle. "Come on, come on! A thousand of you at a time! Die, villains, die!" Again he dashed furiously by, covered in a cloud of dust, and again he returned to the charge; and again, driven to the last extremity by the terrific manner in which Saladin wheeled around and followed every charge, I seized hold of the bridle and tried all my might to stop him, but this time he not only danced about on his hind legs, but made broadside charges to the left for a hundred yards on a stretch, and then turned to the right and made broadside charges again for another hundred yards, and then reared up and attempted to turn a back somerset. All this time there was not the slightest doubt in my mind that sooner or later I should be thrown violently on the ground and have my neck and several of my limbs broken. In vain I called to Yusef; in vain I threatened to discharge him on the spot; sometimes he was half a mile off, and sometimes he passed in a cloud of dust like a whirlwind, but I might just as well have shouted to the great King of Day to stand still as to Badra, the Destroyer of Robbers. By this time, finding it impossible to hold Saladin by the bridle, I seized him by the tail with one hand, and by the mane with the other, and away he darted faster than ever. "Badra, Badra!" screamed a voice behind; it was Yusef in full chase! Away we flew, up hill and down hill, over banks of sand, down into fearful hollows, and up again on the other side; and still the battle-cry of Yusef resounded behind, "Badra, Badra forever!"

SALADIN IN ACTION

On we dashed till the pine grove loomed up ahead; on, and still on, till we were close up and the grove stood like a wall of trees before us. "Thank Heaven," said I, "we'll stop now! Hold, Yusef, hold!" "Badra, Badra!" cried the frantic horseman, dashing by and plunging in among the trees: "Badra, forever!" Saladin plunged after him, flying around the trees and through the narrow passes in such a manner that, if I feared before that my neck would be broken, I felt an absolute certainty now that my brains would be knocked out and both my eyes run through by some projecting limb. In the horror of the thought, I yelled to Yusef for God's sake to stop, that it was perfect folly to be running about in this way like a pair of madmen; but by this time he had scoured out on the plain again, and was now engaged in going through the exercise of the Djereed with a party of country Arabs, scattering their horses hither and thither, and flourishing his stick at their heads every time he came within reach. They seemed to regard it as an excellent joke, and took it in very good part; but for me there was no joke about the business, and I resolved as soon as a chance occurred to discharge Yusef on the spot. Saladin, becoming now a little tamed by his frolic, slackened his pace, so that I got my feet back into the stirrups, and obtained some control over him. There was a Syrian café and smoke-house not far off, and thither I directed my course. A dozen boys ran out from the grove, and seized him by the bridle, and at the same time Yusef coming up, both horses were resigned to their charge, and we dismounted. "Hallo, sir!" said I "come this way!" for to tell the truth I was exceedingly enraged and meant to discharge him on the spot.

"Bless me! what's become of your hat?" cried Yusef, greatly surprised; "I thought your excellency had put it in your pocket, to keep it from blowing away!"

"The devil you did! Send after it, if you please; it must be a mile back on that sand hill."

A boy was immediately dispatched in search of the hat. Meantime, while I was preparing words sufficiently strong to express my displeasure, Yusef declared that he had never seen an American ride better than I did, only the horse was not used to being managed in the American fashion.

"Eh! Perhaps you allude to the way I let go the reins, and seized him by the mane?"

"To that most certainly I do refer," replied Yusef; "he doesn't understand it; none of the horses in Syria understand it."

"No," said I, "very few horses do. None but the best riders in America dare to undertake such a thing as that. Did you see how I let my feet come out of the stirrups, and rode without depending at all upon the saddle?"

"Most truly I did; and exceedingly marvelous it was to me that you were not thrown. Any but a very practiced rider would have been flung upon the ground in an instant. But wherefore, O General, do you ride in that dangerous way?"

"Because it lifts the horse from the ground and makes him go faster. Besides, when you don't pull the bridle, of course you don't hurt his mouth or stop his headway."

Yusef assented to this, with many exclamations of surprise at the various customs that prevail in different parts of the world; maintaining, however, that the Syrian horses not being used to it, perhaps it would be better for me in view of our journey to learn the Syrian way of guiding and controlling horses; which I agreed to do forthwith. We then sat down and had some coffee and chiboucks; and while I smoked Yusef enlightened me on all the points of Syrian horsemanship. how I was to raise my arms when I wanted the horse to go on, and hold them up when I wanted him to run, and let them down when I wanted him to stop; how I was to lean a little to the right or the left, and by the slightest motion of the bridle guide him either way; how I was to lean back or forward in certain cases, and never to trot at all, as that was a most unnatural and barbarous gait, unbecoming both to horse and rider. Upon these and a great many other points he descanted learnedly, till the boy arrived with my hat; when, paying all actual expenses for coffee and chiboucks, we distributed a small amount of backshish among the boys who had attended our horses, and mounted once more. This time under the instruction of Yusef, I soon learned how to manage Saladin, and the ride back to Beirut was both pleasant and entertaining.

CHAPTER XXII.

THE ARAB STORY-TELLER.

This is, among his countrymen, a most important character. Every body who has traveled through Egypt or Syria, will bear witness that the accompanying pencil-sketch is a faithful repre‑

sentation of the class. The old gentleman whose name is attached to it lives in the neighborhood of Beirut. He is called Ben-Hozain, the King of Talkers. The handwriting is his own; and you will admit that the name looks as much like Ben-Hozain as it does like Benjamin Huggins, of which I think it must be a corruption. Ben is conspicuous chiefly for the length of his mustache. His tongue is long, but his mustache is a good deal longer; in fact, it is such a mustache as any Arab in Syria, however distinguished, might be proud to swear by. It is to be regretted that people should swear at all; but if they will swear, it is better they should be profane on the subject of beards or mustaches, than on matters of higher import. By profession and inclination Ben-Hozain is a story-teller. I do not mean to say that he is given to willful lying, or to any malicious misrepresentation of facts; but the business of his life is to entertain the public of Beirut with traditional romances of the country. Where people read but little, they make up in some measure for the deficiency by talking and listening a good deal. This is especially the case with the Orientals. In the absence of a general circulation of newspapers, of printed histories of wars, philosophical essays on man, and books of travel, they must have professional story-tellers, or romancers; that is to say, men whose regular business it is to deal in tradition or fiction. Throughout the whole East there is not a more important personage than the story-teller, or one who wields a greater influence upon the public mind. He is a walking newspaper, a living history, a breathing essay, a personified book of travels, which evolves its stores of knowledge on self-acting principles. As such, being considered a responsible agent, he is entitled to the confidence of the community, and generally enjoys it to the fullest extent. The more marvelous his stories are, the greater credit they obtain; the more rabid his political satires, the greater his circulation; the more incomprehensible his theories and illustrations of human life, the profounder his philosophy. He is always a popular character, and is indispensable at every smoking-house. The grandest Pashas listen to him with profound attention; the morals which he points and the tales which he adorns find their way even into the sacred precincts of the Harem. In the highest circles and in the lowest his traditions and anecdotes are swallowed with avidity. Men who have listened for years to the same stories and the same jokes, continue to listen for years again with undiminished delight and always applaud at the same points and laugh at the same strokes of wit. No child of ten years, in our cold clime of common sense, could devour his first fairy-tale or ghost-story with half the delight that an Arab grandfather devours the oft-told romances of the old story-teller.

The way I happened to take Ben-Hozain's portrait was this: One afternoon I rode out with our dragoman to the pine grove, where the towns-people go to smoke the narguilla and display their feats of horsemanship, and where I had already displayed some feats of horsemanship myself. It was shady and pleasant under the trees, and I dismounted and amused myself taking a view of a Syrian coffee-house, near which were seated a number of Turks, Greeks, and Arabs, in all their picturesque varieties of costume. An old man sat in the midst of the group, chanting at the highest pitch of his voice the famous romance of the White Princess and the Grand Vizier. Sometimes in the excitement of the love parts he screamed, and sometimes pretended to faint; and when he was depicting the more tragic parts, where there was murder and suicide, he howled like a hyena, and counterfeited all the agonies of death in a most thrilling manner. When he got over the principal difficulties, he moderated down into a species of billing and cooing, winking and ogling, that reminded me forcibly of representations that I had seen of the passions in the Astor Place Opera House. I could not but think that nature had intended Ben-Hozain to grace the boards of that establishment, and delight an appreciating audience of the Upper Ten, his delineation of the passions was so exquisitely extravagant. Struck with the picturesque raggedness of his costume, and the length of his grizzled mustache, I began to sketch him. Gradually the listeners dropped off one by one, and gathered around me to look into the mysteries of the art. All kinds of queer remarks were made, of which Yusef gave me a running interpretation. "That's Ben-Hozain," said one; "don't you see how the Howadji puts down his nose?" "And his eyes!" adds another. "And his mustache!" cries a third. "Tahib!" Good. "Adjaib!" Wonderful. "What a sublime genius the Howadji has!" "Tell Ben-Hozain," said I, "to come a little closer, and you shall see him on this paper just as he lives and breathes!" "Adjaib!" Wonderful. "This way, Hozain; the Howadji wants you!" But Hozain had no notion of being interrupted in his story. He went on even louder than before on the subject of the White Princess. "By Allah!" cried the Arabs, "he shall come! Hozain must be done on paper!" With which two stout fellows ran over to where he sat, seized him on each side by the mustache, and hauled him up before me. He was the most comical and good-humored old gentleman imaginable; his face was covered with wrinkles and the stubbles of a white beard, and he seemed quite lelighted at affording merriment to the crowd. Here you have him just as he sat, with his mustache in full; his eyes twinkling with fun, and a tradition in every wrinkle of his mouth. So pleased was he with his appearance on paper that he put his name to the sketch. The Arabs were all in ecstasies, and begged me to take them one and all; but, there being about thirty of them, I had to decline, on the plea of having important business to attend to that evening.

As I was going away, the old story-teller looked wistfully at me. "Well," said I, "what do you want now, my friend?"

"*Backshish*," said he.

"For what? I'm going to put you in a book. Isn't that backshish enough?"

"But I'll never see the book. I'd rather have the backshish now."

"That's strange, Hozain. Have you no pride in the honor of the thing? Think of the fame it will give you! Ben-Hozain will be known in the remotest corners of America."

"Ah, Grand Seignor, Sultan of the United States, Ben-Hozain is already the victim of fame. For more than forty years have I told stories for the public good; Sultans have praised me, Pashas have applauded my romances, beautiful ladies have wept over my love passages, yet here I am, as you see, with scarce a rag on my back. When I'm dead, I don't know that they'll take the trouble to bury me."

"Well, Hozain, I'm sorry to hear so bad an account of your people. In America we take a great deal of trouble about our benefactors after they die. We often spend more money in feasting over their graves and celebrating their virtues than would have made them comfortable during life. Your patrons must be very ungrateful, and as a mark of my contempt for such ingratitude, I shall give you the backshish you require. How much will it take to make you happy?"

"Only two piasters, O sublime Howadji! On that amount of money, Ben-Hozain can be the happiest man upon earth, for he can drink the Coffee of Delight and smoke the Pipe of Content for a week!"

"Very well, take this piece of silver, five piasters (twenty two cents). And remember (said I, proudly,) that in America we never neglect men who live by their talents. We subscribe to their newspapers, read their books, profit by their labors, and when they are dead pay them—a great deal of respect."

CHAPTER XXIII.

THE CEDARS OF LEBANON.

It was our good fortune to become acquainted during our brief sojourn in Beirut, with a young English gentleman, chief officer of an Oriental Steamer, who having a couple of months to spare, agreed to join us in our tour through Syria. His good-humor and intelligence rendered him an invaluable acquisition to our party.

Leaving Beirut in the latter part of November, we passed, not far beyond the suburbs, the spot pointed out as the scene of the remarkable battle between St. George and the dragon, and soon after crossed the pass of Xerxes. The road lay along the sea beach, which extends to the rocky point, five or six miles from the town, called the Roman Pass. On the rocks to the right of the road are some Latin inscriptions carved in tablets, and in some places the remains of basso-relievos. Farther on a few miles we descended into the beautiful little valley of El Kelb, or Dog River, where stand the remains of a bridge built by the Romans. Silk is manufactured to some extent in this country, and our road frequently lay through flourishing plantations of mulberry. The ground is cultivated in a rude manner most of the way along the shores of Syria, and we passed through many small fields of sugar-cane, irrigated by water from the mountain streams, which is conducted in narrow walled ditches through the fields. Covered as the whole face of the country is with stones, yet the tilled parts are apparently fertile and yield abundant crops. On the slopes of Mount Lebanon are many small villages, similar to those met with throughout Syria. The houses are but one story high, built of stone, with flat mud roofs, and at a distance have the appearance of mud boxes put out on the hills to dry. The village of Zuk, which we passed at a distance, is prettily situated, but is like all other Syrian villages, a wretched abode of men, women, and vermin. We met on the road several of those strange beings the Druses, a religious sect wearing a costume peculiar to themselves. The head-dress of the women points upward like an immense horn, about two feet long: the men wore an indescribable dress of ragged robes, picturesque at first sight, but not to be too closely scrutinized. The Druses inhabit the country chiefly around Mount Lebanon and the neighborhood, and sprung originally from the Kamiathians, one of the Mohammedan sects We met also during the afternoon several Pashas and their retinues of servants coming from Damascus and Tripoli, and occasionally traveling merchants with their caravans of merchandise, bound to Beirut from Aleppo and other interior towns. About four miles beyond the valley of El Kelb, we came to another beautiful little valley, sheltered by high mountains, running down to the sea-shore, where there is a small harbor, which our guide informed us was occupied by the British forces after the storming of Beirut in 1841. Here is situated the village of Juna; and the mountain sides are dotted with small houses and terraced with stone walls to a considerable height, the most unpromising patches of tillable ground being thus made available. Yusef soon had our tent up in the midst of a young orchard of mulberry trees; and it was not long before we had on our table a good supper of chicken, rice, preserves, and coffee; for, in justice to our dragoman, I must not omit to mention that he fed us in excellent style, and gave us so many luxuries in the way of tables, bedsteads, chairs, napkins, and different courses of plate, that the poor mules were quite laden down, and we were obliged to protest against this effeminate style of living, especially as we soon found it to be at the expense of time, an important object with us at this season. Contrasted with the sort of traveling to which I had been accustomed in California, it was ridiculously civilized, and made me feel much less independent than when I coursed through the plains of the Ojitas and San José with nothing but my mule and saddle-bags, and slept under the trees. Coffee and chiboucks finished the evening. The clouds had been threatening for some time, and, before we were comfortably in bed, they began to pour down upon us such a torrent of rain that we soon found the tent but a poor protection, and the wind blew in gusts so sudden and violent that we momentarily expected to be covered up in a ruin of canvas. At last we had to make a retreat to a khan down on the beach, where we were fortunate enough to get a tolerable room. The khans, or houses for the accommodation of travelers throughout Syria, are usually large stone buildings, without furniture, and filthy to an extreme. Of course Frank travelers only resort to them when the weather does not permit of living in tents; and many prefer suffering from cold and rain to encountering the vermin with which the khans are infested. It is always best, however, when the season is at all unfavorable, to sleep in houses; for whatever may be the inconveniences of living among mules, asses, fleas, and smoking Arabs, they are not so great as those of sickness in a foreign land, where no assistance can be had. Many a traveler has laid his bones in Syria in consequence of wet nights and sunshiny days. We here took the precaution, as in all future cases, to have the first layer of fleas swept out, leaving the partially dormant layer below; and thus we commenced our first night of Syrian travel. For hours I lay musing over the many scenes I had passed through during the last few years, but the fitful moaning of the wind, mingled with the measured break of the surf upon the beach, at length lulled me to sleep, and I slept well by their familiar music. It rained hard most of the night. Toward morning the wind had moderated, yet several small vessels in the port hove up their anchors and stood out to sea as if they expected worse weather. This was not a cheering prospect for our contemplated tour. We had, in starting from the khan, the first trial of patience to which, in common with all who travel in the East, we were doomed to be frequently subjected—I mean the loss of time. The Arabs, Turks, and indeed all the Oriental races, are singularly independent of time; in fact, with the exception of its use in estimating distances, they appear to have no knowledge of its value whatever. We were to have started at six, but it was nine before we got rightly under way.

Our Arab muleteers were slow, and although Yusef swore himself completely out of breath, and to the best of my knowledge entirely exhausted the vocabulary of strong expressions in Arabic, they made no effort to hurry the matter in the least. On the contrary, I was rather struck with the resigned manner in which they bore his violent reproaches and ferocious denunciations, and the cool air with which they puffed their chibouks after the slightest exertion. On the beach, as we passed along through the village of Juna, we observed the wreck of a vessel—one of the many driven ashore on this coast every winter. In Beirut we were told that not less than eight or ten were lost in this way every winter; the coast of Syria from Tripoli to Damietta affording no secure harbor for shipping. The road beyond Juna to the next point or pass we found rocky and precipitous, much like what we had passed, only still more tiresome. It should be borne in mind that roads in Syria are not like the roads we are accustomed to at home, which, bad as they are compared with the roads through Italy, have yet some pretensions to the name; but here to dignify them by such a name is a complete perversion of the word. The bridle paths of Switzerland are magnificent highways compared with them, and in thus speaking of them I merely adopt the ordinary language of travelers. I have seen nothing like them except in crossing the Isthmus of Panama; imagine that Isthmus extended an indefinite number of miles, and you have some idea of Syrian roads. Fortunately, the horses of this country are remarkable for their sureness of foot and powers of endurance.

Not far beyond Juna is the bed of a river called El Mahmilton, over which is the arch of an old Roman bridge, conspicuous for its massive proportions and fine architectural style. Nothing remained of the river but its bed, most of the streams throughout the country having been dried by the long and uninterrupted drought for the last eight months. In the winter, this stream is no doubt swollen to something like a river by the mountain torrents, although in speaking of rivers here, as indeed throughout Europe and the East, it is not to be supposed that what we call rivers in America are meant Every little creek in the Old World is dignified by the name of river, and every duck-pond is called a lake.

It would be necessary to go beyond the limits of a mere journal of incidents to give an account of the country for the next three days. We stopped at Djbel, Batroum, and Tripoli, long enough to see each town pretty thoroughly, and make some sketches, and on the third day commenced our ascent of Mount Lebanon.

CASTLE OF DJBEL.

At Aheden, claimed by some authorities as the Garden of Eden, we were obliged to take a guide, the path being altogether obliterated in some of the table-grounds by recent floods of rain. As we approached the cedars we went down into a ravine, and soon after passed along the ledge of a profound gorge, extending to the depth of several hundred feet. A village, distant by Syrian measurement two hours from Aheden, lies on the left of the gorge, not far from which is a celebrated grotto, visited by many of the pilgrims as a place of peculiar interest. Our time, however, being limited, we pushed on, and in another hour entered the celebrated grove of cedars— a mere patch of green in the bare and desert hollow of the mountains. It was cold and gloomy within the shadowy inclosure, and quite deserted. Not a living thing was to be seen, and all was silent as death, save an occasional plaintive note from some lonesome bird among the branches. Entering by a ravine below, we ascended some distance among the younger growth of trees till we reached an elevation a few hundred yards higher up, upon which stands a rude stone chapel, built by some of the Frank monks, in the midst of the ancient grove, and still used by Christian pilgrims in their annual visits of devotion. There are twelve veteran and storm-beaten trees pointed out as the original cedars of Lebanon; and the best authorities, I believe, concur in admitting these to be the veritable cedars referred to in the Scriptures. Certainly they bear every indication of extraordinary antiquity; and there is no reason to doubt that they existed in very remote ages. From these have sprung, during the lapse of centuries, the surrounding grove, consisting of nearly four hundred trees of various degrees of antiquity, but all of the same species. The chapel was quite deserted, the priests having left some days before for the more genial climate of Tripoli. It is the custom for all the inhabitants of the vicinity to depart for the valleys below on the approach of winter, which is very severe and protracted at this elevation. Our guide pointed out the height to which the snow reached during the previous winter on some of the trees, and we judged it to be not less than twenty feet. It often covers the walls of the chapel entirely up to the roof, completely blocking up all means of ingress and exit. At such a time, of course, it would be very difficult, if not altogether impracticable, to exist in this region; but, if we are to credit the strange histories related to us by our Arabs, it has been done by the aid of miracles, and may be done again. Eleas, one of our interpreters, assured us that there was once a dark man who came over from a distant country, and who, in consequence of having committed a great sin, was resolved to expiate his offense by starving himself to death in the hollow of one of the old cedars. There he fixed his abode, and prayed in secret, and such was the efficacy of his prayers, that he subsisted for two years on nourishing waters that were sent down to him from the branches of the tree by miraculous power; and he suffered neither from heat nor from cold, but at the expiration of his voluntary penance took his departure, and returned a happy man to his own country. To render the story strictly credible, the hollow was pointed out to us, and Eleas, who was a Christian of the Greek Church, said his prayers under the shadow of the old cedar. With other strange narratives of a similar kind the simple natives entertained us, while we sat down under the wide-branching trees, spread our cloth upon the ground, and refreshed ourselves after the ride from Aheden.

As soon as we had finished our repast, we set out to make a more thorough examination of the ancient cedars, or the original twelve, in which the chief interest is centred. It required no great research to convince us of their great age, which is strikingly apparent in their gnarled and time-worn trunks. Many of the branches have become sapless, and are fast rotting away; others are broken off by the force of many tempests, or have fallen of their own accord from sheer old age; new ones have sprung out, and young shoots continue to supply the ravages worked by time; the trunks are of vast circumference, and are composed of divers parts consolidated, some of them perhaps the growth of different ages. All the old trees and many of the younger ones have large pieces cut out of their trunks, upon which are carved the names of visitors who from time to time have been attracted to this remote region. Among these I noticed the name of Lamartine, said to have been carved by an Arab while the great sentimentalist was going into ecstasies in his comfortable quarters below. There were several American names, but none of very recent date—only two within two years. In the register which is kept on the altar of the chapel I saw several English, French, and Oriental names. Some of the remarks were curious enough. One gentleman, who probably imagined the cedars to be yellow or pink, with crimson tops, like those in the panoramas, says he visited the Cedars of Lebanon, and was greatly disappointed. Another traveler states that he could see much larger and finer trees at home without trouble or expense. What any body expects to see except the Cedars of Lebanon, I am at a loss to conceive. One does not travel three days over bad roads to witness a raree-show, or see simply a few cedar-trees because they are cedars; but, if I understand it, the object is to see the Cedars of Lebanon mentioned in the Scriptures; and there they are without doubt. They can be seen by any body who has eyes to see. It is true they are only cedars, but they are very wonderful, as well from their great antiquity as from the Scriptural interest attached to them.

Messrs. Lansing and Burnett, American missionaries at Damascus, visited this region last summer, and carefully counted the cedars, both old and young. They also made some measurements of a very interesting character. The entire grove, according to their estimate, consists of four hundred trees; the average circumference of the original twelve is about twenty-five feet, and one was found to measure upward of thirty. The trunks of the more ancient cedars do not rise to any great height before they branch out into enormous limbs, commencing ten or fifteen feet from the ground, some perhaps twenty feet. The branches are very crooked and tortuous, partly decayed, as before stated, and gnarled with the frosts and tempests of ages. It is said that no other specimens of the kind are found in any part of the world, except such as have been transplanted from this grove; but Messrs. Lansing and Burnett ascertained to their entire satisfaction that other cedars of the same species do exist in the mountains of Syria. The wood is white, and has a pleasant perfume; and to this odor reference is made in the Scriptures. It is not stronger, however, than the scent of the ordinary red cedar, perhaps less apparent.

From the front of the chapel there is a very fine view of

the valley below, extending entirely to the sea. The reefs opposite Ras Tripoli are distinctly visible on a clear day. Computed by the time required for the ascent, the distance must be about thirty miles from the town of Tripoli. From Beirut it requires three days, at the usual rate of travel, to reach the cedars, but it is not difficult to accomplish the task in less. To Baalbek, across the valley of Bukaa, on the other side of Mount Lebanon, is another good day's ride.

CHAPTER XXIV.

BAALBEK.

BEFORE we left that celebrated grove, we provided ourselves with a good supply of relics. At first we were loth to touch a single twig of those sacred old trees, which had braved the tempests for centuries; but our guides told us that thousands of native pilgrims come from all parts of the country every year, and carry away whole loads of seeds and branches, without the least compunctions of conscience; in fact, that the pruning did them good. With such a precedent, made more certain by the aid of a little *backshish*, we followed the example of other pilgrims, and got the Arabs to cut us some walking-sticks and knock down some burrs, both of which I hope to see flourishing in Washington one of these days.

From the Cedars up to the summit of Mount Lebanon, by the way of the pass that leads into the valley of Bukaa, is nearly two hours of very laborious climbing. It was not long before sunset when we reached the highest part of the ridge. Our horses were pretty well tired down, and ourselves rather the worse of the wear, having walked most of the way from Aheden. The altitude of this part of the mountain we supposed to be about six thousand feet. As yet there was no snow visible on any part of it. The air was sharp and clear, but not unpleasantly cold. Tired as we were, after our hard day's journey, we could not but stop a while to enjoy the view. It was really one of those splendid sights which even a traveler, whose life is spent among the beauties of nature, is privileged to enjoy but once or twice in the course of existence. On the one hand the valley of Aheden, through which we had been ascending for nearly two days, stretched down till it appeared to mingle with the mists of the ocean at the shores of Tripoli; on the other the magnificent plain of Bukaa, bounded in the distance by the mountains of Anti-Lebanon, at the base of which, sparkling in the rays of the setting sun, were distinctly visible the minaret of the mosque and the ruins of Baalbek; while far down in the valley of Bukaa, to the right as we faced the plain, gleamed the bright waters of the Litany, and across the deep gorges at our feet were cast the shadows of the lofty peaks of Lebanon—a vast and impressive scene, within a single sweep of the eye, sterile, waste, and desolate, but sublime in its weird simplicity. It brought to mind, with the vividness of reality, those grand pictures of primeval scenery drawn in the sacred writings; and the lapse of ages seemed now but the lapse of years, passed in a dream. It was like returning after an absence to some long known haunt of youth; for the words of the sacred book, the first impressed upon the memory, were here a sublime reality.

As we descended toward the plain of Bukaa, driving our horses before us, my self-willed old charger, Saladin, took a notion not to be driven down, so he walked up on all possible occasions. In vain I hurled missiles at his head; in vain I begged him not to be foolish; in vain I tried to make him understand that he was only doubling the distance, as he would eventually be compelled to turn back again; it was all to no purpose. Up again to the top of Mount Lebanon he would go, after the most persevering resistance, half way down; and at last he ran away full speed over rocks that seemed quite inaccessible. I had long suspected Saladin of a sentimental turn of mind, and was now convinced that he only wanted to enjoy another view of the sunset; but it was too late, the sun had disappeared and it was fast getting dark. So I darted after him, and the chase became quite exciting. Never skipped a goat with more agility than that slab-sided old horse. It was fully half an hour before I could catch him, and it was then so dark that I found myself lost. Neither muleteers nor guides were to be seen. I shouted till

I could shout no longer, but there was no answer. At last, after tumbling, sliding, and jumping down precipices, till it seemed as if I had reached the sloping-off place of the world, I heard the voices of my friends below. It was evident we must spend the night here, for Baalbek was still six hours distant. The guides and muleteers were nowhere to be seen, and we consoled ourselves with the notion that they had run off with our baggage. After wandering about in the dark for some time we came to the ruins of a village, without a living soul about it. In the hollow a little below the ruins we encamped for the night, our missing Arabs having at length made their appearance. There is a cave here, said to have been not more than a few years since the abode of a large band of those mountain robbers who infest the country. Of late, however, they have not found their business profitable, and they only commit occasional depredations. Our dragoman said he could put to flight any gang of robbers in Syria single-handed, such was the terror in which he was held. He certainly carried pistols and knives enough about his person to kill a good many; but it was not at all dangerous to be shot at by Yusef, for I saw him shoot a good many times and never knew him to hit any thing. The cave was a very nice place for robbers, pleasantly situated, with large trees in front, and a fine spring of water within a hundred yards. At present it is a place of resort for goats and benighted travelers. We lit a fire near the entrance, erected our tent under some fine old chestnut trees, and slept soundly all night in spite of the cold, which was very keen. Next morning there was snow visible on the tops of the mountains.

Yusef having threatened to whip all the Arabs again (for he had already whipped them two or three times), got them to work at an early hour, and, by the force of much talk and desperate flourishing of the stick, they were all ready with their mules as soon as we had finished breakfast. Pushing on rapidly for Baalbek, we were soon made sensible of the deceptive nature of distances from a very high point of view On the preceding evening, from the summit of Mount Lebanon, the plain of Bukaa, reaching to the ruins of Baalbek, appeared to commence at the place of our encampment, and to continue with an almost unbroken surface to the base of the Anti-Lebanon range; but now it seemed as if we were scarcely more than half way down. The road from the ruined village is through a very rocky and broken region, studded over with patches of scrub-oak bushes, and altogether uncultivated. The only signs of habitation we saw were a few miserable huts rudely built of loose stones, the back part being against a hill or mound of earth, and the front barely high enough to admit of a doorway. These wretched hovels are inhabited by a swarthy and half-savage race of Arabs, who live on the flesh and milk of goats, many flocks of which we saw browsing among the rocks. In fact, goats, sheep, dogs, men, women, and children seem to live together upon terms of perfect equality. They were the most uncivilized people we had yet seen, and we had seen a good many on the road from Tripoli.

It was evident that but few travelers in our style of costume had been in the habit of passing, from the apparent astonishment which our appearance created. Some women at one of the huts laughed so immoderately that we were induced to ask them, through our dragoman, what was the occasion of their mirth. Why, said they, we never saw people before with saucepans on their heads for turbans. Do the Christians all wear saucepans? The shape of our trowsers also afforded much merriment. "Don't you burst when you sit down?" they asked, and this sally of wit was so irresistible that we could hear their shouts of laughter long after we had passed. Following for several hours down the course of a small stream, we at length reach in good earnest the plain of Bukaa. This magnificent valley stretches on the left, as we faced Baalbek, as far as we could see; on the right it seemed to merge into a sea of bright water studded with islands, the reflection of which appeared in its surface as distinctly as if it was in reality a sea or lake, reminding me forcibly of the Salinas plains in California. In fact there was much in the general character of this part of Syria to bring up reminiscences of California. The two great ranges of mountains,

Lebanon and Anti-Lebanon, skirting the plain; the vast extent of the view on all sides; the genial sky and bracing atmosphere; the long lines of mules, with their packs, winding over the distant hill-sides; the trails diverging in all directions; the parched and stern character of the scenery, were not unlike an autumn view in the Valley of San José or San Juan, and still more like the Valley of Salinas. But here the resemblance ceases. There is nothing in Syria to remind one of the indomitable energy, the life, vigor, and spirit of progress so strikingly apparent in California. Whatever the plain of Bukaa may have been in the days of the splendor of Heliopolis, it is now a barren waste, dotted over with ruined villages, and of a most melancholy aspect. Portions of it are still cultivated in a rude manner; and we were told it was susceptible of being made to produce good wheat. It is almost entirely destitute of wood and water, and the villages stand out nakedly in the full blaze of an eastern sun. Far in the distance we saw a single column, a tall solitary object on the broad waste, standing like some lonely sentinel to remind the traveler that this land was not always thus desolate. There is a tradition among the Arabs that this column was carried thither after the destruction of Baalbek, on the shoulders of a woman, who placed it where it now stands to commemorate the death of her lover, who was slain on the spot. Her back must have been strong, as well as her love, for on a nearer inspection we found the column to be nearly if not quite as high as Pompey's Pillar. Though of ancient material, so far as we could judge, the blocks of stone had evidently been put together in their present position at a more recent date. It stands on an immense

pedestal, loosely built, and many of the stones appear to have been thrown out of place by some convulsion of nature. The lower block forming the base is broken nearly to the middle, the gap having the appearance of being purposely made to destroy the column by a fall. It is miraculous how it has so long resisted the force of the winds, which sometimes blow with great violence on this plain.

In about an hour more we reached a miserable village, in sight of the ruins of Baalbek, where we stopped to lunch. This was the worst specimen of a Syrian village we had yet seen. There was a pond of green water close by from which the stench was insufferable; and as to the huts, they were literally goat-houses, filthy and poverty-stricken to a degree that can not be conceived; many of them being mere holes cut in the mud-banks partially walled up. The inhabitants corresponded well with the village, being a ragged, unwashed, squalid set of vagabonds, as lazy as Arabs can be, but, like all the Orientals, of handsome features and picturesque and dignified in their rags. Every man, with his turban and chibouck and fine beard, was a living picture. Of the women I can not say so much. They were coarse and ugly enough, and so covered up in dirty rags that the effect was more in distance than proximity. The Sheik was a dignified old man, who sat in front of his hovel smoking with the quiet air of a Pasha or Sultan. And here, let me observe, that I have seldom seen an Arab or Turk of any rank above the mere dregs of society who was not a model of good manners; never evincing any thing like awkwardness in the presence of his superiors, or self-sufficiency over his inferiors. The Sheiks of the villages dress quite as plainly as the best of the ordinary classes and can only be distinguished by the deference shown them by the people generally. In their administration of justice they seem to be actuated by a desire to economize their power by settling all difficulties amicably, and on the principles of common sense. Law is here divested of its tautology, for it is merely an accepted standard of right and wrong recognized by the mass of the community traditionally; and the Sheik who acts with undue severity, or who is governed by inequitable or selfish motives, soon loses all power, and his mandates are disregarded. These village governments are in fact petty republics, though nominally founded and conducted on the principle of hereditary despotisms. This has reference, however, only to their municipal economy; they are all under the sway of the Pashas who govern the large cities in virtue of the powers given them from the Sublime Porte. Strictly as the women were watched, they could not restrain their curiosity, but crowded around us the moment we entered the village. Their sovereign lords now and then sharply reproved them, and added force to the reproof, when it was too often disregarded, by a sharp slap on the side of the head. As usual our dragoman went to the best looking hut, where he procured us a tolerably clean mat, and spread it near the door on a sort of mud seat. Here we were surrounded by all the idlers in the village. Our manner of eating excited the most undisguised astonishment, especially the use of knives and forks, which from the chatter of tongues we imagined to be the subject of much interesting speculation. Every mouthful was watched from its incipient carving to the cutting upon the plate, the trip on the fork to the mouth, its disappearance and mastication there, and final passage down the throat, and presumed lodgment in the stomach. The salting and peppering, the nice turning over with the fork, seemed to be regarded as a miracle of dexterity. Ill suppressed *Mashallas* were heard whenever two pieces could be pinned together and made to disappear at the same time. Yusef was greatly mortified at this annoyance, and told us it was not the Arab fashion, but that these poor devils were no better than *Kelb*, or dogs, and had never seen Christians eat before. He took particular pains to assure us that respectable Arabs, whom he claimed as his countrymen, had as much delicacy about looking at people while eating as any Europeans.

Before reaching the village, we had an indistinct view of the columns of the grand Temple of the Sun; but it was not until we had approached to within a few miles that the whole magnificent pile of ruins and columns loomed up in distinct outline against the slopes of Anti-Lebanon.

It was a soft pleasant evening as we entered the outer walls, and drew up our horses before the castle. Like the Acropolis at Athens, all else seemed nothing compared with the glorious Temple of the Sun. How grandly it towers amid the desolation of ruins! rising in all its majesty from the mighty monuments that lie mouldering around it, with its yet magnificent columns standing out in bold relief against the mountains; its massive walls unshaken by the tempests of ages, its magic ornaments still the perfection of beauty. Looking upward through the mass of ruins, the rugged outline of the mountains was bathed in the rays of the setting sun, and the whole heavens glowed with soft colors. Far across the broad wastes of the valley of Bukaa were miniature islands and solitary trees, reflected in its surface, and long trains of camels passing on their weary way, and the hoary peaks of Mount Lebanon towering high above all.

While Yusef went into the village to search for quarters, we rode around the ruins, more and more confounded with the vast extent and elaborate architectural finish of this magnificent pile. All the associations of the place contribute to inspire the mind with glowing conceptions of the ancient splendor of Baalbek; when those walls of massive stone were perfect; when those broken columns, prostrate now—save a few that stand to show how great the wreck has been—had each a place; when those massive cornices, so exquisite in their finish, those friezes and capitals, wrought with such masterly skill, formed a perfect whole; when the glorious Temple of the Sun stood untouched by the scathing hand of time or the ravages of war, and Baalbek was the glory and the pride of Assyria—such were the associations that filled the mind as we gazed upon this mighty wreck of matter.

Of the origin of Baalbek I believe very little is known. It has been the current belief among the Arabs for many generations that the Temple of the Sun and all the surrounding edifices were built by genii; and in proof of this they point to the immense stones high up in the walls, and ask what human power could have placed them there? The Jews say it was built by Solomon; and it is thought by some that the castle was an impregnable fortress, which Solomon called the Tower of Lebanon. The Greeks believe it to be Nicomedia, where Santa Barbara suffered martyrdom. Pierre Belon, a French traveler, who visited Baalbek in 1548, considered it to be the ancient Cesarea Philippi, where St. Paul makes mention of having been. Some believe it to be the ancient Palmyra; which, however, is now well known to be four days distant. The most reliable authorities agree in the opinion that Baalbek is the ancient Heliopolis.

I was not disappointed in the ruins of Baalbek, and this is saying a good deal. There is very little to be seen in the old world that does not produce disappointment; for I believe any traveler who is willing to confess the truth will admit that reading about places of this kind at home and seeing them with the naked eye are altogether different things. The ruins of Baalbek are among the few sights one sees in the East that will bear the test of scrutiny; the more they are studied the greater is the admiration they excite; and if one can not go into the sentimentalities of Lamartine, he will see enough at least to afford both pleasure and wonder.

Modern Baalbek is totally unworthy the name it bears. I had imagined it to be something like Beirut, or in any event not inferior to Tripoli; but the fact is, it is a miserable village, not much better than the meanest collection of hovels we had seen on the road. A few scattered and ruinous stone huts, with flat mud roofs, the walls broken, and the stones scattered in piles through the narrow and filthy lanes, two or three dilapidated mosques, and a Greek convent, constitute nearly all that exists of Baalbek, exclusive of the ancient temples. Travelers, in consequence of the difficulty of procuring accommodation in any of the Mohammedan houses, are generally compelled to camp outside, or seek for quarters in the Greek convent, which is about as tempting as a comfortable pig-sty. The hill-sides are covered with the ruins of the ancient walls, and the whole town is so dilapidated that it is difficult to distinguish the houses from the general wreck. Many portions of the ancient ruins are built in among the hovels, forming a curious melange of the sublime and the ridiculous. In the midst of mud-roofed huts may be seen standing out in solitary relief the remains of a beautiful Corinthian column; and over some miserable doorway the choicest specimen of a cornice, supported by blocks of rough stone. Some of the inhabitants, loth to destroy the work of the genii, have built their huts around the standing columns, scattered here and there, so that in projecting through the roof they form a very pretty ornament. Old arches and gateways are so patched up and remodeled that little else save the material remains to show their origin. The principal mosque is evidently all, or nearly all, rebuilt from the ruins of some ancient edifice, portions of it being so put together as to destroy all the harmony of the different parts. I believe this is the work of the Turks; it looks very much as if it was done by people who were ignorant of the difference between a column and a cornice.

From an elevation a little beyond the chief ruins there is a fine view of the Castle of Baalbek and the Temple of the Sun. These are the principal objects of interest. I made a sketch of them, which is now before me; but I can not undertake to describe them. It is a mighty mass of ruins of walls, of columns, and towers—a picture of desolation made more desolate by all that survives the ravages of time. The castle, or palace, is a long rambling edifice, composed of immense walls and mouldering towers; parts of it have probably been rebuilt by the Saracens, and some recent patching in white seems to have been done by the Turks, who evidently have a great taste for putting columns where cornices belong, and patching up dark old walls composed of immense blocks with little pieces of white stone about a foot square. The enormous size of some of the blocks of stone in the main walls of the palace is one of the chief objects of interest. Three of these, in the wall at the rear of the grand temple, measure sixty feet each, and form together a surface of a hundred and eighty feet in length and fifty-four in width, all of solid stone. Considering the distance these have been carried from the quarry, and the height to which they have been elevated in the wall, it would seem that the people of those days must have had some very powerful mechanical means of overcoming the difficulty.

We took an Arab boy of the village with us as a guide, and made a thorough exploration of the ruins. I have an imperfect recollection of long subterranean passages, arched over with tremendous stones, very dark, and full of niches and queer places at the sides, with broken busts of old kings, and ruined ornaments, and dim flashes of light through the openings, and a very strong smell of goats; and this is all that I can tell you of the palace. It was, no doubt, a wonderful place once, and is yet; but it is hard to get all the bearings of it in a day or two. There are hundreds of intricate passages to explore above and below, grand old chambers to see, stairs of solid marble, inscriptions in Roman, marble tombs of old kings or emperors, grand old columns, cornices, and friezes; and I don't know how many other things, to crowd the brain with and confuse the memory.

The broken columns on the outside are scattered about in melancholy profusion. Some of the best have been taken away to ornament the mosque of Sultan Soliman in Constantinople; but there is still enough to astonish the beholder. The Doric and the Corinthian orders of architecture are apparent throughout the ruins; the pure and elegant taste of the Greeks prevailing in some parts, and the profuse magnificence of the Romans in others; but always with such an admirable disposition of the parts as to preserve the tone of harmony, and still afford a pleasing variety.

The entrance into the Temple of the Sun is one of the grandest things imaginable. It is almost incredible the amount of labor bestowed upon this single part; the curious carving, the basso-relievos, the intricacy and ingenuity of design, and the wonderful delicacy of finish. Over head is an immense block of stone displaced by some convulsion of nature, and it hangs by a few inches on each side, forming a remarkable feature in the ruin. The carving is minute and beautiful; the eagle and the Cupids are universally admired. Chief of all, however, is the frontispiece, consisting of an immense number of figures in basso-relievo, representing the mysteries and sacrifices of Paganism. There is a mass of men and animals, in most Paganistic confusion, very well exe cuted and very strangely designed. Within the walls of the sacred temple are niches where stood in former times statuary, and some beautiful specimens of friezes and other decorations. In order to get on top we were obliged to creep into a little hole near the grand entrance, and ascend by a circular stairway. From the top of the Temple of the Sun we had an imposing view of the ruins that lie in confused masses around. It is in every respect a scene of utter and hopeless desolation. I could not but think with a melancholy interest of the difference between what I now saw, and what stood there in centuries past, when those ruined walls encircled the pride of Assyria; when those parched and arid plains were covered with gardens, and irrigated by fountains and flowing streams; and the heroes, whose deeds have given a romance to Oriental history, moved in triumph there, amid the swell of music and the homage of the multitude. Now what was it? a desert wilderness—a city of crumbling walls, of battered and time-worn castles, and broken columns—a ruin amid ruins. Camels were browsing lazily on the stunted bushes near the ruins, and groups of Arabs sat smoking on the broken columns; goats ran bleating in and out of the palace-chambers, and the startled crows flew from their nests as we approached. It was ruin every where; the spirit of desolation hung over all, and the proud City of the Sun lay dead in the

"Wide waste of all-devouring years."

CHAPTER XXV.

YUSEF DANCES THE RAAS.

WHILE we were looking at the ruins, Yusef came back from the village, which is a little way off on the slope of the hill, with news that he had found a lodging place for us at the house of his niece. By this time we began to have a suspicion of Yusef's nieces, he had so many all over Syria. At Batroun he had nieces, at Tripoli and Aheden he had nieces, and now here was another at Baalbek, and the strangest part of it was that they were all very pretty. However, as we had no prejudice against beauty, we followed our dragoman up into the village, where we found his niece and her husband living in a stone hut, rather a more decent sort of hovel than most of those in the neighborhood. It was, in truth, a very respectable little stone box covered over with mud, with a place for fire in one corner, and a great many little pockets in the walls all round, where there were stowed onions, tobacco, and sundry small notions for pleasure and sustenance. The host was an Arab of the country, a very good sort of fellow, who seemed to have but two objects in life to accomplish— one to see that his wife kept her face covered, and the other to keep the roof of his house from leaking; I hardly know which troubled him the most. The wife was a pretty buxom young woman, with fine black eyes and a beautiful mouth, which she took every opportunity to display, in spite of the vigilance of our host, who was constantly on the watch, when he was not on the top of the house. He kept a round stone —a piece of an old pillar found among the ruins—which he was almost continually rolling over the top of the house; sometimes he would roll it for an hour, and then come down and look after his wife and smoke his chibouck; but the presentiment was evidently uppermost in his mind that it would rain some time or other, and to work he would go again, hopping all over the roof with one foot while he kept the stone in motion with the other. The poor fellow was actually a victim of conjugal felicity.

In traveling through Syria, as in other parts of the world, I always carried my flute with me to relieve the lonely hours at night and excite a social feeling among the natives. I had fluted my way, after the fashion of Goldsmith, through many a difficulty; and now I was resolved to see what the magic of music would do in removing the prejudices of the Arabs. As soon as it was dark we had a good fire lit in the corner, and, pulling off our shoes, as custom required, we spread our mats close by, and sat down cosily to enjoy the cheerful blaze, my friends (the Southerner and the English Captain) smoking their chiboucks, while I brought forth my knapsack and commenced putting the pieces of my flute together. The Arabs, who had begun to crowd in, were greatly interested in the strange instrument that I was getting under way; and Yusef, who was rather proud of his superior civilization, sat by enjoying their remarks and giving us a running interpretation. Some thought it was a sort of pistol, with a large touch hole; but this notion was ridiculed by the more knowing ones, who said it was plain enough to see that it was a new-fashioned pipe, and that they would soon see me put the bowl to it, and begin to smoke. At last I got all the pieces adjusted, and, commanding silence by a mysterious motion of the hand, commenced playing that classical air of "*Old Zip Coon*," which I dare say never was heard before among the ruins of Baalbek. There was the most breathless attention on all sides, interrupted only by suppressed exclamations of *tahib! tahib!* (good! good!) whenever I blew a very shrill or false note and soon the women and children from the neighboring houses began to crowd in, and there was gradually a large circle formed around the room, the audience squatting down in rows, till there was scarcely space enough left to breathe. I blew away with all my might, for not only was I excited by the success of my experiment, but rather inspired by the music I was making, which I assure you was not bad. The familiar airs of home made me sentimental, and I merged into the doleful air of "Give me back my heart again; oh! give it back again!" which was a miserable failure; not a damsel seemed disposed to listen to it. They commenced, in the very middle of the most pathetic strain, to call for the first tune; so I had to return to "Old Zip Coon." When I had concluded, there was no end to the *tahibs:* Mr. Coon was a decided hit. In order to vary the entertainment, silence was commanded again, and Yusef was desired to explain that there would be a song; that it was a song of an old black gentleman who lived in America, who was a Pasha among the blacks; that he was called Uncle Ned because he was so venerable, and, being very old, the hair all fell out of his head, and there was no hair at all in the place where the hair ought to grow; that he hadn't any eyes to see with, and, consequently, was as blind as a post, or a stone wall, or any thing else that is supposed to be deficient in eyes; that neither had he teeth to eat bread with, and he had to let the bread alone and eat something else; that his fingers were as long as canes in the brake, which was about an average of sixteen feet; and, eventually, that one day when he was out in the field, a horrible monster called Grim Death came along and caught him by the heel and carried him away, and he was never heard of any more except in this song, which was written in commemoration of all these facts. Thereupon, having excited the most profound interest in the history of Uncle Ned, I launched forth into the song, keeping as near the tune as possible, and going through all the motions descriptive of the baldness of his head, the absence of his teeth and the length of his fingers. At length, when I arrived at the final catastrophe, where Grim Death seizes the old gentleman by the heel, I made a sudden motion at the heel of our worthy host, who was sitting near by, completely upsetting him with fright, and causing a laugh from the audience that seemed as if it would never come to an end. It was the best hit of the evening, and completely removed all constraint

The women had gradually uncovered their faces, and the men were in such a good humor that they paid no attention to it; and we were all as jovial as possible—showing that people all over the world are pretty much the same by nature, and that there are few races so barbarous as not to be moved by music and a spirit of sociability. I never found it to fail any where; and never knew an instance of any advance being made in a hearty, off-hand way, where it was not returned even more cordially—from the fact, perhaps, that it is so rarely done by travelers. But my triumph was of short duration. Yusef became inspired by the bright eyes of the Arab damsels, and soon carried away all my laurels. Standing forth in the centre of the room, he addressed the audience in the most impressive manner—stating that with their permission he would perform the celebrated dance of his country, called the *Raas*, for which it was necessary that he should have a space cleared in the middle of the floor. This proposition was greeted by a general murmur of approbation. A space was soon cleared, the audience crowding back on top of each other against the walls, but all in the most perfect good-humor. Yusef now began to unwind himself. He was in his choicest Arab costume, and fairly dazzled with armor. His sash was almost interminable. Francesco, the boy, pulled for five minutes, unwinding him all the time, as a spool of cotton on end might be unwound; and when the armor was all taken off and the sash at an end, Yusef called for his sword, and stood forth ready for the dance. Never was there such a sensation among the damsels of Baalbek. He was the very cut of an Arab beau, whose attractions and accomplishments were not to be resisted by vain and foolish woman. Poising his sword in the air, he called for music, and the music struck up—your humble servant being the musician. Whiz! went the sword through the air, cutting and slashing in all directions; up cuts and down thrusts within an inch of the retreating noses of the audience, who were now tumbled over in regular heaps. The women could scarce suppress their screams; the men cried Tahib! Tahib! and Yusef cut away in a perfect frenzy, till the first part of the performance, commencing with the sword exercise, was concluded. He then began in good earnest the dance of the Raas; gradually at first, with a tremulous motion of one side and a convulsive quivering of the other that seemed quite miraculous. I really began to think the fellow would go to pieces. His right leg kept running all round in a circle, while his right shoulder and arm danced a jig; the whole of his left side kept rising and falling convulsively, and his back worked as if every joint had a distinct and independent movement. Tahib! Tahib! shouted the audience, and round and round ran the independent leg faster than ever; and the left side worked, and the right side danced, and the back wriggled into the most convulsive motions, and Yusef looked just as much like one of the figures in a show, worked by wires, as any thing I ever saw, only a good deal more wiry. Some of the motions in this part of the dance were so ludicrous that the music had to stop suddenly for want of breath; but the dance went on to the clapping of hands kept up by the Arabs. The concluding part of the performance consisted of dancing, fighting, and love-making all together. The *djeered* is thrown, the sword whirled over the head, hundreds of foes slain, skulls split open, and terrible wounds received in the heroic attempt to carry away the daughter of a Grand Sultan, who seems to be surrounded by difficulties. At last Yusef is mortally wounded, and he begins to die by throwing his head back and getting very weak in the knees. Every bit of his body is convulsed with dying tortures; shoulders, breast, elbows, legs, and all are writhing horribly; by degrees he drops on one knee, and then on the other; and his arms fall loosely, and his head tumbles over on his breast, and he is about to roll over perfectly dead, when he catches a glimpse of his lady-love. With a wild yell he springs to his feet again, seizes his sword, and lays about him so desperately that the audience begins to think it is no joke at all. It really seemed as if Yusef had entirely lost his senses; the perspiration streamed down his face; he snorted like a horse, and his eyes had something horribly wild and insane about them. I expected each moment to see him cut somebody through the skull—knowing it to be a common piece of entertainment in these outlandish countries. But it was only a dying effort, this fit of desperation; down he fell on his knees before his lady-love, gasped out the madness of his love with his last breath, and died like a true lover with his head in her lap. The sensation was tremendous. Hands were clapped, *tahibs* shouted from all quarters, and the clatter of astonishment, admiration, and sympathy from the Arab damsels was perfectly overwhelming. Never did I feel so cut down in all my life; old Zip Coon was completely forgotten in the torrent of admiration drawn forth by the performances of Yusef. I quietly put the flute in my knapsack, and came to the conclusion that all triumphs are fleeting, and that the *Raas* dance is the greatest dance that ever was invented.

YUSEF DANCING THE RAAS.

Such were the demonstrations of satisfaction on the part of every female in the room, and the undisguised delight with which they returned Yusef's sidelong smiles, that there was not a male member of the audience who was not fired with jealousy and mistrust. Low murmurs began to arise between man and wife; smothered rebukes were given by friends and relatives; and fair faces began reluctantly to disappear, but not without parting glances at the Adonis of Arabs. That there was not a female heart in the crowd unseathed by his graces of person and flashing silks, as well as by the heroic courage which he had displayed in the affair of the Princess, was perfectly apparent. Even the husband of Yusef's niece, who was well acquainted with the relationship existing between his wife and that distinguished adventurer, did not seem altogether satisfied that their consanguinity would prove a barrier to all danger; indeed, he looked at both parties with extreme suspicion; but perceiving that there was no indication of any immediate danger (for they were discreet enough not to notice each other) he hastily left the house, climbed up on the roof, and relieved his mind in some degree by rolling the broken pillar over it furiously for the space of half an hour.

Alas, I wish I could conscientiously say that there was no danger; I wish Yusef had never stopped there; I would blot out that night in tears more copious than were shed by the great poet who wept when he found Baalbek in ruins; but a stern sense of duty compels me to proceed; it shall never be said that I have smiled at human weakness, or attempted to shield the culpable from just and merited reproach.

The guests having at a late hour retired to their respective homes, Yusef spread our mattresses on the floor, and fixed us comfortably for the night. His own mattress he left for future consideration. The husband of Yusef's niece carefully noted the manner in which we were arranged, and apparently satisfied that all was right so far, he looked into every little pigeon-hole in the walls to make assurance doubly sure, and then looked at the door between our room and that in which himself and wife slept. There was a large wooden bolt attached to it, which he carefully fastened, and then pulled back and fastened again, so that he might be sure there was no deception about its being fast; and then bidding us all good-night, he reluctantly departed through the front door—came back again in five minutes for a drink of water, looked at the door that was bolted, at the tall Southerner, the English Captain and myself, then at Yusef—departed once more, and before we were asleep, slyly peeped in again to be quite certain that there was nothing wrong, closed the front door softly, and retired to the adjoining room, where he talked seriously to his wife—probably about the leak in his house—for more than an hour. By the time he had concluded, every body was apparently asleep. There were two, however, who were very far from being asleep. One was myself; I could not help thinking that the inner door, although bolted on the right side for us, in case of an invasion from that quarter, was bolted on the wrong side for the husband of Yusef's niece, in case of an invasion from our side, which I regarded as much more to be apprehended. The other member of our party referred to as not being asleep, was Yusef himself. He had pulled his mattress up within a few feet of the bolted door, after every body was quiet, covered himself up carefully in the blankets, and commenced snoring immediately; which was precisely what kept me awake—not the snoring but the suspicions aroused by it. Yusef never snored when he was asleep. I knew him too well for that; he was always as wide awake when he snored as he ever was in his life. Consequently I kept a very small corner of my weather-eye open; it was impossible to close it while the snoring continued. A dim light from the dying embers in the fire, enabled me to perceive, in the course of time, that Yusef was getting restless; the snoring gradually stopped; the blankets began to drop off, and he sat up on his mattress and looked cautiously around. Satisfied that all was right, he crept to the door, fumbled at the bolt for some minutes, and eventually drew it back, without making any more noise than a mouse would have made under the same circumstances. The difficulty was to get the door open; it was hung on wooden hinges, which, perhaps, had not been greased for some time. Yusef breathed hard a few moments, gathered

K*

fresh courage, and commenced pulling cautiously at the door. It opened a little way; another pull; it opened a little more; another yet—it creaked—it creaked dreadfully! Quick as lightning Yusef pushed it back, bolted it, covered himself up in his blankets, and commenced snoring again; but there was evidently a commotion in the other room. The voice of a man shouted something fiercely—it was in Arabic—but doubtless it was—Who's there! Under some circumstances it is difficult to answer such a question; under the present circumstances Yusef considered it impossible; he only snored the louder, and heard the less. There is no doubt that the owner of the voice labored under the impression that some of us intended to rob him, for I heard him, both in my sleep and in my waking hours throughout the remainder of the night stumbling uneasily about the room. In the morning, Yusef, who had snored to the best of my belief without stopping from the moment he had so suddenly covered himself up in the blankets, set to work and beat the muleteers; but not with his accustomed alacrity. His mind was depressed, and he looked so little refreshed by balmy slumber that I was induced to ask him what was the matter. He evinced some little confusion at first; but quickly rallying, stated that he had suffered from a bad dream; that he dreamt he saw a lion; and the lion was going to attack us; that he was unarmed at the time, but inspired by his courage, which never forsook him in any emergency, he crept toward the lion in the hope of getting him by the mane and choking him; that just as he was about to put the lion to death, some invisible spirits pulled him back, and so they tormented him every time he got near to his foe, throughout the entire night.

It was certainly an extraordinary dream. Possibly Yusef really dreamt it. I hope so; many stranger dreams than that have been dreamt; but I have never been able to rid my mind of the impression that the lion was very pretty, and not at all ferocious.

CHAPTER XXVI.

A SOCIAL CHAT WITH YUSEF

WITHOUT exactly claiming to have control over the morals of our dragoman, I nevertheless considered it my duty to point out to Yusef the evils of those stringent measures adopted by the Arabs in their matrimonial relations, and to show him how much better it would be to abandon those absurd customs at once. When the conversation ran on congenial subjects, such as love and war, his sagacity and enthusiasm were very remarkable; and I was often surprised at the quickness of his perception, and the readiness with which he met all my arguments.

"It seems to me, Yusef," said I, after we had finished breakfast, "that you Arabs are the most barbarous people on the face of the earth. Why, even the Hottentots give their women some liberty. You, however, not only cover their faces, but keep them in a state of abject slavery. How can you ever expect to be a virtuous people when your wives are nothing but slaves!"

YUSEF (with spirit).—"They are not such slaves as your excellency thinks. We shut them up and keep them at home when strangers are about—especially gentlemen like your excellency, who perform on the flute, and sing songs of an inspiring and captivating nature; but, as a general thing, we treat them kindly. They exercise power enough over us now, and if they had greater liberty they would exercise a good deal more."

GENERAL.—"Of course they would, and why not? It is the very perfection of civilization when unlimited power is given to woman. In America we never think of shutting our women up and keeping guard over them. They would soon mutiny against that. Though they are free as air, many of them consider that they are barbarously limited in power, even now It is nothing uncommon for them to hold conventions, for the purpose of denouncing the male sex, and asserting their right to seats in our National Legislature. Some of them even aspire to the Presidency. For all I know, there may be a female candidate nominated for that high office at this very moment."

YUSEF.—" Don't you whip 'em, sir? Don't you lock 'em up, and give 'em the bastinado?"

GENERAL (indignantly).—" The bastinado, forsooth! I'd like to see such a thing as that tried in our country. Why, we have ladies who would cowhide a man if they knew he entertained such a thought; and we have newspaper editors who compliment ladies for distinguishing themselves in that way. No, Yusef; we never use the bastinado. On the contrary, there are persons of the male sex, or who assume to be of that sex, ever ready to join these spunky ladies in their conventions, and act entirely under their dictation. That such men will eventually aspire to petticoats is not at all improbable."

YUSEF (highly excited).—" I'd shoot 'em; by Allah, sir, I'd gut 'em! Miserable dogs! I'd—no matter!—proceed, sir—proceed!"

GENERAL.—" Tell me, Yusef, in the name of common sense, which you know is the grand object of my crusade in this benighted region, what do the Arab women cover their faces for? Fain would I probe to the bottom all these strange customs, and learn the reason thereof."

YUSEF.—" Now, verily, O General, hast thou asked me a question that it is difficult to answer. It is the custom of the country, and, to the best of my belief, has been the custom for many centuries past."

GENERAL.—" But the custom is absurd, and ought to be abandoned at once. Don't you think so?"

YUSEF.—" Again, that question is a poser. I have never considered it in the light of an absurd custom, having been used to these things from infancy. To me, it seems exceedingly strange that the women of America don't cover their faces."

GENERAL (somewhat nettled).—"Why so, pray? They're not ashamed of their faces: why should they cover them?"

YUSEF.—"Pardon me! I only meant that to my uneducated and untraveled eyes, it looks a little indiscreet. Beauty, O General, is a rare and precious jewel: it doesn't do to show it too often."

GENERAL.—"But what use is it if it be hidden under a mask, and never seen at all except by the lady's husband? Every husband admires the beauty of his wife when other people admire it. If other people don't admire it, what incitement is there for admiration on his part? He must get accustomed to it in a month or two, just as the shepherd who lives on the mountain-top gets accustomed to the beauty of the scenery. To cover a woman's face up, is what we call hiding a light under a bushel."

YUSEF.—"This we regard as the philosophy of the thing: Every pretty woman is vain of her charms. It is the weakness of the sex. If we don't keep a sharp look-out, she'll cast them forth as snares to entrap mankind. That's woman's nature, when she's admired. Now, we hold that a wife has no right to cast snares upon any body but her husband." (I quite agreed with Yusef in this, and involuntarily thought of his strange dream concerning the lion.) "Hence, not being restrained by reason, because of her vanity, she must be restrained by masks, and sometimes by bolts and bars."

GENERAL.—"True, very true, Yusef. I must confess that there is some foundation for your argument. There are extreme cases when bolts may be necessary."

YUSEF.—"It stands to reason, sir; it arises from the love of flattery, which is the great weakness of woman. Have you no customs in your country, sir, equally strange and incomprehensible at first sight?"

GENERAL.—"No, Yusef; thank heaven, we are clear of all such absurdities as this. Our most fashionable ladies not only keep their faces uncovered in public, but frequently appear in ball-rooms and opera-houses, with scarcely more than a piece of gauze above the waist."

Yusef.—"And don't they feel ashamed at all?"

General.—"By no means. Those who desire to be distinguished in the world of fashion, never feel ashamed of any thing that is fashionable. They take great pride and pleasure in making the exhibition. It shows a consciousness of purity; because, if they were not certain that they could resist the effects of this display, of course they would not make it on any account."

Yusef (with flashing eyes).—"I'd like to live there! Above all things, I'd like that—in another people. Most wonderful are the diversities of custom. An Arab woman would be disgraced were she to adopt such a fashion."

General.—"Of course; that results from the benighted condition of the female sex in your country. Your people are behind the times, Yusef. As civilization progresses, we cast aside all these barbarous prejudices. We approximate toward first principles. There was a time, even in our country, when a lady could not display her charms in public; but of late years we have become fashionable tourists. We go to Europe every summer, and import the latest improvements in fashion and morals. No female now is considered worthy to mingle in the most stylish society, until she is up to the Parisian standard. We dance by Paris—dress by Paris—eat by Paris—drink by Paris—and I rather think the most fashionable of us will soon sleep by Paris."

Yusef.—"*Inshalla!* where is all this to stop—especially in the matter of dress?"

General (a little confused).—"Where is it to stop? Oh, that I can't tell you. Perhaps it won't stop at all till we reach that primitive state of simplicity from which we originally fell. The Parisians are an extremely natural people, in some respects—not at all restrained in social life."

Yusef (with a sigh).—"It must be a Paradise upon earth. But, then, I am told, that no man is entitled to more than one wife, by law. Can he send her home, or sell her, as we do, when he sees another more beautiful?"

GENERAL (smiling).—"No, Yusef; he can't sell her, but he can get a divorce. If he be rich, he can buy it without much trouble; and if he be poor, he can get drunk and maltreat her, and then swear she is not a good and true wife; so that the law, which is very sagacious in these matters, perceiving that there are faults on both sides, and that the parties can never live happily together, grants a divorce."

YUSEF.—"A most admirable law! But, yet, it seems to me, it would be better to have several wives. Woman is an evil at best—indeed, I may say, the root of all evil. Now, your excellency knows that by mixing two or more poisons together, a very harmless beverage may be produced. We consider that if a man be afflicted with a quarrelsome wife, who poisons his happiness, the best thing he can do is to get some more poison, and mix the two together; if two poisons won't answer, he should mix an additional number in the same way. The remedy is certain to effect a cure. When a woman has two or three fellow-wives to quarrel with, she can't spare much time to quarrel with her husband. Let a man act discreetly, and profess to love one a little better than another whom he originally professed to love best, and there will soon be a very lively state of hostility between the ladies of his household. While they are fighting, he can take it easy, and smoke the pipe of peace. That, sir, is the philosophy of combining evils: curing a wound by making another; the true principle of counter-irritation."

Somehow, it was useless to argue with Yusef. He always got the better of me; and this naturally excited my indignation. I, therefore, decided the matter by telling him it was useless to talk such nonsense to me; that the Arabs were a very wicked and ignorant race at best, and he was the more to blame for entertaining such monstrous doctrines, as he had enjoyed the advantages of intercourse with a more enlightened people.

CHAPTER XXVII.

THE GREEK BISHOP.

BEFORE leaving Baalbek I went to the Greek convent to have a social chat with the patriarch, who was represented to be a very hospitable and intelligent man. It is situated down toward the lower part of the town, not far from the Temple of Santa Barbara. The entrance is through a dilapidated court-yard, which serves as a sort of caravanserai for camels and mules; and the convent is little better than the rest of the hovels around it, except that it is larger and higher. There is a church attached to it of ancient and ruinous appearance, with a few tawdry ornaments and miserable pictures in the interior. A Greek monk, who acted as our cicerone, told us that this church contained the most valuable relic of any church in Syria; that it was not commonly exhibited to strangers, but he would take the liberty of showing it to our excellencies. Having thus excited our curiosity, he proceeded, with great caution and solemnity, to draw back some small black curtains that covered a hole in the wall, and by degrees revealed to us the hole, which was cased around with a black frame and covered with a pane of glass; but I candidly confess I could see nothing in it, nor could I, after the most persevering inquiries all round, ascertain that any body else had seen any thing, or that there was any thing there to be seen. It was a good deal like some of the wonderful things one is called upon to admire now and then in Italy—you go a great way to see them, and are expected to be in raptures, but for your life you can't find out what all the talk is about; there is nothing to be seen. We paid a piastre, however, for the information, and I would recommend all travelers who go to Baalbek to do likewise; they may see something, probably a bone of the ass that Baalam rode, or a reflected image of the face, with its full complement of ears.

The reception room of the convent was furnished in the Turkish fashion, with a low platform extending round the walls on three sides, upon which were spread rugs of every variety of color. There were no chairs, nor any other furniture except a few bad prints, and a good supply of chiboucks hung up around the walls. It was a great nuisance to be obliged to take off our shoes, as on all occasions, no matter how many houses we went into, how dirty they were, or how cold it was: whether there were rugs on the ground, or mats, or, what was most common, puddles of mud, our dragoman protested that if we kept on our shoes it would be a mortal offense to the inmates of the house. I was often disposed to rebel against this insane practice; but you know when one is in Rome he must be romantic; when one is in Syria he must bear with serious inconveniences, not the least of which is keeping up a good understanding with the natives by keeping the feet bare.

The bishop, a venerable man, with a beard of patriarchal length, received us with great kindness and cordiality. He said it was seldom he had the pleasure of meeting American travelers there, and regretted that we had not taken up our quarters in the convent. While we were talking, coffee and chiboucks were brought in by a domestic, and gracefully presented to us in the Oriental style. As it is characteristic of the East, I may as well tell you the manner in which one is honored on paying a visit. You enter the room, furnished, as above stated, with rugs all round, make your bow, and are politely motioned to a seat; that is, to a seat on the floor. If you can do it, you squat down as much like a tailor as possible; if you can't, you stretch out both legs and get your back against the wall. Do let me persuade you to try it, if you want to know how odd it feels. The form of salutation depends pretty much on the relative rank of each party. Where there is not much ceremony it is merely a bow and the hand is placed over the breast; where the civility is intended to be very marked, as in the native form, the visitor makes a dive at the hem of the host's garment as if he would catch it up and kiss it; but the host, perceiving the intended honor, dives down at the same moment to prevent it, and, as if by accident catches the hand of his guest and helps him up with it part of the way; when each touches his breast, mouth, and forehead with his own hand; sometimes repeating the dive, but this is only when a man is electioneering for some office, or calls to borrow a few hundred piasters, in which case he dives down a great many times.

Supposing you to be seated now, a servant enters, bearing a tray, upon which are several cups of coffee about the size of egg-cups, and these are handed round and presented with a graceful bow to each visitor. The coffee is as thick as chocolate, and at first it may lodge in your throat, but after a while one learns to like it. Chiboucks are then brought. The stems are about six feet in length, and the bowl being placed on the ground in a little brass pan at the proper distance, the mouthpiece is whirled around dextrously by the domestic, who calculates the distance so nicely that he brings it within the sixteenth of an inch of its destination. The smoking begins, and if you have good Djebel or Latakia tobacco, it is, as my friend the English captain says, quite stunning. Conversation goes on between the whiffs, and is as lively as such conversation can be where one naturally thinks in English, communicates his ideas to his dragoman in Italian or French, has them translated into Turkish, Arabic, or Greek, and learns the result in about ten minutes from the time of starting. I often, after a good deal of difficulty, got out a joke and made my interpreter understand the full bearings of it; when he would set to work, jabbering in some horrible unknown tongue, taking so long to tell it that the whole thing would quite escape my memory, and it was only in about a quarter of an hour after, that an explosion of laughter would startle me out of my cloud of smoke; for a joke is never so stale or so trifling as not to cause a laugh in the East. As I made it a point, however, never to talk French or Italian to Yusef where there was a probability of these languages being understood (by which means I passed for rather a learned man), he translated from English in the present case. The worthy patriarch felt a good deal interested in the fact, usually announced by Yusef in terms of great pomposity, that I had traveled a long way, and had been in California. The old gentleman had heard some fabulous accounts of California, and, after some exclamations of wonder at seeing before him a live person from that strange land, he delivered himself as follows: "It is a wonderful country, I know; thousands of miles off; away at the other side of London. They dig up whole mountains of gold there, and catch fish without eyes. God Almighty kills them because they are wicked; also food is scarce. The sun is very hot; there is great thirst; likewise men burrow holes in the ground the same as rats. Oh, I don't want to go to California. It is a bad country. Better stay here in Baalbek and praise God." I thought so too, and desired Yusef to tell his Reverence that it would be better for him not to go to California, if he had any notion that way; in fact, that he would do much better reclaiming benighted Arabs in Baalbek than digging for gold on the banks of the Sacramento, and would find a more fertile harvest in his own professional line.

We had further conversation on various topics, after which, with many kind wishes, the patriarch bid us good-by, and wished us a pleasant tour through Syria; expressing at the same time his regret that we had not found it convenient to come at once to the convent instead of going to a native house.

I went down again during the forenoon to the ruins, and made a sketch of the Temple of the Sun and a general view of the whole of Baalbek. Near the main ruin is a very beautiful little Temple, which I omitted to mention before, built chiefly of marble, and very highly decorated. It reminded me a good deal of the Temple of the Winds at Athens. The form is octagonal, and there is a portico all round, supported by eight Corinthian columns, between which in the niches are the remains of pedestals upon which formerly stood statues. The Greek priests suppose this to be the tower of Santa Barbara. By some travelers it is compared to the Temple of Janus at Rome. Two little streams of water run through the town, one of which passes under this temple.

One of the most remarkable ruins in Baalbek is that of the ancient mosque, in which is seen the tomb of Saladin. I had some doubts as to this being the ruin of a mosque; but, in the absence of any better information than that of our dragoman, had to take it as such. There is a high wall, inclosing a space of some hundreds of yards square, in which are rows of vast arches, sustained by pillars, covering the entire interior. Looking through underneath it has the appearance of a perfect forest of pillars. Near the entrance is a little tomb, built of rough stone, apparently of Saracenic construction, upon one end of which is an inscription in Arabic. This is said to be the tomb of the famous Saladin, the conqueror of the Christian hosts on the fields of Hatin and of Esdraelon. I did not read the inscription; so I am unable to tell you what it means.

There are some few objects of interest in the way of ruined walls and arches, containing patches of the antique, scattered about through the town and the neighborhood, all of which we thoroughly examined; but they are so much like any other ruins that the interest depends mainly upon their being in Baalbek, where every body can not go to see them, as in Rome or Athens.

Tired of rambling about, I sat down on an eminence overlooking the ruins, and began to think seriously and soberly of all that I had seen, and to divest myself of the first enthusiastic impressions, so as to arrive at some reasonable idea of what Baalbek must have been in the days of its glory. Sober second thought is a good deal like a written contract; it brings both parties (the imagination and the judgment) to a proper understanding, and leaves no room for visionary speculation or loose interpretation.

That Baalbek was a city abounding in fine edifices is sufficiently apparent from the magnificence of its ruins. One can not but deplore the desolation of those splendid temples, and the loss of the many works of art buried there, among which must have been some of the choicest of ancient times; and while there is so much left to admire it is not improbable that, in the lapse of centuries, there may have been much destroyed equally worthy of admiration. But that Baalbek ever was a very extensive or very important city is not, I think, rendered probable by any evidence now existing. The foundations of the ancient walls, which can be clearly traced, embrace but a small area of ground, certainly not sufficient for a very large city; and its position, shut in among the mountains of Lebanon, two days distant from any seaport, and not on the usually traveled route from the interior cities of Asia Minor, indicates that it was not supported by commerce. It is also probable that the Temple of the Sun and the Palace were the most important of all the public edifices; and that the streets were narrow and badly paved, without side walks, as in all the cities of the East, and the residences of ordinary construction; because even a small city could not be embraced in so limited a space with any thing like fine streets or large houses. If the implements of agriculture were not a good deal better than any that exist in Syria at the present day (and it is said they are about the same as were used in scriptural times), the plain of Bukaa must have been more indebted to Nature than to the cultivation of man for its reputed fertility. Probably there were more trees on it, and some gardens and vineyards for the supply of the town. The inhabitants must have lived on something, and it is not likely they had much else to eat except what they produced on this plain. But there is no evidence of a luxurious style of living. If ever there were carriages, they must have traveled in the air, with mules or horses at each end, as they do now; for there is nothing to show that there were roads fit for wheeled vehicles to run on. Sometimes a piece of an old Roman road is seen along the coast, and poor enough it must have been in its best days; but I could discover nothing of the kind about Baalbek. I think the inhabitants of the glorious City of the Sun rode on donkeys. At all events, donkeys must have been convenient in climbing through the streets, unless the style of paving was a good deal better than any thing done throughout the East in modern times, of which there is no evidence in the specimens that remain.

In sober truth, the more I thought about Baalbek as it was, the more I became impressed with the idea that we are apt to magnify the grandeur of every thing ancient, and encourage false impressions by feeding the mind with the poetry of the past. There was as much reality then as there is at present; men were human and all their works were human; and the ruins of those works derive much of their effect from the lapse of time. To an imaginative mind a broken column is more beautiful covered with the mould of ages, than one of precisely the same form, new and complete. There must have been a time when those works were new, and when contemporary architects and critics held the same opinion of them, compared with something more antique, as we do now of what is done in our day, compared with what was done then. The enchantment that distance lends is lent to all these temples and relics of ancient grandeur with a most liberal hand. I saw in Jerusalem a picture of Baalbek rebuilt as it originally stood, beautifully drawn by a competent artist; and, comparing it with drawings of the ruins, I must say that Baalbek in ruins, with a little room for the imagination, is much grander and more imposing than Baalbek, complete as it existed in ages past, with nothing beyond mere reality to look to.

But it will not do to indulge in this train of thought. Strip the past of all its romance, and there is little left to write about. What reader will be satisfied with plain facts? what reader will be satisfied with the simple unadorned truth—except the few that I hope to honor me with a perusal of these pages? and it is only to that rare but enlightened class that I dare to address such unpopular views.

In my rambles about the village of Baalbek I was struck with the beauty of the children, and the extreme youthfulness of some of the Arab mothers. I saw several young females, not more than twelve or fourteen years of age, with babies in their arms, evidently their own; and I was told that this is quite common throughout Syria. Many of the women are very beautiful—much more so, I think, than either the Circassian or the Turkish women. It was quite enchanting, their fine complexions, dark eyebrows, and flashing eyes; and for regularity and delicacy of features I have seldom seen them equaled, except in other parts of Syria. In Nazareth I saw some of the best formed and most beautiful women I had ever seen in any country; I believe it is noted as much for the beauty of its female population among tourists as for its historical interest; but at no place did I see what I really thought approached the perfection of beauty in so high a degree as in Bethlehem. The women of Bethlehem are absolutely bewitching. I never saw such perfect profiles, such eyes and eyebrows, and such delicate little hands and feet. Not that I mean to say that they are at all to be compared in all the higher attributes of beauty to our own fair countrywomen, for that would be sacrilege. There is nothing in the East, or in Europe either, or any where else that I have ever visited, to compare with the ladies of Philadelphia, Baltimore, and Washington. Talk of Parisian beauties! Lively and vivacious they are, to be sure; but not dignified, not queenly, not gentle and modest. Talk of English beauties! Grand enough and fair, but not graceful. Italian beauties; dark, dull, and greasy. German, fat and florid; Turkish, tallowy and buttery; all well enough in their way; but, Mashalla! it won't do to mention them in the same breath with American beauties.

And now good-by to Baalbek. We are off for Damascus, galloping out through the ruins and over the prostrate relics of the past as merrily as if they were only so much rubbish.

CHAPTER XXVIII.

THE ARAB MULETEER.

A MOST indispensable and striking character in Syrian travel is the Arab muleteer. Every party of Frangi has its baggage train of mules; and generally every mule has its

MUSTAFA, THE ARAB MULETEER.

separate owner, who does the driving, feeding, loading, and smoking. These mules are hired at Beirut, or wherever the starting point may be, by the dragoman, who makes his own bargain with the muleteers. For a mule and driver the usual price is ten to fifteen piasters a day. On this sum the muleteer must feed himself and mule, and pay all his ordinary expenses throughout the journey. It is not much to be sure; only forty or fifty cents a day for personal attendance, expenses on the road, and risk and interest on capital; but it seems to be enough, for at the end of the journey our men appeared to have sufficient left to keep them till the next trip

The Arab muleteer is a practical philosopher and man of the world. There is nothing to trouble him but his mule, and that only troubles him when it wakes him up by running off the road or throwing him into a ditch. He wants but little here below, and has a happy knack of getting that little almost free of expense. His mule must be fed or it will die in the course of time, but that want he supplies by taking the oats and barley out of the trough where the horses of the Howadji feed at night, and putting them in the place where his mule ought to be feeding. He does this when the dragoman is not present, because if the dragoman saw it, there would certainly be an unpleasant state of feeling between the parties. The muleteer is a man of peace; he wishes to get along in the world as quietly as possible; hence he feeds his mules as far as practicable at the expense of others, and says nothing about it, from a natural repugnance to disturbances of the peace. To be sure the horses of the Howadji sometimes look unaccountably lank and dispirited; and the mules unaccountably thriving and frisky, but what difference does that make to the muleteer? If it makes any difference at all it is in his favor; it prolongs the journey, adds so much to his pay, and affords him in some degree an equivalent for the beatings which he daily receives from the dragoman. Besides what the horses lose in flesh the mules gain. Sometimes the dragoman swears that he gives the horses a bushel of barley apiece at night, and they don't seem to be a bit the better for it next morning; there must be thieves about; he determines to watch them, and to shoot the first man whose hand he sees in the horse-trough. At last the horses grow so lank and dejected that he does watch; he sees a hand in the barley;

L

it is the hand of the muleteer. The shooting is postponed till next morning on account of the danger of wounding the horses; but the muleteer is whipped with a cane till he swears by the beard of the Prophet he will never do so again. For a few days the horses look better; but this doesn't alter the general principle, because the mules begin to look just as lean and spiritless as the horses did before. The muleteer is willing to be honest; he would like to be on good terms with the world generally; but it is not in his nature, or any other man's nature to stand such treatment as this. Hence he resumes his previous policy as soon as he can safely do so, and continues to be whipped occasionally when caught with his hand in the wrong place. Whipping, however, is one of the ills that the flesh of the muleteer is heir to. He takes it hard apparently, but it goes easy enough in reality. A good deal of the pain of whipping is mental, as any school-boy can testify. With him, it is only skin deep; his skin is tough from exposure, and is not readily affected.

He takes life easy, as a matter of personal convenience; sometimes sleeping on the top of the baggage, which is on the top of the mule, and sometimes trotting along with his comrades, listening to pleasant stories of genii and dragons, or telling some pretty tough ones himself, but always in that happy and contented frame of mind which evinces an entire absence of care. Clothing never annoys him at all; a shirt or two and an old sash last him a lifetime; breeches he wears little or none; shoes are superfluous, except when his circumstances are affluent. What if he have nothing to eat now and then? He can smoke the pipe of bliss, and sleep the sleep of oblivion. What if he be out of tobacco? No matter; the Howadji will give him some. Moreover, he knows where the bag is kept, and can help himself, provided nobody be looking on. Food is the least of his wants. A bunch of grapes or figs and a piece of leather bread satisfy all his necessities in this respect; and occasionally there are pots and pans that come in as a sort a relish, to be licked when the dragoman has been drinking a little arrack, and feels unusually good-natured. A very happy fellow is the Arab muleteer, take him altogether, sleeping and smoking his way through life on a capital of one mule. When he gets rich by making a fortune of ten dollars, he buys a small ass, so that he can ride after his mule, and boast an ass of his own; and then he assumes the honorable position of a Howadji among muleteers, and is, to all intents and purposes,

A GENTLEMAN OF ELEGANT LEISURE.

CHAPTER XXIX.

FROM BAALBEK TO DAMASCUS.

ABOUT noon we left the ruins of Baalbek behind us, and proceeded through the plain of Bukaa toward Damascus. Our road lay along the base of Anti-Lebanon. The aspect of the whole country was sterile and desolate in the extreme. There was not a shrub on the wayside to relieve the utter barrenness of the scene, or intercept the dazzling glare of the sun, which even now in midwinter had something left of its summer fierceness. The weather was not warm; but the whitish cast of the earth and the unclouded brilliancy of the sky, gave that intensity of light so characteristic of Syria, and which is so destructive to the sight that nearly half the inhabitants are afflicted with ophthalmia. Not far from the outer walls of Baalbek, we saw the quarries from which the stone for the Temple of the Sun and all the public edifices was taken. Large gaps, in the form of an amphitheatre, are cut in the solid rock, from which the immense blocks of stone in the castle were taken. The ground or bottom of the quarries is covered with detached blocks, cut away, trimmed, and ready for transportation. It is a strange sight to see these pieces there, just as they were left in ages past, fresh from the hands of the masons. One block of stone is of immense length. It is said to be larger and longer than any found in the ruins of Baalbek I think our dragoman said the length was sixty-seven feet. The Arabs have another legend connected with this stone, rather harder to credit than the story of the column. They say that the Sultan, when he was building the Castle of Baalbek, found all the men in his kingdom unable to remove this stone, so great was its weight. A woman, standing near, and seeing all their efforts unavailing, said; ".Upon my soul! a nice set of fellows you are not to be able to carry a little stone!" "Little!" quoth they; "do you call this little?" "To be sure I do," said the woman; "a mere nothing. If you were men you could carry it." "Hear her!" said they. "Why, one would think you could carry it yourself, the way you talk." "Carry it! Of course I can," said she; whereupon she laid hold of the stone, lifted it up on her back, and trotted all the way with it to Baalbek, where she laid it down by the castle-wall. "Now," said she to the Sultan, who was superintending the work, "give me ten thousand piastres for carrying this stone here." "May I be kicked like a dog if I do," said the Sultan, in a rage. "What! have all my men disgraced, and then pay a slave of a woman for doing it! Get thee away, wretch!" "Oh, ho!" said the woman; "is that the way you talk?" Whereupon she seized the Sultan by the back of the neck, and pitched him headlong into a neighboring ditch, giving him a kick as he went. "By my soul!" quoth she, "men are forgetting their place nowadays. They are getting as impertinent and conceited as popinjays." With that she seized hold of the stone again, tumbled it over on her back, and trotted all the way back with it to the quarry, where the workmen were still looking at one another in silent astonishment. "There," said the woman, pitching the stone down; "I told you so! You had better go now and help the Sultan out of the ditch. He's floundering about there like a mud-turtle." Saying which, she slapped the chief workman heels over head, because he was staring at her, and went off dancing the Raas, since which time the stone has remained just as she left it. The Arabs pointed it out to us, and said there was no doubt about the truth of the story, for the stone was in the very same spot. That they believed every word of it themselves was quite evident; and we, of course, believed as much as we could.

Passing some ancient tombs on the left, we descended into a rocky valley, called Wady Ain Tihebeh, or the valley of the well. Here there were some camels feeding near by the fountain. They had come over from Damascus with packs of merchandise for Baalbek; and so picturesque they looked, all lying down in a circle, with their masters sitting on the ruined fountain smoking, that I fain had to stop and make a sketch of them. Soon after, we came to the village of Tihebeh, a miserable collection of huts, with the white dome of a mosque in the centre. About this point we struck off to the left from the plain of Bukaa, and shortly came to the valley of Nebusheet; from which we climbed up a very rocky path, hardly practicable for our horses, to the village of Nebusheet. In this village there is a mosque containing a large tomb, called by the inhabitants the Tomb of the Prophet Nebusheet. None others but the followers of Nebusheet live in the village, and they are known as Meitmaleh. They revere the tomb of their prophet as the Mohammedans do at Mecca; but it is only in secret or among themselves that they dare to avow their belief. When among the Turks they pray like Turks, and profess to acknowledge the superior power of Mohammed; but they are looked upon generally as heretics, and are not admitted to all the privileges of the Mohammedan faith. For instance, they can not go to Mecca, or enter the Mosque of Omar at Jerusalem. In the valley beyond Nebusheet there is a rapid stream of good water, from which the village is supplied. The labor required to carry the water up the rocky path, a distance of nearly a mile, must be prodigious. The Arab men know very well that it is harder work than smoking the chibouck; so they attend to the smoking, and make the women and children carry the water. We met in the pass some thirty or forty women and children, with scarce any thing but rags on them, bearing great earthen pitchers on their heads; and yet they toiled up the rocks singing merrily, as if theirs was as happy a life as any; perhaps it was. About the same number were going down, being thus continually engaged in the hardest possible labor, while the men were sitting up in the village, smoking or doing nothing. I thought that in warm weather it must keep half the population of Nebusheet thirsty to keep the other half supplied with water. The stream below is called the river of Surgoya; and is a pretty strong stream for its size, driving several mills. At one of these mills we stopped to lunch. The hoppers were going at a great rate, and I peeped in to see how the grinding was done. The miller wore a turban, and had so much dust in his beard that he looked like an old Pasha. "*Marhabba*," said he, which means how d'ye do, or good morning, or something of the kind; "*Marhabba*," said I, and I crept in through the low doorway. Now, I had seen some few mills in my time, but never such a mill as this. The whole machinery consisted of a round rough stone, with a hole through it, in which was wedged a thick shaft of wood. At the bottom of the shaft were some paddles, against which the water dashed at one side, turning the shaft, and with the shaft the grindstone. A bag of wheat was hung over the hopper, to which was fastened a piece of stick that ran over the stone, and by its vibration jerked out the wheat. The miller, seeing my wonder, thought it arose from inability on my part to understand the complexity of all this machinery; and with great good-nature he explained the whole process in Arabic, pointing with much satisfaction at each part, and showing me by a whirling motion of the arm that it was the going round of the grindstone that ground the wheat. This idea of the wonderful manner in which the wheat was reduced to meal had such a hold upon his imagination that he jumped on the grindstone to stop it, in order that I might see for myself. But the stone wouldn't stop immediately, and it was only after being tilted on his back once or twice that the worthy miller succeeded in getting himself braced against a post so as to stop the mill. Then he took up a handful of the meal, and showed me that it was really ground by that same machinery, which he made still clearer to my mind by a copious dissertation in Arabic on grist-mills as a general thing. "*Tahib!*" said he, signifying "good." "*Tahib*," said I, and crept out through the same hole that I entered, very much pleased with my visit.

On leaving the mill, we passed through a long winding valley, hemmed in on the right and left by low monotonous hills, dotted over with oak bushes, and uninhabited for many

miles, save by a few goat-herds. We were so disgusted with
the monotony of this valley that we forgot to ask the name.
Ascending and descending through several passes, we at
length entered another valley, through which runs a stream
that waters the valley of Zebdene. Yusef had gone on to
the village to look out for lodgings; and my two friends and
myself, tired of lagging behind with the mules, pushed on
for Zebdene, in hopes of reaching it before dark. Crossing
the stream in half an hour or so, we ascended a hill on the
other side, and here we found two roads going nearly in the
same direction and of nearly equal size. We took the upper
one, which of course was the wrong one. By the time we
had ridden a mile it was quite dark, and we found from the
lights in another direction that we had made a mistake.
There being no other path, we had to retrace our steps, which
is not pleasant in Syria, where every step is a matter of study
for both horse and rider, and stepping in the dark especially.
We returned again to the valley, from which we heard the
muleteers coming down the side of the mountain, shouting
loudly to the jaded animals. They reached us presently, and
we all pushed on together for Zebdene. It was one of the
most pleasant rides we had enjoyed during our tour. The
moon came out, as we ascended the banks of the stream, and
it became a mild, clear night, with the towering mountains in
full view all around us, and the snow-capt heights of Djebel-
esh-Sheik glimmering in the distance. The sharp cry of a
jackal from the ravine on the other side of the stream had a
wild and startling effect in the stillness of the night; and the
strange stories of Eleas and the muleteers about robberies
and murders in these lonesome glens made us involuntarily
look toward every thicket on the roadside. It was not an
agreeable idea, take it altogether, that of having our legs cut
off, as was done with one traveler, or our skulls battered in
with clubs, as another was served not long before, or even to
be politely requested to give up our money, and compelled to
make the rest of our tour on charity. Yusef had taken with
him all the guns, pistols, and swords—and, worse than that, all
the propensity for fighting that was in the party. We might

have fought upon a pinch, but I believe we preferred not fighting. For my own part, I had made up my mind, if attacked by the robbers, to offer them my old coat, two shirts, a toothbrush, a small pocket comb, some sketches of Baalbek, and a few short-hand notes from which these pages are written, together with a draft on my friend the Southerner, who was kindly paying my way to Alexandria, where I expected a remittance. I had likewise about me some small paper money, amounting to twenty kreutzers (sixteen cents), payable in Austria in the course of forty or fifty years; a letter of introduction to the Pasha of Egypt, two Seidlitz powders, and a pocket-compass, which, together with an expired commission as third lieutenant in the revenue service, I intended delivering to the chief of the robbers sooner than shed one drop of blood, and requesting him as a favor to take any thing else about my person or in my knapsack that he might find useful. Fortunately, however, for the reader and myself, we met no robbers, or, if we did, they were so terribly afraid of us that they passed on without shooting.

We soon came into the beautiful and fertile neighborhood of Zebdene. Signs of civilization, such as we had not seen since leaving Beirut, began to appear on both sides of the road. Every thing quite reminded us of home. The road was broad and plain, and the gardens were well hedged with bushes. Rustic gateways, covered with running roses, peeped out from clumps of trees; the gurgling of springs and the soft echo of distant voices made a pleasant music in the night air; and as we rode along under the shade of overhanging trees, and looked through the vistas of foliage on each side, the running vines hanging in festoons through the vineyards, and the groves of fig trees and olives were lit up with a glow of moonlight, and vividly brought to mind our early impressions of the beauties of Eden. As we entered the village, it was a pleasant variety to find none of that shadowless and parched appearance about it that characterized all the villages we had seen before. The houses were half hidden among trees, with little green patches of ground about them, and though rudely constructed of mud and stone, like all we

L*

had seen, yet they were evidently larger and more commodious. We rode on some distance looking around us for Yusef, starting up sleepy dogs, and exciting the wonder of the natives in our search, calling Yusef, Yusef! as we went, but it was not until we had reached the farthest extremity of the village that Yusef made his appearance. Alas, I grieve to tell it! his face was very red, and he staggered a good deal, and labored under some difficulty in getting out his words; in short, it was quite plain he had been drinking arrack—a thing that he did a little too often for our satisfaction. "Come dis way genelmen," said he, "I'm got you a very good house. My niece live here—she gone down to Damascus now, but her husband very good man." Here was another of Yusef's nieces; I was not sorry to hear that she was gone to Damascus; for somehow Yusef always wanted to delay us when his nieces were at home. The house was very nice and comfortable—one of the best we had seen in our travels; it was situated in an inclosure, fenced in by high hedges, with a rustic gateway in front covered with rose bushes, and had altogether a rural and picturesque effect in the moonlight. The Arabs sitting about the door smoking their chiboucks, and the mules standing under the bushes with their packs, while the muleteers ran about shouting at a great rate and doing a great deal of work that amounted to nothing, were all that reminded us that we were in a foreign land. Without them we might readily have fancied that we were in a quiet little country village at home.

The husband of Yusef's niece received us with great kindness and hospitality. A good fire was blazing in the corner, near which he spread mats for us, and while we were enjoying the cheeful glow of the fire, he brought us coffee and pipes. Here let me tell you that you who take your ease at home, don't know the luxury of coffee and tobacco. Syria in the month of December is the place to find it out. You get up in the morning, after suffering all the tortures that vermin can inflict during the night, eat a hasty breakfast, and are off before sunrise. For six hours you climb scraggy mountains and descend horrible precipices, and then sit down on a rock by the roadside or near some ruined Khan, to eat a chicken and some leather bread; then the same riding is repeated till night, when you feel as if a piece of horse or a well-cooked dog would be a positive luxury. While you are warming yourself by the cheerful blaze of the fire, hot coffee appears as if by magic—the very thing to brace up the system for dinner, which comes in about an hour. Now, blessed be the man that invented coffee! It goes down with such a relish after all the troubles of the day; warming the throat, sending a thrill of delight into the stomach, filling body and soul with joy, and inspiring a proper appreciation of the chibouck and Djebel tobacco. All these delights we enjoyed at Zebdene, and very grateful and happy we felt that night, in spite of the prejudices of the untraveled against the use of stimulants. I shall long look back upon Zebdene as a bright spot in our pilgrimage through Syria. In the month of May it must be one of the most charming places imaginable.

Having a spare hour next morning, while the mules were being loaded, we walked out to see the village by daylight, and were quite enchanted with the fresh and verdant hedges of wild rose, the rustic gateways (which seemed to be the ruling passion of the Zebdenes), the pomp of groves, the garniture of fields, and "all that the genial ray of morning gilds." On our return to the house the horses and mules were ready, and we rode off merrily toward Damascus. Clouds began to gather upon the mountains, as we passed out of the shaded avenues of the village into the open plain, and it was not long before a heavy rain swept down upon us, accompanied by a strong cold wind that was very piercing. Three hours from Zebdene we came to the river Berada, another small stream, running between high and precipitous rocks of very marked geological character. Parts of the mountain sides were distorted as if by violent convulsions of nature, and we observed in the rocks distinct marks of trees and impressions of leaves. Our guide pointed out to us the place where the river formerly gushed through the mountain on the left, after we had passed a bridge; and on the right, on a high peak, the tomb of Abel. We had no data to authenticate the burial of Abel on the mountain, but it was the current opinion among the Greek Christians that this was his tomb. On the left, beyond the bridge, we saw a number of holes cut in the rocks like doorways, in which the Jews in old times buried their dead. They are called the tombs of the Jews. Farther on we came to the village of Suharadan —a dirty gathering of dilapidated hovels; and soon after, the village of El Sanean, situated on the slope of a hill. The valley on the left is well watered, and is fertile and beautifully wooded on the banks of the rivulet, having a fresh and verdant appearance, that contrasts pleasantly with the barren mountains on each side. El Sanean is made memorable to us by certain curious tombstones that we saw there, and by the vilest abuse that ever unoffending pilgrims received. An old woman, literally a living skeleton, covered with leather, followed us up all the way from the spring in the hollow, shaking her clenched hands at us, and shrieking at the top of her voice, "Dogs that you are—get away from here. Begone, filth of the earth!" Seeing that we merely laughed at this (partly for the reason that it was all in an unknown tongue, and partly because when translated it sounded so ludicrous to hear this skinny old hag denounce us as barbarians and dogs, without the slightest provocation, so much like what we were in the habit of doing toward the Arabs ourselves, and so palpable a hit at travelers in general), the old wretch actually danced with rage, flinging about her arms and working her jaws like some galvanized mummy. Our dragoman was so overcome with laughter that it was some time before he could give us the gist of her remarks. "Oh, yes!" she shrieked, "you may laugh, you dogs—you don't know any better. You are nothing but dirt, scarce fit to be spit upon! Begone from here, you grinning dogs, before I defile my hands by scratching your eyes out! What do you come poking about here for? Why don't you stay at home, where you are all dogs together? You want some bread, eh? Ha! ha! that's good?" And here the ferocious old hag laughed so horribly with her toothless jaws that we fain rode off to escape further abuse.

In an hour we came to the stream of Zeita, where we stopped to lunch. From this point on to the village of Dummar is a winding valley, highly fertile and picturesque, the road running along a ledge at the base of the mountain on the right, the river on the left, its banks covered with trees, and numerous springs gushing from the rocks and running over the road, making one of the most refreshing combinations of agreeable sights we had yet seen. At length we entered the village of Dum-mar, the most beautiful spot on the whole road from Baalbek to Damascus, not excepting our favorite Zebdene. We saw little of the houses, for they are nearly covered up with trees and running vines; but the gardens, wild and uncultivated as they are, teemed with richness of vegetation; and the ruinous old walls by the roadside were overrun with luxuriant vines and wild flowers. As we passed out of the village near the bridge we saw a large gathering of the native Arabs, lounging and smoking their chiboucks under an immense wide-spreaking tree in front of a Khan, with groups of camels laden with merchandise from Damascus feeding in the shade, and at a short distance from the crowd an Arab story-teller, shouting, at the top of his voice, the famous history of Hassan, the Robber of Camels. The bridge crosses the River of Dum-mar, a considerable stream, watering a fertile tract of country above. Leaving the village we had a pretty hard ride up to the top of the mountain called Jebel-el-Nazir. It was here we had the first view of the magnificent plains of Haroun—a sight that can never be forgotten; one that is truly a joy forever.

CHAPTER XXX.

DAMASCUS.

In the midst of an extensive wooded valley lay the beautiful city of Damascus called by the Emperor Julian the true city of Jupiter, the eye of the whole East. What can I say of the first view of Damascus, the bright glowing paradise of the Orient, the famous city of the Caliphate, that from early youth had haunted us in our brightest dreams of Eastern travel! There it lay before us at last, outspread at the base of Jebel-el-Nazir, upon the broad plain embosomed in groves of olives and cypress; with its mosques and minarets and castles, its white domes and giant old gateways, rising from the mass of foliage, and glittering in the sunbeams like a fairy city of snow in a summer garden. It was enough to inspire even a practical man like myself, whose mission in the East is to rake up stern facts and expose all visionary fancies—enough, I say, to strike poetry into the unpoetical—even into a determined foe to romance. On this very spot, cr close by, it is said that a famous Sheik, whose tomb we saw as we passed down, exclaimed on beholding Damascus: "I will proceed no further; I will die here, for if I go on I shall be unable to enjoy Paradise." And sure enough he died, for there stands his tomb. Like the first sight of Constantinople, it is gorgeously Oriental; different indeed in position, but scarcely less beautiful. Surrounded by luxuriant groves, and embosomed in gardens, its white spires and domes stand out with wonderful distinctness and sumptuous profusion from amid the waving mass of green; and afar on every side from the base of Jebel-el-Nazir stretches the splendid valley of the Seven Rivers, variegated with green fields and woods and villages; while on the one hand gleam the bright waters of the River Burada and the Bahr-el-Merj, or Lake of the Meadow; and on the other the snow-capt summit of Jebel-esh-Sheik, the ancient Hermon; and dim ranges of mountains loom up from the plains of Hauran, and a purple glow from the setting sun hangs softly over the vast amphitheatre of mountain and valley, giving more than earthly beauty to a scene that seemed the baseless fabric of a vision. Such is the approach to Damascus, " the right hand of the cities of Syria."

Here, before we pass beyond the Mausoleum of Abut-el Nazir, the guide of the Prophet, let us take a long, lingering look over the plain, and drink deep into our souls draughts of heavenly beauty; for within the walls of Damascus, as within the city of the Sultan, all is "of earth, earthy."

Descending by a narrow pass to the left of the Mausoleum of Abut-el-Nazir, we rode for about a mile along the base of the mountains, and then turned to the right into the groves of Damascus. Here reality at once gave a check to our enthusiasm. All travellers bound to Damascus, in search of the beautiful, should take a good look at it from the summit of Jebel-el-Nazir, and die as soon as possible, like the Sheik, but not go a step farther. There is certainly nothing to die for within the walls of Damascus, though a good deal to produce death, in the way of filth and disease. Instead of handsome villas, surrounded by flower gardens and adorned with works of art, as we were led to expect from the view above, we saw nothing but high mud walls, broken and dilapidated gateways, and trees covered with dust; with a few breaches in the walls by the way-side, exposing some wretched huts within the inclosure, as dirty as mud and dust could make them. There was not the least attempt at ornament or comfort visible any where; scarce sufficient cultivation to sustain life; lazy dogs and lazier Arabs lay basking in the sun by the roadside, sharing mutually the luxuries of dust and flies; and the whole aspect of the neighborhood, as we approached Damascus, was neglected and barbarous in the extreme. The narrow and mud-walled roads crossed each other in all directions; dust covering them to the depth of six inches; and the air was so filled with it that we were well nigh stifled before we entered upon the principal paved road leading into the city. At the gate called by the Franks the Porta di Baalbek, we were stopped by some Turkish guards, who entered into a social conversation with our dragoman concerning our business in Damascus, past history, and future prospects, all of which seemed to afford them the highest satisfaction, as they resumed their chiboucks, upon being paid the sum of two half-piasters, or four cents and a quarter, with an evident determination to remain satisfied with the information they had received (and the half-piasters) all the rest of their lives, and never to stop smoking again on any account.

If our disappointment was great upon entering the groves in the neighborhood of Damascus, it was greater still upon entering the city. The streets are not more than eight or ten feet in width, badly paved in parts and not paved at all generally; dirty beyond description, and abounding in foul odors and disgusting sights of lepers and beggars. Overhead throughout most of the city were hung ragged mats for the purpose, I believe, of keeping out the air in summer, and making the streets wet and gloomy in winter. It was as much as our lives were worth to ride through these streets over the slippery stones; spraining our horses' legs, and getting jammed on each side of the street every dozen steps, sometimes carrying away the shutters of a shop or a basket of fruit, and now and then compelled to jerk up the off leg and hug the wall to avoid being crushed by a drove of camels. The loads of these animals seemed expressly designed to rake both sides of the streets; and where there was not room for them, mules and donkeys supplied their place. We had often heard of the hostility of the inhabitants of Damascus to Christians; their hatred of all sects except their own, their intolerance toward foreigners, and their bigoted attachment to Islamism; but we had been told that of late years they had greatly improved in consequence of increased intercourse with the Frank nations of Europe. Ibrahim Pasha taught them a good many lessons, without doing their religion or morals much good. The British Government, in 1841, gave them some notion of the importance of good behavior, which seemed to make some impression upon them. They still vent their hatred, however, upon foreigners, as we found from our experience, whenever they can do so without incurring risk. In passing through some of the more obscure streets we had stones thrown at us by the boys, and were repeatedly spit at by the children, and insulted by derisive shouts of Frangi! Frangi! The men stood by laughing, evidently quite pleased with the conduct of the rising generation, though it is due to them to say that they were too lazy or too cowardly to take any part in these annoyances themselves. After passing through several of the quarters in which the different sects reside, we arrived at a wall with a door in it, upon entering which we found ourselves in the Court of the *Hôtel de Palmyre*, the only tolerable place for Frank travelers in the city. From the streets the houses have the appearance of mud forts, most of them being bare mud walls with holes in them, presenting a most forbidding and gloomy aspect to the stranger, who is not aware of the pleasant surprise that is in store for him when he passes the obscure little doorway. We were quite charmed upon entering the Court of the *Hôtel de Palmyre*. In truth, it seemed as if we had made a mistake and stumbled into the palace of some Pasha. It was a very ordinary house, as we afterward found, but appeared really magnificent, after what we had been accustomed to. There were orange trees, laden with tempting fruit; a large reservoir full of water, with a fountain in the centre; a paved court and various archways, leading into the different apartments, all on the ground floor; and then there were Arab and Greek servants, who were lounging about; and the host, with a flaming red fez in his hand, received us as visitors of high distinction—all very gratifying things to way-worn travelers, who had been for eight days wandering about over the mountains of Lebanon. The air was fragrant with the scent of oranges and rose water—we suspected the host of havnig sprinkled the pavement or himself with attar of roses when he heard we were coming—fountains were bubbling away in the rooms and out of the rooms; in short, without going into particulars, the whole was quite Lalla Rookhish—that is to say, like all things Oriental, the first sight was full of enchantment. It was so strange and showy, every thing so fashioned out to captivate the senses ; the rooms extending clear up to the top of the house, with domes above ; the walls cornered and curved into all sorts of shapes, and painted with brilliant colors, in stripes and grotesque devices; marble floors, alcoves for the beds, running gauze curtains drawn across, to keep off the spray of the fountains; divans to lounge and smoke upon, with a pleasant mingling of the useful in the way of narguillas and chiboucks. Oh, you have no idea how luxurious it was! Such was the effect of these glowing features of Eastern life upon my nervous system, aided by two cups of excellent black tea from a box presented to the host, as he solemnly declared, by Mi-lord Bath, that I lost all sense of the dignity of Oriental travel in the enthusiasm of the occasion, and gave vent to my joy in such extraordinary flourishes on the flute as to arouse every smoking Arab and son of an Arab about the establishment. They pronounced it, as I solemnly aver on the responsibility of our dragoman, the most *tahib* music that ever was heard within the walls of Damascus, not excepting the famous dead march of the Turkish band, consisting of three notes, with variations. That beautiful air, called Ezepa Kouna by the Arabs, and so much admired by them whenever I played it, rolled magnificently round the dome of our chamber, and reverberated with ten-fold effect throughout the court, to the great astonishment of two English gentlemen who had just returned from Palmyra, and who had probably never heard it before, or only knew it by the vulgar name of Zip Coon. My friends— the Captain and Southerner—were quite charmed, but none so delighted as I was myself. We all declared it was a glorious life, this riding, and smoking, and fluting our way through the land of turbans, and went to bed as jolly as possible, to dream our first dream in Damascus.

What we dreamt it would be impossible to say with any degree of accuracy. If I remember right, the English cap tain was troubled about getting in all his coal by 2 p. m., at which hour the steamer was to sail; the Southerner slept soundly in a cane-brake; and it fell to my lot to dream that the grand Caliph of Damascus had ordered me to be bastinadoed for misrepresenting him in the report of a speech which he had just delivered in the United States Senate, on the subject of free-soil. At all events, whatever our troubles were (and I assure you, our *night-caps* had nothing to do with them), we all woke up next morning in a very serious frame of mind; and, upon ascertaining that we had bad colds, and our beards were dripping wet, and our heads ached, we arrived at the following conclusions: That, however charming a fountain may be in a bedroom in summer, it is apt to be damp in the month of December; that cold marble floors are more pleasant in August than in mid-winter; and the total absence of chimneys, stoves, and all means of warming a room, except a miserable pot of charcoal, is not productive of comfort, however pretty and Oriental the whole thing may be. All the glitter of colors on the walls looked very tawdry this morning; the fountain sent a cold shudder through us; the Arab domestics looked as lazy and filthy as ever, and in spite of the repeated assurances of our landlord, that "indeed Mi-lord Bath had slept in this very chamber," we changed our quarters for another room less showy but much more comfortable.

We took for our guide through the city a methodical old gentleman called Ibrahim. In his book of recommendations he is represented to be a "regular old Jew," "as honest a man as any body could expect," "not the brightest guide in the world, but the best in Damascus, and one who knows the way through the city;" and, in justice to him, I must say that he deserved these testimonials, and that his knowledge of the languages is equal to his knowledge of the antiquities of Damascus.

The old gentleman (for he claimed to be a Reis) was very slow and dignified in his movements, and wore a long beard and large turban, that gave him a most imposing aspect; we called him Ibrahim the Solemn. He showed us the bazaars,

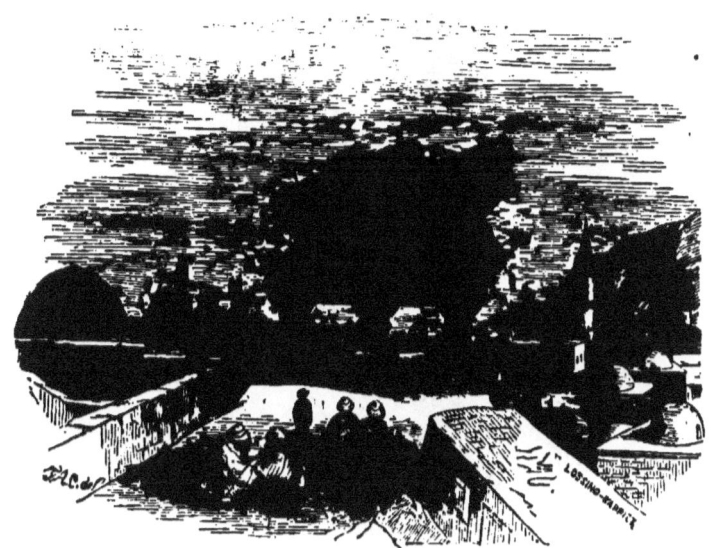

ANCIENT ARCH IN DAMASCUS.

and told us, with great solemnity, that they were bazaars; the mosques, too, he pointed out, and informed us that they were mosques; some old walls, likewise, he showed us, and said they were walls; after which, satisfied that he had imparted to us much valuable information, he took us to a native smoking-house, and with our permission, called for coffee and narguillas for the whole party, which he paid for out of his own purse, charging us afterward only double the amount; according to a custom prevalent among guides all over the world.

I was greatly struck with the majestic and dignified appearance of old Ibrahim; and thought he would look very much like a distinguished person, on paper. Indeed, I secretly entertained the belief that he was really some extraordinary man, in reduced circumstances; probably one of the learned Rabbi that I had read about in books on the East. My chief ground for the latter opinion was, that he seemed always to be wrapt in a profound study; and had a great antipathy to any thing like learning in others. Nothing so excited his contempt (if I might judge by the gravity of his countenance, for

IBRAHIM.

he never manifested his excitement in any other way) as any allusion to the history of Damascus. In a happy moment of inspiration, I got an exact fac-simile of his features, which will enable the reader to see precisely how he looked upon being asked by one of the party, if he remembered at what date St. Paul preached from the house-top. On the subject of Roman antiquities he was especially reserved. It was evident that he had an antipathy to the Romans, and would in no degree contribute to the perpetuation of their fame. That he will come out one of these days in a book against that people for building useless walls and arches in Damascus, and thereby setting idle tourists all agog, about ruins that don't exist as well as those that do exist, I have no doubt whatever. I observed it in the expression of his countenance on several occasions when I solicited his opinion about Herod the Great.

Actuated by the purest motives—chiefly by the desire to dissipate the mists of fancy, as you know has been my object all along—I took the liberty of asking Ibrahim if the ladies of Damascus were pretty; to which he replied by throwing up both hands in horror, and saying, "God forbid that I should know. People say they are, but I don't know; never saw them in my life." Now, I gave Ibrahim credit for sincerity in a good many things; for instance, being in earnest when he smoked the narguilla, hating the Mohammedans with a bitter hatred, loving the Armenians with a Jewish love, and in believing that there was not a more honest man than himself in the city of Damascus; but it must be admitted, that I had room for doubt on the point above stated. Strange stories are told about some of the English nobility who have visited Damascus of late; and nobody knows more about them than our old friend, "except," as our *maître d'hôtel* was in the habit of saying on all occasions, "Mi-lord Bath." Here is the last, translated from the original Arabic:

There was once in the East an elegant beast, and Beckford was his name; a harem he took, and then wrote a book, which won him some little fame; Corruption was tired, till an earl it inspired to follow in his path; when soon to shame it put his name, then washed it in a Bath.—Moral: Because a nobleman is in Damascus, he needn't be a Damascus Blade.

The following lines, from a book published in India, entitled, the "Shurboo Muit Amil," may be taken as another specimen of Oriental wit. The translation is from the modern Arabic:

ON A LITTLE MAN NAMED DAVID, WITH A VERY LONG BEARD.

  How can thy chin that burden bear?
   Is it all gravity to shock?
  Is it to make the people stare,
   And be thyself a laughing-stock?

  When I behold thy little feet,
   After thy beard obsequious run,
  I always fancy that I meet
   Some father followed by his son.

  A man like thee scarce e'er appeared;
   A beard like thine, where shall we find it?
  Surely, thou cherishest thy beard,
   In hopes to hide thyself behind it.

CHAPTER XXXI.

BATHS OF DAMASCUS.

We arrived at the *Hôtel de Palmyre*, as already stated, after eight days' wandering over the mountains of Lebanon, and among the ruins of Baalbek, covered with the dust of travel and the filth and vermin of Turkish khans. The first consideration next morning was a Damascus bath. My English friend had been in Syria before, and knew all about the native baths. He said they were "stunning," a word signifying every thing wonderful, in an Englishman's mouth. "Stunning" baths are supposed to be baths that knock into a cocked hat all a man's preconceived ideas of the luxuries of bathing, and it is an expressive word, as I soon discovered. The tall Southerner preferred enjoying his nap, so we left him in his glory. An Arab youth accompanied us from the hotel, with special injunctions from the padrone to show us to the baths patronized by his late master, Lord Bath. I don't know how often his lordship went there, but it is to be hoped that he went often enough to be cleansed of the impurities of rather a prolonged sojourn in Damascus. We followed our guide through a confusing maze of narrow and dirty streets, till he disappeared in a most forbidding doorway; and it was not until he re-appeared and had repeatedly urged us to enter, that we could consent to patronize such an unpromising place. He assured us, however, that we would find the baths *tahib, mucha tahib*—very good; a great deal better, we hoped, than they looked from the outside. Passing through an open courtyard, in which were countless Arabs, half-naked, up to their elbows in dirty clothes and soap-suds, we entered a large circular hall, the public dressing and undressing saloon, where payments were made, and coffee and chiboucks handed round. A fountain of cold water stood in the middle, into which dark unshirted men of the establishment plunged their arms and heads to cool themselves, and out of which they now and then dipped up water for thirsty customers. Around the saloon was an elevated platform, upon which stood a circular row of low bedsteads, most of which appeared to be occupied. It was a strange sight altogether; on every side extraordinary apparitions of dusky bearded men rising up out of the sheets, wild-looking Arabs with bald heads running about screaming horribly, gray and grizzled old Turks falling on their faces toward Mecca; a mist of cold steam rising from the sloppy marble floor; and the whole space overhead filled with dangling clothes hung up on lines to dry in the reeking atmosphere. In a retired part of the room, behind a huge pile of smoking towels, sat the master of the establishment—a venerable Arab, with a beard reaching to his middle. He also was smoking calmly amid all the turmoil, and only stopped at long intervals to note down something on a pile of paper which he held on his lap. I believe that man was writing a book—probably a learned work on hydropathy, showing the absurdities of Preisnitz and his followers in chilling the blood with cold water, when they might comfortably boil it up to the proper temperature in hot water. To this venerable man of letters we made known our wants as best we could in a broken mixture of Italian and French, through our guide, who understood something over a dozen words of each, stating that we had come a long way, and hearing in Damascus of the famous repute of his baths, had determined to try them. The old man raised his head, looked at us solemnly for some time, as if he suspected that we might be tinctured with the heresies of Preisnitz, and then waved his hand gravely toward a subordinate functionary who stood near. The subordinate was covered up high over the head in a pyramid of towels. "Friend," said we, "can't you show us into a private dressing room? We Franks don't like to make models of ourselves in public." "Impossible," said he (through our guide, of course), "every body undresses here." "But we are *howadji* of rank, and mustn't be confounded with common people; besides, we are willing to pay double for a private room." "Oh, as to that," replied the man, very much affected by our allusion to *backshish*, "I knew you were mi-lords; but I am very sorry indeed; this is the custom in Damascus. We never have private rooms here." "And do you expect us," said we sternly, "to strip ourselves before all those naked wretches?" "Praised be Allah," retorted the man, "we bathe none here but Reis and Pashas! Don't you see his highness there?" pointing to the apparition of a living skeleton, very dirty, sitting up in a pile of sheets, "that's a Pasha; and his excellency on the left," directing our attention to a greasy, bald-headed old Turk, who was amusing himself picking the fleas off his shirt, "that's one of the chief officers of the government; and there, and there—all Pashas and men of distinction. "Enough," said we; "strip us and boil us. Be quick about it, and see that we are well scrubbed." Mounting the platform, we selected two beds, and, with the assistance of the chief of sheet-holders, were soon reduced to bare legs and short linens. Further than that we stoutly protested against till screened from either a real or supposed gaze of wonder on the part of the multitude around us, who appeared to think that the *Frangi* might develop some new features in human anatomy. At last we made a compromise by denuding and sheeting ourselves. This done, we thrust our feet into some wooden clogs, to keep them clear of the floor, and were conducted into the first bath-room. Here was a blue mist, through which all that we could discern were shaven heads, naked and dusky figures looming through the warm soapy atmosphere, with a grim and horrible effect. There was a hot, heavy, oppressive smell, that quite disheartened one of us at least as to the prospect. I instinctively held my breath, for fear of inhaling some plague, leprosy, or other loathsome disease peculiar to Oriental cities. While thinking seriously of darting out, paying the *backshish*, and considering the thing done, a gaunt figure emerged from the fog, and seized me with the grasp of a vice. He was the most frightful looking monster I ever beheld—a perfect living mummy; dark, lean, and

M

shriveled, with sharp-pointed yellow teeth, and only one eye, the other having been dug out with some rough instrument; but that single eye was enough: it actually seemed to glare with triumph at the idea of a Christian subject. Another naked wretch seized hold of my friend the English captain, and we were both dragged rapidly into an adjoining apartment.

I sincerely hope that the impression made upon my mind on entering this den of satanic visions will never be effaced by any future experience. It was quite sufficient to give me a general idea of the state of things to which a man may be reduced by an evil course of life. In truth, it was worthy to be ranked with Martin's illustrations of Milton. At one end was a seething caldron of hot water, in the shape of a dark marble vase, from which arose hot clouds of steam; the marble floor was wet and soapy, and of a smarting heat; the walls were reeking with a warm sweat; high overhead was a concave ceiling, pierced with round holes, in which were colored glasses, and through this the light poured down in streaks of every hue; a mist of hot vapor hung in the atmosphere, lit up by flashes of colored light, and gave the moving figures an appearance of wretches roasting in flames of fire and brimstone; and all around, in every direction, were bare bodies, and limbs, and shaven heads glistening through the obscurity, and great naked monsters torturing them with dippers full of scalding water or blinding lather from huge basins of suds; some scraping with razors a bald crown, some scalding down a leg or an arm, or rubbing off the skin from the backbone of a prostrate victim; others stretching out limbs and trying to disjoint them, or scrubbing them down with hard brushes —all working with a fiendish zest, increased to a malicious grin of triumph when a groan or involuntary yell of agony could be elicited. "Surely," said I to the captain, "they are not going to put us through here in this diabolical crowd?" "Oh, this is nothing," said he; "there's another place yet, if I'm not mistaken. We can go into that if you like, only it's a good deal hotter." "Hotter! Why, good heavens! there's not air enough here for a musquito." "Nonsense;

you'll not mind it directly; it's quite stunning, I assure you, when you get used to it." Now, I had a painful misgiving of absolute suffocation in the act of getting used to it, but it was too late to retreat. At some magic word in Arabic from the captain, who was not much pleased himself with the assemblage here, we were seized again by the naked monsters before mentioned, and dragged into a room still further on, and of much smaller dimensions. There were only two or three victims in this branch of the establishment. It seemed to be the finishing-up place, where people who chose to go through the whole operation were subjected to the final and most exquisite ordeals; but we, as a matter of favor, were permitted to suit ourselves by having the whole thing concentrated. The fact is, in the rooms through which we had passed there was such an odor of impure flesh that we were both a little haunted by visions of plague and leprosy. Here, however, we were past all odors; there was no further use for the organs of scent. It was of such a fiery temperature that for a few minutes it was a sufficient labor to struggle against suffocation. Soon the big drops of sweat rolled down from my forehead; I was covered with a flow of steam and sweat that quite blinded me. The captain vanished in a white mist, leaving a parting impression on my mind of a man gasping for life in a sea of soap-suds. I saw no more of him for a quarter of an hour. Meantime I was jerked out of my winding sheet by the one-eyed monster, and thrust down into a sitting posture, close by the vase of hot water "Hold, for God's sake! What—" It was too late. A perfect deluge of foaming lather came pouring down over my head and face, running into my eyes, ears, and nostrils, and stopping up my mouth beyond all hope of speech. I have an indistinct recollection of a confusion of agonies through which I went for the next five minutes, but can not depict them with any thing like the force of reality.

From the crown of my head to the soles of my feet, I was enveloped in a bank of hot lather, which the horrid wretch who had me down was rubbing into my flesh with a small rake, or some other instrument of torture. At last he reached

BATHS OF DAMASCUS.

my eyes, and here he rubbed so effectually that the pain was too exquisite to be borne. "Water, water!" I roared, in the very extremity of agony, "water, you villain! quick, or I'm blind for life! "*Mooè*," suggested the captain from his bank of suds on the other side, "call for *mooè*, that's the Arabic; he'll understand it better than English!" "*Mooè!*" I screamed in the madness of anguish; "*Mooè!* you rascal!" There was a guttural sound of assent from outside the coating of lather; it was impossible to see an inch; but I heard a dabbling as if in water, and thought I detected something like a fiendish inward laugh. Next moment my brain seemed to be scorched with a hissing flame of fire, and my body felt as if a thousand devils were tearing strips of skin off it with red hot pincers. For a while I was entirely incapable of utterance. I could only writhe madly under the grasp of the live mummy, who held me down with one hand, while he continued to pour the scalding flood over me with the other, till a momentary cessation of the torture enabled me to call for aid. "Captain! oh heavens, captain! he's boiling me in earnest!" "Cold water!" said the captain in Arabic; "put some cold water on him!" There was a pause now, while the man went in search of cold water, during which I sat simmering in a puddle of suds, afraid to stir lest my entire suit of skin should drop off. In a few minutes he returned, and, holding the bucket over my head, he poured down a stream of fresh water that sent a shock into my very core. It was a relief, however, as it eventually enabled me to open my eyes. When I did open them, the first object in view was that diabolical wretch, grinning horribly, and squinting with a malicious satisfaction at the results of his labors. I was red all over, a perfect boiled lobster in external appearance. "*Tahib?*" said he, signifying, Good, is'nt it? "*Tahib*, hey?" And then he took from a large bowl of suds a familiar-looking instrument, a brush, which he fastened on his hand, and seizing hold of me by the arm, commenced rubbing with all his might. To be carded down in this manner with a hard brush, the wooden part of which now and then touched up some acute angle, was not productive of agreeable sensations, but it was a vast improvement on the hot-water process. Such exquisite delight did the villainous old mummy take in it, that he strained every muscle with zeal, and snorted like a racer, his fiery eye glaring on me with a fiendish expression, and his long pointed teeth, glistening through the steam, as if nothing would have afforded him half so much satisfaction as to bite me. Stretching me on my back, he scrubbed away from head to foot, raking over the collar bones, ribs, and shin bones in a paroxysm of enthusiasm. This done, he reversed the position, and raked his way back, lingering with great relish on every spinal elevation, till he reached the back of my head, which event he signalized by bringing the end of the brush in sudden contact with it. He then pulled me up into a sitting posture again; for by this time I was quite loose, and felt resigned to any thing, and drawing the brush skillfully over the beaten track, gathered up several rolls of fine skin, each of which he exhibited to me, with a grin of triumph, as a token of uncommon skill. "*Tahib, Howadji? Tahib?*" Good; isn't your excellency cleverly done, eh?

Having arrived at this stage of the proceedings, the indefatigable monster again covered me up in a sea of lather, and while I was writhing in renewed agonies from streams of soap that kept running into my eyes, in spite of every effort to shut them off, he dashed a large dipper, full of hot water, over me, following it by others in rapid succession, till, unable to endure the dreadful torturing, I sprang to my feet, seized the dipper, and shouted, "*backshish!*" at the top of my voice. The word acted like magic. I never have known it to be applied in vain throughout the East. It opens sacred places, corrupts sacred characters, gives inspiration to the lazy, and new life to the desponding; in short, it accomplishes wonders, no matter how miraculous. From that moment I was a happy man; rubbed down with a lamb-like gentleness, smoothed over softly with warm sheets, dried up from head to feet; turbaned like a Pasha, slipped into my clogs, and supported through the various chambers into the grand saloon, where I had the pleasure of greeting my friend the captain, of whom I had enjoyed but a confused notion of proximity for some time previously. An attendant now handed us chiboucks and coffee, which, together with the delightful sense of cleanliness and relief from all further suffering, produced a glow that was quite ecstatic. Covered up to our necks in warm sheets, we lay back, supported by pillows, sipped our coffee and smoked our chiboucks with a relish to which all the past pleasures of life seemed absolutely flat. A thorough feeling of forgiveness, a quiet sense of happiness, and an utter indifference to the world and all its cares, pervaded the entire inner man, while the outer was wrapt in that state of physical beatitude which the Koran promises to the devout followers of the Prophet in the seventh heaven. "Stunning, isn't it?" said the captain, calmly puffing his chibouck.

Being Frangi, of course we *backshished* every body, and were immoderately cheated. The entire expense, however, did not exceed thirty cents, including coffee and pipes—little enough, one would say, for such an ordeal. As for the effect upon the system we found it very pleasant and salutary; but I have no doubt the old gentleman whom we left writing behind the smoking pile of sheets will do full justice to that branch of the subject in his work, which, it is to be hoped, will be translated into English. There is only one objection to the boiling process; my hair has been falling out ever since, and I am apprehensive of total baldness before any young lady will be moved to pity, by these "hair-breadth 'scapes," these "dangers by flood and field." The baths of Damascus are stunning; I fully agree to that; but it is with an inward reservation, a fixed intention to flog that old mummy out of his skin the very first time I meet him in Washington.

CHAPTER XXXII.

THE MISSIONARIES IN SYRIA.

I HAD the pleasure of becoming acquainted, during my sojourn in Damascus, with several of the American missionaries; and I feel that it would be ungrateful to omit a passing tribute to their kindness of heart, unpretending piety, and noble exertions in the dissemination of Christianity among the Arabs. Prejudiced, in some degree, against the missionaries as a class—partly from having paid but little attention to the subject, and partly because I had seen some very bad specimens in other countries, yet I had never doubted the high and praiseworthy aim of the system; and it was a source of genuine gratification to find that there are a great many more sincere people in the world than I had supposed in my younger days. A good cause often suffers from the unfitness or insincerity of its followers; but if it be founded upon true and righteous principles, it must triumph in the end. It has been well remarked, that "if men who are set apart to instruct others, instead of entertaining them with what neither teachers nor hearers understand, and (what is worse), stirring up the latter to dislike and hate one another for difference in opinions, would preach the true Gospel of Jesus Christ, which is 'peace on earth and good-will to men,' and also enforce this excellent doctrine by their own examples, and all other virtues by the same means, we should undoubtedly soon experience a great alteration in the world." Nothing can be more injudicious than to attempt the reformation of a barbarous people by threats, or by confounding them with abstruse doctrinal mysteries. The Christian religion is simple and easily understood; the most ignorant may be taught to comprehend it, if it be presented in the unpretending language of its best and greatest teacher. But in order to do this, it would seem necessary that the mind of the barbarian should be prepared in some measure to receive it by a knowledge of the principles upon which it is founded; by some practical, tangible showing of the difference between right and wrong; by such preparatory lessons in civilization, as would enable him to perceive the temporal, as well as the spiritual advantage of what he was learning.

The schools attached to the missions throughout the East are, in this view, of incalculable service to the cause of Christianity; and, although there is perhaps no other part of the world where so many difficulties have to be contended against, the success which has attended the missionary teachings is most remarkable. In Athens, Mr. Hill, by his judicious and admirable system of education, gradually inspiring in his pupils a love of virtue, and a thirst for spiritual knowledge, has made an impression on the hearts and minds of the rising generation of Greeks that must eventually spread and become general throughout the land. Evangelides, the Greek-American of Syra, has also done much by his teachings; and the same may be said of all the missionaries and teachers whom I met with in the Levant.

One of the most memorable and delightful evenings of my whole pilgrimage was spent in the church of the Rev. Dr. Smith of Beirut. There, for the first time in my life, I heard the Christian religion expounded in the land of its origin. Attracted, as I was strolling by the door of the humble little church, by the chaste and classic eloquence of the preacher, with whom I was entirely unacquainted, I stepped in and took my seat; and I may safely say, that never had I listened to a more delightful or instructive discourse. Among the congregation was a large number of intelligent-looking Arabs, in their native costume; and the profound attention with which they listened to the teachings of their pastor, and the strict decorum and good-breeding evinced in their manner, struck me as the most impressive instance of progress in a land of darkness and ignorance, toward a better state of things, that

I had ever witnessed. Who can measure the good that each one of these Arabs may, by his influence and example, do for his fellow-men, even in his own day and generation?

Damascus has always been noted as the stronghold of Islamism; and the inhabitants have ever been distinguished for their bigotry and intolerance. Until very recently, Christian pilgrims were not only subject to insults in passing through the streets, but frequently assaulted and maltreated without provocation. A great improvement has become perceptible in this respect within a few years past. Missionaries from every civilized nation are now permitted to preach, and educate the native children without molestation; and although the result of their labors is not so encouraging as in other portions of Syria where there is less intolerance, yet there is every reason to believe that the great cause of civilization is taking root, and that a few years more will develop a growth equal to the most sanguine anticipations of those who are interested in it.

Mr. Burnet, who has been in Damascus only six or seven years, now preaches to a respectable congregation of Arabs in their own tongue. Dr. Shephard, Mr. Lansing, and others, are making rapid progress in the education of the Arab children; and when the system which they have adopted is thoroughly in operation, there can be no question as to its beneficial results.

To each and all of these gentlemen I am indebted for much valuable information in regard to the social condition of the Syrians; and I shall always remember with unfeigned pleasure the delightful and profitable hours which I was so fortunate as to spend in their society.

After seeing all that travelers, limited in time, can be expected to see in Damascus and the neighborhood, we bade good-by to our kind friends, mounted our horses once more, and proceeded on our journey.

For three days nothing particular occurred. A heavy rain-storm set in as we left Damascus; and we were drenched to the skin, and compelled at last to seek shelter in a miserable village up in the mountains, called Far-how-ar. On the following day, the rain turned to a cutting sleet, and we were forced to stop at Beit Jem. Taking the rough bridle-path from that village, we ascended Jebel-esh-Sheik, or Mt. Hermon, where we suffered intensely from the cold. The mountain was covered with snow; and the whole aspect of the country was wild and barren. We saw a few jackals among the rocks, and shot at one that came snuffing the air rather close to us, but, with our usual luck, missed him.

On the evening of the third day we descended near by an old castle, to the village of Baneas, the ancient Cesarea Philippi. We saw here the grotto from which flows the spring said by some authorities to be the source of the Jordan. I had promised to meet Doctor Mendoza and the Madam at Philippi; but they had passed on the day before, evidently because it was "imposs to remain tranquil" in such a place. I had also on various occasions during my life agreed to meet friends and foes in Philippi. The friends were not there: I was not disappointed in regard to the foes. We all had an abundance of them during the night, and in the morning had no cause to complain of having met nothing in Philippi.

CHAPTER XXXIII.

THE BATTLE OF THE MULETEERS.

This morning, before leaving Baneas, a terrible battle took place between my dragoman Yusef and the muleteers. I caution the reader not to be alarmed for my safety, when I state, that on an average, we have a battle every day. Neither do I claim any great merit as a military man, on account of the coolness with which I witness the strife of the contending parties; because, to be candid, I always contrive to occupy some elevated position at a safe distance from the scene of action, where I sit smoking my chibouck very pleasantly till the conclusion of the fight. Besides, I know that Yusef is bound to conquer, because he not only carries all the arms, but is perpetually so boiling over with courage, that even when there is no real enemy at hand, he shoots the air and kills a great many imaginary enemies. Under these circumstances I feel a confidence in the result that is very cheering. The cause of the present difficulty was this, as well as I could learn : The muleteers having found some old acquaintances at Baneas, had spent the night in smoking and talking. When the time arrived for starting they were in a sound sleep. Yusef tried, by all manner of pushing and shouting, to wake them up; but the more he tried the more they remained fast asleep. The effect seemed rather to be agreeable than otherwise. At last, bereft of all patience, and aided by Francesco, he caught them by the legs and dragged them out of doors, where he eventually brought them to life, both by personal violence and a fierce torrent of abuse. "Now," said he, as I judged from his tone and manner, "if those mules are not ready in ten minutes, I'll flog every one of you ! I'll then cut

your throats from ear to ear. After that I'll tear out your
livers, and give them to the dogs; I'll make mince-meat of
your hearts, and hang your bodies up by the heels, as a warning to all muleteers throughout Syria. Yea, by the beard of
the Prophet, if that won't do, I'll tie you to the tail of my
horse and drag you to Jerusalem, and when I get you there
I'll—no, I won't bury you in holy ground—I'll *eat you!* By
Allah, I'll EAT YOU!" This last threat was evidently made on
the spur of the moment; it was too dreadful to be premedi-
tated, and must have had its origin in the difficulty of getting
rid of the bodies after dragging them to Jerusalem. I could
not think that Yusef really meant to eat the muleteers; for,
leaving aside every moral consideration, they were the dirtiest
set of vagabonds I ever saw, and must have been thoroughly
saturated with smoke. However, they seemed to think a little more smoking would do them no harm; for the moment,
Yusef turned his back and went into the khan to pack up the
cooking utensils, they very coolly filled their pipes and began
to smoke again, conversing at the same time with great good-
humor. At the expiration of half-an-hour, having waited
patiently all this time, I ventured mildly to suggest that we
ought to be on our way, or we would never be able to reach
Tiberias. Upon this hint Yusef became suddenly fired with
unconquerable indignation toward the muleteers. He rushed
furiously out of the khan, the veins swollen in his forehead,
and rage depicted in every feature. I followed at a reasonable distance, thinking there would certainly be bloodshed this
time. "Where are they?" he shrieked. "Show me the rascals! Ho! Yakob! Hassin! Mustapha!" "Here we are,"
said they; and, behold, they were sitting in the same spot,
smoking their chiboucks. "Dogs!" cried Yusef, drawing his
pistol, "didn't I tell you I'd kill you if the mules were not
ready in ten minutes? Die, dogs, die!" But they had no
idea of dying; on the contrary, they rose to their feet, and
began to expostulate with Yusef on the violence of his conduct, which brought forth a counter expostulation from him,
and a retort from them, and then a retort from him again,
which brought up old scores, and the battle raged fiercely in

words for the space of half-an-hour. It became by that time perfectly furious. Yusef howled and shrieked, and spat at the muleteers; and the muleteers howled and shrieked, by turn, and then smoked. The pistol evidently was a failure; it was returned to its case. The battle of words now waxing fiercer, Yusef lost all patience. Drawing his sword, he flourished it thrice over his head, shut his eyes, and rushed blindly at the rebels! But there was no sign of a panic; they stood very calmly while he flourished his sword around their heads, as if they thought the cuts and thrusts that he made at them had no foundation in reality. Having completely exhausted himself by the effort, he eventually returned the sword to its scabbard and sat down. One of the muleteers, Mustapha, was conspicuous for his docile temper. He was a comical old fellow, always in a good humor, and ready to bear any amount of ill-treatment. Now, in cases of difficulty, Yusef always ended the matter by beating Mustapha. Already he had beaten him several times; and in Damascus, apprehending trouble on the road from a growing disposition to mutiny on the part of the muleteers, he had provided himself with several tough sticks, to encourage discipline. In the present emergency, seeing Mustapha close at hand, he sprang to his feet, calling to Francesco to bring him his best stick, and seized the poor fellow by the coat. The stick came; Mustapha begged; Yusef stormed; Mustapha promised; Yusef foamed and spat upon him; Mustapha howled most piteously; Yusef raged most furiously; Mustapha called upon the Prophet to save him; Yusef struck him for his impiety, in taking the name of the Prophet in vain. The more Mustapha begged and wept, the more Yusef beat him; till, apprehensive of serious consequences, I called upon him sternly to desist, on the pain of our sublime displeasure. It was not without reluctance that the whipping was brought to a conclusion.

At ten o'clock we were packed and mounted, and on our winding way just as if nothing had happened. Mustapha cracked pleasant jokes with every body, and laughed heartily behind Yusef's back at the idea of the beating and shooting, going through a great many pantomimic motions, showing how people died when they were shot, and, when they were not shot, how they were beaten with a stick, and how they wept at the pain thereof.

Meantime Yusef entertained us with some remarkable instances of his courage, touching incidentally upon the affair of the Djereed, in which he had killed four men and disabled six for life—the best men that could be produced by the great Prince of Lebanon. He also pointed out the precise spot where he had recently shot a dead man under the most singular and appalling circumstances. It seemed that in returning to Damascus, after leaving a party of travelers at Jerusalem, he had occasion to pass this way in the middle of the night, which was the time he usually chose for traveling when alone, as it increased the danger of robbers. He knew there were robbers waiting for him here, and in order to give them notice of his approach he was singing merrily as he rode along. All at once he saw a very tall man, as he thought, standing under an olive tree, with his face turned up, looking at the moon. "Ho, villain!" shouted our traveler, "is it me you want? Fall down on your knees, wretch, and beg for mercy. Behold! I am Yusef Badra, the destroyer of robbers!" The man instead of falling upon his knees seemed to grow taller as the destroyer of robbers approached "Fool, that you are!" cried Yusef, riding up still closer and drawing his pistols; "don't you know I never miss killing when I shoot." Still the man made no reply. "Then die! die like a dog!" Saying which Yusef fired six times, and each time he heard a ball strike. "Oho!" said he, perceiving that the man only moved a little without falling down or uttering a single groan, "you are the devil; I'm very glad to see you, old gentleman! Yusef Badra is not afraid of the devil, or any body else; besides, we have a small account to settle." Upon which, drawing his sword, he urged his frightened horse up to the spot and ran the mysterious stranger clean through the body. It was not until then that he discovered his mistake. He had shot and pierced through the body a dead man! The corpse was hung to a branch of the tree by the neck, and the feet, being in the shade, were invisible at a short distance. It was a poor traveler whom the robbers had murdered that night. Yusef cut the corpse down, as he informed us, and pinned upon it these words, which he wrote upon a piece of paper by the light of the moon : "If ever Yusef Badra meets the wretches who murdered this man, he will cut their heads off and hang them by the heels to this tree."

On the road leading down into the valley of El Huleh we crossed, near Baneas, the chief source of the Jordan. At this point it is nothing more than a good spring of clear water, enlarged to the size of a rivulet by contributions from several smaller springs. It comes from a large cave in the mountain a little beyond Baneas. In an hour and a half, having descended a long slope over a bed of rocks, we reached an old bridge with three arches, which crosses a stream called by the natives the true source of the Jordan. It is a disputed point among biblical writers which of the two is in reality entitled to the name, the size being nearly equal; but the best authorities seem to concur in giving the distinction to the stream nearest to Baneas. Before reaching the bridge we passed several fine olive groves, and had a distant view of the lake El Huleh, whose bright waters gleamed like a sheet of silver in the hollow of the great plain.

From the bridge we struck out into a marsh, directing our course toward the base of Jebel Egil, the range of mountains on the right of El Huleh. We soon found that the recent heavy rains had flooded all the low grounds, and our horses and mules were sometimes scarcely able to extricate themselves from the mud. Our baggage was frequently thrown off the backs of the mules in their struggles, and recovered with great difficulty and delay. We saw waterfowl all around us, chiefly cranes, snipe, and such as are common in swampy grounds; and by dint of a great deal of firing, at the expense of an immense quantity of powder and shot, accidentally killed two cranes that flew up suddenly within ten feet of our sportsmen. In the afternoon we saw for the first time a Bedouin village. It consisted of a dozen or fifteen low black tents, in the midst of the marsh, with a population of lean and savage-looking Arabs, who looked scowlingly at us as we passed. Soon after, we passed another encampment—an extensive village of tents and straw cabins. Horses were tied to stakes about the doors, and herds of buffalo, with short thick horns twisted back, grazed in the surrounding marshes. Several lean and wolfish dogs ran fiercely at us, but fled howling as we presented our guns. These Bedouins are not the genuine descendants of Hagar, or the supposed wild Ishmaelites who still roam the deserts of Arabia. They are partially civilized by intermixture with the Syrian Arabs, and lead rather a pastoral than a predatory life. Those who abide in the valley of El Huleh pay tribute to the Turkish Government for the use of the land, and reside upon the plains permanently, moving their villages from one part to another as the sheiks direct. Large herds of tame buffalo find excellent pasturage here during the entire year, and upon the produce of these and the cultivation to some extent of the soil they contrive to obtain a tolerable subsistence. The land in some parts of the valley is exceedingly fertile, and seems well adapted to the production of Indian corn, of which the Bedouins raise a small quantity. Around the bases of the mountains, where the land is not too marshy, wheat thrives well by the mere scratching up of the ground with rude wooden plows (such as were used in scriptural times), and sufficient flour for the people of the valley is produced with very little labor. Rice is grown in the marshy lands, and grass abounds naturally throughout the plain. In the vicinity of lake El Huleh tall rushes and flags grow in great quantities, which are found useful in building and roofing the huts. It seemed a little strange to us that these people should live in the low grounds, their tents and cabins floating in water half the time, exposed to the full glare of the sun in summer and the piercing winds in winter, while not more than a few hundred yards distant, on the sides of the mountains, were some very pretty sites for villages, pleasantly shaded by bushes, and protected from floods and storms. But there is no accounting for tastes, certainly no accounting for the tastes of the Bedouins. Some of the women and children were remarkable for the beauty of their features; the men had also fine features and a commanding air about them even in their rags; but they were a swarthy, unwashed set of vagabonds at best, and lived in a style more suitable to a village of beavers than to any thing of the human kind.

In the winter the greater part of the plain of El Huleh is covered with water; all the small streams from the mountains swell the lake till it overflows its low banks and spreads around for many miles. The sources of the Jordan may be considered as flowing chiefly from the neighborhood of Baneas; but every stream that runs into the lake of El Huleh forms in reality an additional source, as they all unite in the lake, and eventually find their way, through the Sea of Galilee, into the main river Jordan, which winds from thence a distance of seventy miles into the Dead Sea.

On leaving the Bedouin villages we rode on toward Ain-el-Malaha, or the Stream of the Mill. Our dragoman, who had maintained a profound silence for some hours, while in the vicinity of the Bedouins, now gave vent to one of those sudden paroxysms of fury which had frequently alarmed us with apprehensions of an attack from some hidden enemy. We were riding along very pleasantly, not dreaming of the least danger, when Yusef, without the slightest warning, dashed madly out of our ranks, yelling like the very demon of wrath, and whirling his gun fiercely over his head. The war-whoop of an American Indian could not compare at all with the battle-cry of our ferocious dragoman. Away he scoured over the plain, causing the earth to fly up from his horse's hoofs in a perfect shower, turning and rearing, charging and chasing the enemy. Arrived at close quarters, he fired his gun; then drew his pistols and fired them, and then with a savage yell drew his sword, which he flourished with one hand, and his dagger, which he flourished with the other, and then he laid about him in front and behind, and on the left side and the right side, cleaving skulls, ripping, cutting, and thrusting, and charging over dead bodies, and shrieking madly for more live ones to come on. "Villains, cowards, dogs! the whole of you together come on! come on!

and die by the avenging hand of Yusef Badra!" I declare, on the veracity of a traveler, it was the most desperate and exciting conflict I ever beheld. By the time I had ridden up to the assistance of our friend who was so bravely defending us, I could not perceive that there was a single live person left, and even the dead had disappeared. "Why, in the name of common sense," said I, "what have you been shooting at and killing all this time?" "Killing!" shouted Yusef fiercely, his eyes starting from their sockets, while he panted and foamed with rage; "killing! I could kill forty thousand of them! There never was a Bedouin yet that could stand before me. I only wish I had some of the rascals here now!" "Keep cool, Yusef," said I, alarmed at the frightening demonstrations he was making, "keep cool, it's much the best way." "Cool, sir! By Allah, I'll go back to the village this very moment and kill a dozen of 'em for pastime. Do you think, prince of Generals! that I'm afraid of a beggarly set of Bedouins!" "No, certainly not, Yusef," said I, soothingly. "Nevertheless," cried he, fired by another sudden burst of fury, "I must, by the beard of the Prophet, I must, go back and kill a dozen of 'em, or I can't sleep to-night!" Saying which he clapped heels to his horse, and was about to dash off again, when I shouted, "Hold, Yusef, hold! I insist that you leave those Bedouins alone, and don't attack them. Remember what our defenseless condition would be during your absence!" "True, General, true; I won't attack 'em to-night for your sake. I respect you, oh, glorious General! commander of all the military forces in America! I love you better than the brother of my heart! This night you shall sleep soundly in Ain-el-Malaha."

We rode on peacefully for some distance after this, and encountered no other immediate danger than that of being walked over by several caravans of camels heavily laden with produce for the markets of Damascus, which we met in some of the narrow passes as we approached the Mill of Malaha.

When there was nothing particular to occupy our attention in the way of ruins or scenery, it sometimes happened that we became sleepy from the monotony of our journey, and lagged along in pairs, conversing drowsily upon various topics suggested by the occasion. I was very fond of drawing Yusef out, when he was in the proper spirit, not only because he was well informed upon the every-day affairs of Syrian life: but from a habit of argument into which I have fallen, in consequence of three years' experience as a reporter in the United States Senate. If I sometimes become a little disposed to indulge in flights of eloquence, not strictly called for by any existing emergency, it is altogether through the force of example.

The tall Southerner and the English Captain, having both fallen into a doze, while they jogged along about a mile behind, I took advantage of the occasion to indulge in one of my customary chats with Yusef, who seemed in an uncommonly good humor, considering that all the Bedouins were out of sight. But this conversation being of an important character, I must give a verbatim report of it in a separate chapter.

CHAPTER XXXIV.

THE GRAND SECRET OF HUMAN HAPPINESS.

General.—"How is it, Yusef, that your countrymen never think of bettering their condition? See that lazy wretch basking in the sun there; why doesn't he go to work and do

TAKING IT EASY.

something useful? I verily believe he smokes all day and sleeps all night."

Yusef.—"And wherefore, O General, should he trouble his head about any thing more? The very philosophy of life is to be content with as little as possible in this world."

General.—"Then he must be a great philosopher, for he

certainly has no visible means of support. It takes uncommonly little to satisfy him, so far as I can see."

YUSEF.—" Yet that little appears to be enough. He takes it easy, as you may perceive, and doesn't seem at all unhappy."

GENERAL.—" Faugh! what a barbarous life! A fine looking fellow like that fooling away his time basking in the sun like a great mud-turtle. Why, in our country he might earn his dollar a day."

YUSEF.—" True, O General, but he'd have to work."

GENERAL.—" Of course he would—ten hours a day, at least. Then you see he'd have the pleasure of spending his money. He'd pay a tolerably high price for a small cabin to live in; and a tolerably high price for something to eat, and tolerably high prices for clothing for himself and family, and at the end of a week, after six days of honest toil, digging a well or down in a coal-pit, perhaps, he'd feel tolerably tired and sleep soundly till the morning of the seventh."

YUSEF.—" To my poor understanding, O General, that seems rather a melancholy life—not a hopeful one at least. I can only say that touching the matter of labor, I am in the dark as to what it ends in."

GENERAL (smiling).—" Why, it ends in labor, to be sure; the man labors for money; and when he gets it he labors either to keep it or spend it. But don't you perceive the difference between a mere animal existence, and that noble ambition which inspires a civilized people to seek for active, positive, or palpable happiness—something they can hold in their hands and look at. In our country, there are men who go thousands of miles by land and water (some try to go in the air) to dig up gold in order that they may be happy When they get a hundred thousand dollars they only want another hundred thousand, and when they get that they only want half a million more, by which time they might be perfectly happy only for some other want. Sometimes when they haven't any other want in particular, they lose all their money by some visitation of providence—a fire or flood, or die of a fever just as they are going to be perfectly happy."

Yusef.—"Adjaib! wonderful! And do they pray, too, as well as do all this?"

General.—"Why—yes: they contrive to spare one day out of seven ostensibly for that purpose; some of them can't spare even that. While you barbarians spend most of your time in idleness, taking it easy, as the saying is; stopping what little work you do at least five times a day to pray and smoke, no matter how important may be your business, we work hard early and late, and never stop our labors (especially if they be profitable) to pray at all, and very seldom to smoke, though we economize time by chewing a little. I never knew a man in our country to think so much of his soul or any body else's as to stop short in a bargain amounting to ten dollars, or even ten cents, for the purpose of communing with his Maker. We don't do it; we haven't got the time; can't spare it. Time is money, Yusef. Every day is a dollar, or five dollars, or ten dollars; every minute is a cent or the fraction of a cent, more or less.

Yusef.—"But, in the name of the Prophet, when you get all this money together, what do you do with it? Don't you ever stop working?"

General.—"Oh, yes: we retire from business sometimes; purchase a country seat—build a handsome villa, and live there a month or two, by which time we become perfectly satisfied."

Yusef.—"Then you take it easy, and smoke the pipe of content at last?"

General.—"Why, no—not exactly. We become perfectly satisfied that it's a dull business—that it won't pay: too slow, entirely too slow; can't get through life fast enough doing nothing in the country. Go back to town. Speculate; make more money—or lose what we've got. The fact is, life is a bore at best; we know it; we get through it as fast as we can, in order to skim off what cream there may be in it, and enjoy it in a concentrated form; we live a good deal in a short time."

Yusef.—"But what becomes of all the money you make by living fast?"

GENERAL.—" Oh, we leave it to our children. We can't well spare the time to eat it or wear it on our backs, so when we die we bequeath it to our sons, who, being rather younger in the world, don't know its value, and spend it. They spend it tolerably fast sometimes, Yusef; they live very rapidly on it, indeed—railroad fashion, using a good deal of steam to help them along: they get over the track with considerable velocity, you may depend upon it."

YUSEF.—" And then what do they do?"

GENERAL (with a yawn).—"*Bust!*"

Yusef whistles with astonishment, but says nothing.

GENERAL (finding Yusef so favorably disposed toward a peaceful and contented mode of life).—" I consider this an appropriate occasion, Yusef, to let you know my utter abhorrence of the system of flogging which you adopt in your management of the muleteers. It is extremely repugnant to my feelings, and I beg you will not repeat it hereafter."

YUSEF.—" Inshalla ! they are nothing but brutes. It does 'em good, sir. They couldn't get along without it. Fain would I do any thing to oblige your Excellency, but if I quit whipping them they would raise a mutiny directly."

GENERAL.—" A most absurd argument—fit only for a barbarous people. These muleteers are freemen, and not slaves. You have no moral right to whip them. If they were slaves it might be another question. What do you think would be the result if we Americans, a free-born people, were to seize up a free-born sailor or soldier and flog him like a slave?"

YUSEF.—" Think, O General? Doubtless I'd think he deserved it. Discipline, sir, must be kept up in all the relations between master and man. If a man won't do his duty, he must be whipped into it; that's the way I always serve these dogs."

GENERAL.—" It wouldn't do for you to undertake such a barbarous thing in our country. Thank God! we are a civilized people. Public sentiment and the laws of the land would soon put down such tyranny. The captain of a whale-ship, or of any other ship, who flogs a man and accidentally kills him by too much flogging, is tried by the laws of the land, and fined from five dollars up to fifty! Think of that! I have known naval officers to be tried by Court Martial for cruel and unusual punishments, and even REPRIMANDED, in certain extreme cases where death resulted; yes, Yusef, sometimes actually informed in writing that they were to consider themselves severely CENSURED!"

YUSEF.—"To me, O General, that seems to be a most unwise and oppressive state of things. When I pay a man for his services haven't I a right to do what I please with him, body and soul? If I hire him to work and he won't do it, haven't I a right to take satisfaction out of his hide? If I take a dislike to him, haven't I a right to beat him upon any pretext whatever?"

GENERAL (excited).—"Great heavens! Is it possible that even a brutish Arab can maintain such monstrous doctrines as these? Do you know, miserable barbarian, that the very walls of our Capitol would cry out in execration of doctrines so absurd and inhuman? Senators would rise in their places, and call for the opinions of naval and military commanders; Secretaries would hold official councils, and proclaim to Congress and the world their devotion to the interests of the service; Lieutenants, Captains, and Generals would avow their abhorrence of cruelty in every form, and indignantly contend against sapping the foundation of our national defenses, by depriving them of an established privilege. Never let me hear you utter such abominable sentiments again, or, by all the rights of humanity, I'll put you in a book! I'll do it, Yusef, as sure as fate! Your name shall figure on the title-page!"

YUSEF (turning pale).—"In the name of Allah, beloved General, Light of my eyes and Friend of my heart, wherefore this extreme displeasure? Surely, thou hast mistaken my meaning. I didn't intend to say that I'd make whipping a general thing; that I'd whip any respectable person of my own class. My observations were designed to apply exclusively to low brutes of muleteers, without friends or influence; mere dregs of society, destitute of brains and feeling. Your Excellency does me gross injustice, if you think that.

because I would whip a muleteer for insolence or disorderly conduct, that I would, if placed in command of a ship, or at the head of a regiment, whip any of my officers for the same, or even a much greater offense."

GENERAL (somewhat pacified).—"Of course not, Yusef; certainly not. · I never knew any commander, holding a position of high authority, either in America or England, to contend for such an indiscriminate exercise of power as that. It gratifies me to observe, that ignorant and debased as you are, there are yet some enlightened principles of civilization not altogether unfamiliar to you."

YUSEF (warmly).—"Bless your generous heart, O General; I knew you'd do me justice! I knew it by instinct! What, sir, flog an officer for getting drunk or insulting me? No, sir. I'd take him aside and reprimand him; I'd talk to him, like a brother, with tears in my eyes, or challenge him to mortal combat."

GENERAL.—"Such is the practice in all enlightened communities; and I must say, that with such principles, Yusef, you would be an ornament to any community,· however skilled in the noble science of human destruction."

YUSEF (enthusiastically).—"A noble—a glorious—a wonderful science! O great and effulgent Chieftain! brightest ornament of the City of Magnificent Distances! not a night passes over the head of Yusef Badra that he doesn't wallow in rivers of blood! His bed is a bed of human skulls! his pillow is the cold and clammy corpse of a fellow man! the sweetest breath he inhales is the putrid effluvia of the dead! the grinning and fleshless jaws of his enemies are smiling flowers to his heart; the ribs and joints that lie scattered around him are pleasant verdure to his eyes, refreshing them after the scorching heat of battle; the wailing of the widowed for the dead, the moaning of the bereaved for lost friends and kindred, are dulcet sounds that thrill sweetly upon his ears; all—all the visions that can give hope and inspiration to the warlike soul, diffuse themselves through the soul of Yusef Badra. Yet he wakes to find himself without a foe; his very soul thirsting for blood, he finds but a dastardly muleteer to chastise for theft or laziness! Fain would he plunge his sword through the miserable dog; tear out his bowels, and fling them to the crows; but the baggage of the Howadji must go on; it won't do to gut the wretches yet awhile. I'll gut them at the end of the journey; by Eblis, sir, I'll do it in Jerusalem! yea, O General! I can't wait even so long as that! I'll do it in Nazareth! No, by heavens! I can't wait till then. I'll gut 'em in Tiberias! Two days from this date I'll—what? wait two days? Nay; by all the glories of war! I'll do it at Malaha—the very first stopping-place we come to. I'll rip them open from head to foot! I'll cast their entrails out over the house-tops, to be devoured by birds and beasts of prey! I'll drink their blood to cool the fever of courage and defiance that forever burns within me! I'll do it at Malaha! nay, by all the horrid luxuries of murder, I'll gut 'em NOW—this very moment—Ho! Mustapha! Yakob!"

GENERAL (seizing Yusef's horse by the bridle).—"Hold, Yusef, hold! Are you mad? In the name of humanity, don't commit such an outrage as that. Calm yourself, Yusef—calm yourself. Now, I beg you, as a friend, not to shed the blood of innocent men. We may meet some robbers before long, and if we do, I promise you, on my honor, I shall not strike a blow; I'll get behind you, and you may slay them all single-handed."

YUSEF (foaming).—"I'll do it, General; I'll do it. What? only single-handed? Is that all the odds your Excellency intends to give them? Tie my hands, sir—tie my hands behind my back! I'll fight the rascals without hands! Come on, sir! come on! By heavens! I think I see some now behind that rock! So—ho—o, Sulemin, So—o—ho; gently, my boy, gently—So—ho!"

GENERAL (getting behind Yusef).—"Verily, I do believe they are robbers. Now, don't sacrifice yourself, Yusef! Be calm; be deliberate. Take good aim when you shoot; aim at their heads. Remember my life is in your keeping."

Hitherto Yusef had evinced his excitement by turning very red in the face; he now evinced it by turning very pale, on account of the intense character of the pleasure he experienced in catching a glimpse of two muffled figures, crouching behind a rock on the road-side. But, somehow, Syed Sulemin, usually so docile and obedient, began to cut an extraordinary number of flourishes, and actually refused to proceed a step further Saladin, inspired by the capering of his rival, and supposing that it was preparatory to a race, dashed off without further notice, and in a few moments was close up to the rock. The figures rose; there were four. They were not robbers; they were only two Bedouin women, an old man, and a donkey, resting with a sack of wheat, on their way to the mill. I had scarcely noted these facts, when Syed Sulemin came thundering up with Yusef, who had drawn his pistols, and was ready for slaughter.

YUSEF.—" Where are the wretches? Let me at 'em! Pooh! only two women! only one old man! only a miserable ass! Come on, sir! come on! We'll find better game than that before long."

GENERAL.—" I sincerely hope not. Certainly, if we again discover human game, I shall dismount from Saladin, and let him proceed alone. On the whole, I think we are rather fortunate in not finding robbers on this occasion."

YUSEF.—" But the delight—the glory of the thing! The exquisite satisfaction of shedding blood. On, Sulemin, on. By heavens! if there's a robber within ten miles, we'll have him!"

GENERAL (seizing Yusef's bridle again).—" Now, I protest against this insane courage, Yusef; this flying in the face of Providence. Take it easy—take it easy. The very philosophy of life is to be content with what you've got. If you have friends instead of enemies around you, it is the will of Allah. Smoke the pipe of content. Be assured, good and evil fortune enough will come in due time; don't make yourself unhappy by bad dreams and sanguinary hopes. Bask in the sunshine of peace, while it lasts; cease that constant chafing for human blood. Sleep while you can sleep, and smoke while you can smoke. Depend upon it, there is no happiness in steaming it through the world this way; living at a railroad speed; wearing yourself out with internal fires; besides running the danger of bursting up, by destroying the escape-pipe of your courage. Take it easy, Yusef—that's the true philosophy of life."

Yusef (a little confused).—" But what is ease? A sitting hen takes it easy; it's her business—she likes it; she has a natural propensity for sitting. A mud-turtle basks in the sun; it suits him; he feels comfortable; he doesn't like running; his legs are too short. A snail travels slowly; he's a slow coach; he takes it easy, because he can't take it fast; he carries his house on his back, and it makes no difference where he goes or how long it takes him; he's always at home. But, do you think, O General, that I, Yusef Badra, renowned in history and in song throughout Syria, could take it easy if I were alone upon a desert, with six armed Bedouins bearing down upon me?"

General (thoughtfully).—" Why, no, Yusef—I don't see that you could well take it easy under those circumstances. In fact I rather think you'd take it fast. I'm tolerably certain that I would where the odds were so great against me. This is an extreme case, however."

Yusef (proudly).—" That's the beauty of it—there's where the principle lies. I couldn't stand it, you see. If there was only one Bedouin, I might sit still, and let him strike me the first blow, for pastime; but six!—six to one! No, sir, I couldn't take it easy in the common sense—I'd have to kill 'em; rip 'em up, gut 'em, scatter their brains on the four winds of heaven: Every man takes his ease in a different way, according to his capacity, inclination, or courage. The coward takes his ease in peace; the brave man in war. My case lies in blood—human blood, sir. When I wallow in it, I feel comfortable and happy—I'm perfectly easy then, only I want more—that's the only difficulty; I always want more; if it wasn't for that I'd be the happiest man living."

General.—" Certainly a very unfortunate propensity, as regards its operation upon the rest of mankind. Happily, we are differently organized, as you say; for if we all took our ease in killing, the world would be pretty easy before long."

Yusef.—"That's the beauty of it—the very principle of existence! A Turk takes his ease in smoke; a Frenchman in dancing; a German in beer, talk, and pipes; an Englishman in beefsteak; an American—pardon me, O General, I mean no disrespect in referring to your own words—an American in being uneasy. When he is uneasy he is easy, and when he is easy he is uneasy."

General (puzzled).—"Really, Yusef, I hardly know which side of the question you have placed me upon now. We seem to agree, and yet we don't agree—no—we differ and—I don't know! that's not right. One of us must be wrong —there's a mistake somewhere."

Yusef.—"Your Excellency is wrong."

General.—"Upon my word, it seems so; though I'm certain I started right. The fact is, Yusef, we must come to a compromise, and allow that there's right and wrong on both sides. All nations have their merits and their faults; there is good every where, if mankind would only profit by it. Extremes of laziness, or of restless ambition, are alike inimical to happiness. The whole universe is founded upon compromise; the harmonies of nature are compromises. Every tree and flower that springs from the earth yields its verdure or its fragrance by compromise with the elements. Life is a compromise; society, government, nations—all are compromises; and they who base their conduct upon an adherence to the lessons taught by the harmonies of nature, are most apt to enjoy what we call happiness in this world."

Yusef (enthusiastically).—"Most sublime and beloved General! Verily, that last touch of eloquence hath aroused my inmost soul! I am intensely enlightened and inspired by this discourse! By all the compromises! by all the harmonies of existence, I swear that this moment I could slay Hassin the Dragon-killer. I could devour the seven-headed Dragon, and wallow in the blood of Rabadab, the four-handed Giant! Nay, by all the ghosts of the gory dead—"

General (alarmed).—"Be calm, Yusef! be calm. Compose yourself! It was not my intention, in speaking thus, to arouse you in that frightful manner. Suppress those dreadful thoughts, I beseech you, and tell me what object that is in the distance. There! don't you see something like a stone box?"

Yusef.—"I do, most certainly. That, your excellency, is not a stone box, but a mill—the famous Mill of Malaha—where this night you shall sleep soundly, or my name's not Badra, the Destroyer of Robbers!"

From all I had heard respecting the accommodations of the mill, I naturally supposed that it was an extensive establishment kept by some wealthy miller, who, for the purpose of enjoying society in this remote region, had built an addition to it, where he entertained travelers of distinction, and perhaps furnished them with choice bread and wine of his own manufacture. I need not say that I was a little disappointed when we rode up and took a general survey of the premises. But as this again is an important matter, involving adventures of a very stirring character, I must reserve it for another chapter.

CHAPTER XXXV.

* THE MILL OF MALAHA.

I WISH it to be distinctly understood that I entertain no vindictive or revengeful feelings toward any body on account of the disappointment I experienced in the first view of the Mill of Malaha. To be candid, it arose partly from a credulous faith in every thing that the Arabs told me, however wonderful, and partly from a natural disposition to invest every thing with the charms of romance. Notwithstanding the practical sense of my companions, who believed nothing at all that was not in print, and who were continually producing authorities on every doubtful point, I secretly swallowed every thing miraculous, and filled up all the obscure parts with glowing anticipations, that were doomed never to be realized. Even at the time, I often suspected that such things were only to be found in the Arabian Nights; but somehow I could not help thinking they might turn out to be true, and on that hope hung an immense amount of anticipation. Bearing in mind, however, that my mission was of a practical character, I was always ready to admit the facts in the end, and to denounce the Arabs for their extravagant indulgence in hyperbole, as also to expose the fallacies of all travelers who make a practice of investing commonplace realities with the glowing absurdities of fiction. It may be set down as a rule that when a writer on Oriental life tells you what a pleasant thing it is not to be civilized; when he even professes to have some savage propensities in his nature, and has an unconquerable desire to be a wandering Ishmaelite, there must be something wrong in the man. Either he is making a book to be read by a public that continually thirsts for something strange and new, or wishes himself to appear in the light of a dark-minded, restless, unhappy man, so high above all the conventionalities of society, that to be a savage is the only condition really worthy of him; or, worse than all, there is so little of the genial and kind in his nature that he finds few to love him at home, finds fault with others for what he owes to himself, and becomes smitten with a morbid contempt for civilization. It reads very prettily, all this—especially if it be cleverly done. But let me tell you, my friends, there is a dreary, commonplace, comfortless reality about Arab life, with all its barbarous romance; a beggarly vagabondism that is entirely unworthy of being aspired to by any person of good principles or common sense; a bestiality that must make any one who has a respectable home turn to it with a grateful heart and an inward thankfulness that he was born in a tolerably decent country, and among a people, who, with all their affectations and absurdities, are yet something better than savages.

And now for the Mill. Behold it, as we wind down the rugged pathway toward the stream of Malaha—a little square stone building, half in ruins, with a flat top, perched over the water among the rocks, a camel browsing on the bushes near it, and a dozen lazy Arabs squatted down by the door smoking their chiboucks. That single glance was enough. Every thought of the hospitable old gentleman and his accomplished daughters; the flower-gardens, the choice home-made bread and sparkling wines of Lebanon, vanished in a moment. I said nothing; but rode quietly up to the door, where, with a misgiving of the sequel, I resigned my horse to the muleteers, and saw him, together with the horses of my companions, led off to a cave in the neighboring mountains. A very animated conversation now took place between our dragoman and the Arabs. The chief talker, a rugged ill-favored man, whose dark leathern skin looked darker still from the fact that his beard and eyebrows were covered with meal, was no other than the old miller himself, and the others were Bedouins who had come over from an encampment on the opposite side of the stream. As well as I could catch the drift of the conversation from Yusef's man ner and gestures, which I had now learned to interpret with considerable accuracy, it appeared to be this : that we, a traveling party, consisting of the Commander-in-Chief of all the military forces in America, a royal prince, son of the King of the United States, and an English Lord, whose palace at home was built of pure gold, wanted lodging for the night in the far-famed Mill of Malaha, of which we had read in ancient and modern history, and whose proprietor we had always regarded as the sublimest miller that ever the world had produced. On the other hand, it was urged by the miller that he was a devout Mussulman, and would never consent to having his mill defiled by the presence of a party of infidels, who were at best not fit to kiss the smallest toe of the great Prophet; that should he suffer us to sleep there, he would never more have a particle of luck, and ten chances to one the grindstones would fly in his face and kill him stone dead, or the mill itself would tumble down upon him after we had left, and make minced meat of himself and all his family. To which, as I took it, Yusef replied that, praised be Allah, we were convinced of the errors of our ways, and were on a pilgrimage to Jerusalem, where there was no earthly doubt we would join the standard of the Prophet in less than a month; and that, besides, being royal personages of boundless wealth, we would cheerfully pay as high as three piasters each (twelve and a half cents) for the accommodation of his establishment, together with a liberal *backshish* in the morning. In reply to which, the miller, with glistening eyes, stated that he was not that narrow-minded sort of person who could from any religious prejudices be guilty of so inhospitable an act as to turn from his doors a party of distinguished Howadji; that he always regarded the Americans and English as the most liberal and enlightened people in the world, next to the Arabs, and upon the assurance of five piasters each and such *backshish* as we deemed consistent with our rank and dignity, he would cheerfully consent to having the mill honored with our presence. Keeping in view his own interests, Yusef made answer to this by saying that he, being our responsible agent in all pecuniary matters, deemed it incumbent upon him. as a man of honor, known throughout Syria, and even to the remotest corners of England and America, as a dragoman, who never lied or took advantage of the liberality of his employers, to pay just and reasonable prices for every thing, and that he could not reconcile it to a sense of duty to pay more than four piasters; but that he had not the slightest doubt that the *backshish* would amount to treble that sum. At this the miller shook his head dismally, grunted a few words of doubt, which I interpreted to signify that he had become rather accustomed to promises of that kind; then puffed his chibouck awhile, and ended by waving his hand for us to enter. By this time it had begun to rain, and we were glad enough to find shelter.

If the external appearance of the mill was disheartening, the interior was absolutely dramatic and inspiring. Stables I had slept in; caves, haystacks, trees, and the broad canopy of heaven had afforded me lodgings in cases of emergency; but I had seen nothing half so strange or curious in the way of accommodations for a night's rest as the mill of Malaha. It was just high enough to stand up in where the arches that supported the roof ran up to a point; but these arches being very rough and irregular, and the ground, consisting chiefly of holes, it was necessary to crawl into the dark recesses on our hands and feet. The water made a tremendous rush underneath; and, looking through the broken parts of the floor, there was every prospect of tumbling through during the night, and being carried down among the wheels, and afterward deposited in the lake of El·Huleh. Following Yusef, who carried a dim lamp in his hand, we narrowly escaped being ground to pieces by two grindstones, which flew round continually at a tremendous rate, without any covering over them; and in the course of time having worked our way over several holes and through a good many puddles of foul water, we found ourselves on a sort of elevation about a foot high, close by the grindstones again, where we learned that we were to spend the night. The dust and chaff, together with the intense darkness notwithstanding the lamp, and a thick cloud of smoke from a crowd of Arabs, hid away somewhere in the obscurity, afforded me reasonable grounds for thinking that if any one of us ever lived to see daylight again, it would only be through the intervention of Providence: certainly there was nothing here to encourage such a hope.

The ground being somewhat soft, I had the curiosity to feel it, and then take up a handful and smell it; by which means I became sensible of the fact that it consisted of a very rich deposit of manure. However, having a couple of mattresses, we spread them over it, and found that it made a very warm bed, although it must be admitted that the points of rock which came through it did not produce an agreeable sensation when they came in contact with our ribs.

"A stunning place, this," said the English captain, good-humoredly. "Upon my word, I think we'll have a jolly time of it to-night."

"Yes; very jolly: the fleas are getting lively already," said the tall Southerner, scratching himself fiercely.

"Coffee!" said I; "coffee, Yusef. Gentlemen, I hold it as a principle that coffee is an elixir for all the ills that flesh is heir to, provided it be sweetened with the sugar of—"

"Lead," suggested the captain.

"No, sir; the sugar of content. Coffee expands the soul, warms the imagination; sends a cheerful glow throughout the entire man after the toils of travel, and acts as nature's balmy restorer, when sleep is banished by fortuitous circumstances, or by—"

"Fleas," said the captain, suddenly starting, as if stung by a wasp. "What an abominable nuisance they are! I'll venture to assert that they are as large here as humble-bees. Never felt any thing like them in my life! Stunning, quite stunning, I assure you!"

There was no doubt of it. I began to feel them myself, though I had always boasted of being proof against such petty annoyances. They actually began to pierce like a thousand needles. Sometimes they pierced like cambric needles, and sometimes like large sail-needles; and very often they pierced like all the needles that ever were manufactured, put together in assorted bunches. While Yusef and Francisco were absent boiling the coffee outside of the mill, and getting supper ready, we entertained ourselves scratching a trio, and jumping now and then nearly out of our skins in the most desperate efforts to shake off the vermin.

Presently supper appeared; and, I say it in justice to our dragoman, a most excellent supper it was. He was a capital cook and caterer, and fed us like princes, as he always represented us to be. The Arabs crept around us out of holes in the walls and dark corners, and while we ate they looked on with greedy and longing eyes, and said a great deal on the subject which we could not comprehend. They seemed very lean and hungry, and talked rapidly as each mouthful disappeared. It was evident that they built some hopes upon coming in at the end of the feast. We told Yusef to give them something to eat, which he did; when, feeling very happy and comfortable, we had our chiboucks lit, and smoked our Latakia tobacco in great state, as became persons of royal dignity.

I gradually dropped off into a doze, a mere doze, for I scorn the charge of having slept a wink that night. The grating of the grindstones, the everlasting clatter of tongues, the dust, chaff, smoke, and fleas, to say nothing of the roar of the water down below, were enough to banish all hope of sleep; I merely closed my eyes to try how ridiculous it would feel. How long they remained closed I scarcely know; it was not long, however, for I soon heard a heavy breathing close by my head, and felt the warm breath of some monster on my face. I knew it to be no Arab; it blew and snuffed altogether unlike any thing of the human kind. Thinking it might be all fancy, I cautiously put out my hand in the dark (Yusef having carried the lamp away), and began to feel around me. For some moments I could discover nothing, but in waving my hand around I at length touched something —something that sent the blood flying back to my heart a good deal quicker than it ever flew before. To tell the honest truth, I never was so startled in all the previous adventures of my life. The substance that I put my hand on was bare and warm; it was wet also and slimy, and had large nostrils with which it seemed to be in the act of smelling me previous to the act of mastication. With the quickness of lightning I jerked up my hand, and felt it glide along a skin covered with long rough hair; the next instant my ears were stunned by the most dreadful noises, which resembled, as I thought in the horror of the moment, the roaring of a full-grown lion. But it was not the roaring of a lion; it was only the braying of an ass. The monster was a Syrian ass. There were two of them, and they both began to bray; they brayed in concert; and I declare in all sincerity, it was the most intolerable concert I ever heard. Had it been a lion, the consequences might have been serious to the whole party, as well as to the animal himself, for I should certainly have called upon Yusef to bring out his pistols and guns, in which event there is not the least doubt that some of us would have fallen victims to the conflicting wrath of the rival lions.

Oh, Lamartine! Alphonse de Lamartine! if thou couldst have witnessed our sufferings on that occasion, I'm certain thy tender eyes would have shed floods of briny tears! In thy weeping Pilgrimage thou didst weep for the past, the present, and the future; for the great and the little; for the happy and the wretched; for the birds of the air and the beasts of the field; for the great leviathan of the deep and the smallest creeping thing earthly. Thou didst weep when thou wert happy and when thou wert sad; when thy heart was full and thy tongue refused its office; and when thy tongue spake and thy heart in turn was sealed with sorrow; thou didst weep that the land was stricken with ruin, and thou didst weep that the ruin was sublime—that thou wert gifted with the power to weep, and that there was cause to weep—that mankind was wicked and Alphonse de Lamartine the only living mourner in the land of desolation; that the little wren was happy and the Great Philosopher miserable; that the Great Philosopher was a Poet, and the little wren neither a poet nor a philosopher but a simple wren. Thou didst weep from the beginning unto the end of thy Pilgrimage; thou wert born with tears in thine eyes, and thou hast shed them copiously unto the present day; wherever thou hast

MILL OF MALAHA.

roamed, thy footsteps are marked in tear-drops; thy whole life has been a constant overflow of tears; thy lachrymal ducts have never yet been dry, and never will, until the tear-bags within are withered up in dust; nay, even then thou wilt start new floods from that feeling heart, and weep that the world hath lost a Poet and a Philosopher. Wherefore, I —a simple General in the Bobtail Militia, following in thy footsteps on a Crusade against the Mists of Fancy—do venture to assert that hadst thou seen us in this old mill, beset by fleas, donkeys, and filthy Arabs, thou wouldst have opened thy flood-gates of sympathy and refreshed us with balmy sighs and copious showers of gentle tears.

Now, as long as our grievances were confined to vermin, dirt, and noisy Arabs, we bore them very cheerfully, and even admitted that little afflictions of that kind add materially to the spice of travel; but when it came to making asses of us by placing us on a par with such animals, it was altogether too much to be borne. I had often heard that traveling makes one acquainted with strange bed-fellows, but in all my previous experience I had never been subjected to the mortification of sleeping in the same bed with two genuine asses.

"What," said I, fired with honest indignation, "are we to stand this? Breathes there a man with soul so dead that he'll voluntarily sleep with a pair of vile asses?"

"Ho, Yusef!" cried the Captain, "we'll be ass-assinated if you don't turn these abominable beasts out. We are in danger of being devoured bodily."

Yusef declared that he was very sorry, but it was a Mohammedan custom to show great tenderness and respect to animals of the brute kind; he would ask the miller to put the asses out, but could not insist upon it as a matter of right. Another exciting conversation now took place in which all the Arabs participated. Yusef stormed, threatened, and swore; the old miller protested, remonstrated, and finally declared that he could not be guilty of any thing so inhuman; that he would sooner drive out of his house on a rainy night the brother of his affections than the asses of his heart; so, to make peace, the asses of his heart were suffered to remain.

I will not undertake to describe how we spent the rest of that memorable night: how the grindstones came within an inch of grinding us to death every time we stretched our legs out; how in attempting to escape from the furious attacks of the fleas we got ourselves involved under the hoofs of the asses; how the old miller stopped smoking about midnight, and by the united assistance of all his Arabs succeeded in the course of two hours in getting his mill stopped; how every one of them talked all the rest of the night, and went to sleep about daylight; and how we got up at the same time and made a vow never again to stop at the Mill of Malaha.

At sunrise we were mounted, and on our way toward the Sea of Galilee.

CHAPTER XXXVI.

THE REBEL SHEIK.

Our road this morning lay along the base of Jebel Egil, on the right side of the valley El Huleh, as we faced toward Tiberias. We met several caravans of camels and mules, and passed numerous herds of cattle and a few Bedouin villages. The weather was mild and pleasant, with a slight sprinkle of rain during the forenoon. On the ridge dividing the valley of El Huleh from Lake Tiberias, or the Sea of Galilee, we had a fine view of both lakes, the one lying in the broad plain through which we had passed, gleaming brightly through a mass of verdure; the other, famed as the sacred waters of Galilee, almost encircled by barren mountains, dim in the haze, and still and desolate as it lay outspread before us in the noonday sun. Far and near, which ever way we looked, the mountains were blanched with the scorching heat of summer; and all the rains of autumn were still swallowed by the thirsty earth, and still there was the same dreary waste of whitish stones and sodless heights; dreary and shadowless, yet rich beyond all that earth could yield in the history of Him who had stilled the tempest and walked upon the waters.

As we wound our way among the barren rocks we saw several Arabs skulking about the cliffs, armed with long guns, and apparently watching our motions with keen interest. By certain signs they seemed to communicate with others in advance; and now and then, when they thought we were not looking, they disappeared and ran along on the other side of the ridge, so as to keep pace with us. Our dragoman looked uncommonly anxious and downcast, which made me think he was very much afraid that some of these suspicious vagabonds would get away before he could get a good chance to shoot them. On this account, as I supposed, he kept very close to us, we being altogether unarmed, so as to be on the spot when the attack commenced, and at the same time afford us protection with his courage and fire-arms.

But it seemed as if we were doomed never to enjoy a good adventure in the way of an attack from the Arabs. No matter how fervently we wished to be robbed (having only a trifle of small change about us), I verily believe had we hung bags of gold on our backs, and invited every prowling thief we met on the way to shoot at us; had we proclaimed aloud that it would greatly oblige us to be peppered with slugs or knocked on the head, so as to have a genuine adventure, to put down in our journals, and talk about when we got home, not one would have dared to undertake such a thing, so efficiently were we protected by our dragoman. These fellows, who watched us so closely, were, as we soon discovered, the followers of a noted refugee from the Turkish Government, formerly the Sheik of Baalbek, who had fortified himself in the ruins of Khan Jub Yusef.

As we rode up in front of the Khan, the Sheik came out and received us with great civility. He was followed by a few armed men, who, upon seeing that there were no spies in the party, dropped off quietly, and sat down on the rocks, some distance off. A long conversation took place between the two heroes (our own and the hero of the Khan), the substance of which appeared to be this: that the Sheik, unable to endure the oppressive sway of the Turks, had taken up arms against them, resolved to die fighting for the freedom of his country. All the followers that he could prevail upon to join his standard amounted only to nineteen; yet with this handful of men he had fought and slain more Turks than he could count. Himself and his party were sentenced to be hunted throughout the land, and shot down, tortured, or mutilated, wherever they could be found. Several had been killed at different times in battle; three had recently been captured in a foraging expedition down by Tiberias, and, after suffering the cruelest tortures, were shot and hung upon poles, as a warning to the rest of the band. For himself (the Sheik), there was no hope but to kill a few more Turks before he died. Already he had been hunted like a wild beast throughout the length and breadth of the land; his comrades had been scattered and shot down till only himself and six or eight remained; but they were resolved to sell their lives dearly.

The Sheik was one of the finest-looking men I had seen in the East. He was about thirty years of age, tall and well-proportioned, and easy and dignified in his manners. His features were of the true Oriental cast, regular and pleasing in repose, but indicative of a fiery temperament, and the unlimited sway of the passions when once aroused. Nothing could be finer than his eyes—dark, brilliant, and piercing; at times gentle as a woman's, yet alternately, as he changed from calmer themes to the oppression of the Turks, flashing with a savage hatred that was perfectly withering in its ferocity. His costume was rich and picturesque. It consisted of a handsome turban, which set off his dark flowing beard to great advantage; loose trowsers, profusely embroidered; a costly vest, ornamented with braid and silver buttons; and over his shoulders an ample robe, resembling a poncho, of rich and beautiful colors. There was a natural ease in all his movements, an unaffected dignity in his manners, a genuine eloquence in the rich tones of his voice and the copious flow of his language, that I have seldom seen equaled, and never surpassed, in any other part of the world.

Within the Khan we caught a glimpse of his wife, a beautiful young creature, who bounded away like a frightened fawn as we entered. No wonder the Sheik guarded well his ruined Khan, for it held within it a living treasure—a being of grace and beauty—whom he doubtless loved with all the passion of his race, whose gentle and confiding eyes were all that smiled upon him now.

No: there was another treasure, dearer to him perhaps than his wife. An Arab may have something like a true regard for a woman; there is no reason why he should not, except that it is not the custom of the country, and an Arab regulates his affections pretty much like ourselves—according to custom. In Oriental countries it is customary to love a favorite horse with great constancy and devotion: the Sheik of Baalbek had a beautiful horse, and the probability is that he was even more attached to it than he was to his beautiful wife. Nor is it (to reduce every thing to the pure ore of truth) at all unlikely that he had two or three more wives, equally charming, hidden away in some dark corner of the ruins. The reason why my suspicions were aroused on this subject was, that he took a great deal of pride in introducing us to his horse, while not the slightest intimation escaped him that such a thing as a wife was any where about the premises.

It was my first sight of a genuine horse of the desert. I had seen in Zanzibar, and even in Washington, horses called Arabians, and probably they were of Arab blood; but there is just as much difference between the ordinary Arab horse and the true Bedouin breed (so seldom found except in the deserts) as there is between a cart-horse and a racer. This was certainly one of the most beautiful animals of its kind. The delicacy of the features, the fine flashing eye, the small sharp ears, the proudly arched neck, the clean and symmetrical limbs, were all indicative of the purest Arabian blood. What struck me most was the fierce pawing of the ground, the perpetual chafing, the restless and constant swaying to and fro of the head, all so fraught with a high spirit yet unbroken by the cruelty of man; so like the motions of a caged beast, that frets and sways unceasingly in its barred prison, and ever pants for liberty, till the fire within burns away, and it dies untamed and savage to the last. Yet with all this chafing, this eloquent appeal for a return to desert-life, he seemed to know and love his master well: a word, a touch, a motion of the hand, even a glance of that flashing eye, thrilled through him, and caused him to snuff the air, and quiver as if burning with some ungovernable impulse.

The ordinary Syrian horse possesses many fine qualities, though of course it can bear no comparison with the pure Arab. For powers of endurance, sureness of foot, spirit, and gentleness under proper management, it is difficult to find his equal. At Beirut almost every variety can be found at reasonable prices.

CHAPTER XXXVII.

THE SYRIAN HORSES.

WHILE on the subject of horses, it may not be amiss to mention that we were extremely fortunate in that respect. No person who saw us mounted, and on our journey, would, for a moment, have supposed so, from the physical aspect of our animals; but it was in remarkable points of character, rather than in the remarkable points which adorned their forms, that their chief merit consisted. Indeed, it would have been difficult to find four horses, either in Syria or any other part of the world, to compare with ours in general intelligence and reflective powers. That there was something akin to the noble faculty of thought, something of a much higher order than mere instinct, in every one of them, was beyond all question. As for Saladin, it is but simple justice to him to say, that he had a head that would have done honor to some of the Howadji whom I had met during my wanderings in the East. Not only did he carry an uncommon amount of brains in it, but he possessed, in an extraordinary degree, the faculty of doing himself credit by the manner in which he made use of them. His brains and his judgment went in partnership, as a general thing; though, as all great mortals have their weak points, so I am forced to admit that Saladin had his. Strong in his passions, he sometimes suffered them to have unlimited sway over both his brains and his judgment, which is a weakness common to genius; but if he was bitter in his resentments, he was also devoted in his attachments. There was no nonsense or affectation about him of any kind; he professed nothing that he did not accomplish, in a zealous, off-hand manner. An enemy to the back-bone, he was a friend to the very bottom of his stomach. God bless old Saladin! I love him, with all his faults! Day after day how he toiled for me up-hill and down-hill, over beds of rock and beds of mud, in sunshine and in storm, wherever I wished to go—save in those extreme cases, already referred to, when the fire of genius or the excess of vindictive passions caused him to forget, for the moment, that he carried so true a friend upon his back.

The horse upon which the English Captain rode, was the most classical in form of any in the party; that is to say, there was a rotundity of body in him that continually reminded me of the fat horse in front of the Roman Capitol, and of the bronze horses in Naples, which were probably modeled upon animals of the horse species that had recently been drowned. The Captain, doubtless, in view of this fact, as well as on account of his warlike spirit, called him Waterloo, but it was chiefly for fleetness of foot that Waterloo was distinguished, in the eyes of the Captain. This conceit I always regarded as a weakness on the part of my friend; because, to tell the truth, Waterloo was the only really clumsy animal in the party. The Captain, however, was firmly persuaded that Waterloo was born for a racer; that he, Waterloo, had been a racer in early life, and had strained the muscle of one of his fore-legs, which accounted for the fact that he always came in at the end of every race on the journey. All that was necessary was, to keep the switch going; and certainly it did seem essential, for the moment the Captain stopped switching, Waterloo stopped running. The switch was just as indispensable a part of his machinery as the piston-rod to a steam-engine. When we set out in the morning, the right arm of the Captain commenced working, just as regularly as machinery could work, and it only stopped when it was requisite that Waterloo should also stop. By night both parties were entirely exhausted with the labors of locomotion. But the most singular part of it was, that my friend would never admit that Waterloo was not naturally a full-blooded racer. He would even go so far as to bet his hat on a trial of speed with Saladin, which was a proposition so preposterous that I never could listen to it without a smile of disdain.

The little iron-gray, upon which the tall Southerner rode, was, perhaps, the most ferocious and determined of the whole cavalcade, when aroused from his habitual sobriety, by any inspiring cause. We never came in sight of the Portuguese party, consisting of Dr. Mendoza, the Madam, Emanuel Bal thos, and their muleteers, that the iron-gray did not become perfectly frantic, and cause all his companions to become frantic by his capers. I don't know what was the reason—I only know that there was no beautiful little palfrey called Zulieka in our party.

Yusef's famous steed of the desert, Syed Sulemin, was part and parcel of himself. They certainly must have been born at the same time; nursed in the same manger; educated in the same school; inspired by nature with the same warlike spirit and the same savage propensities; so congenial were their souls, so well adapted the one to the other; so thoroughly identified were they in all the relations of life. If Yusef said, let us go, it was go; if he said, let us stay, it was stay; let us dance, it was dance; let us fight, it was fight. No matter what he thought, said, or did, Syed Sulemin thought, said, and did the same—not that they spoke exactly the same language, but there was a perfect understanding of tongues between them. The only material difference that I could discover in their points of character was, that when any thing like a real enemy appeared, Syed Sulemin never stopped until Yusef said stop, rather decidedly; and it was evident that he did so then more from habit than any positive desire he had to avoid a hostile meeting. It was really affecting to witness the tenderness that existed between our dragoman and his beloved horse. Every morning, regularly, before mounting, Yusef greeted Syed Sulemin in the most brotherly manner. He asked him how he felt; how had he slept; what was the general state of his health; had any body stolen his oats; and upon being answered, as Syed Sulemin was in the habit of answering, by a peculiar working of the ears, a neighing and nickering, and other well-understood signs, Yusef could never restrain his affection, but invariably hugged him round the neck, exchanged kisses with him, and shook hands with his fore-foot to show him that they were still devoted friends, and never could be separated by any adversity of fortune. Often as this was repeated, Yusef never seemed to tire of it; on the contrary, whenever we arrived at a Khan where there was a concourse of people, the very first thing he did upon dismounting was to say: Kiss me, you beauty! and when Syed Sulemin had kissed him, Shake hands with me, you rascal! and when Syed Sulemin had shaken hands, Fight me, you coward! and when Syed had fought him, Dance for me, you cripple! and when Syed had danced, Now fall down on your knees, and say you love me, you brute! and when Syed had finished doing and saying all these things, and a great many others, Yusef looked triumphantly upon the assembled Arabs, as much as to say: Wretches! did you ever see the like of that before? Filthy barbarians! did you ever hear a horse talk English like that? Miserable bumpkins! don't you perceive that *I* am Yusef Badra, the renowned Dragoman and Destroyer of Robbers? Benighted dogs! don't you understand, at a glance, that this is the famous Steed of the Desert, Syed Sulemin—that cost ten millions of piasters before he was born!

The only time I ever knew Yusef and Syed Sulemin to disagree was on the occasion of an extraordinary display of horsemanship in which Yusef seldom indulged. It was at a small village on the road-side, where a large concourse of the inhabitants, including a number of women, had gathered on the house-tops to see the Frangi pass, especially to see Yusef, who had friends here, and who was generally regarded as a miraculous and most astounding character by all villagers throughout Syria. On this occasion, he was resolved to show them his best specimen of horsemanship. Dashing up gallantly in front of the whole crowd, he whirled the *djeered* over his head, and then flung it up in the air to a prodigious height. As soon as it struck the ground he was on the spot; when, with a proud smile of conscious skill, he hung over in his saddle till his hands reached the earth, and grasped the stick firmly so as to lift it up and whirl it over his head again. The Arabs were astounded; but the sensation was premature.

Yusef neither lifted up the stick nor whirled it over his head on that occasion. Had he even lifted himself up without the stick, he might have sustained the illusion by a series of fictitious flourishes; but he remained hanging there by the saddle in the most pitiable state of helplessness. He tugged, and writhed, and struggled, much in the style of a cat hung by the tail. It was all one: there he dangled entirely unable either to lift himself up or extricate his feet from the stirrups.

It was an awkward position for any man; positively humiliating for one who was regarded as an Admirable Crichton by the whole female population of Syria; more than awkward and humiliating in the presence of a large concourse of experienced riders; but intensely deplorable as a display of horsemanship on the part of the renowned Badra, the Prince of Dragomans and Destroyer of Robbers. The Arabs on the house-tops laughed aloud; the women tittered and screamed, and, to the best of my belief, asked Yusef if he stood in need of their assistance, which was an exceedingly satirical and feminine question; for the truth was, Yusef didn't stand at all; if he needed any assistance he rather hung in need of it.

Fortunately, however, Syed Sulemin stood. It was admirable to behold the resignation with which he turned his head and contemplated the struggles of his friend and master. What else could he do? It was not in horse-flesh to lend a helping hand on such an occasion. Syed Sulemin could not reasonably be expected to take hold of Yusef in his teeth and throw him up on his back again; hence, like a philosopher, he calmly awaited the result.

Mustapha, the muleteer, happening to come along about this time, and perceiving his renowned master hanging by the leg in that critical position, stood by and contemplated the scene for some moments in profound astonishment. Had he been a vindictive or revengeful man, he would, in remembrance of the beatings he had received in Baneas and other places, have passed on; but Mustapha had a kind and forgiving heart. As soon as he discovered that it really was not an intentional display of horsemanship, he seized Yusef in his arms and extricated the embarrassed leg from the stirrups.

I am sorry to say that Yusef, owing, perhaps, to a flow of blood to the head, took his stick immediately upon regaining the saddle, and struck Syed Sulemin several times with great fury; which Syed Sulemin resented by running away from the scene of the disaster, and never stopping till he reached the next village. Furthermore, that soon after our arrival at that village, where we spent the night, Yusef, who had never spoken a word since the disaster, now broke forth and charged Mustapha with having stolen his oats on the previous night. This Mustapha denied most indignantly. Yusef said that to deny so palpable a fact was to call him a liar; whereupon he fell to work with his stick and beat Mustapha; nor is it probable that he would have desisted until he had fairly flayed the poor fellow from head to foot, had I not interfered and sternly protested against such a severe mode of punishment. Next morning Syed Sulemin and his master kissed and made up; and Mustapha relieved his feelings on the road by riding on top of the baggage on his mule, some distance in the rear of Yusef, and convulsing himself and all the other muleteers with silent laughter; as also by showing every body, except our dragoman, how a *djeered* may be picked up in certain cases.

To complete this sketch, I may as well add that, besides the four horses above described, we had three baggage mules, all respectable animals in their way. They belonged to the Arabs who drove them, and were much like their masters—rugged and unpromising in appearance, but capable of enduring any amount of fatigue, when driven to it by the force of circumstances. The only fault they had, was an unprofitable habit of lying down with our baggage in the middle of every marsh and river that lay across our road. It was a habit equally unprofitable to both parties, because it damaged our provisions, saturated our bedding, ruined our books and maps, put us out of temper, and did the mules no good whatever, inasmuch as they only increased the weight by the amount of water soaked up in that way, besides the beatings they received for the trouble. But it was no use to reason with them; they would do it; somehow it afforded them satisfaction.

Before proceeding on our journey to the Sea of Galilee, I must not forget another remarkable feature that usually was prominent in our travels. While we are winding our way toward Tiberias, with nothing but bare and desolate rocks on both sides, permit me to introduce you to our friend and fellow-traveler, Tokina.

Attached to our party was a small donkey, which often excited my wonder by his great spirit and powers of endurance. Tokina was his name; and, although it could not be denied that he was an ass—a perfect ass, I may say—yet he was a most sensible little fellow, and had a soul very much above any common ass. He was not much bigger than a Newfoundland dog; but he had an amount of ambition concealed beneath his shaggy little hide that would have done honor to any horse in Syria. If his ears were long, so was his head; he carried a good deal in it as well as on it.

There was not an inch of the way from Beirut to the summit of Mount Lebanon, and from the summit of Mount Lebanon to Damascus, and from Damascus to Jerusalem, that he did not bear himself bravely under all circumstances; never once flagging, however great his burden; always trotting along briskly, tumbling into rivers and ditches, and climbing out again as much alive as ever; carrying immense lazy Arabs on his back up hill and down hill, and running away now and then, and kicking all the mules within his reach. Tokina was not only a remarkable ass, but a transcendentalist. There was no telling what he was about half the time, he maintained such an aspect of profound wisdom, and used such obscure and uncouth language to explain himself. He was also something of a politician; that is to say, he was very fond of any body that gave him oats, and always wagged his ears and smiled pleasantly when he expected little attentions of that kind. When imposed upon by unmerciful riding, he would bear it all patiently, never tripping until a good opportunity occurred of making something by it; and then he would stumble into a ditch, as if by accident, and come out rejoicing without saddle or rider. I often imagined when he brayed on occasions of this kind that he meant to say: "Bismillah! you are in the mud now! See how I throw dirt on you! You needn't think to impose upon me because I'm little. By the beard of the Prophet! a pretty fellow you are, truly! Two hundred pounds' weight nearly riding on a little chap like me! But don't think because you're a bigger ass than I am that you can come it over me in this way much longer. I won't stand it; if I do may I be turned into a two-legged animal, and walk on end all the days of my life!" Whereupon he would kick up his heels and dash off, laughing to himself in such wise that it was perfectly human. Then to catch him was a job that afforded us infinite diversion; to see him dodge under the mules, and run behind and before the horses, and upset the Arabs that were on foot; it was such innocent relaxation for a great mind. Being ridden upon he seemed to regard as one of the necessary evils of society, and bore it always as long as he could; the greatest ass in the world could not do more. Doubtless he saw how the big people around him rode on the little people, and how the principle extends from the highest to the lowest of the living kind—those with vertical as well as those with horizontal backs. If he made use of his senses, he could not help perceiving that the various governments of Europe rode on Turkey; that Turkey rode on the Pashas of Syria; that the Pashas of Syria rode on Yusef Badra, the Destroyer of Robbers; that Yusef rode on Mustapha, and Mustapha on the back of his mule; that life is a general system of riding and being ridden upon, and even the smallest of asses has a weight of despotism to bear upon his back.

I have often thought that the auto-biography of a Syrian ass would be most interesting and instructive. What strange revelations he could give us of character, adventure, and book-making! What valuable reflections on the antiquities of Palestine! What rich and copious notes on affairs of Government! Pardon any thing thou may'st deem amiss in these remarks, O Tokina! for I know and love thee well, and mean thee no offense. If thou should'st feel at all hurt, remember that I, your best friend, who have saved thee many a beating, am of the human species myself; and accept as a peace-offering the sketch herewith appended, in which I have endeavored to do justice to thy personal beauty, and at the same time show the world that thou art grievously imposed upon!

TOKINA.

CHAPTER XXXVIII

THE SEA OF GALILEE.

Soon after leaving the ruins of Khan Jub Yusef, we entered upon a bed of solid rock. It was a perfect picture of desolation. Scarcely so much as a blade of glass was in sight. All was blanched and barren around for many miles, and there was no sign of life save the bleating of a few sheep, and the sad lowing of camels from the valley. The pathway was marked by holes worked in the rocks by mules and caravans. It had been traveled over in the same way for centuries upon centuries past. As we came out toward the brow of the hill overlooking the lake there was a change in the scene more like some enchanting optical illusion than any thing real. There lay outspread before us in the calm of the evening the beautiful valley of Genesareth, its green fields and groves of olives glistening, after the morning showers, in a flood of rich sunshine. The lake was placid and clear, and light clouds were sleeping calmly on the tops of the mountains. Bare and desolate were those craggy heights, yet rich beyond all the powers of art in the glow of the evening sun. Descending by a stony path, we at length entered the valley, leaving to the left the village of Tell Hum. We stopped a while at an old ruin called the Khan Minyah, where we saw a few ragged Arabs sitting out on the roof, smoking their pipes, and listening to the traditional romances of some old story-teller. A few compliments passed, some questions were asked and answered, on both sides, when we rode on through the low and well-watered plain, amid groves of fig-trees and olives. The air was deliciously soft and balmy. A fresh scent of flowers arose from the earth, and around us there were green slopes of grass, and banks of fragrant herbs, and thick shrubberies of oleander in full bloom. Camels browsed lazily among the bushes; herds of sheep were scattered over the openings of meadow, and lambs ran frisking from us as we passed; the cackling of hens and the distant barking of dogs about the villages fell pleasantly on the ear; and sometimes we crossed little streams of limpid water, lingering like ourselves to catch each beauty by the wayside, yet ever journeying on to the Sea of Death. Here and there we saw a swarthy Bedouin, seated upon the rocks with his pipe in his hand, watching the smoke from his lips as it curled upward, and vanished in the air. Pelicans stood upon the shores of the lake peering into the clear water in search of prey; and the dapper duck sported about on its surface, diving out of sight as we approached. Yusef meantime entertained us with the wonderful history of Hassin, the Dragon-killer; telling us all about the way in which Hassin outwitted the Grand Vizier, and slew the most ferocious seven-headed dragon that ever existed; how he went off to court the daughter of the Sultan, a cruel Princess who had a palace built of the skulls of her lovers, and only wanted one more skull to finish it; how she set him to work to test the sincerity of his professions by ordering him to eat at a single meal forty cows, four hundred sheep, two thousand chickens, and a thousand baskets of bread; also to drink twenty or thirty hogsheads of wine, and empty every well of water within a circuit of ten miles; how Hassin, by helping a giant out of a cobweb, in which he (the giant) had become entangled under the disguise of a fly, so won upon the regard of that distinguished person that he made himself as small as an ordinary man, for convenience, and disguised in Hassin's clothes did eat all the cows, sheep, chickens, and bread, and drink all the wine and water, and then call for more, protesting that such trifles as these only gave him an appetite; how Hassin eventually carried off the Princess, and lived with her in a palace of gold ornamented with diamonds and precious stones, and became known throughout the whole world as the greatest of Sultans, and was called ever after Hassin, the Dragon-killer.

In due time we emerged from the bushes, and came out upon the pebbly beach of the lake, not far beyond Ain-et-Tin. We rode at once into the clear sparkling water. It was pure as crystal, and so calm that the mountains on the other side seemed suspended in the air, and the reflection of the sky was as rich in quiet beauty as the sky itself. The ruined villages along the shores presented strange and mystic pictures in their inverted shadows; palm-trees overhung the deep with all their mirrored richness of outline; white ruins of mosques glittered in the distance; the naked and craggy mountains behind were steeped in an atmosphere of purple; and the waters and the mountains were wrapt in the sublimity of repose and the hallowed associations of the past.

Much of the pleasure we experienced in viewing these scenes, it must be admitted, arose from the physical comfort we enjoyed in the genial glow of the evening, after our sad experience in crossing the snow-capped heights of Jebel-esh Sheik, and our sufferings in the Mill of Malaha. Apart from the scriptural interest so interwoven with every spot around the Sea of Galilee, and the gratification of finding some place upon which to refresh the eye, after days of travel through desert regions of parched earth and sterile hills, there is in reality but little in the natural scenery about the lake, unaccompanied by freshening rains and a glowing sky, to attract attention. The valley of Genesareth is certainly a charming spot, but the charm is greatly heightened by the predisposition to be enchanted in the eye of the beholder. Around the shores of the lake the mountains are much the same as all the mountains throughout Palestine; and it is only in certain conditions of the atmosphere that they acquire that beauty which had so delighted us. This I think it due to the reader to state, in order that he may not be disappointed should he ever visit that region.

Continuing along the shores of the lake for a few miles, we took to the road again, and soon arrived at the village of Medjdel, a collection of miserable huts pleasantly situated a short distance from the water, under the brow of an abrupt cliff. Medjdel is interesting as the birth-place of Mary Magdalene. We had no time to explore the caves or artificial grottoes in the cliff.

Passing over a rocky and precipitous path, along the shores of the lake, we at length beheld the castle and ruins of Tiberias, once the capital of Galilee.

Tiberias is handsomely situated on a slope facing the lake. It is a filthy and dilapidated town, built in the Saracenic style, and is at present in a wretched state of ruin and decay. One or two mosques in the upper part on the hill-side, and a few scattering palm-trees among the ruins of the ancient city, give it something of an Oriental character. The foundations of the old walls and the remains of the ruined gateways are still standing; and the broken columns and friezes scattered about the outskirts of the town bear evidence of its grandeur in by-gone centuries. The first view, on the approach, embraces the ruined castle on the top of the hill and the immense gateway and fortifications. From these it would appear that in the days of its prosperity Tiberias must have been a city of considerable importance. Columns and cornices of massive proportions, beautifully cut, lie partially imbedded in the ground; and large blocks of stone, which evidently occupied in remote periods a prominent place in the temples and palaces, are scattered about for many miles. Portions of the ancient walls are nearly perfect; but the greater part seem to have been shaken down by some convulsion of nature—probably the great earthquake which destroyed Safed—or shattered into ruin by the ravages of the wars between the Turks and Syrians. This city was once the capital of Galilee, and was famed in later periods of its history as the principal seat of Rabbinical learning. It contains at present a population of several thousand, chiefly Jews, who hold it by sufferance of the Turks. Some of the most learned of the Rabbi composed and promulgated their works here, and at one period it boasted institutions of learning and historical research unequaled by any in the East. The streets are narrow and unpaved, the houses are of filthy appearance, and the aspect of the inhabitants sickly and emaciated. Unlike the larger towns in Syria through which we had passed, Tiberias showed no symptoms of European influence. The turbans and fezzes, the loose flowing robes and Oriental slippers, the sashes of rich silks, and all the peculiarities of costume which distinguish a purely Oriental people, existed here without change or innovation. Many of the Jewish women, whom we accidentally saw as we passed by the doors, had fine features but seemed wasted and haggard from sickness. The children were gaudily dressed in red and yellow robes, and were remarkable for their beauty. The shops are mean and filthy. A lethargy apparently hung over the place. Turbaned and dark-bearded men, with downcast eyes and sallow faces, walked slowly through the narrow streets, and seemed to sigh as if they bore some weight upon them that an eternity of years could not remove. Vailed and shrouded women glided in from the doorways, and the ghosts of shriveled old women sat crouchingly in the sun, shaking their palsied heads, and moaning as if they never more could feel its genial warmth. Starved and hairless dogs staggered about through the filth, stopping here and there to scratch up the bones of some carcass; foul odors filled the air, and green and fœtid pools of water lay stagnant among the ruins.

We stopped at the only tolerable house in the place, a sort of hotel for Frank travelers, kept by one Wiseman, a German Jew. Our arrival occasioned the liveliest commotion throughout the establishment. Women and children ran all about, screaming at the top of their voices that the Howadji had come—to be in a hurry—to get out of the way—to stop making such a noise—to be stirring about, and not stand staring at one another like fools; while we, calling for water, sat down in the big room, and heard water echoed all over the house in German, Italian, and Arabic; but saw nothing of it for half an hour at least. Herr Wiseman, our host, was all that a host could be, good-humored, busy, and obliging. He showed us, among other important evidences of the reputation of his establishment, the register of names, from which it appeared that Lord Somebody and suite had spent three days here *en route* to Damascus; explored the Lake of Tiberias; were highly gratified with their visit, especially his lordship, who, with the exception of a bad night's rest in consequence of the fleas, enjoyed himself exceedingly ; would recommend all travelers to take a boat and view the lake by moonlight. *Tres contents* with the hotel, but his lordship could not, in justice to his friends, say that the beds were altogether free from the nuisance of fleas. That Mr. Somebodyelse, chancellor to a British Consulate, fully concurred in the opinions and sentiments expressed by the aforesaid lord, and would add, for the benefit of the traveling public, that excellent fish might be caught in the lake, and sportsmen could find capital shooting on the other side, but on no account to venture out without a flask of brandy, London brand. That the Hon. Lady Blank, attended by her dragoman and servants, was on her way from Jerusalem and the Dead Sea to Damascus, and hoped to spend the summer in Constantinople ; was highly gratified by her visit to Tiberias, and considered Herr Wiseman a most accommodating and obliging person, but would advise all travelers to call for fish, and by no means to order beefsteak, as the beefsteak here was positively ruined in the cooking, unless personally superintended.

From the windows of our chamber we had a good view of the lake. There were two or three boats down by the water; but, not having romance enough in our party to go on a moonlight excursion, we spent the evening in writing up our journals. At an early hour next morning after breakfast, our mules being sent on to Nazereth with the baggage, we mounted our horses, and rode down to see the famous warm baths of Tiberias. These baths are situated about two miles from the town, at the extremity of the valley. They have long been celebrated for their medicinal virtues, and are much resorted to by invalids. At present a good building, erected by Ibrahim Pasha, covers the chief spring. In the centre of the largest apartment is a spacious reservoir, into which the water, warm from the mountain, falls from the mouth of a stone lion. The floors are of marble, and all conveniences are found for bathing. The visitor may swim about in the pure element if he likes, and, for a few piasters, become thoroughly saturated with sulphur. There is an inner apart ment of smaller dimensions where the water is of still higher temperature—so warm, indeed, that at first it is painful to bear the hand in it. Invalids may be parboiled here to perfection; and it is said that they come from all parts of the country for that purpose. The water is clear and pure, and is strongly impregnated with gas and sulphur. Doubtless its medicinal virtues are not exaggerated: and the day may come when some enterprising Yankee will purchase the premises, and have out his bills throughout the hotels of the East, "Sulphur Baths of Galilee—Pavilion of Tiberias: boats, horses, and bowling saloons always ready for visitors; the best liquors kept at the bar; pleasure trips to Safed only 12½ cents; steamer Pasha leaves for Tell Hum and all the intermediate ports twice a day: Fare 25 cents. Zachary Doo!.. tle, Proprietor."

BATHS OF TIBERIAS.

CHAPTER XXXIX.

JOURNEY TO NAZARETH.

FROM Tiberias we ascended by a mountain-pass toward Nazareth. It was a day of deadened sunshine; sallow in its light, but not cloudy; so still that the hum of life rose up from the valley and followed us to the height, where we turned to look back upon the sacred waters. On the right, over on the mountain, lay the ruins of Safed.

Years ago, I forget how many, occurred the great earthquake that laid it desolate. It was a scene of terror well-remembered by the survivors and by the inhabitants of Tiberias. I stopped awhile to trace out the sad havoc that had been made there; and, while I gazed upon its mouldering vestiges, the past seemed to rise before me in all its terrible reality.

A murky gloom hung over the shores of Galilee. No gleam of sunshine rested upon the sacred waters. The hot air was stagnant upon the mountains, and the valley of Genesareth lay parched in the stillness. Its groves of olives were withered; its herds were motionless; its ruined temples without shadow. From the heights of Safed down into the pulseless waters below there was a hush of life; for the presage of Doom was spread abroad A death-pall lay upon the blanched earth.

Then there came a low sighing out of the gloom, but none knew whence it came. Fear smote upon the hearts of the people, and they fell prostrate and prayed. There was a feverish trembling of the earth, and it was still again; and again it trembled and moaned, and again it was still. The hour was come; it came not with a sudden shock, but with the slow certainty of fate. A deep, sad wail of death rose upon the air. All living things fled, but they knew not where to flee. The plains opened in smoking fissures, and the mountains were cleft asunder by a hand that man hath never seen, and great rocks rolled crashing down into the depths below. Shrieks of terror mingled with the crash, and smoking masses of earth were upheaved, and buried beneath them houses and temples, and all that stood upon its sod. Men rushed from their abodes and smote their breasts, crying, Woe! woe! a judgment hath fallen upon Safed! Women fled shrieking with their children into the dark caverns. But there was death in the noonday light, and there was death in the darkness; all was desolation and death; wherever they fled, desolation and death. Crushed beneath the falling masses, they lay buried in a sepulchre of ruins. The dread doom had come; there were no sounds but the sounds of woe. Woe to the highest and the lowest; woe, woe to Safed; woe to all that were there that fatal day. The living were buried, and the dead were cast up from their graves, and the living and the dead were entombed in the convulsed earth to moulder henceforth together. Days after, putrid corpses were dragged from the ruins: strong men, crushed and maimed, grasping masses of ruin in their clenched hands as they died; the corpses of mothers, with their skeleton arms still twined around their babes; blackened and bleeding, some were dragged out to drink in the light of heaven once more, and die raving mad. O happy fate for them that were crushed to rise no more! For days after, the living lay maimed in the sad chaos, and smothered cries were heard when Safed was no more—wailing for the lost that were never to be seen again; for the dead that never more could know the bitterness of life.

The dream was ended: I turned and rode on toward the plain of Hatim.

On the ridge, as we left Tiberias, we had a fine view of Mount Tabor, which, from its regular outline, standing alone on the plain of Esdraelon, is easily distinguished from the neighboring mountains. We passed some rich spots of ground on our way this morning, and saw the Arabs at work scratching it up for the spring crops with their rude wooden plows and stunted oxen. On the left, two hours from Tiberias, we passed the village of Lubich, pleasantly situated on a mountain slope, and surrounded by groves of olives. Sometime during the forenoon, we passed through the famous plain of Kurim Hatin, where was fought one of the bloodiest of the battles between the Christians and the Saracens that occurred during the Crusades. Saladin, the hero of the Saracen hosts, here added to his fame by deeds of bravery scarcely paralleled in the history of those sanguinary wars. It was on the plain of Kurin Hatim, according to some writers, that Christ fed the five thousand with the loaves, and on one of the neighboring heights preached his Sermon on the Mount; but the best authorities deny that there is any satisfactory evidence of this.

In the valleys that swept down on the left, we saw a number of Bedouin encampments; and on the road met straggling parties of ragged and suspicious-looking fellows, armed with guns, who eyed us scowlingly, but always passed on when they caught sight of Yusef. The missionaries in Damascus had advised us to take a guard from Baneas to Nablous, as that was the most dangerous part of the road. We had heard a good many stories, especially of the dreadful state of things between Tiberias and Nazareth, where, it was said that it was an every-day occurrence to be knocked on the head and beaten within an inch of one's life, if not killed outright, by the banditti who infested that region. Confident, however, that Yusef would slay them all if they attacked us, we dispensed with the guard, and encountered every risk, under a most agreeable sense of security.

Early in the afternoon we passed through the village of Ker Kenna or Cana, and stopped at the lower part, near a fine grove of pomegranates, where we found excellent water. It was here that Christ turned the water into wine, and we could not but feel as we drank from the flowing spring, that there was something in its scriptural associations to make it a memorable event in our journey. There was a luxury in sitting here by the fragrant pomegranates smoking our pipes after our morning's ride, and watching the children as they came down from Cana with their earthen pitchers, as in olden times, to carry up water from the well. A few lazy Arabs gathered around us to see what we were doing; they watched with particular interest the progress of a sketch that I made of the well, pronouncing it, as I supposed from their manner, the most wonderful work of art they had ever beheld. These people, like all we had seen in this part of the world, seem to recognize no difference between winter and summer. They were clad in loose rags, although the weather was cool, and in their huts seldom used fire, except a few coals to boil their coffee and light their pipes. We gave them a trifling *backshish* for looking at us, and, wishing them a pleasant time of it, went on our way toward Nazareth.

CHAPTER XL.

NAZARETH.

LEAVING Mount Tabor several hours on the left, we passed through the village of Remeh, and descended into the valley beyond. On again ascending we came in view of Nazareth. Apart from its scriptural associations, there is little about Nazareth to attract attention. It is a mere village of square, flat-roofed houses, situated on the side of a hill, with a mosque and some large buildings, occupied by the monks, in the lower part. The valley is well-wooded with olive trees, which extend up beyond the houses toward the top of the hill. A few palm trees present a picturesque outline near the mosque. The general appearance of the valley of Nazareth is similar to that of most of the valleys through which one passes in Syria. Before reaching the town we came to a square plat of ground, inclosed by a stone wall, within which stands a convent. We were met at the door by a Greek priest, who invited us to enter. This convent is said to cover the spot on which the Virgin Mary was born. We took off our hats and went in. Places of this kind are turned into mere catchpenny shows, and there is no evidence of their being the identical places referred to in the Scriptures, other than the traditional testimony of the monks. The convents built upon them are sustained chiefly by the contributions of pilgrims and travelers, and these contributions depend of course upon the skill of the monks in maintaining the authenticity of the localities. That the position of Nazareth is well established, I believe admits of no doubt; but farther than that is uncertain. The spot upon which it is said the Virgin was born is in a sort of vault in the back part of the chapel; it is covered with a square marble slab, over which is erected a canopy. There is a well of fine water underneath, from which we drank. While we were looking on, several priests entered with lighted wax candles, and went through various ceremonies; kneeling and kissing repeatedly the marble slab. A poor old woman, covered with rags, forced herself in through the crowd, and fell groaning upon the floor, kissing the cold stones and the robes of the priests with frantic eagerness. She seemed to be under the influence of religious excitement, and would probably have left us in that belief had she not, when we turned to depart, bounced up with activity, and headed us off before we reached the door, begging vociferously for alms. The change in the expression of her countenance was quite miraculous. She was no longer the groaning devotee; it was plain enough to see that there was method in her madness. We gave her a few piasters, and also a trifle to the worthy priest, who was equally assiduous in his attentions. Both of them wished us a happy journey, and we wished them a continuance of their profits.

We stopped at the house up in Nazareth built by the Latin monks for the accommodation of pilgrims; a very clean and convenient stone building, with rooms that seemed grand, after the wretched places we had slept in since leaving Damascus. It was a long time before the keys came, but they came at last, very much to our satisfaction. It was too late to see any thing that evening; so promising ourselves a pleasant trip to Mount Tabor next morning, we turned in after dinner, and slept soundly through the night.

The monks of the Latin convent treated us very kindly. We were visited by several of them, and found them friendly and obliging. Of course we paid well for every thing we had; but we got the value, besides pleasant smiles and kind words.

In the traveler's register we saw the names of several acquaintances, among others that of our excellent Minister to Constantinople, Mr. Marsh, and his family, and some tourists from Kentucky. Mr. Marsh was taken ill here a few months before on his return from Egypt. He bears testimony to the kind treatment which himself and family received from the monks during his stay in Nazareth. We saw also the name of an American gentleman who appeared to be a most indefatigable traveler in the East and throughout Europe. Very few registers that I saw any where were without his signature. I saw it on the ruins of Baalbek, and on various other ruins; and met with no minister, consul, traveler, dragoman, or guide who was not acquainted with him personally or by reputation. Among the Arabs he was generally known as my Lord Willoughby, a mistake that doubtless originated in the passion for titles displayed by his dragoman, Emanuel Balthos. I also frequently met with the name of a much-esteemed traveling companion from Boston, who, doubtless from the same cause, was remembered throughout the East as the Prince of Wales. Not only do I believe that this will be news to both of these gentlemen, but caution all travelers who may come after me through that land of metaphor not to misconstrue the fact in any way should they find it reported that General Sir John Brown, of the City of Magnificent Distances, accompanied by the Prince of Wilmington and Lord Captain Bullfinch, had just passed; but to attribute it all to our dragoman, whose passion for display in matters of this kind is perfectly incorrigible.

It is recorded in the register of the Latin Convent by a Mr. Alwyn, of Quebec, some six or eight months ago, that he was robbed and cruelly beaten by the Arabs near Djenin. I had heard of the affair in Smyrna, and now read it in his own handwriting. It appeared that he was traveling through Palestine accompanied only by his dragoman. Three miles from Djenin he was attacked by four Arabs, who dragged him from his horse and beat him with stones and clubs till they thought he was dead. The dragoman made his escape, and it was supposed he was an accomplice of the robbers. Mr. Alwyn found, upon coming to his senses, that his skull was fractured in several places, and he lay for some hours unable to move. At length some traveling Arabs passing that way took him to Djenin. The Sheik refused to let him have a horse to take him to Nazareth, without an assurance of forty piasters, which he had to promise on the prospect of obtaining it from the Latin monks, as he had been plundered of all his money. On his arrival in Nazareth he was most kindly and hospitably received by the monks, who paid for his horse, dressed his wounds, fed him, and took good care of him for three months, when he was sufficiently recovered to proceed on his journey. Our companion, the English Captain, was chief officer in the steamer in which he took passage, and bore testimony to the truth of the narrative.

On the day after our arrival in Nazareth the weather was so unpromising that we were reluctantly forced to abandon our visit to Mount Tabor. It is only a ride of three hours; but we thought a rainy day could be better spent on our way to Jerusalem, especially as there was every prospect of the wet weather setting in for the winter.

First, however, we went to take a look at the sights. Nazareth is one of the worst specimens of a Syrian town; it abounds in abominations of all kinds, and is the abiding-place of as dark and villainous a population as we had yet seen. The difference was very striking between the inhabitants of this part of the country and those about Tripoli and Mount Lebanon. There they seemed pastoral in their habits; they were polite and affable, and had a frank and cheerful expression that was very pleasing. As we advanced southward from Damascus the people were of a darker complexion, and had a scowling and morose cast of countenance. We found their religious prejudices stronger as we approached Jerusalem, and sometimes had difficulty in obtaining lodgings in the native houses, though the magic effects of *backshish* never failed in the end to open their doors.

The women of Nazareth, as far as we had any opportunity of seeing them, are extremely beautiful. They are carefully masked, however, and it is only accidentally that the traveler can catch a glimpse of their faces.

During the forenoon we went to the Latin convent, which is reputed by the monks to be built upon the spot where stood the house of the Virgin Mary. The chapel has some tolerable paintings; incense is burnt continually on the altar, as in the chapels throughout Italy, and, altogether, it reminded me of the ordinary Italian churches. Most of the monks are Italians, from the Tuscan and Roman States. A school is attached to the convent, where the Christian children of the town are educated free of expense; a medicine-shop or infirmary also forms a part of the establishment; and we saw around the doors crowds of sick and afflicted creatures, to whom the monks were distributing medicines. It must be admitted, that whatever may be objected to these institutions throughout Palestine, their effect is beneficial to the poor people; and, in general, the monks who occupy them are kind and humane to all who need their assistance.

By noon we were on our way toward Jerusalem. Ascending the hill on the east, I stopped in a grove of olives to make a sketch of the town. The weather was raw and chilling, and I barely had warmth enough left in my hands to take a rapid outline of the principal points. My companions becoming impatient, I had to spur up old Saladin, and push on to make up for lost time. We soon came to the high range of bluffs overlooking the plain of Esdraelon. The view was very fine as we commenced our descent. On the left loomed up the beautiful and moundlike outline of Mount Hermon; in front, at a distance of ten or twelve miles, the barren peaks of Little Hermon; and beyond, inclining to the right, the vast and prairie-like plain of Esdraelon, a wilderness of rich land covered with wild-grass and weeds, and dotted at remote intervals with the ruins of castles and villages. Our road lay close by the reputed Rock of the Precipitation. Dr. Robinson discredits the authenticity of this as the true location, and believes the Rock of the Precipitation to be not far behind the Greek convent. He very justly argues, that an infuriate rabble would have had no object in carrying their victim so great a distance from the town, when there were precipices in the immediate vicinity quite as well adapted to their purpose.

CHAPTER XLI.

A GAZELLE HUNT.

DESCENDING by a rough and stony path, we commenced our march across the great plain of Esdraelon. There was little to relieve the monotony of this part of our journey; sharp gusts of wind swept over the plain, and the only sounds we heard were the lowing of cattle at a distance and the rattling of the withered weeds along our path. By accident somebody in the party who had the gun let it off at the right time and killed a hawk; and occasionally a gazelle would start up and bound off over the plain. On one of these occasions the excitement was so strong that it came well-nigh costing us more than the game would have amounted to had we succeeded in capturing every gazelle within a range of ten miles. It was the first time we Frangi had seen this beautiful animal in its native wilds; and so impressed were we by the remembrance of the "gazelle-like eyes" we had left at home, that we agreed to capture one if we could, dead or alive. With this determination the tall Southerner took Yusef's double-barrel gun, well loaded with slugs; the English Captain a stick to make his horse run them down; myself nothing at all, because I was not skilled in hunting; but I had a penknife in my pocket, with which it was possible I might be called upon to bleed somebody in case of a bruise or fracture. Yusef had his small gun, his Allen's revolver, sword, daggers, knives, and other arms. Thus equipped for the chase, we rode along keeping a sharp look-out among the weeds on each side of the path. It was an anxious time, for every moment we expected to see a fine herd of gazelles bounce up. But not the sign or shadow of a gazelle was to be seen for miles. Eventually our enthusiasm was cooling down in the chilling air, and we began to despair of seeing any more gazelles, when a thumping sound struck upon our ears. It was sudden and distinct, almost like a shock of galvanism. Per Baccho! what a glorious sight! Four splendid gazelles, not fifty yards off, in the act of bounding away! Shoot 'em! Catch 'em! Stop 'em, somebody! O Jupiter! what splendid animals! There was a sudden pause, and then a shout of excitement from the whole party, and away dashed every body, shouting at the utmost power of his lungs, and shooting to the extreme extent of his powder and fire-arms. The mules, heavily laden as they were with baggage and the additional weight of the muleteers who were asleep on top, pricked up their ears and began to caper about, till, no longer able to control their enthusiasm, they started off to join the chase. The muleteers were thrown from the baggage, and were suddenly waked up by finding themselves on their heads; when jumping to their feet they ran after the mules as fast as they could, shouting at the top of their voices, like the rest of us. It is not to be supposed that Tokina, the ass, was proof against all this. At the very first intimation of a general stampede, he dropped down on his head, and deposited Francesco, the boy, in a mud-hole, and then springing up again, ran off toward Nazareth with his tail straight out, his ears pointed forward, and his mouth wide open, braying in the most hysterical and frightful manner. Thereupon Francesco likewise started off at full speed, shouting madly for somebody to stop the ass; so that there was not a single living object in the party, two-legged or four-legged, that was not chasing something. It was a general chase all round, of the most exciting character, for which it must be admitted some of us were altogether unprepared. The mules evidently were not in a proper condition to undertake a rapid and tortuous run of this kind; for the baggage being carelessly fastened to their backs by means of various small cords, soon began to slip off on either side, and to hang dangling underneath in a way that was not only inconvenient to the mules themselves, but extremely perilous to our cooking utensils and stock of provisions. One mule especially labored under an unusual combination of disadvantages. Yusef had purchased several chickens in Nazareth, of which he designed making a stew that evening, and in order to keep them fresh he had tied their legs together and fastened them in a live state on the top of the cooking utensils. The pans and kettles, sliding down on each side of the mule, remained hanging by the handles underneath, and banged away there against each other in the most terrific manner; and the chickens, having nothing to balance them on top, slipped over behind, and hung between his hind-legs, where they got up such a cackling and fluttering that the unfortunate animal, driven to distraction by the noise and other causes, went perfectly insane with fright, and ran all round in a circle for ten minutes, by which time every cord was broken, and our entire stock of provisions and implements of domestic economy deposited at intervals over nearly a hundred acres of ground. The other mules had knapsacks, mattresses, bundles of clothes, and a variety of other articles hanging over them and under them; but by dint of hard kicking, and an occasional fit of rolling, they got rid of them at last, and went their way at random. Meantime the horses branched off in different directions, and made the most frantic efforts to overtake the game. The horse of the English Captain, though equal in spirit to any in the party, seemed least likely to accomplish the general object, on account of some peculiarity in the construction of one of his fore-legs, the chief tendon of which had been growing shorter and shorter every day from the time of leaving Beirut, and was now so short that he was forced to do all his running on three legs. The animal upon which the tall Southerner was mounted was a slender little iron-gray which also had a very remarkable peculiarity. It was the misfortune of this horse to be possessed of a body that tapered off toward the hind part without the slightest symptom of a stomach. No matter how much corn or barley he ate of nights, or how tight the saddle-girths were drawn in the morning, he was always so deficient in stomach, that in two hours from the time of starting, the girths invariably reached his hind-legs, and the saddle occupied the space directly over his tail. It was in this condition that he was compelled to make chase after the gazelles. The legs of the tall Southerner were somewhat long for so small a horse, and having no natural support from the saddle, on account of its position, he was forced to tie them in a hasty knot underneath, by which means a constant spurring and goading was kept up, and an irregularity of motion on the part of both horse and rider extremely curious and picturesque at the distance of half a mile. Yusef's famous steed of the desert, Syed Sulemin, was perhaps the only animal in the party that could be said to keep the run of the gazelles, but he kept it at so great a distance that they must have been entirely out of sight when the firing commenced. The last I saw of Syed Sulemin and his master they were rapidly disappearing in a cloud of smoke; and it was not until the chase was entirely over that I began to entertain the most remote idea of ever beholding them again. While all this was going on, it is not to be inferred, from the minuteness of the details into which I have entered, that my horse Saladin stood still in order to afford me an opportunity of noting down all these facts; for such was not the case; so far from it, indeed, that he had been tied by the hind-legs with a thick rope to a stake, and his fore-legs bound together with a strong chain, and his tail fastened in some way to a heavy wagon, I am certain he would have carried them all with him sooner than be left behind. What I saw was at a single glance, but the whole thing was of an unusual and impressive nature, which enables me to recall the details without difficulty. That Saladin was bound to be in chase of something was a self-evident proposition. He was not an animal mentally or physically calculated to stand still when there was any prevailing excitement. In the present case, however, he made a mistake at the very beginning which was the chief cause of all the misfortunes that befell the mules. These animals, as ill luck would have it, were some two or three hundred yards ahead of us, a little to the left of the path, when the stampede commenced. Saladin, entirely indifferent as to what he was running after, provided he overtook something, started off briskly at the very first shout; and having but one eye, which was the left eye, it happened that he caught sight of the mules just as they became fired with ambition to join the chase. I have no doubt whatever that he thought they were legitimate game, and that the grand object to be achieved was to run them down and then run over them. Such small game as gazelles probably never occupied the attention of so great a head as his. At all events, no sooner did he catch sight of the scampering mules, than he neighed as if ready to burst with impatience; and, tossing up his head and tail simultaneously, dashed after them full speed. All his previous efforts in the way of running seemed ridiculously tame, compared with the prodigious bounds which he made on this occasion. Accustomed as I had in some measure become to his fits of insanity, this so far surpassed any derangement under which he had hitherto labored, that I was forced to let him have his way, and confine my energies to keeping myself in the saddle. The mules, startled at the clatter of the baggage about their legs, and panic-stricken at the thundering of hoofs behind them, tried hard to head off; but Saladin kept his left eye on them and never ceased to head off after them, till every one in the train was running round in a circle at the utmost extremity of his speed. No equestrian corps in a circus could have presented half so extraordinary a spectacle. It was utterly in vain that the muleteers kept running round inside the ring, calling upon me in the name of Allah to give over running their mules down in that way, and swearing by every hair in the beard of the Prophet that if I kept it up much longer the poor animals would drop dead on the spot; for Saladin, driven to the very climax of enthusiasm by the noise of the tin pans and the screaming of the chickens, rushed furiously after the mule upon which they were hung, and never left off biting him until the unfortunate beast was entirely rid of his load and crazed beyond all hope of recovery. By this time the rest of the party began to gather in, and by their united assistance both Saladin and the mules were stopped. In the course of half an hour we gathered up the scattered remnants of our baggage and went our way, greatly dejected in spirits. We never saw either the chickens or gazelles again.

The unhappy issue of this adventure had a very depressing effect upon the whole party. We had lost a good deal of time, as well as chickens and cooking utensils; and, from all we could ascertain in regard to the prospect of getting any thing to eat at Djenin, or any reliable means of cooking what we might get, it was a very doubtful prospect indeed. There was every reason to apprehend that we should be compelled to go to bed supperless; which was by no means a pleasing view of the case, considering the exercise we had taken in our hunt after the gazelles. In consequence of this state of feeling, there was very little said on the subject by any body, except the muleteers, who, for as much as half-an-hour, did nothing but beat the unfortunate mules, in the hope of obtaining the satisfaction in that way which was properly due them by Saladin. But, as well as I could catch the drift of their conversation, both from the way in which they looked at me, and the violent manner in which they belabored the poor animals when they saw that I was composed under the circumstances, there was not the slightest doubt, on my part, that their resentment was directed against myself, as the chief cause of all the trouble, rather than against either Saladin or the mules; and that being denied the privilege of relieving their minds upon a Howadji, they relieved them upon their own personal property.

As for Saladin, I regret to say, that he did not evince such a spirit of resignation as I expected from a horse of his greatness of character, especially from a descendant of the renowned Ashrik. From the moment of being stopped in his attempt to get a piece out of the mule, which he had driven mad, he fretted and chafed in an unusual manner, as if under the influence of some fierce and insatiate passion for flesh, which could only be appeased by a large mouthful out of some animal in the party.

The English Captain was the first to break the silence by any direct reference to the affair of the gazelles. He said that it was the most stunning circumstance within his knowledge how it was that he had missed overtaking the largest of the gazelles, which was the one he had in his eye all along. He had kept that gazelle in his eye from the very beginning, and was gaining on it rapidly, when it suddenly disappeared;. it must have perceived that it was quite useless to run away from him any longer, and hastily concealed itself in a hole till he passed by. The tall Southerner was of opinion that the whole difficulty was owing to the want of stomach in his iron-gray; which was the cause of the saddle slipping back, so as to prevent him from taking good aim. He thought that had the saddle remained in its proper place, he could have steadied himself by the stirrups; instead of which, it required most of his attention to keep his legs tied together underneath. However, he believed that he had wounded one of the gazelles very severely, for he saw it leap more than thirty feet when he fired.

Yusef, during this conversation, lost much of his dejected expression of countenance; and when the tall Southerner spoke of having wounded a gazelle, he was no longer able to suppress his enthusiasm. He declared, in the most emphatic manner, that he had wounded two, one of which he had no doubt dropped dead in five minutes after, for he had broken one of its hind-legs, and crippled both the fore-legs, in such a manner that it was utterly impossible for it to run more than a quarter of a mile farther. The other was not so badly wounded, having only lost its eyes by a slug (he knew that the eyes were destroyed by the way it ran); and there was some probability of its living, but it could never see where it was going. He would have gone after the dead one, and, in fact, did go some distance after it, but—

Here Yusef stopped. Had he been struck with lightning he could not have stopped more suddenly, or more unaccountably to himself. It was well for him that he was not thrown headlong over his horse. The cause of the interruption was this: being a little too far behind to hear distinctly all he said, I had thoughtlessly ridden up rather near; and precisely at the most interesting point (for I felt exceedingly curious to know why the dead gazelle was left running about with one broken leg and two crippled legs), the very point that most required explanation, my horse Saladin, still chafing under his recent disappointment, seized that moment to obtain satisfaction; and the way he obtained it was, by seizing in his teeth that portion of Yusef's horse which was nearest to him.

Now I have never said that Syed Sulemin was a cowardly horse: I do not say so now; his spirit was beyond question. But there are times when the bravest of horses, as well as the bravest of mankind, are apt to betray a natural weakness incident to the flesh. So sudden and so exquisite was the torture inflicted upon Sulemin by this unprovoked attack, that he not only yelled in the excess of his anguish, but jumped at least two feet from the ground. Nor did he cease his convulsive throes when he lit upon the ground again; but continued to rear and plunge in such a frightful manner that it was quite evident the pain had driven him mad. Every horse in the party, either from astonishment at this unexpected turn of affairs, or fear of consequences, began to rear and plunge at the same moment. The result was, that the horse of the English captain, having only the perfect use of three legs, was unable to plunge sufficiently far out of the way; and Syed Sulemin in the fury of his wrath, upon discovering, as he thought, the author of the insult, gave that unfortunate animal a kick that sent him staggering into the midst of the other horses, where he was kicked again by the iron-gray, and afterward bitten by Saladin. It was with the utmost difficulty that we were enabled to restore order among the contending parties.

When order was at length restored, we resumed our journey; but such was the jealousy and ill-feeling, not only between the horses, but between the riders, each of us protesting that it was the fault of the others, that a general gloom prevailed in the end, and we rode on for several hours in silence. What conclusion my companions came to, I am unable to say: for my own part I was determined never again to join in a gazelle-hunt to the latest hour of my existence.

CHAPTER XLII.

DJENIN.

THE great plain of Esdraelon is one of the finest tracts of country in the East. In its general aspect it reminded me of some of the vast plains in California, after the summer heats have withered up the grass. Some portions of the land seem to be rich and arable. We saw a few fields covered with stalks of Indian corn, from which we inferred that this grain might be produced here in large quantities by proper cultivation. No part of Palestine that we had yet seen appeared so well calculated to sustain a large population. Railroads might be run through it at a very trifling cost, and an easy communication opened with the seaboard. In some places I noticed wild cotton, which naturally suggested thoughts of cotton mills. Tunnels might be cut through the mountains to Jerusalem, and a profitable trade thus opened with the inhabitants of Judea; and by removing the sands from the Desert the line of communication might be carried to Cairo, Suez, the East Indies, China, and California. The hot-baths of Galilee would be a pleasant place of retreat in the summer; and good hotels would soon spring up throughout the country as the blessings of civilization progressed. I sounded the inhabitants on the subject of annexation, but they did not seem disposed to discuss the question; in fact the only answer they gave me was, *backshish!* There seemed to be no hope at all of reclaiming the poor creatures.

Passed during the afternoon the villages of Yafa and El Mazraah, mere gatherings of hovels like bee-hives, situated on mounds or elevations, resembling islands in the plain; also, El Fuleh, a pretty looking village, picturesquely situated in a sort of oasis on the left. Stopped to refresh ourselves at

Mukeberteh a filthy and miserable village, inhabited by the most ragged and scowling set of vagabonds we had yet seen. Saw in the distance beyond Little Hermon, the ruined castle of Bizan. It stands upon an elevation in the valley of Jezreel, which is a part of the great plain of Esdraelon. This is celebrated in scriptural history as the spot where Saul's body was hanged by the Philistines, after his defeat and death Saw Mount Carmel on the left; also Gilboa, noted in scriptural history as the place where the battle took place in which the Israelites were defeated and Saul slain. This spot is also famous as the scene of a sanguinary battle between Saladin and the Crusaders.

Late in the afternoon, after a ride of six hours from Nazareth, we arrived at Djenin, the ancient Ginea, a town of considerable size, handsomely situated at the base of a range of mountains on the south side of the plain.

We found it somewhat difficult to obtain lodgings here, in consequence of the hostile feeling of the inhabitants toward Christian travelers. Djenin is one of those places occasionally found in Palestine where this religious intolerance has been in full force for centuries, and still remains unchanged, notwithstanding the progress of a more liberal and enlightened state of feeling throughout Syria and the East. A few days before our arrival two English travelers, who had encamped outside the town in their tent, were beset during the night by a heavy storm, which blew down their tent. It was so dark and cold, and the rain poured down so heavily, that they were obliged to give up all hope of erecting it again, and they proceeded to the town with their dragoman, to try and find shelter till morning. For some time they walked about through the dark and filthy streets, applying for lodgings at every door, but as soon as it was found that they were Franks they were driven away with abusive and insulting language, and sometimes threatened with violence if they did not at once get away out of the town. Wet and cold as it was, they were forced to return to their wreck of a tent, pack up their baggage as well as they could in the dark, and proceed on their journey in the midst of the storm.

Our own experience in Djenin was not quite so bad as this, though bad enough. Upon entering the town we rode up to a fountain, where we waited nearly an hour, while our dragoman went in search of some lodging-place. He had a niece here whose husband was a Christian; but he feared they were not at home, having heard that they were on a visit to Jerusalem. While we were waiting at the fountain, a great many ragged children and women came to get water and stare at us; and before long, a number of cadaverous and thievish-looking men began to gather around us, smoking their pipes, and remarking upon all our peculiarities of costume and manners. It was a great comfort to think that we had near us the means of striking terror into the hearts of these lazy vagabonds, in case they should undertake to treat us with any sort of disrespect. In all truthfulness, they were the most squalid, miserable, scowling set of villains it was ever my fortune to behold; ragged to the very extremity of raggedness; dirty to the foundation of dirtiness; smoked and smoky to the essence of smokiness; and beastly in all respects to the lowest pitch of beastliness.

Yusef returned in due time, bringing tidings that his niece had really gone to Jerusalem; but that he had, after great difficulty, obtained lodgings for us at the house of a Christian Arab from Nazareth.

Djenin afforded us a fair example of the extent to which mental and physical persecution may be carried without absolutely producing insanity. Expecting every moment to be robbed by the natives, who are the worst in all Palestine, we lay in the hut of a Christian Arab, where we were literally in danger of being devoured by asses, cows, goats, and smaller animals, such as cats, dogs, rats, and lizards, as well as by the vermin, which completely obliterated all my remembrances of South America and California. Never before had I been conquered by annoyances of this kind; I had always slept through them, and laughed at my companions next morning for being troubled about such trifles. But, O Lamartine! Lamartine! if thou hast tears to shed—and I know thou hast yet a few more left—in the name of humanity, shed them now! It was pitiable to behold us; it was more than pitiable—actually heart-rending. To this day I can not think of that miserable little town and the night we spent there without an itching to get farther away from it. In the middle of the night, after tossing, rolling, and groaning, without even so much as a wink of sleep—for the fleas actually covered me as a live coating of black mail—I started up and looked around in search of sympathy. The tall Southerner was sitting up on the mud floor, his hair disheveled, his eyes wild and and haggard, and his face dreadfully scarred and emaciated; he was in the act of aiming a blow, with an empty bottle, at the head of some hungry animal that had been trying to eat him. The English Captain, jolly as ever, was scratching himself with one hand, while with the other he held a pipe, which he smoked with great calmness and good-humor.

"Hallo!" said I, "what's the matter, Captain?"

"The fleas," said the Captain; "they're quite stunning, I assure you. Never saw so many in all my life."

"Why don't you catch 'em?"

"Too strong for me; can't hold 'em. 'Pon my honor, they won't let me sleep a wink. Awfully ferocious animals; stunning, quite stunning, I assure you. Sir, I don't think any thing short of hot brandy-punch will cure them."

The proposition was so gratifying that we all immediately agreed to it. Francesco and Yusef were aroused, and commanded to produce fire and water in ten minutes, on the pain of our displeasure. Very soon we felt quite happy, in spite of the vermin—happier, a good deal, than we did next morning.

I have looked in vain for a scientific description of the Syrian flea. Surely it deserves a place in natural history: and, although unskilled in entomology, I shall here notice briefly this extraordinary animal. The *Pulce granda*, or Syrian flea, is of a lively disposition and irregular in his habits, given to late hours and disturbances of the peace. He sleeps occasionally during the day, but is always wide awake at night, when his vivacity is very remarkable. Human blood is his food; he prefers Christians to Arabs as an article of diet; has great vigor of muscle and capacity for digestion; carries in his mouth a long harpoon, which he throws with great skill; uses likewise a boarding-knife and patent forcing-pump. He never dies naturally, but is subject to diseases of the brain, from too great a flow of blood to the head. Wounds produced by this ferocious animal are unpleasant, but not fatal. Constant depletion, however, may destoy life; hence, by repeated attacks, a man may be altogether dried up; in which case he becomes a dry subject. One should always, when he feels the harpoon thrown into him, seize hold of the flea by the hind-legs, tear him out by main force, and deposit him secretly upon his neighbor. I always did so, as nearly as practicable, upon the English Captain or the Southerner. Sometimes I dropped him into their ears, so that they might have odd dreams to tell when they waked up.

We had fleas all through Syria; we were flayed by fleas from Beirut to Jerusalem. They are the living embodiment of the nights in Palestine, which are now the nearest approximation to the knights of Jerusalem.

In the morning, after a hurried breakfast, I went to take another look at the town. The weather was wet and gloomy, and nothing could exceed the comfortless and melancholy aspect of the whole place: the narrow streets, half-filled with ruins and piles of filth; dead carcasses sopping in green pools of mud; the dark alleys reeking with a sickening stench; the walls of the houses blackened with smoke, and tottering to ruin; a few half-naked wretches, scarce bearing the semblance of human creatures, wallowing about the doorways amid the foul abominations; stagnation, decay, ruin every where—the earth polluted, the air accursed, the very dogs sneaking into darkness, as if to hide their degradation.

We were glad enough to take our leave of so unpleasant and inhospitable a place. It rained hard all the forenoon, and our ride was uncommonly dreary.

CHAPTER XLIII.

ADVENTURE WITH THE SAMARITANS.

WITHIN three miles of Djenin we passed the spot where the attack was made by the Arabs upon Mr. Alwynn. It was a lonesome and desolate valley, between two ranges of barren mountains, and seemed a fit abode for banditti. Keeping a sharp look out, however, on both sides, and occasionally behind, we were determined to seize at once upon any bad characters whom we might discover prowling about, and hang them up to the first tree on the roadside; but they must have suspected from our general appearance and the efficient manner in which we were guarded, that we were people not to be trifled with, for we saw nothing of them.

In about two hours we reached Kubatayeh, a village inhabited chiefly by a population of Turks. Soon after, we came to a mountain pass, from which we had a fine view of the rich plain below. The village of Sancan on the opposite side is prettily situated on an eminence, and is surrounded by ruinous walls and the remains of an old castle, which any person who has the time to spare may find worth looking at. On the left, two hours farther on, is the village of Jeba, a picturesque collection of ruins embosomed in olive groves. This part of the country abounds in groves of fig-trees and olives, and we saw a number of Arabs plowing in the fields, very much as the fields must have been plowed three thousand years ago. What would a farmer think at home, in this the nineteenth century, to see the ground rooted up with a forked branch of a tree, with a pair of oxen fastened to it by a string?

At Jeba, we diverged from the main road, sending on our

mules to Nablous, and took a by-road to Sebustia. From the summit of a mountain not far from Jeba we had a fine prospect of the valleys on both sides, with their flowing streams bordered with green shrubbery. The mountains were terraced in every direction, and fig-orchards and vineyards flourished luxuriantly on all the arable grounds. In the distance gleamed the bright waters of the Mediterranean—the most welcome sight we had enjoyed from the time of leaving the cedars of Lebanon. It is wonderful how the heart is gladdened by a glimpse of a familiar object, after one has been shut in for some time among strange scenes. I really felt as if I could hug old ocean, when I beheld his honest face shining in the sunbeams.

On our descent from the ridge, we passed through Burka, where we were stared at by the inhabitants with vacant wonder; and some distance below we crossed a deep valley and ascended on the other side a mound-like hill, upon which was situated in ancient times Samaria, the capital of the Israelites. Nothing now is left of the ancient city but broken columns and cornices, scattered throughout the fields on the hill-sides, some of which are partially imbedded in the ground; and a double row of columns, said to have formed a portion of a temple built by Tiberius. The whole site of Samaria, covering several hundred acres of ground, now rudely cultivated, is strewn with these relics of the ancient city. One of the most picturesque objects to be seen there, is a ruined mosque, built perhaps during the time of the Saracens. The view in every direction is very fine; and the position of the old city must have been one of the most charming in Syria for salubrity, convenience, and scenic effect. Of the present town of Sebustia, little need be said. A description of one Syrian village, answers with little variation for all the rest; low square huts, with flat tops; a lazy, beggarly population of picturesque Arabs, are the principal features in all these villages. The inhabitants of Sebustia seemed to be still more rude and debased than any we had yet seen in our wanderings, probably from being farther removed from the ordinary traveled route. Some had a brutish and idiotic appearance.

We sat down by the ruins of the old mosque, and spread our table-cloth and provisions on a stone, and while we ate our lunch, the natives began to gather round us in large numbers, and stare at us with undisguised astonishment. Yusef was very much disgusted with their rudeness, and gave vent to his displeasure in English, which struck us as somewhat remarkable, inasmuch as it was not to be supposed that these poor wretches were learned in that tongue. The number increasing, we began to think they meditated a descent upon our chicken, and I assumed the responsibility of telling Yusef that he had better drive them away. He looked embarrassed and distressed (doubtless he felt humiliated by their want of manners), but mustering up his usual spirit, he addressed them in Arabic, and they all talked together with great violence for some time. At last I saw that the Arabs were getting very forward and excited, and our dragoman very pale. I knew that Yusef was going to be furious, and that the next thing would be a general fight, which, considering the odds against us, I was rather anxious to avoid. With this view, I told him to let them alone, and by no means to attack them. At the same time, in order to appease their ferocity, I threw them the bones of a chicken which I was picking and some crusts of brown bread, which I told them in good English was the best I could do for them, as I was very hungry, and had eaten most of the provisions. Instead of being thankful for small favors, they became perfectly incensed at this, and asked Yusef, as he declared himself, if I meant to say that they were dogs. I have reason to suspect that he denied the charge most emphatically; for after a great deal of exciting talk, he picked up the chicken-bones and the bread, and in their presence, devoured both the one and the other with amazing avidity. No sooner had he done this (and I was certain it was not from hunger), than his jaws began to chatter, and he said: "Gentlemen, we had better go on. It will take us till night to reach Nablous;" and at the same time he pulled out his purse and distributed a large amount of *backshish* among the crowd; caught up the remnants of our lunch and thrust them into a bag, which he cast over his saddle, then mounted Syed Sulemin, dashed spurs into the sides of that noble animal, and led the way down the hill with uncommon celerity. My friends and myself mounted as fast as we could; for to tell the truth we did not altogether like the appearance of these modern Samaritans, and we departed in the rear of Yusef, with a very ticklish sensation about the backs, as if it would be unpleasant to be peppered with slugs out of the long guns, with which some of the Arabs were armed. It took us at least half an hour to catch up with him; and he then told us that we had made a most fortunate escape; that the rascally beggars at Sebustia had threatened to insult us, and that he (Yusef) had told them that if they did so he would not only cut their throats from ear to ear, but raze their village to the ground; in which event we might possibly find ourselves in difficulty with the Turkish Government upon our arrival in Jerusalem. This was the reason that he had compromised the matter—had he been alone he would never have rested content without their blood, but taking our interests into consideration, he had refrained from making an attack, and had ridden away hastily lest he should be provoked into it by their demonstrations of hostility. We were very glad that the adventure had turned out so well, and saw at once how prudently our dragoman had acted.

CHAPTER XLIV.

NABLOUS.

WE had a very pleasant ride of two hours through the valley of Nablous. It was one of the richest and most luxuriant valleys we had seen in all Palestine, abounding in fine groves of olives, fig-trees, and thriving vineyards and gardens; the grounds were fenced in with good stone walls, and we passed several mills, situated on the bank of a stream, which courses down through the middle of the valley. In the spring it must be a perfect little Paradise. Travelers who have passed through it at that season, dwell with delight upon the beauty of its gardens, and the abundance of rich flowers that bloom on the roadside.

It was near sundown when we entered the old stone gateway of Nablous. Passing through a labyrinth of narrow, ill-paved and filthy streets, we found comfortable lodgings at the house of one Asam, a Protestant Christian. Learning that Dr. Mendoza and the Madam had arrived on the previous day, I lost no time in finding them out. They had procured tolerably good quarters not far from the house of Asam; and when I was ushered up the stone stairway, I had the pleasure of beholding them in all their glory, seated at a table, and glowing radiantly in the fumes of coffee and omelette. The Doctor's head was buried in a red night-cap; his face was of the purest olive color, and he bore evidence of having suffered the most intense physical privations. The Madam wore a large hat, about as broad in the brim as an umbrella, in order to preserve her complexion, which was already rather dark; and I saw with distress that her amiable features were dreadfully lacerated by the attacks of vermin. However, she smiled as sweetly as ever, and met me with her accustomed politeness and cordiality ; and the doctor, although rather depressed in mind, became eloquent very soon on the subject of the accommodations of Palestine.

" 'Tis a 'orrible country," said he ; " I no want to voyage here again. De ruin are interess, but the hotel not good. Very bad hotel. I shall be content to arrive in Jerusalem. De Madam are a little indispose ; but he shall be better when he arrive in Jerusalem. Sit down ; take some coffee. Mon Dieu ! very bad country dis. To-morrow we shall depart on our voyage. 'Tis imposs to remain longer in Nablous."

We had some further conversation as we sipped our coffee, relative to the inconveniences and discomforts of Syrian travel ; and it was a great source of pleasure to both parties to find that we had all endured the most intense physical tortures from the time of our departure from Damascus.

It rained hard all night. In the morning, it cleared away, and we went out to explore the town. Nablous, called in Scriptural times Sychar, is a town of considerable importance, with a population of about eight thousand—chiefly Jews, Christians, and Turks. There are some good stone buildings in the principal streets ; and it has some pretensions to bazaars. It is well supplied with fruits and vegetables from the neighboring gardens, and oranges are brought up in large quantities from Jaffa. The streets are rendered rather more convenient for walking than those of most towns we had seen, by means of a deep pathway cut in the centre for camels and mules.

On the left, as we faced toward the Jerusalem road, is Mt. Ebal ; on the right, Gezeroum, on which is situated the synagogue of Samaria. Ebal is barren and rocky ; Gezeroum, also rocky, but cultivated to some extent. We visited the Samarians, a sect claiming to have no relationship with any living tribe, and whose family records, it is said, extend back more than three thousand years. They are much like the rest of the population of Nablous, in physiognomy and dress ; the number now living is about a hundred and fifty.

CHAPTER XLV.

A STRIKING SCENE.

ON leaving Nablous we visited Jacob's well, where Christ gave the waters of life to the Samaritan woman. The situation of the well accords with scriptural history, and there is very little doubt as to its great antiquity. It is dug in the solid rock. A large stone covers the mouth; and this is all that now marks the spot.

We also visited the reputed site of Joseph's tomb. A rude stone building covers the pretended sepulchre; but the best authorities deny that there is any evidence that Joseph was buried here.

The road, as we struck off to the right toward Jerusalem, passes over a mountainous and unpromising country. Some fertile valleys are seen at distant intervals; but for the most part the face of the country is barren and rocky. Leaving Kubelan to the left, we stopped to rest at the picturesque ruins of a Khan, in sight of El Lubban, in the valley of Lubban. This valley is cultivated and fertile; and we saw in it many thriving groves of olives. Ascending a precipitous mountain beyond the Khan of Lubban, we had a fine view from the summit, of the strange old village of Singil, which for scenic effect can scarcely be surpassed in Palestine. In about an hour we reached the stair-like road of stones leading up into it. Singil is a curiosity. Situated on a pyramid of rocks, it bears the appearance at a short distance of one mass of ruins; and indeed it is little better upon a nearer approach. The entire village is in the last stage of decay. As we climbed up the barren and rugged road, and entered the mass of ruined walls, we were struck with wonder at the wretched appearance of the hovels on either side. Some of them are built of mud and straw, in the shape of bee-hives, scarcely ten feet in diameter, and only five or six in height. In these miserable dens of filth whole families of men, women, and children were living like so many pigs, and quite as dirty.

We found rather good quarters in the ruins of an old Khan, among goats, chickens, and smaller nuisances; all of which we endured with great resignation after our experience in Djenin.

At an early hour in the morning we took our leave of Singil, and from the top of the mountain saw the sun rise in his most inspiring style, gilding the mountain peaks in the vast circle around with all the radiant glory of his rays. Stopping awhile at Ain-el-Haramayeh, we enjoyed a sight less grand, but scarcely less striking. It was washing-day with the women of the village. About three-score of leathern-faced and skinny old hags were standing up to their knees in water at the foot of the fountain, scolding one another, or more probably (as I took it) abusing their husbands; and pounding their husband's breeches with great clubs, as if nothing would please them better than to be pounding legs in them at the same time. I saw one ferocious old hag take up a ragged shirt, wring it maliciously by the neck, then place it on a flat stone, and mash it into a shapeless mass by the desperate and malignant blows that she gave it with her club. I was really very glad that her husband was not inside of that shirt, while she was wringing and pounding it; for I should have felt called upon to expostulate with her, and there is no telling how such interference from a stranger would have been received by the excited bevy of furies who were flourishing their clubs all around. The probability is that I should have been compelled in the end to seek protection behind Yusef; who by this time, however, was a long way off, because, as he afterward admitted, he always kept clear of women on wash-day. He disliked the female sex every day in the year; he disliked them on wash-day more than ever; because it always brought to mind a favorite sash that he wore, which he gave to one of his nieces to wash some time ago, telling her at the same time to be careful how she rubbed it, as it was of very rare and delicate texture, and he never would wear any thing with holes in it. Now this niece, being of a malicious turn, like all womankind, took the sash to a neighboring fountain, and belabored it with a club till she pounded a small hole in one end of it; and then she brought it to him, with tears in her eyes, and said: "I am very sorry, Uncle Yusef, but I've spoiled your sash. If you'll forgive me this time, I'll never do it again. You see what a great hole there is in it!" "Yes," said Yusef, "I see there is; a pretty business you've made of it. You may take it now and wear it on your head as a token of my displeasure; when I have any more sashes to wash I'll wash them myself." And so he did, to the best of my belief; for, during the whole journey, I never saw him give a sash to one of his nieces to wash, though I sometimes detected him giving them handkerchiefs and other nice little presents that were perfectly new.

On leaving Ain-el-Haramayeh, we passed through some fine valleys, abounding on both sides of the road with luxuriant groves of fig-trees. The inhabitants of this part of the country seemed to be more industrious and thriving than those living between Nazareth and Nablous. Some very good pieces of ground, fenced in with rough walls of stone, were frequently to be seen on the sides of the hills; and it was pleasant to hear the songs of the native laborers who were engaged in sowing the grain for the crops of the coming season.

Passing to the right of a dirty village called Jibia, we stopped awhile at Sinca and Infua, and thence continued on to Bireh, rather a larger and better looking village than we had seen since leaving Nablous. A short distance below Bireh is an old Khan, with a fountain near it, where we dismounted to refresh ourselves, and had the satisfaction of being abused for half an hour by a crowd of washerwomen, still more ferocious and alarming in their appearance than those of Haramayeh.

Beyond Bireh, toward Jerusalem, we entered a rocky plain entirely destitute of wood. This, with little change, continued till we began to ascend the mountains overlooking the sacred city. Several caravans of camels, laden with merchandise for the interior towns, obstructed the narrow passes in the rocks, and sometimes obliged us to turn back in order to avoid being walked over. It was very Oriental, this sort of thing, but not pleasant. I had a great notion to put some of those camels to death—especially one that walked both Saladin and myself off the road, and sent us rolling down a steep hill, in such a dangerous way that it was a miracle our necks were not broken.

The camel is an oddity in his way. He looks very well in a picture or on a desert standing under a palm-tree; he looks well at a distance with a family of Bedouins on his back; he looks well lying down by the ruins of an old mosque; in an artistical point of view, he looks well almost any where; yet, when you come to analyze his character, and consider all the fine descriptions that poetical writers have given of his patience, his gentleness, his powers of endurance, his admirable physical construction, and all that, I am rather disposed to regard him in the light of a humbug; and I take the more satisfaction in expressing this opinion because it has a healing influence upon the bruises that I received when Saladin and myself were rolled down the hill. As to his gentleness, he is gentle from pure laziness. He can be vicious enough at times. Let any body who would test the mild spirit of the camel, place his fingers between the teeth of that gentle animal, at certain periods, when he has been fretted, and there will soon be no further room for doubt on the subject. The camel is gentle, when he is not savage; patient, when he is not impatient; affectionate, when he wants something to eat; docile, when he is taught to understand that the absence of docility is usually filled with a stick. As to his physical strength and powers of endurance: Can he jump as far as a flea? can he carry as heavy a load on his back; can he endure half the amount of heat or cold? I mean in proportion to his size. Let any body who admires the beauty of the camel stand behind one and see him go down a hill; cast a look at his feet and legs; and ask himself, Is that beautiful? is that picturesque? is that graceful? and he will see how ridiculous the idea is, and what an awkward, ungainly, absurd animal the camel is. I hold that Tokina, the Prince of Asses, has more beauty in his person and more sense in that long head of his, than all the camels in Syria. I am perfectly satisfied with my experience in camels. Once, during a sojourn in Zanzibar, I mounted a camel, and was thrown over his head before I had traveled ten paces. On another occasion, as I was walking by the sea-shore one morning, three frisky old camels, by way of a frolic, ran after me. I was rather brisk at running—especially when three large animals with whose habits I was not familiar were after me—and I gave them a very fair race of it for as much as a mile, and probably might have made them run a mile or two more, had I not run into some quick-sand. The camels ran all round the quick-sand twice or three times, and then went away about their business, which was more than I did, for I was up to my arm-pits in the sand by that time; and I remained there perfectly satisfied that I was gaining on them up to that period, and that I would eventually have beaten them had I retained the free use of my legs. I was not satisfied, however, with the way I was going then, so I shouted to some Arabs who chanced to be near, and they pulled me out. Ever since that period I have been prejudiced against camels, nor has that prejudice been removed by my experience in Syria. I would recommend all camels in future to keep clear of any body that looks like a General in the Bobtail Militia.

CHAPTER XLVI.

JERUSALEM.

From a mountain-pass above the plain beyond Bireh, we rode out on a wide waste of whitish rocks, and beheld in the distance a walled city, dim in the shades of the coming night.

VIEW OF JERUSALEM FROM THE GROTTO OF JEREMIAH.

"How doth the city sit solitary, that was full of people! how is she become a widow! she that was great among nations, and princess among the provinces, how is she become tributary!

"She weepeth sore in the night and her tears are on her cheeks; among all her lovers she hath none to comfort her:

all her friends have dealt treacherously with her, they are become her enemies."

The resident population of Jerusalem is about seventeen thousand; consisting chiefly of Turks, Armenians, Arabs, Greeks, Italians, and Jews of all nations. It is estimated that the average number of pilgrims who visit the Holy City every year is about fifteen thousand. On particular occasions the influx of strangers is of course much greater. Sometimes, when the accommodations of the city are insufficient for so many pilgrims, encampments are formed outside the walls; and many find shelter in the Convents of Bethlehem and St. Saba. The uncertain tenure upon which each sect holds its right of worship in Jerusalem; the mingled severity and laxity of the Turkish laws; the fanatical zeal with which all the sects are inspired, and the bigoted hatred that exists between them, give rise to perpetual hostility of feeling, and often to sanguinary feuds. It is deplorable and melancholy to see how profaned are the precepts of Him who preached peace and good-will toward all men in this very spot; whose voice still lingers upon Zion and the Mount of Olives; to witness in their worst form envy, hatred, and malice practiced in His name, and the outward worship of God where sin and wickedness reign triumphant. Perhaps upon the whole face of the globe there could not be found a spot less holy than modern Jerusalem. All the fierce bad passions that drive men to crime are let loose here in the struggle for immortality; all the better traits of human nature are buried in fanaticism; all the teachings of wisdom and humanity are violated in a brutish battle for spiritual supremacy.

In the Holy Sepulchre the hatred between the sects is fierce and undying. The Greeks and Roman Catholics, the Copts, Armenians, and Maronites, have each a share in it, which they hold by sufferance of the Turkish Government; but this union of proprietorship, instead of producing a corresponding unity of feeling, occasions bitter and constant hostility. The Greeks and Romans, who are the two largest sects, and in some sort rivals, hate each other with a ferocity unparalleled in the annals of religious intolerance. The less influential sects hate the others because of their power and repeated aggressions; the so-called Frank Catholics hate the Copts and Armenians, whom they regard as mere interlopers, without any right to enjoy the Christian mode of worship; all hate each other for some real or imaginary cause, and each indulges in the self-glorification of believing itself to be the only sect that can find favor in the eyes of the Creator. Such is the bitterness of this sectional hostility that for many years past it has been impossible to keep the building in a state of repair. The roof is dilapidated, and the rain pours in through the windows; yet so it remains. The Latins will not permit the Greeks to undertake the necessary repairs, lest the mere act should give an implied ascendency of power the Greeks refuse to give the Latins permission for the same reason; the Copts and Armenians are too feeble to contend with the more powerful sects; and the more powerful sects refuse to grant them any liberty which they do not already hold in despite of them through the Turkish Government. During the ceremony of the Holy Fire, which takes place once a year, the scenes of ferocity and violence that occur are indescribable. Religious insanity, and all the horrors of bloodthirsty fanaticism, destroy many of the devotees. Crimes of the darkest character are committed with impunity. Half-naked men and frantic women struggle madly through the crowd with live coals of fire pressed to their breasts; bodies of the stabbed and maimed are dragged out dead; the chanting of priests, the howling of the burnt, the groaning of the crushed, fill the thick and suffocating air; and from the swaying mass arise dying shrieks of Immanuel! Immanuel! Glory to God! Sickened with the disgusting and humiliating spectacle, the beholder turns away with the startling words of Ferdinand upon his lips—

Hell is empty and all the devils are here.

We were not long installed in our quarters at Signor Stephano's hotel, when we were beset by dealers in all sorts of relics; crosses of pearl and olive-wood, fruit-beads from Mecca, ear-rings of asphaltum from the Dead Sea, polished flint and petrified olives from the Mount of Olives and the Garden of

Gethsemane, and small trinkets, manufactured of lead, from the Convent of St. Seba. These relics, which are purchased in great quantities by the pilgrims, form an important source of revenue to the convents of Jerusalem. A considerable portion of the population also obtain a living by making and vending them. The most skillful carvers of pearl are said to be the inhabitants of Bethlehem. Some very beautiful specimens are carried about by the Jewish peddlers who frequent the Frank quarters. The pearl is imported on the backs of camels from Cairo and the Isthmus of Suez. In general, the designs are taken from the pictures in the various convents, and, considering the rude instruments used in executing them, and the prevailing ignorance of the principles of art, they are wonderfully well done. I saw many that gave me a high opinion of the natural ingenuity of the Arabs. Olive-beads and the fruit-beads of Mecca and Bethlehem are hung up for sale in all the bazaars. A few piasters will purchase quite a collection Enough of walking-sticks, paper-cutters, and snuff-boxes, purporting to be cut from the ancient olive-trees in the Garden of Gethsemane, are sold annually to freight a ship. It is rare to find any thing in the way of a relic that can really be traced to the original olives; for, being only eight in number, walled round and well-guarded, no portion of them can be taken without permission from the guardians, who are careful not to destroy a very profitable source of income by destroying the trees. For a few piasters, however, a good deal can be done even in the Garden of Gethsemane; twigs and leaves and pieces of roots can be bought by a little persuasion, and a little more *backshish* to overcome any lingering scruples of conscience on the part of the custodians. Wicked as it was to do it, I thought so much of my friends at home, that I violated my own conscience and that of an old priest several times, in order to get a good supply of the sacred relics.

Near the Golden Gate, which faces the valley of Jehosaphat, stands the ruin of a Mohammedan sepulchre. I was greatly struck by the lonely and desolate aspect of the place; and made a sketch of the ruin, including a few of the surrounding objects.

MOHAMMEDAN SEPULCHRE.

In my rambles about Jerusalem, I passed on several occasions through the quarter of the Lepers. Apart from the interest attached to this unfortunate class of beings (arising from the frequent allusion made to them in the Scriptures), there is much in their appearance and mode of life to attract attention and enlist the sympathy of the stranger. Dirt and disease go revoltingly together here; gaunt famine stalks through the streets; a constant moan of suffering swells upon the dead air, and sin broods darkly over the ruin it has wrought in that gloomy and ill-fated spot. Wasted forms sit in the doorways; faces covered with white scales and sightless eyes are turned upward; skeleton arms, distorted and fœtid with the ravages of leprosy, are outstretched from the foul moving mass; and a low howl is heard, the howl of the stricken for alms; alms, O stranger, for the love of God! alms to feed the inexorable destroyer! alms to prolong this dreary and hopeless misery! Look upon it, stranger, you who walk forth in all your pride and strength and breathe the fresh air of heaven; you who have never known what it is to be shunned by your fellow-man as a thing unclean and accursed; you who deem yourself unblest with all the blessings that God has given you upon earth; look upon it and learn that there is a misery beyond all that you have conceived in your gloomiest hours—a misery that can still be endured; learn that even the Leper, with death gnawing at his vitals and unceasing tortures in his blood, cast out from the society of his fellow-man, forbidden to touch in friendship or affection the hand of the untainted, still struggles for life, and deems each hour precious that keeps him from the grave.

The quarter of the Lepers is a sad and impressive place. By the laws of the land, which have existed from scriptural times, they are isolated from all contact with their fellow-men; yet there seems to be no prohibition to their going out beyond the walls of Jerusalem, and begging by the roadside. Near the gate of Zion, on the way to Bethlehem, I saw many of them sitting on the rocks, their hideous faces uncovered, thrusting forth their scaly hands for alms. Their huts are rudely constructed of earth and stones, seldom with more than one apartment, and this so filthy and loathsome that it seemed unfit to be occupied by swine. Here they live, whole families together, without distinction of sex; and their dreadful malady is perpetuated from generation to generation, and the groans of the aged and the dying are mingled with the feeble wail of the young that are brought forth branded for a life of misery. Strange and mournful thoughts arise, in the contemplation of the sad condition and probable destiny of these ill-fated beings. Among so many, there must be some in whose breasts the power of true love is implanted; love for woman in its purest sense, for offspring, for all the endearments of domestic life which the untainted are capable of feeling; yet doomed never to exercise the affections without perpetuating the curse! some, too, in whom there are hidden powers of mind, unknown save to themselves; ambition that corrodes with unavailing aspirations; a thirst for action that burns within unceasingly, yet never can be assuaged; all the ruling passions that are implanted in man for great and noble purposes, never, never to give one moment's pleasure unmixed with the perpetual gloom of that curse which dwells in their blood

As I plodded my way for the last time through this den of sickening sights, a vision of human misery was impressed upon my mind that time can not efface. I passed when the rays of the sun were cold and the light was dim ; and there came out from the reeking hovels leprous men, gaunt with famine, and they bared their hideous bodies, and howled like beasts ; and women held out their loathsome and accursed babes, and tore away the rags that covered them, and pointing to the shapeless mass, shrieked for alms. All was disease and sin and sorrow wherever I went ; and as I passed on, unable to relieve a thousandth part of the misery, moans of despair and howling curses followed me, and the Lepers crawled back into their hovels to rot in their filth and die when God willed.

CHAPTER XLVII.

ARAB GUARD TO THE DEAD SEA.

A MESSENGER from the Sheik of Jericho called upon us this morning to let us know that the Arab guard was ready to conduct us to the Dead Sea and the Jordan. He assured us we would have no trouble with the Bedouins with such a guard; they were all terrible fellows, whom the Bedouins knew too well to attack; for, praised be Allah, they had killed some hundreds of the rascals already, and would kill some hundreds more before long. It was a great source of consolation to be protected in this efficient manner; for I must confess it was rather startling to hear the strange stories that were told of the way in which travelers were attacked and murdered, or carried off into the deserts and never heard of again. I expected to see twenty able-bodied men, well-drilled, and armed to the teeth, because it seemed as if it would require that number of men, and men of that kind, to slay so many Bedouins. They were down at Job's well, he said, waiting for us; and meantime he would receive the two hundred piasters for the Sheik, and forty piasters for the men. The latter sum was to be devoted to the purchase of a sheep, and the sheep was to be roasted on the banks of the Jordan, and the men were to eat it. This was my understanding of the case when I paid my share of the forty piasters; and I did it the more willingly because I was fond of sheep roasted in this way, and anticipated taking some part in the feast. But here let me record a notable fact: the sheep is a humbug. To the best of my belief, there never was such a sheep killed or roasted by the Arab guard. If such a sheep be in existence at all, it is just as likely to die a natural death as the Bedouins when shot at by these same Arabs.

Bidding good-by to our worthy comrade, the English Captain, who had made up his mind to return to Beirut, we passed out of Jerusalem by the Jaffa gate, and went down to Job's well. There was no guard there; not the sign of a guard; nothing but the well and two asses. So, having nothing better to do, we (my friend and myself, and not the asses) sat down on the top of the stone wall and amused ourselves throwing pebbles into the well. It appeared to be very deep—perhaps about a hundred feet. I had no doubt at all of its antiquity. It looked old enough; but whether Job had authorized the naming of this spot after him, or whether it was merely a freak of fancy on the part of the Latin monks, we could not tell. Historians differ so much touching the location of these wells and their right names, that I was always content to let them settle the knotty points, and thank God for the fresh water, when I found any. A queer, ruinous old place Job's well was, consisting of a very deep hole in the solid rock, with a pile of broken walls and a moss-covered dome over it, in the Judean style, built perhaps some few centuries ago; for I believe no historian pretends that any thing but the well itself can be traced to scriptural times. It lies in a blanched and arid valley of rocks, close down by the foot of Mount Zion.

PILGRIMS ON THE ROAD TO JERUSALEM.

All along the road coming from Mar Saba were long lines of pilgrims, mostly on foot, some mounted upon camels and donkeys, and all wending their way toward Jerusalem. They had been to the Greek convent, and were returning after the ceremonies. The priests wore long beards and flowing robes, and the common pilgrims were ragged and barefooted, and walked at a weary pace with their heads bowed down. I never saw any thing that so impressed me with the idea of earnest devotion. With scarce clothes enough to cover their nakedness, poor and friendless, many of these way-worn pilgrims had wandered from their far off-homes, over mountains and deserts, through scorching suns and dreary wastes, to lay their bones near the Sacred City.

While we were sitting upon the top of the ruin, there came out from among the rocks close by a ragged Arab, of most uncouth aspect, with a long gun hung over his shoulders and a rusty sword swinging by his side. An old pistol and a crooked knife were thrust in his sash, which was long and flashy, but defaced by the dirt of ages. All the colors of the rainbow were combined in his turban, his tawdry vestments, and scanty breeches, and his nose was hooked like an eagle's, and his eyes flashed and wandered like the eyes of some wild beast that had been caught not long before. I declare, within bounds, that he was the most ferocious, unshaved, unwashed, and dilapidated looking vagabond I had seen in all my travels, and it was not without suspicion that I watched him as he approached, and a lurking fear that there were more of the same kind not far off. Sure enough, out came another pretty soon, just as if the ground had opened and let him through from some infernal region below; and another soon after, rubbing his eyes; and then another waking himself up too, all armed like the first, with long guns mounted all over with brass, and rusty swords, and old pistols fastened in their sashes, and all looking so ragged and hungry, and so much like genuine robbers, that I involuntarily turned to see if Yusef had brought his fire-arms to bear upon them. My chief dependence was upon Yusef, for I never carried any weapon of defense except a penknife, and my companion was likewise unarmed. Besides, Yusef had a courageous and blood-thirsty disposition, as he repeatedly avowed, and delighted in nothing so much as in killing people, which I was not naturally fond of, apart from the risk of killing myself by carrying deadly weapons. I had always felt a presentiment that, if I carried a revolver or pistol of any kind in my pocket, it would go off and disable me for life; hence I never carried any thing more deadly than a penknife, and that I was resolved not to use in the way of violence unless driven to the last extremity.

Instead of rushing upon these fellows, however, brandishing his guns, pistols, and swords, as was his habit when nothing was in sight, Yusef greeted them with a kindly salaam, saying, "Good-morning, friends; how do you do?" to which they answered in the same friendly strain; and a great many compliments passed, as I supposed from the flowery style of the conversation that ensued. Yusef passed his chibouck around, and they all sat down and began to talk with great animation and a rapidity of utterance that would have astonished me had I not become rather used to it. Even as it was, I thought some of them would certainly choke in getting out so many raking gutturals at once. The talk did not seem at all likely to come to an end short of two or three hours. At last I made bold to come down from the top of the wall and ask what they wanted. "Nothing, O prince of Generals," said Yusef; "only to take you to the Dead Sea." "Do you mean to say, thou vilest of dragomans, that this is the Arab guard sent here by the Sheik of Jericho to protect us against the Bedouins?" "I do, O General! It is verily the Arab guard." "For which we paid two hundred piasters, and forty piasters for the roast sheep?" "Yea, the same; verily the same, on my sacred honor as a dragoman; only there will be another man before we reach Mar Saba."

I looked at their guns, which were pointed in various directions; said nothing, but secretly hoped the other man would not be a corpse. For you perceive the expected guard of twenty that were to insure our lives had been reduced to eleven imaginary men before we arrived at Job's well. It now consisted of four actual beggarly varlets. Each carried a long gun, as already stated, and each had a dangerous way of carrying it across his back, or over his shoulders, or under his arms; so that there were stocks and muzzles ranging all round. It was utterly impossible for one of these guns to go off without killing somebody. As we rode on down the valley the fifth man joined us; and when I saw that his gun was longer, if any thing, than the rest, and was carried so as to take a still wider range, I at once committed myself to Providence, under the conviction that if there was any shooting to be done it would not be the Bedouins that would suffer, but we who rode behind the guard; and especially I dreaded this result when I came to think that there might be powder in the pans and slugs in the barrels, and that the powder might take fire if the locks should once get to going. In faith, so impressed was I with this idea that I fully made up my mind to call these fellows aside the very first chance, and prevail upon them by a heavy *backshish* to discharge their guns at some rock or tree, and keep them unloaded until we were attacked by the Bedouins; and it was my settled determination, in the event of such an attack, to join the Bedouin party at once, and remain on that side till the conclusion of the fight.

THE ARAB GUARD.

CHAPTER XLVIII.

THE DEAD SEA AND THE JORDAN.

Our ride to Mar Saba, notwithstanding the guns of the Arab guard, was devoid of any incident worth relating. The distance in point of time is about three hours from Jerusalem. The road lies mostly between two ranges of craggy bluffs, almost destitute of vegetation, and entirely uninhabited. On the left we saw the caverns in which the monks lived, before the general massacre by the Turks, in which some thousands were brutally butchered. These caves are now only inhabited by goats. Some of the bones and skulls of the murdered monks are still scattered about the rocks. The Wady is of a very singular geological formation, and bears the appearance of having at some remote period formed the bed of a river. I am not aware of any theory having been formed on the subject, but it struck me as not improbable that this may have been the original outlet of the Jordan, after passing through the Dead Sea. That a stream of water so deep and rapid should continually pour into so small a sea, and lose itself in evaporation, does not seem reasonable. But the question remains, where it does it go now, or how can it fall into the Mediterranean, if the surface of the Dead Sea be, as scientific explorers have determined, considerably below the level of any other sea into which it could flow? According to the most authentic English measurement the depression is 1311 feet, 9 inches. Lieut. Lynch gives it at 1316 feet, 7 inches. The subject involves some curious questions, but is rather too profound for a casual traveler. Having seen it stated, however, that a recent corps of French engineers have decided the depression to be much less than either of these estimates (I have forgotten the exact measurement, but believe it is about ten or fifteen feet), may it not be that there is a mistake in the instruments? that by a little more measuring it may be discovered that the Dead Sea is rather higher, if any thing, than the Mediterranean?

If a difference of five, ten, twenty, or fifty feet can be made by half a dozen corps of learned explorers, the only question that remains is, how many will it take to bring it up to its proper level, so that the water may flow out naturally, without subjecting the unlearned traveler to perplexing and unprofitable conjectures.

Turning off a little from the highway, we took a walled road on the right, to Deir Mar Saba, and were soon in front of the convent gate. We had a letter of introduction from the patriarch of the Greek convent in Jerusalem to his brother of St. Saba, for which we paid about a dollar. This precaution of an introduction is deemed necessary in order to provide against any secret attack upon the monks. The gate is always kept closed, and a guard is stationed on the watch-tower who gives notice of the approach of strangers. Repeated depredations committed upon the monks by the Bedouins and others, and the isolated position of the convent, have given rise to these precautions. Our letter was pulled up in a little box to a high window, and read by the patriarch; after which we were let in through a small door, and led down a great many stone steps into the little building set apart for the accommodation of travelers.

We found our quarters very clean and comfortable; the fare good and the Greek patriarch very friendly and obliging. He showed us all the curiosities of the convent, including the room-full of skulls, the date-tree planted by St. Saba, the skull of St. Saba himself, the pictorial temple in which the works of that distinguished saint are duly represented on the walls, and numerous strange grottoes and chapels dug into the solid rocks. A very queer, picturesque old place is the Convent of St. Saba; and any traveler who has the time can not better employ it than by spending a few days there, rambling through its vaults and chapels, and studying the remarkable history of its founder, which is full of wild romance.

At an early hour in the morning, we mounted our horses, outside the gate, and set off with our Arab guard for the Dead Sea. The road is wild and desolate beyond conception Not a living thing was to be seen for miles on the wayside All around was blasted and sterile. A few sickly shrubs grew along the ravines, through which we passed on our journey. From the top of the highest mountain we beheld a glistening sheet of water, far down below, encircled by rocky heights. It was the *Bahr el Lut*—the Sea of Lot.

Winding out from a deep gorge, we came upon the plain. As we toiled slowly along the dried bed of a water-course, we saw behind the banks of earth some Arabs, armed with guns, but as we drew near they skulked away, and we saw them no more. Doubtless they were spies from Jericho, watching to see if we were accompanied by the usual guard. A jackall, started from his lair, fled up on a bare mound, where he sat licking his lips. Nothing more occurred till we arrived at the shores of the Dead Sea.

We dismounted and walked down upon the beach. A sultry mist hung over the mountains, and the air was still and heavy. There was a low sad moaning from the surf, as it rolled over upon the long slopes of mud with its thick and slimy foam; and when I dipped up a handful of it and swallowed it down, I was not surprised that there were no fish to be found there. It did seem even that a few strange birds that came wheeling down over it, turned away again out of the pestilent air. Dwarfish shrubs, gnarled and leafless, grew in the mud, back from the beach. Along toward the Jordan was a low morass, with dank weeds in it, and all around the weeds and rushes were stricken with the death-spirit, and drooped and withered, or lay rotting on the foul earth. Verily the ban of God is upon the land; "it mourneth and fadeth away."

We filled our tin cans with the bitter water; and, upon returning to the mound of earth upon which our horses stood, saw in the distance a large party of mounted horsemen. At first we thought they were Bedouins, and there was the most intense anxiety and consternation on all sides. Yusef turned ghastly pale, and said that the water made him sick; but no sooner did he catch sight of a horseman, who dashed out of the front ranks of the approaching party, than he set up a frightful yell of defiance, plunged spurs into his horse, and set out furiously to meet him, and settle the thing by single combat. Long before the rival warriors met, they commenced firing their pistols and guns in the air, and when they did at last come together, they grappled each other by the neck, and I thought it was the most dreadful scene I ever witnessed to see them thus twisted up in a struggle of life or death. But it was neither a struggle of life nor of death, as we soon discovered; it was only a struggle of love—pure devotion of heart between Yusef Badra and his friend Emanuel Balthos.

In a few moments the whole party came up, headed by the Catholic Bishop of Jerusalem, and a dozen priests. It was the party of Dr. Mendoza. Nothing could exceed the devotion of the Bishop, and all his followers, to the interests of Dr. Mendoza and the Madam. Being all of the same religion, there was a bond of sympathy between them from the first moment of their meeting in Jerusalem. They guided the Doctor and the Madam all about Jerusalem, showed them all the relics of antiquity, gave them the best rooms in the convent; never let them go out of sight a single moment; attended them even to the Dead Sea, all from motives of the purest regard, and without even a hint at money. What could the Doctor do in return but make a handsome present of a hundred pounds to the convent, and a little pocket-money to these strangers in a strange land?

We were all delighted at this meeting on the shores of the Dead Sea. No sooner had we met and shaken hands, than Doctor Mendoza expressed himself in the following manner:

"Bad countree dis. Convenience for sleep in Jericho not good. I have drink de water of de Dead Sea and no like. De Madam also drink: consequent he are indispose. We shall proceed to Jerusalem. 'Tis imposs to exiss in dis countree. I shall be content to depart for Beirut."

After much pleasant conversation in the same strain, we shooks hands again and parted; Doctor Mendoza and his devoted followers for St. Saba, and we for the Jordan and Jericho.

We rode along the beach for some miles, and then struck off into a morass, through which our horses plunged and staggered for some miles farther, till we reached a higher part of the plain and found a mule-path leading to the Jordan. Our Arab guard evinced the most intense anxiety as we drew near the boundary of the Bedouin country. As to Yusef, he never was more cool and collected in the absolute presence of the most dangerous foe. For more than an hour he scarcely uttered a word; but with looks of the most profound indifference, reined up his steed of the desert, and rode along in our very midst, as if he had no further thought of the Bedouins than to be the central point of attack when the fighting commenced.

In good time, we drew up our horses on the banks of the river. While our guard were busily engaged in disposing of their forces on the tops of the neighboring hills, so as to be as far away from the Bedouin country as possible in order that they might enjoy a more extended view of it, and cut off all stragglers that might come in their direction, we dismounted and indulged in various reflections concerning the Jordan. The conclusion that I came to was this: I was greatly astonished to find the river Jordan no bigger than what we call a creek in the back-woods of America; and resolved in all my future readings about rivers, lakes and seas in the old world, to look at them through an inverted imagination. I stood at the water's edge, and tossed a pebble across to the other side with all ease. It was not more than thirty yards wide at most; and although the current was swift, yet it was impossible to get quite rid of the idea that the Jordan, so famed throughout the whole civilized world, must be somewhere farther on, and this little stream only one of its tributaries. Why it was I thought so, it would be impossible to say; but I certainly must admit that I never was so disappointed in regard to the size of a river in my life.

The sheep for which we had paid the messenger of the Sheik of Jericho, forty piasters, was not roasted here by the Arab guard according to contract; but fortunately Yusef had provided himself with a cold leg of mutton for us in Jerusalem, which we devoured with amazing relish after our ride, and he also gave us some brown bread which he had thoughtfully smuggled into his bag at the Convent of St. Saba, and which we washed down with copious draughts of water out of the Jordan. While we were thus sitting on a conspicuous part of the bank, eating our lunch, I could not but think that we afforded an excellent mark for any prowling Bedouins that might be concealed in the bushes on the other side; and on that account, as well as because of my original disappointment, I sincerely wished that the river was as wide as the Ohio. Every time I looked over into the Bedouin country, I expected to see a dozen guns pointed at my head; and this notion became at length so unpleasant, that in order to divert my thoughts from so painful a view of the subject, I called to Yusef, who was standing behind a tree not far off, priming his pistols, to come and sit down opposite to me, and give me a detailed history of the affair with the six Bedouins, whom he had slain on his last journey through Syria. It struck me as a little singular that he did not exhibit his usual alacrity in obeying this summons, especially on a subject so congenial to his nature; I therefore repeated it with some warmth; upon which he reluctantly left his station, and seated himself close behind me, when he immediately began to give me a rapid account of this remarkable affair. Finding myself unable to hear him distinctly, with my back turned toward him, I requested him to sit opposite me, which he very reluctantly did. Indeed it was evident that something preyed upon his mind, for often as I had heard him repeat the story, I never before knew him to omit the part where he had pinned two of the Bedouins to a tree with a single thrust of his sword. On this occasion, his chief concern seemed to be to get through as soon as possible; and he frequently looked behind him to the other side of the river, as if he thought we might eventually be compelled to depart for Jericho without even a skirmish with the rascally inhabitants of the Bedouin country. I afterward found that I was quite right in my suspicion as to the cause of his anxiety; for he assured me, after we had mounted our horses and left the river some distance behind us, that such indeed was the case, and that he had a great mind to go back again and spend the night there watching for them.

Having finished my lunch about the same time that Yusef got through killing the six Bedouins, I took my tin can which I had purchased in Jerusalem, and accompanied by my friend the tall Southerner, who was quietly smoking his chibouck most of this time, went down to the river and filled it with water for the benefit of some acquaintances at home. Every drop of that water, I intended distributing with miserly discretion, and when I came to the last drop it was my design to fill the can again with fresh water out of the nearest pump, and still protest on my veracity, as a traveler, that it contained water which I had myself dipped up out of the **Jordan.**

CHAPTER XLIX.

THRILLING ALARM IN JERICHO.

A PLEASANT ride of three hours from the banks of the Jordan brought us to the reputed site of Jericho. Nothing remains of the ancient city, and I believe it is admitted by the best authorities on scriptural history, that there is no ground for the assumption that this was the location of Jericho. It is not even rendered probable by any reasonable conclusions from historical evidence. Without entering into that question, we had sufficient to do to credit our senses, when we were told that we were in the midst of the village, and that there was no other village than what we saw around us. A ruinous old Khan, eight or ten wigwams built of mud and bushes; half a dozen lazy Arabs lying about on piles of rubbish, smoking their pipes; a few cows, sheep and goats, browsing on the stunted bushes; some mangy-looking dogs, engaged in devouring the careass of a dead mule, and a few hungry crows waiting near by for a share in the feast, were all the signs of habitation and life that we could see about Jericho. The Khan stands at a distance of a few hundred yards from the huts or wigwams, and is said to be occupied at present by a Turkish guard of twenty-five soldiers, stationed there by the Pasha of Jerusalem, to protect the people of Jericho from the Bedouins. We saw nothing of the soldiers. Doubtless they were asleep, and the probability is that they had been asleep ever since their departure from Jerusalem. It appeared, from all we could learn, that in consequence of the depredations committed by the Bedouins upon travelers visiting the Dead Sea and Jordan, and also upon the Arabs, living in the villages on this side of the river, that the Turkish authorities of Jerusalem had agreed to furnish the Sheiks, numbering five, with this guard for their protection, and as an equivalent had caused them to enter into stipulations for the safe conduct of all travelers to those places, holding them responsible for any loss by robbery or plunder, and allowing them to exact a hundred piasters from each traveler in payment of their services. This tariff upon pilgrims affords the Sheiks and their dependents their principal means of support. The guards are not very expensive, in point of equipment, as may be seen from the specimens with which we were favored; nor does it appear that they exercise any very salutary effect upon the Bedouins, since there appear to be quite as many robberies committed now as there were before this arrangement. It is essential to have them, nevertheless, for depending as they do chiefly upon Frank pilgrims for their support, they contrive when cheated of their profits by a refusal to take advantage of their protection, to do the robbing themselves; and this being regarded by the Turkish authorities as a matter between themselves and the Franks, it is seldom noticed. Each of the five Sheiks, belonging to the different villages on the Jericho side, takes his turn in furnishing a guard, and receiving the emoluments, so that the profits are pretty equally distributed. In addition to the sum of a hundred piasters to the Sheik (about four dollars American money), there is, as before stated, the further sum of forty piasters to the men, for a sheep that is never either killed or roasted; which I shall always regard in the light of a gross imposition upon the credulity of strangers. Besides this, there is there an unlimited amount of *backshish* to be paid to the guard individually at the end of the journey, for taking good care of the Howadji. I paid the *backshish* without reluctance, because I felt extremely grateful in being permitted to reach Jericho without being shot through the head—not by the Bedouins but by the guard; and I could not but feel sensible of their kindness and discretion in keeping away on the distant hills when we were down by the Jordan, and thereby exposing us to but one danger at a time—that from the guns of the Bedouins on the other side of the river.

It was a mild pleasant evening as we reined up our horses before the palace of his highness the Sheik of Jericho. The sun was in the act of setting, and to do him justice he did it as well as ever I saw it done. The whole valley of the Jordan was steeped in a glowing atmosphere of purple; and the mountains beyond the Dead Sea were admirably finished off on top with cities of gold made out of naked rocks and sunshine; and the Bedouin country, take it altogether, to its most distant point of view looked very much like a land of wild, undefinable beauty, and glowing romance.

Regarding the palace of the Sheik of Jericho, of which I have made mention, it was a mud hut about thirty feet in length, ten feet high, and roofed with a combination of bushes, straw, manure, mud, gravel, and old rags. It had three walls altogether—the back wall and the two end walls. The whole of the front part was open, or rather would have been open, had not the Sheik with a degree of shrewdness and ingenuity very characteristic of the citizens of modern Jericho, placed some bushes in a pile there, with an inside partition of the same, and formed a sort of connection between them and the roof by another pile on top, so that in point of fact he had a front wall and porch at the same time, where he could sit in warm weather, and smoke the pipe of content. This was to be our lodging-place for the night; it was the best and only lodging-place we could find. The Sheik and his family lived in one corner of the bush part, which was the part of which he seemed to be most proud; and some cows, goats and chickens lived in the main or mud part. The only remaining part, being the other corner of the bush-work, which, in the absence of any tourists from foreign countries, was temporarily occupied by an ass, we had to wait awhile till the Sheik and the ass came to an understanding in regard to the right of possession. The Sheik in order to make room for us, was in favor of removing the ass to that part of the house which was occupied by the goats and chickens. The ass was in favor of staying where he was. The Sheik endeavored to remove him by force. The ass being the heavier body, stood his ground and wouldn't be removed by force. In vain the Sheik expostulated with him; the ass was not to be humbugged in that way; his head was too long for that; so he remained doggedly where he was, and seemed to have made up his mind so to remain as long as he chose. At this crisis, the conflict of opinion in regard to the right of possession, appearing to be direct and positive, and to admit of no compromise between the parties, the Sheik went up to a bag that hung upon a post, and took out some barley, which he held out in his hand as an additional argument. The ass looked at the barley, smelled it, found that it was good, concluded that the argument was based upon just principles, and quietly followed the Sheik into the goat and chicken department, where he was tied fast to a post, and severely flogged by that individual for refusing to be convinced at first. I considered that there was a moral in the incident, and noted it down for future study.

By the time we had scraped up the ass's bed, and made our own beds in place of it, Yusef had boiled some coffee, which was very refreshing to us after our day's journey. We had a good supper of stewed chicken in due time, which we shared with the Sheik; and about ten o'clock, being tired, we turned in to sleep. In order to give a proper understanding of the startling adventure that befell us during the night, it will be necessary to go back a little, and mention that not more than three or four nights previously a large party of armed Bedouins had made a descent upon the village, and in spite of the vigilance of the Turkish guard, who were sound asleep and not to be wakened by the cries of the villagers, had captured and driven off a number of cows and sheep, and threatened to kill every body in the village the next time they came down. A similar invasion, or perhaps a worse one, was nightly apprehended; so that the alarm was general, and all the live stock was driven into the houses for safe keeping. This the old Sheik communicated to Yusef with great coolness, considering the danger; but it was not so taken by Yusef. His eyes seemed as if they would start out of his head, when he was informed of this unpleasant state of things, and it was some time before he could calm himself sufficiently to give us any idea of the dangers that threatened us. I have no hesitation in confessing that it was not a piece of intelligence calculated to make me sleep soundly. Nothing but the implicit confidence I had in the courage of Yusef, could have induced me to risk my life in such a place a single hour longer; although it was now dark night. As soon, therefore, as he had interpreted for us the startling information which he had received from the Sheik, I came to the conclusion that our only hope of safety lay in Yusef. Calling him up close to where we were seated, I stated to him in substance that being unarmed, and in no way prepared to resist an attack from the Bedouins, I was willing, as doubtless also my friend the Southerner was, to yield to him the post of honor; which was directly across the entrance into our quarters.

"If it should unfortunately happen," said I, "that these Bedouins should make a descent upon us to-night, they will unquestionably come in through the first hole or doorway that they find open. Now as there is no door here to put in this gap, and no means by which we can secure ourselves for defense, the only possible chance of escape we have depends upon you. Arm yourself well, Yusef; load and prime your guns and pistols carefully; see that your sword and knives are properly disposed for action: spread your mattress directly across the gap in front of us, and keep watch as long as you can. Should you fall asleep, which is not likely under the circumstances, the Bedouins will no doubt wake you up, as soon as they step on you. While you are grappling with them, my friend and myself can tear away the bush-work behind us, and make our escape. Should you survive the conflict, you will overtake us in the morning on the road to Jerusalem; but should you fall, we will take care to mention all the facts to your family in Beirut; and hand them over any funds that may be due to you."

I can not say that Yusef took this proposition with the avidity which was to be expected from one who had been thirsting so long for the blood of a Bedouin. He looked confused and astonished at first; then turned very pale and trembled all over; and when I spoke of conveying the melancholy intelligence to his family regarding his fate, he was more affected than I had ever yet seen him. All this I attribute to that remarkable feature in human nature which causes us, after we have long cherished any fond anticipation, to feel something of a re-action when it is likely to be realized. Seeing clearly that this was what affected Yusef, I laid hold of his mattress myself, and fixed it across the gap in the bush-work, and told him not to despair; that there was every reason to believe that the Bedouins would be down upon us before morning. I then assisted him in fixing his weapons of defense; and all being arranged to my satisfaction, directed him to give the alarm the moment the attack was made.

Yusef, without saying a word, lay down, and was perfectly quiet for about ten minutes, as if in profound thought. At the expiration of that time, he suddenly began to snore, which aroused me from a doze into which I had fallen. I instantly thought of his singular dream in Baalbek concerning the lion; and on that account felt some doubt as to his being asleep. Not content with snoring, he began to mutter broken sentences, and what was a little singular, he muttered in English, which was not his habit generally when asleep. "Poh! Bedouins! I only wish they'd come! Cowardly rascals! I'd like to see them walk over me—I'd soon kill 'em—rip—shoot—" and so on, till I put out the light, fell asleep myself, and left him thus talking to himself in the dark. My friend, the tall Southerner, who took things easy, generally, had fallen asleep some time before, and thus we slept on, and might have slept soundly till morning but for what followed.

I fancy that it must have been about midnight that I was aroused from a pleasant dream of home, by something like cold flesh lightly moved over my face. In the panic of the moment, I grasped at the invisible object, and, to my intense horror, found that it was a human hand! Great heavens! it must be a Bedouin feeling for my neck! "A Bedouin! A Bedouin!" I shouted, holding on to the struggling hand with all my might. "Help, Yusef! help! I've got him! A Bedouin, by all that's horrible!" The tall Southerner sprang to my assistance in a moment. It was intensely dark;

by reason of which, not being able to see, he stumbled against the struggling man, whom he grappled by the throat, and we all three rolled over in a heap together. Finding it utterly impossible to distinguish friend from foe, I again called to Yusef for help. "Help, Yusef, help—we've got him! Strike a light quick, or he'll get away! A light! a light!"— It was all in vain; there was neither an answer nor a light, and the dreadful thought occurred to me that this Bedouin had stabbed Yusef, or cut his throat, and then crept over to serve my friend and myself in like manner. "Never mind," said the tall Southerner, coolly; "he's all safe. I have him by the throat. You grope about and find my knife, General; we'll fix him presently." I can not say that I approved of this proposition. It was not pleasant, the idea of groping about in the dark, after what had happened. I might find something more than a knife; perhaps I might find another Bedouin. The struggle that had just taken place, quite satisfied me that one Bedouin was as much as I could conveniently manage. "No," said I, "you keep him down while I strike a light. I have a match in my pocket, if I can only find it. Hold on to him, if you can." It was as much as the tall Southerner could do to retain his grasp of the man's throat, who, upon hearing the word "knife," struggled like a maniac; but my athletic friend was too strong for him. He held him down with the grip of a vice. While they were struggling, I got the match out of my pocket, and succeeded in lighting it; by which time the old Sheik and his wife, alarmed at the frightful noises that we made, were calling upon us in the most heart-rending tones to spare their lives The sight that met my eyes, upon holding up the match, was one that I shall never forget. Had I beheld a grizzly bear in the hands of my friend, or a rhinoceros, or even a seven-headed dragon, it might possibly have surprised me; but I was completely stunned and overwhelmed with astonishment at the actual spectacle. There, in the extreme corner, lying on his back, his eyes starting from their sockets by reason of being choked in the iron grasp of the tall Southerner, who held him down by the throat, was no other than our faithful dragoman and protector, Yusef Badra! It was clear enough, even at a glance, why he did not come to our assistance when called upon at the first alarm ; it was clear enough why a supposed Bedouin should understand English, and struggle like a maniac when he heard that his throat was going to be cut; it was all clear enough now, except the cause of this singular mistake which had well-nigh cost us the life and future services of Yusef Badra. I need not say with what astonishment the tall Southerner relaxed his grasp; how Yusef sat up with blood-shot and starting eyes, looking all around him, and gasping for breath; how we immediately lit the lamp, and pacified the old Sheik and his wife, who were perfectly frantic with fear ; in fine, how we called upon Yusef to tell us, in the name of the seven wonders, how he had fallen into this difficulty.

"Spirit of Eblis!" he gasped, panting for breath, "what a horrible—a—a—what a—a very dreadful night-mare I've had! By the beard of the Prophet!—I—I—thought I was ch—choking! It even seemed to me that I was al—almost st—strangled ; for I protest I c—c—couldn't get my breath! I do believe—I—I—would have d—d—died, if your Excellencies hadn't w—w—aked me up!"

In the course of a few minutes, when he had somewhat recovered, he gave us some further particulars in regard to his dream, which was certainly of a very extraordinary character. It appeared that as he lay upon his mattress thinking how he could best protect us from the Bedouins, the idea occurred to him that, being very cunning fellows, they would, in all probability, upon seeing a door-way open in the bush work, naturally suppose that he, Badra, the Destroyer of Robbers, was lying there waiting for them ; that they would, therefore, endeavor to effect their entrance through that part where the Howadji lay. In order to meet them upon their own ground, therefore, he had cautiously crept over into that corner, behind us, where he sat waiting for them ; that while he was thus watching over us, he fell into a doze, but imagined it was into the river Jordan; and feeling himself going down, he began to swim; that the moment he moved his

R

hand for that purpose, it was seized hold of by a large snapping-turtle, which held him fast, and was pulling him down under the water, when another turtle, still larger, seized him by the throat, and got on top of him, and doubtless would have strangled him had he not, as he supposed, awakened us by his groans. He felt very thankful to us for saving his life, and would take care in future not to eat so much supper, which he imagined was the cause of his sleeping so badly.

Having thus satisfied us as to the cause of the whole alarm, and proved that the result of the adventure was a subject of congratulation to both parties, we all lit our chiboucks, and enjoyed pleasant conversation on the subject of strange dreams, till day-light warned us that it was time to get breakfast and depart for Jerusalem.

CHAPTER L.

CHRISTMAS NIGHT IN BETHLEHEM.

ON our return to Jerusalem, we devoted the few days intervening before the 25th of December to a more thorough exploration of the neighborhood. So familiar now to every reader of Oriental travels are the Tombs of the Judges, the Mount of Olives, the Grotto of Jeremiah, the Mount of Zion, and all the places famed in sacred and classical history, that it would be a difficult task to add any thing new to what has been written on these subjects.

I had heard much in regard to the ruinous aspect of modern Jerusalem; and, strange as it may appear, was rather disappointed in not finding it so dilapidated a city as I had supposed it to be. Indeed, it seemed to me in quite as good condition as most of the cities which I had seen in Turkey and Syria. The first view on the approach by the Damascus road, is strangely beautiful and impressive.. The white mosques, and minarets, and rounded domes, and the fine old gateways, are strikingly Oriental. The houses and bazaars in the upper and middle parts of the town, toward the Jaffa gate, are as good as any in Beirut, and not at all like what one might expect in Jerusalem.

On Christmas afternoon, having made up our minds to spend the night in Bethlehem, we set out with a crowd of Frank pilgrims, and in due time arrived at the convent. This building is very large and of irregular form; and is said by the monks to be built over the Grotto of the Manger. The most reliable authorities deny that there is any reasonable ground for the assumption. We found the whole village of Bethlehem filled to overflowing with pilgrims from all countries; and it was not without difficulty that we obtained a room in the convent, which was already overflowing with visitors.

In that old convent I passed the most memorable Christmas of my life; and I sincerely hope it was the last of the kind that I am destined ever to spend. To give the remotest idea of the ceremonies would be utterly impossible; and if I thought that a single reasonable being in any civilized country, no matter of what persuasion, could look upon them with other feelings than those of disapproval and humiliation, I would not even acknowledge that I was there.

Long before midnight the crowd was dense and crushing. Hundreds of monks, bearing candles, were assembled around the main altar. There was a waxen image there; a strange disgusting thing, with staring eyes of glass, tawny skin, and wrinkled neck; its cheeks puffed out, and its mouth slightly open, as if it had been suffocated with thick incenses. A string of beads was coiled up on its breast. It was dressed in white, and glared strangely with silver spangles and tawdry lace.

They laid it on its back on the altar; and they talked to it, and chanted, and prostrated themselves in its presence; and the wild glare of many lamps glistened upon their pale greasy faces and shaven heads; and anon they turned to the pictures on the walls, of bleeding and mutilated saints, and bowed down again with closed eyes, and chanted their heathenish rites, and moaned for the wickedness of the unbelieving.

In jostling crowds they put aside the staring and affrighted Arabs, and went from alcove to alcove in a scorching halo of light; and hour after hour, as the incense and foul air rose thicker and thicker over the heads of the swaying mass, they fell prostrate before the ugly wax image, and chanted the glory of the new-born.

On the floor, surging around the many feet, was a sea of human heads, bald and blue with recent shaving, and the grizzled beards of the old were frothy as the foam wrought by a fierce tempest.

There was something intensely brutish and disgusting in the whole spectacle. I could not but think that it was rank blasphemy, this exhibition of pretended divinity in a miserable wax image; a thousand times more barbarous than the heathenish rites of savages. The great fat monks, in their coarse sackcloth, with their shaven heads and bare feet; the sweat standing in big drops on their faces; their eyes rolling wildly in their heads; their hoarse chants grating harshly upon the air; the lustful expression with which they turned from the altar, and on their bended knees gazed into the faces of the women, presented a scene too sadly impressive ever to be forgotten.

At the hour of twelve, they lifted with awful looks the tawdry babe from its resting-place on the altar, and held it up for the multitude to gaze upon; and then they bore it off in clouds of incense, through long winding passages, and descended into the cave, and laid it down upon a rock; and the wax candles cast a pale and ghastly light upon it, and as it lay there with its round glass eyes staring at them, they fell prostrate and worshiped it, and chanted, and moaned, and wept at the feet of the panting crowd. Again they rose, and with hot, blood-shot eyes, scowled malignantly upon the heretics that pressed down upon them to see the strange spectacle; and in the thickness of the foul atmosphere, and the gloom of the dark, reeking cavern, they looked slimy and monstrous, and I thought it was the most sickening exhibition of brutish superstition that the eye of man could behold.

Parched with thirst and dazzled with the unceasing glare of lights thrust in my eyes for hours before, humiliated by the degrading spectacle, and sick at heart, I struggled out from the crushing mass, and groped my way up the winding passages to our quarters in the convent. I lay down, my brain burning with visions of monstrous and unholy rites, and strove to sleep; but, hour after hour, I started up and wondered what strange, unearthly sounds fell upon my ears; what fearful spectres were painted upon the air; what weight of horror lay like a night-mare upon my breast. Can it be, I thought, that—

"———Some tormenting dream,
Affrights me with a hell of ugly devils?"

Or is it that men are driven mad by the terrors of death; that they thus draw darkness out of the future and swallow it into their souls? Is it that all this is done in the name of that merciful Redeemer, whose words fall like balm upon the heart?

And then, as the night waned, and the sounds fell fainter and fainter upon the air, a soothing calm stole over me, and closing my eyes, I wandered back in thought to a happy home across the waters, and saw around the peaceful fireside on a Christmas night, a circle of familiar faces, all gentle and smiling, all radiant with hope; and kindly greetings passed; and pleasant words were spoken, and the happy past was revived, and bright anticipations of the future beamed upon every face; and I inwardly thanked God that so much of good was yet left upon earth, so much of bright promise in the future; and in the soothing of those happy memories and the hopefulness of better things to come, I committed myself to the keeping of Him who showeth the path of life, in whose presence is fullness of joy, at whose right hand are pleasures for evermore.

CHAPTER LI.

CROSSING THE RIVERS.

THE heavy rains during our stay in Jerusalem had swollen the rivers, so that on our journey from Jaffa along the coast we were frequently stopped, and compelled to make a detour of several miles in order to find a crossing-place. Even then, owing to flats and marshes, we were subject to danger and inconvenience, and sometimes reduced to the necessity of dismounting, and hiring some of the neighboring Arabs who were acquainted with the fords to drive our horses before us and carry ourselves across on their backs. The mules usually contrived, about midway in these difficult passages, to get

fast in the mud, and upset themselves and the baggage; which always occasioned the most intense excitement among the Arabs. To give any idea of the shouting, and shrieking, and flourishing of sticks; the frantic lamentations on all sides; the thundering reproaches of Yusef; or the remonstrances of the Howadji against the damage of their precious curiosities, would be entirely out of the question. I shall content myself by leaving all that to the imagination of the reader, and presenting a sketch of what impressed me as the most picturesque feature in the scene.

The position is striking, and not altogether ungraceful. It has the advantage of making one pair of legs answer a double purpose—that of carrying the owner across the river, and at the same time the Howadji who is mounted upon the back of the owner; and it presents the Howadji in rather a more elevated point of view than if the legs of both parties were in the water; which, however, sometimes happens before they reach the opposite bank. Should the Arab who acts the part of carrier in these cases, accidentally step upon the point of a sharp stick, and suddenly let go his hold, the probability is, that the hold of the gentleman upon his back will reduce both parties to a level, but not to an equality; because the more elevated naturally falls underneath, and he not only suffers from the disaster, but is obliged in the end to pay *backshish* for a back that failed to carry him over, and no deduction made for getting his own back saturated with mud and water.

At one of these fords we met our old friend Maximilian, the celebrated Greek patriarch, who, in company with a highpriest of the same church, performed his pilgrimage to Jerusalem in a basket. Experience had taught him the danger of depending upon a mule when a river was to be crossed; for, on one occasion, the mule upon which the two baskets were hung—that of Maximilian on one side, and that of the high-priest on the other—took it into his head to lie down, which he did in spite of all the Arabs, and it was with difficulty that the venerable pilgrims were rescued from a watery grave. Hence, the wily old patriarch, being too infirm to stand much moving, hit upon the expedient of having himself carried across all future rivers in the following manner:

He caused a stout Arab to get under the basket when they arrived at a river; and at a given signal the ropes being unfastened from the mule, and placed in the hands of the carrier, so as to form a secure way of balancing the load, the basket and the patriarch were borne off at the same time.

and safely landed on the opposite side, unless in case of accident. If any accident occurred we heard nothing of it. My impression is that Maximilian reached Jerusalem in safety.

Any person unacquainted with these circumstances, would, perhaps, at the first glance, imagine that the sketch is designed to represent a peculiar race of men never before heard of; with long beards, basket bodies, and an unusual number of arms and legs, and the knees of the two principal legs turned backward, so that these singularly-constructed people may see what is going on behind them while they walk. There are many curious races of men in the world, according to the narratives of enterprising travelers; but I will not undertake to say that such a race as this is to be found in Palestine. Although fully impressed with that belief when I saw the Greek patriarch mounted in his basket, upon the back of an Arab, I now give this explanation to caution the general reader, as well as all physiologists and scientific men, to be careful how they fall into the same error.

R*

CHAPTER LII.

THE DESOLATE CITY.

This was a dreary day; from the rising of the sun nothing in sight but a waste of waters on the left, a desert plain on the right, and the blanched and rugged heights of Carmel dim in the distance. Our road lay along the coast of Phœnicia, over barren rocks and beds of sand, all parched and shadowless.

Evening came, and thick clouds covered the sky; the sun was hid in the gloom; there was neither heat nor cold, nor glare nor darkness; but a dim, death-like pall was outspread upon the earth. No bird of the air or beast of the field was in sight; no sound broke upon the stillness but the sad moaning of the surf; no sign of life, or hope, or promise was within the last sweep of desolation around.

We rode silently on our way; and about the seventh hour of our journey from El Mukhalid, we beheld afar upon the shore a ruined city. Fragments of walls and towers rent asunder, and masses of ramparts, shattered by earthquakes and the ravages of war, loomed darkly through the haze. The Arabs stopped, and, pointing to the ruins, said that there lay all that was left of *Cesarea*.

VILLAGE OF EL MUKHALID.

THE DESOLATE CITY.

We rode on, and drawing near saw that ghostly city was walled around with ramparts, and masses of ruin were scattered round about over the plain. A few sickly weeds grew among the banks of broken columns and shattered walls; but there was neither shrub nor leaflet nor green sod there; all was withered and lifeless.

I stopped awhile to sketch the ruins, while my comrades passed through and went their way toward Tantura. When I had finished, I entered through a crumbling archway, and wandered about, lost in wonder at the utter desolation of the place. Not a living soul was there; not a living thing that I could see; not a sigh, or whisper, or sound of life came from out of the ruins. The silence of death was every where; not even the low wail of the surf now reached me through the masses of shattered walls; and I thought how terrible was the wrath that had thus smitten the abodes of men with destruction; how "the Lord maketh the earth empty, and maketh it waste, and turneth it upside down, and scattereth abroad the inhabitants thereof."

There was nothing but ruin every where; high walls rent in gaping fissures; towers shivered asunder to their bases; great archways cast down in rugged masses; streets choked and filled with shattered columns or covered over with blasted earth, all waste and sodless. Not a bird of good or evil omen sat upon the fragments; not a beast haunted the ruins; it was all still, all silent and without life.

Ruined cities there are, scattered broadcast throughout this land of desolation; yet all that I had seen had some remnant of vitality within their walls. Dark and squalid men and masked women haunted them; dogs and wild beasts of prey and birds of evil omen fed upon the dead things that were cast out from the doors; but here there was nothing of the present; all was silent, all dead. No foul odors from dark and narrow streets; no bearded men with downcast faces, stalking sadly through the fallen city; no dark-eyed women to steal a flashing look at the stranger; no human voice to utter a word of welcome, or say, Depart in peace; no moody follower of the Prophet to scowl his hatred, or stalk unheeding by; all was of the past.

I sat upon a broken column, and looking with a saddened heart upon this scene of desolation, wondered what had become of all that had lived here; the good, the wicked—the brave, the beautiful, and the gay; how lived they; how died they; were all the records of their deeds for centuries past buried with them, and nothing left; was there happiness within these walls; did they feel as we who looked upon these ruins felt; did they look back over the past and forward to the future, and in their ambition encircle the wide world, and turn to dust at last to feed the worms of the earth and nourish the weeds; and was this mass of ruins all they had left to mark the spot?

There was not a breath to answer; not a leaf to whisper of the past; all gone, never to be seen upon earth again: not a soul but myself was there—a stranger from a distant land the only inhabitant now.

In the grave-yard there is only the gloom of death; silence is all we look for there; but here, in the abiding-place of men, where once there was the din of life, there was the silence of death and more than its gloom; for these walls were built for the living. I had wandered through ruins in another clime, where two thousand years ago a city was buried, and all were buried within it in the midst of life; yet I saw their homes unchanged; the frescoes upon the walls; the marks idly made by the soldiers; the bedrooms, the wine-cellars, the signs upon the doors, the tracks of the carriage-wheels in the streets, as they were buried two thousand years ago; so fresh, so life-like, that one would scarcely be startled to see the dead arise and resume their avocations. But here nothing but the bare and ruined walls was left to tell of the past; there was no connecting link to unite it with the present; nothing within the shattered gateways, or abroad over the desert around, but fragments of columns and massive stones—a waste of ruins; all dreary and voiceless—all wrapt in desolation.

The silence of a ship upon the sea at night, when all are buried in sleep, and the waters have ceased their dirge, is without gloom; for the stars in the heavens are worlds where thought may wander; where the soul may drink in the beau-

THE DESOLATE CITY.   397

tios of the firmament; and if the darkness be upon the deep, then its mysteries are eloquent; in its unfathomable caves lie wonders that can never cease to inspire glowing thoughts of the greatness of the Omnipotent.

Not such is the Desolate City; the city of the silent dead. Here is nothing to tell of them that dwelt there. The land is laid waste, and the earth mourneth and fadeth away. "The Lord hath done that which he had devised"; he hath fulfilled his word that he had commanded in the days of old : he hath thrown down and hath not pitied."

Such is Kaisariyeh—once a proud city of the Phœnicians; now all that remains of Cesarea Palestina.

KAISARIYEH.

CHAPTER LIII.

A SERIOUS CHARGE

At Tantura an incident occurred which any gentleman of respectable standing in society might well be excused for passing over in silence. I do not believe a similar case is to be found in all the records of Syrian travel, though, doubtless, many a traveler has had personal experience of the same kind. It was an unpleasant charge, to say the least of it; a provoking and unmerited charge; one that touches the very soul of an honorable man in the tenderest part. Fain would I proceed on the journey, and leave Tantura to future travelers; but a desire to maintain that spirit of candor and truthfulness by which it has been my constant endeavor to distinguish this narrative from all others, induces me to give a full exposition of the facts.

Tantura is a small village by the sea-side; the houses are also small and very dirty, like all the houses in Palestine. Such a thing as a hotel is not known in Tantura, or even a common tavern, or the remotest approach to any thing like it. There ought to be a Khan there; the traveling public require it, and would patronize such an establishment, but Tantura is Khanless; there is not even a can of milk to be had for love or money. The only place we could find to stop at was a small hut, situated in a pond of green and stagnant water. There was room for improvement all about the house, but not much room inside; at all events, not any to spare, considering that the occupants for the single apartment of which it consisted were already two mules, four goats, several dozen of chickens, and the owner and his wife. Add to this our party of Howadji, servants and muleteers, and there is little left to subtract except the vermin, which might be continually subtracted for many years, and yet leave a remainder. The old Arab, who claimed to be proprietor, was a cadaverous and unwholesome-looking person, broken down in spirits, and evidently laboring under a complication of domestic miseries. His wife was a leather-faced, sharp-featured, shrewish sort of body, who seemed to be continually spurring and goading the old man on to make himself useful, never ceasing for five minutes to keep him at work, and always extremely enraged when he sat down to smoke. I had strong reason for believing that she had bought him with money, and was taking the worth of it out in petty installments; or, it might be, that she really thought the affairs of the house required constant and laborious attention, or they might in the course of time become deranged.

After our evening repast was over, being rather tired, we spread our mattresses and lay down, as we supposed, for the night. But it was not for the night, nor for more than a very small part of it; because, as I said before, the house itself was unpromising, the landlord was unpromising, his wife was unpromising, and the whole establishment gave no promise whatever except that of vermin, which was faithfully fulfilled. We had a great abundance, and were not at all disappointed. I was so little disappointed myself that long after my companions fell asleep, which they did at last, I rolled about in extreme bodily anguish, wishing that some of the genii said to exist in those countries would transfer me to the meanest stable-loft at home. There was a dim wick burning in a small earthen lamp, in one corner of the house, by which I was enabled to look about and see if there was any possibility of bettering my condition. Rubbish and dirt abounded in every direction, so that it was some time before I could make out what there was in the opposite corner—rather a darkish sort of place, with some mud cupboards or shelves, not very clearly defined. The thought struck me that there might be some cavity or elevated hole there in which I could stow myself away above ground. It was a very happy thought, and a very bright thought under the circumstances, but not a lucky one, take it altogether. Wishing to disturb nobody, I crept cautiously over two or three snoring Arabs, and reached the corner without waking a living soul, so far as I knew. It was a capital place; indeed, I may say such a snug sort of spot for a quiet nap as would have enchanted any man of imagination. In the corner, and extending along the wall to the length of six or seven feet, was a kind of mud cupboard, with two or three large cavities or shelves in it, a good deal like the place for dead bodies in the catacombs of Rome. But it was not the holes that I was so pleased with; they were all filled with old earthen vessels, kettles, pans, and other loose rubbish; it was the space which I supposed to be on top that charmed me. The mud-work was very frail, and shook a good deal when I began to climb up, but by groping my way cautiously, and balancing the whole structure whenever it began to give way, I got on top at last, about ten feet from the ground, and was greatly rejoiced to find that it was a most admirable place for a night's rest. All it wanted was to be cleared up a little, the surface being covered with onions to the depth of two or three inches. I had thrown my coat up before me, which I often used as a pillow, and, having nowhere else to put the onions, began forthwith to gather them up in a pile at one end, and stow them under the coat, so as to make a comfortable resting-place for the head. This I was doing as quietly as possible, from a desire not to disturb my friends who were asleep down below. While I was raking up the last of the onions, and carefully balancing myself lest the cupboard should fall over and kill somebody, I distinctly heard a voice in the opposite corner of the house; a woman's voice, low but sharp enough to be the voice of the old man's wife, which it unquestionably was. Then there was a guttural response; then the woman's voice again, a little louder and a good deal sharper; another guttural response; a thumping sound, followed by a groan, and then out of the darkness crept the old man, looking up at me as he approached with an expression of countenance in which terror, anxiety, and astonishment predominated. He kept staring at me for some moments to my great surprise, mumbling over something to himself in

Arabic, of which I understood not a single word except Howadji. "Well," said I, leaning over the top of the cupboard, "what do you want with the Howadji, old gentleman? Can't you let me make a bed here?" To this he responded as before, only with more spirit, having apparently taken courage at the gentle manner in which I addressed him. Unable to understand him, I resumed the gathering up of the onions. The female voice in the corner again reached my ears, and the old Arab became quite violent. "My friend," said I, rather annoyed, "you are wasting breath. Really I can't understand a word you say. Ho, Yusef! wake up. Ask this old gentleman what he wants." Yusef woke up and rubbed his eyes. "What's the matter, O General? Where is your Excellency?" "Here," said I, "up here on top of the catacombs in the corner." "Bless my soul! And this old fool, what does he want?" "In faith, Yusef, I don't know. He's been growling at me like a bear for ten minutes." Yusef turned fiercely upon the old Arab, and addressed him in tones of thunder. What the answer was I don't know; it certainly was not of a satisfactory nature, for I never before saw Yusef so enraged and indignant. He drew his sword, and would doubtless have put the poor man to death on the spot had not the voice of the woman broken in at this juncture, which caused him to return it to the scabbard in some trepidation, and cover himself up as quickly as possible in his blanket; upon which the old Arab made the best of his way back to the dark corner where his wife was. Yusef now raised up his head again, looked cautiously around him, and indignantly uttered these words: "By Allah! this is too bad! O General! General, my blood boils; for heaven's sake, let me kill somebody; quick, let me kill somebody; I can't stand it, I must—" "Stop, Yusef! There must be no bloodshed here! What did the man say to you?" "Say? O wherefore do you ask me? How can I repeat it? I'm ashamed of my country. In six months, O General, you shall see Yusef Badra in America." "Nay, but I command you to tell me. Out with it, if you choke in the effort. What did he say?" "He said, O General! he said you were *stealing his onions!*

he declared by the holy beard of the Prophet that he saw you at it himself; that with his own eyes he beheld you gather them up and put them in a bag." "Good heavens, Yusef!" "Yea, he called upon his wife to save him from my just wrath; and what do you think she said, O General? Can you guess what she said?" "No, indeed, Yusef; I am perfectly confounded." "She said she missed some of them about a week ago, and had no doubt now that you were the same fellow that stole them, as nobody else knew where they were. Likewise she said, O General, that if I molested her husband she would proceed at once to tear the eyes out of my head, and then enter a complaint against me before the Turkish authorities at Acre, and, at the same time, have your excellency bastinadoed for theft."

It was enough; I got down from the top of the cupboard; mildly reproved my companions for making a laughing matter of so serious a charge; requested Yusef to light my chibouck and say no more; calmly seated myself on a spare mat. and gave free indulgence to melancholy reflection. Oh destiny! had it come to this?—to this at last! That I, who had spent four precious years of my life in the Treasury Department of the United States; whose chief study was the study of the banking system; whose most earnest hope was, never, by any visitation of Providence, to be Secretary of the Treasury, president of a bank, or signer of a circulating note; that I, whose only ambition was to be thought an honest man as well as to be one in reality; that I, who had chased the mighty leviathan of the deep, slept in the veritable castle of the renowned Crusoe, dug the glittering ore out of the gold mines of California, explored the remotest corners of the earth for the benefit of mankind, ; that I, who had smiled at the Queen of Greece, and frowned at Otho, King of Greece; who had entered upon the grandest Crusade against the Mists of Fancy that ever was conceived by the soul of Chivalry, should at last be accused of stealing onions! Enough! enough! I turned over, put my pipe away, and went fast asleep; for I was callous to fleas now; they might bite me by millions; rats and mice might gnaw at my vitals, but

A SERIOUS CHARGE. 403

I was totally resigned to all earthly afflictions that could be piled upon me; and the consequence was, I slept soundly till morning.

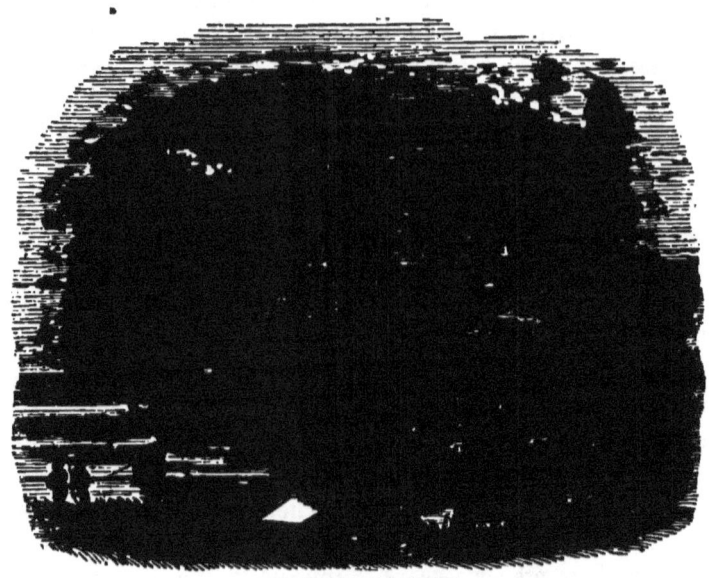

RUINS NEAR TANTURA.

CHAPTER LIV.

AN EXTRAORDINARY AFFAIR.

DOCTOR Mendoza and the Madam occupied the house next door. I was going to say they slept there; but they slept nowhere at all on the present occasion. They were wide awake all night; there was no sleep in Tantura for persons of fastidious taste on the subject of hotels: the contrast indeed was rather striking between the accommodations of Tantura and St. Petersburg. Perhaps there never was a more wretched house made by human hands than that occupied by Doctor Mendoza and the Madam—except ours, and I defy the whole world to produce such lodgings as we had.

In the morning at break of day, I went out to shake off some of the acquaintances of the night; the Doctor and the Madam were sitting upon a pile of baggage in front of their hotel, groaning in a most disconsolate manner. We were always strictly Parisian in our politeness—no matter under what circumstances we met—especially the Madam, who had been educated in the true French school. It would have done any man of feeling good to see her when she rose from the baggage and returned my salutation; it was the most striking exhibition of politeness under difficulties that I ever beheld. Her skin was perfectly green, spotted over with red bites; her nose swollen to an unusual size by repeated attacks made by noxious reptiles; her hair disheveled and uncombed, and her dress and general exterior, covered with dirty straw and mud. Yet she bowed as gracefully and smiled as pleasantly, as ever bowed and smiled a lady in the dress circles of a Parisian Opera-house. It was really charming to behold such unruffled politeness. " Oh, Monsieur Général! Monsieur Général! was all she could say—"Quel jolie ville, Tantura! Quel hôtel Parisien! Oh, Mon Dieu!" and throwing up her hands, she sank down again upon the baggage in the most graceful manner. I verily believe if it were the fate of the Madam to be seized by a Royal Bengal tiger she would melt him by her politeness, or die gracefully in his teeth.

Doctor Mendoza's skin was greener than ever; that is to say, the green predominated, but there were yellow spots, and red and black spots all over his face, which gave some variety of color to his features. There was but little variety in the expression, however, for it was that of unmitigated disgust for Tantura and its accommodations. The corners of his mouth almost tied themselves in a knot under his chin, and his under lip formed a perfect representation of a piece of beef-steak thoroughly saturated with water.

"Good-morning, Doctor," said I; "how did you pass the night?"

"No pass de night!" replied the Doctor gloomily, "'tis imposs to sleep. Very bad place dis. Hotel are not good in Tantura. Very bad hotel. De Madam is indispose. He shall have pleasure to arrive at Beirut. Very good hotel in Beirut. I no like dis country. Tis interess for the ruin, but I no like the ruin for sleep in, cos 'tis imposs to sleep. Very much pulee for bite. No get much to eat here; no much flesh on the Arab for manger. 'Tis necess for cat de traveler. I shall be tres contents to leave Tantura—'Tis imposs to remain here."

I really felt very sorry for the Doctor; he looked so green and dejected, so utterly incapable of enjoying misery, so wrapt up in that single idea of a comfortable hotel, that I declare upon my honor had it been in my power I would have built a hotel on the spot, and given him the very best room in it. There was no help for him, however; and expressing my sympathy for his unhappy condition, I returned into the hut to dispatch a hasty cup of coffee before starting upon our journey.

Yusef had prepared a good breakfast of stewed chicken and

rice; but having no appetite, I contented myself with the coffee and a small piece of bread; after which I called for a chibouck, and endeavored to soothe my nervous system by a comfortable smoke. The conversation turned incidentally upon the affair of the onions. I was averse to any allusion to so humiliating an episode in our tour, and made several attempts to change the subject. It was no easy matter, as may be supposed, to silence our dragoman when any thing unusual was weighing upon his mind; he had to give vent to his indignation in some way, and the most natural was by talking.

Although he spoke in English which it was not likely the old Arab woman understood, he had hitherto kept a guarded watch upon his tongue; but now finding she had disappeared, he broke forth in his usual strain of violence. He denounced the whole female sex as the root of all evil; he protested that he would sooner be tied to the tail of a wild horse than to any female that ever breathed; he swore that the insult offered by that old hag to his beloved friend and master, would rankle in his breast until he had slain every male member in the family. I was greatly moved at this avowal of sympathy and devotion, and did my best to soothe the excited feelings of Yusef, by telling him that the greatest of mankind were subject to the caprices of fate; that charges alike humiliating had been preferred against high officers of state and other great men, who required far more to be distinguished for integrity than myself; that in the present case this was an ignorant old woman, who was more to be pitied for her ignorance than blamed for the injustice she had done me; that it was very true many evils in this life could be traced to the gentler sex, yet we could not well do without this source of trouble, for were we alone in the world we would find ourselves much more miserable, and in all probability would pine away for want of something to make us only as unhappy as we were before, and in the end become totally extinct. To this Yusef replied that he felt the full force of my remarks, and would even go as far as to admit that perhaps this was one of the necessary evils of life; but what he most insisted upon was, that there was no other evil that did not spring from the female sex; in illustration of which he related the well-known case of the Persian Shah, who had repeatedly demonstrated the truth of the axiom. I had read about this case somewhere, and it was already known to me, but inasmuch as the reader may not be familiar with it, I may as well add that this renowned Shah was in the habit of asking, whenever any disaster occurred—Who was she? meaning thereby, who was the female that caused it. On one occasion a poor stone-mason fell from the top of a house and broke his leg. The Shah demanded the name of the woman. His attendants said it was not a woman, but a poor stone-mason. "Who was she?" repeated the Shah. "Go find out what woman caused this accident." The attendants did so; they inquired of the poor mason, and ascertained that while he was at work on the top of the house, he saw a beautiful woman in the street, and in leaning over to see her the better, he lost his balance and fell to the ground. Such was the cause of the accident; "And" said Yusef, alluding perhaps remotely to a certain feat of horsemanship, and a certain bad dream concerning a lion, in the earlier part of the journey, " such is the cause of all the disasters that have ever ——."

Here the conversation was cut short by the most dreadful series of noises that I had heard during the whole journey. My first impression was that we were besieged by a party of mounted Bedouins; for the yelling of horses and the shrieking and screaming of Arabs were perfectly deafening. I looked appealingly to Yusef.. He was our only hope of salvation in the terrible emergency of the moment. At first he turned pale, evidently with joy at the prospect of a fight; then hearing the noises more distinctly, he sprang to his feet, seized his sword and rushed out, foaming with rage. The tall Southerner and myself, loth to see him sacrificed in our defense, without striking a blow in our own behalf, followed him with what weapons we could snatch up in the hurry of the occasion. Upon reaching the open space in front of the hut, we beheld a sight that might well astonish and confound the most experienced of travelers.

Several of the horses belonging to Dr. Mendoza's party, and our own three, were twisted up in a convulsed group, in all the fury of mortal combat! Syed Sulemin was standing on his hind-legs in the very midst of the contending parties, striking out frantically with his fore-legs in every direction. The iron-gray, with his head outside of the circle, was kicking behind him to the extreme extent of his power; and Saladin—alas, that I should be called upon to narrate so disgraceful a proceeding on the part of a descendant of the renowned Ashrik! Saladin, regardless of that high fraternal spirit which should prevail even among horses against a common enemy, was biting Syed Sulemin! actually tearing and torturing with his teeth the very flesh out of the rear of a fellow-warrior! Well might the noble Sulemin keenly feel this unkindest cut of all—the common enemy bearing down upon him on the right and on the left and in front; and a sharp fire in the rear from one who should have given him all needful aid and comfort.

All the Arabs belonging to both parties were running around with cudgels in their hands beating the horses, and striving by that means, and by the most terrific shouts, to separate them. Emanuel Balthos, the dragoman of the Portuguese party, was also running about; but he was judiciously beating the Arabs for suffering the horses to fight, and not the horses for fighting. Yusef upon seeing that some of his own Arabs received the chief portion of the punishment, rushed into the battle and cudgeled the Arabs of Emanuel Balthos! Doctor Mendoza, apprehensive that the fight was becoming general, danced all about, tearing his hair, and calling upon Yusef and Emanuel and the Arabs and the horses—all to stop fighting for God's sake, or it would frighten the Madam out of "his wits." He shouted in Portuguese, in French, in Italian, in English; he protested that the "Madam was indispose;" that it was "necess to remain tranquil," but all in vain—there was no stopping the fight; and in the extremity of his despair, he wrung his hands, and groaned—"'Tis imposs! 'tis imposs!" The Madam shrieked wildly, in her anxiety for the safety of the Doctor; she shrieked alternately, "*Mon Dieu! Mon Dieu!*" and "*Docteur! Docteur!*" and strove several times to faint upon the pile of baggage, but was unable to do so on account of the interest she felt in the progress of the contest.

Eventually the whole affair was brought to a conclusion in a very singular manner. Tokina, the ass, having received a kick from one of the horses, doubtless, for casting ridicule upon the battle by incessantly braying, ran to the mules for satisfaction: they being tied fast to a shed, were rather more contracted in their sphere of action. The sudden and violent attack which he made upon this party, caused them to show their resentment with one accord; and so unanimous was the strain upon the shed, that it fell to the ground with a tremendous crash, filling the air with dust and fragments, and totally confounding every animal and every spectator on the entire premises. The strife was at an end. The horses were led away panting; the mules were unfastened from the wreck of matter; and Tokina, the peace-maker, ran off as fast as he could toward Acre, braying hysterically at the absurd issue to which he had brought the whole affair, and the contempt which he had thereby cast upon every body concerned in it except himself. I could not but feel vexed and mortified at this insulting conduct on the part of Tokina: and I really thought when I caught the last glimpse of his ears in the distance that he was as great an ass as anybody.

It is hardly necessary to add that upon a general review of the circumstances, it was ascertained that the whole difficulty orginated in a matter of jealousy between Syed Sulemin and my horse Saladin.

CHAPTER LV.

RISE, DECLINE, AND FALL OF YUSEF BADRA.

NATIONS have had their good and evil fortune, and, according to all the evidences of history, the vicissitudes of prosperity and adversity which have attended them, have invariably resulted from in their own good or evil conduct. So we find it even more immediately apparent in the case of individuals. The fate of my renowned dragoman, friend, and leader, Yusef Badra, furnishes, perhaps, one of the most striking illustrations on record.

I have endeavored to show in the course of this narrative that Yusef was, by nature and education, fierce and unrelenting in his prejudices; that the two ruling prejudices of his life were, an innate hostility to the female sex, and an insatiable thirst for the blood of his fellow-creatures; that to restrain him from the indulgence of these unfortunate propensities, was my constant endeavor throughout the entire journey. From the time of leaving Jerusalem, this task, partly of friendship and partly of self-preservation, became daily more arduous; and so much trouble did it occasion me, that I often felt disposed to abandon him to his fate. All the nieces, whom he failed to meet on the road after leaving Damascus, he met in Jerusalem. Despising the whole sex, as he did, he nevertheless felt it to be his duty to call upon his relations, for the sake of his deceased uncle, whose memory he considered himself bound to honor. Now, these nieces, as well as all that he had previously met in Baalbek and elsewhere, knowing his repugnance to the sex, always maliciously contrived to make him drunk with arrack, so as to humble him in the eyes of the world. It was entirely in vain that I represented to him the weakness of suffering himself to be caught by their snares; he declared that they were as cunning as so many devils, and that a man might as well undertake to live without eating or drinking, as to avoid the snares of woman; in short, as he had often said before, that the female sex was the root of all evil.

Scarcely a town on the coast, as we drew near Beirut, was free from these temptations. At Acre, we slept in a very fine house, owned by the husband of Yusef's most beautiful niece. This one he hated more than all the rest, because she was more malicious. She made him drunk so soon, that when he brought us in our supper, it was with difficulty he could stand upright; and all the English he remembered was the burden of a song which I had taught him on the road, in the hope of overcoming his absurd prejudice against womankind. Even that he was puzzled to get exactly right. At first he had it:

"Oh, believe me, if all those endearing young arms,
 Which are twined round me fondly to-day,
 Were to change by to-morrow, and lose all their charms—"

And then finding himself at a loss for what was to follow, he began again:

"Oh, endear me, if all those believing young arms
 Were to twine round me fondly to-day,
 I'd change by to-morrow, and fleet in those charms—"

But that was not right; he thought he must have been right at first:

"Oh, gaze on me fondly, if all those young charms,
 Which are twined round my arms to-day—"

And so on, till I was forced in self-defense to request silence, and sing the song myself, which so inspired Yusef that he danced all around the room; then made a fierce and sudden attack upon Francesco, the boy, whom he conquered in a moment; and finally declared he loved his glorious General, he loved the tall Southerner, and he loved Francesco, and he loved Syed Sulemin, and he loved Tokina the ass; nay, by heavens! he almost loved his niece! In this happy frame of mind, he retired to remote and unknown parts of the house.

and we saw nothing of him again till morning; when, as usual of late, he looked morose and gloomy, and beat all the muleteers. Truly, saith Socrates, doth intemperance rob us of our reason, that chief excellence of man, and drive us to commit the very greatest disorders.

Thus, it will be seen, commenced the decline of Yusef Badra. His rise took place on the journey to Jerusalem. At Baalbek, he rose rather high. At Damascus he rose higher. At Jerusalem he rose highest. Now commenced his decline. That very day, on the journey to Tyre, as we were going through a narrow pass, we met a caravan of camels. Yusef, incensed at the driver of the first camel for not getting out of the way, came very near slaying both the man and the camel on the spot; and would have done so, had not the man exhibited so much spirit and courage that it struck the warlike soul of Badra with admiration; he not only pardoned the offense, but cordially shook hands with the offender and passed on. I saw with pain and anxiety that Yusef was daily giving way more and more to his fierce passions; and that sooner or later, it must end in his utter ruin. On the occasion of this difficulty, therefore, I deemed it my duty to warn him of the results that would probably ensue from this unlimited sway of courage.

"What," said I, "would have been the consequence had that man been a coward? You would have slain him on the spot—run him through the body with your sword. I saw it in your eye, Yusef; don't deny it; I saw that you meant to do it."

"Do it?" cried Yusef, smiling proudly. "Fight a single man? a miserable camel-driver? No, sir; I merely intended to cut his head off with one blow, so that he never would find out till he sneezed that it was off at all; the camel I should simply have ripped open."

"That's precisely what I mean. The man was not a coward, and, therefore, you admired him, and felt that he was a congenial soul. You spared his life; you shook hands with him; you loved him as a brother. But had he been a coward, as I before said, what would have been the consequence?

A momentary pleasure to you, would have been death to him. For I certainly could not have arrested your arm, situated as we were in a narrow pass."

"It is even as your Excellency says," replied Yusef, with deep contrition; "such, indeed, was my intention. I freely confess it. But consider, beloved General, the circumstances, I may say the character and extent of the provocation. For nearly forty days have I restrained myself to gratify your Excellency. Never before have I performed the journey through Syria without killing at least six men. This time what have I killed? My sword and fire-arms are fairly rusty for want of use. Not a single life have I taken up to the present date."

"You are certainly mistaken in that, Yusef. I saw you cut the heads off of more than a hundred chickens before we reached Jerusalem, and I have your own word for it that you killed a gazelle on the plains of Esdraelon. Besides that, you struck terror into the soul of every suspicious vagabond on the road; and I'll venture to assert that many of them have since died from fright, which, the experience of medical men sufficiently demonstrates, has frequently produced that result. Now, I hold, that you might as well kill a man as frighten him to death."

"Your Excellency is right," cried Yusef; "I did do some trifling service in that way, merely to keep my hand in. I likewise killed a couple of men in Jerusalem, as a matter of amusement. I had forgotten the circumstance. However, I shall never be able to show my face in Beirut, or sleep soundly on my arrival there, without killing at least one more; and I ask it, as a special favor, that your Excellency will not deny me this pleasure."

"Most emphatically I forbid it, Yusef. Furthermore, I take this occasion to declare that if you attack or molest in any way a single unoffending person between this and Beirut, I shall put you in a book. Not one of your daring and intrepid acts has escaped my notice. These frightful exhibitions of chivalry—these perils that you are continually rushing upon, endangering not only your own life but the lives of the whole party, shall be fully described and held up to the traveling community, to warn them of the evil effects of misguided courage. Yusef Badra shall become a name not only feared throughout Syria, but a terror throughout the whole civilized world!"

This threat, which I made with all the force and emphasis necessary to give it full effect, did not allay in any degree the fiery zeal of my dragoman. Scarcely had I concluded, when he seized my hand in the most enthusiastic manner, and said—

"By all the compromises of Earth, O General, I would slay ten thousand men, and die ten thousand deaths to oblige your Excellency! If you deem me worthy of figuring in this important history of which you speak, I only ask that you will call me by my proper name, and give me no fictitious title."

"I'll do it, Yusef—I'll certainly do it; so I warn you; be on your guard."

With that, to my great surprise, he gave vent to his fearful war-cry, Badra! Badra for ever! and before I could utter a word, dashed off at full speed. It was in vain that I shouted to him to stop; there was no stopping him now; and as I rode along, restraining by every possible means the fiery spirit of Saladin, my mind was filled with the most gloomy forebodings I felt quite sure that something dreadful was going to happen Oh that insatiable thirst for fame! How it

"—— Heaps the plain with mountains of the dead,
Nor ends with life, but nods in sable plumes,
Adorns our hearse, and flatters on our tombs!"

As we drew near Beirut, we stopped at every house on the road-side to inquire if Yusef had passed. The muleteers had gone on; and the party now being reduced to the tall Southerner and myself, we were compelled to depend altogether upon signs for the information we sought—pronouncing in various different ways the name of our leader and the word dragoman, and then pointing up the road. The answers were invariably to the same effect, and being communicated in signs they were singularly dramatic. We judged, from the frantic manner in which these signs were made, that a furious horseman had passed, that he was armed with guns, pistols, and knives; that he flourished his sword at every body in the most terrific manner; that he smote the very air for breathing in his face, and vanished in a cloud of dust. The description was not to be mistaken. No other horseman than Yusef could be meant.

Within six miles of Beirut, we overtook a withered little man, hobbling along and talking strangely to himself: he stopped when he saw us, and running up began howling frantically at us in Arabic, and flourishing his hands in the air, and beating his sides by turns in the strangest manner, as if entirely bereft of his senses. Our first thought was that the poor fellow was drunk or crazy; our next that he was a beggar, and wanted alms. We threw him a few piastres, which set him to howling louder than ever, nor did he stop his violent gesticulations to pick them up, but ran after us as we rode on, working himself into a perfect phrensy. That he was an unfortunate lunatic we were now thoroughly convinced; he ran after us for as much as a mile, sometimes catching our horses by the tails and trying to stop them; and when he found that we still continued on, he at length flung himself prostrate on the ground, rolled over and over, and howled like a hyena. The whole thing was unaccountable and singular. Not the remotest idea of the cause occurred to either of us. Unable to do any thing for the poor fellow, we rode on as fast as we could to the nearest hut, which was in sight, and made signs to some Arabs there to go back and see what was the matter. To this the only reply we could get was a perfect torrent of Arabic, and the most threatening and indignant looks, mingled with the words—Beirut! Beirut!

I declare, for my own part, that I was completely struck aghast with mystery. Certainly it was the most singular occurrence that had happened during the entire journey. What could it mean? Was the man mad? Were all the Arabs near Beirut bereft of their senses? In truth, it seemed so; and entirely unable to come to any other understanding in regard to the matter we pushed on rapidly; and in about an hour more entered the suburbs of Beirut.

It was a delightful evening. The civilized appearance of the town, after all the ruinous places we had seen, the familiar masts of the shipping, the stir and activity every where, had an indescribably pleasant effect. It seemed quite like returning home, after a long absence. I thought, when we drew up in the neat front yard of Demetrie's Hotel, that it was the cleanest and most pleasant-looking place I had ever seen; that the Arabs lounging about were all dandies of the first rank in the world of fashion; that Demetrie was the finest-looking man, with his splendid mustache and Albanian costume, that could be found in the whole East; and, in short, that every thing and every body looked wonderfully new and civilized.

Yusef was not there. He had arrived; had embraced his friend Demetrie, who admitted that he was a little under the influence of arrack; and, as well as we could understand from the drift of Demetrie's hints, had gone off to see one of his nieces, to whom he had a letter from another niece in Jerusalem.

It was not until after breakfast the next morning, that we enjoyed the pleasure of seeing Yusef. He was standing out in the front yard, dressed in the most gorgeous of Oriental costumes. His turban was of the richest texture and most flashing colors; his vest actually glittered with gilded embroidery and silver buttons; his sash was of flaming vermilion; his sword and atagar of Damascus, dazzled the eye as they swung by his side in the morning sun-beams; his legs were swathed in crimson velvet; and his feet seemed to spurn the earth in the glory of yellow embroidered slippers, the richest productions of Aleppo. I declare, without exaggeration, when I saw him thus encircled by an admiring crowd, rolling out torrents of rich Arabic, as he gracefully waved his hands in the air, showing with what ease he had encountered the Bedouins from Damascus to the Dead Sea, I thought he was the most graceful, warlike, and distinguished-looking man the world had ever produced. When I approached and said: "Good-morning, Yusef; how do you do?" it was really flattering to my feelings, the mingled dignity and deference with which he bowed to me, and the Oriental richness of the figures of speech which he made use of in returning the compliments of the morning.

"Brightest ornament of the glorious land of Liberty," said he, "radiant and most effulgent miracle of Generals, most graceful, extraordinary, and accomplished horseman; thou who fearest neither man nor beast; thou who hast traversed the dangerous and devious windings of the desert mountains of Syria, like the flaming planet that was deemed worthy to be worshiped by the great Zoroaster;—behold! I, who have never bowed to Bedouin foe; I, who would scorn to bend the knee by compulsion before the grand Sovereign of all the Turkeys; I, Yusef Badra, kiss the hem of thy garment, and greet thee with the willing devotion of a heart steeped to the core in human blood!—a heart that seldom throbs save in a crimson sea of gore!"

In this strain he talked for some time, greatly to the admiration of all the surrounding Arabs; after which, we set out, under his guidance, to make some purchases in the bazaars. As we were strolling along leisurely through the streets of Beirut, I took advantage of the occasion to ask Yusef the reason of his mysterious disappearance on the road. He changed color a little at the abruptness of the question; but quickly answered that it was merely for the purpose of killing a man, of whom he had heard strange accounts in Sidon. This man, it appeared, was of gigantic stature, seven feet high at least, and large in proportion; every body on the road was afraid of him; he had even threatened, in case he ever met Yusef Badra, to clip the ears from the head of that individual; which, taken altogether, so aroused the soul of Badra, that he had determined upon putting this braggart to death. After his (Yusef's) conversation with his beloved General, being inspired thereby, and reminded of this giant, he set out full speed for the purpose of carrying his purpose into execution. He had not gone more than a few miles when he discovered the giant, concealed behind a rock, waiting for him. Maddened at the cowardice of this trick, he put spurs to Syed Sulemin, dashed straight up to the spot with drawn sword, and challenged the miserable wretch to stand forth and defend himself. The miserable wretch was even taller than he was represented to be—eight feet high at least. But, in despite of that, finding him unwilling to close in the fight, Yusef dismounted and beat him with the flat of his sword till the poor braggart cried out that he was killed, conquered, overwhelmed, and completely satisfied. "Doubtless he is dead by this time," added Yusef, with great coolness, "it is impossible that he could have long survived the fright and the beating together."

At this juncture, I was astonished to perceive that Yusef turned ghastly pale; his knees knocked together, and he was transfixed to the ground like one who unexpectedly discovers a spectre. Following the direction of his starting eyes, I beheld two Turkish soldiers within a few steps, walking straight up to him. "Excuse me, gentlemen," said Yusef, turning to us, with a ghastly smile, "I—I—have a l-l-little business to settle." At the same moment, the Turkish soldiers laid their hands upon his shoulders, uttered a few words in a low tone of voice, took him each by the arm, and walked off rapidly, leaving both my friend and myself perfectly amazed and confounded.

Alas! need I tell it? this was the fall of Yusef Badra! In two hours the whole town of Beirut was in commotion. It was cried aloud in Greek, in Arabic, in Italian, in French, in English—Have you heard the news? Yusef Badra's in jail! Badra's in jail! Badra! Badra! God help poor Badra! Sad is the fate of Badra! Poor Badra! Unhappy Badra!

We returned toward Demetrie's. The pathway was lined with Arabs, friends, and fellow citizens of the fallen Badra. They cried aloud to us, as we passed, Howadji! Howadji! Badra! Badra!

We entered the yard in front of Demetrie's. It was filled with muleteers who had served under Badra; among whom we recognized our own Mustapha. They cried out to us, O Howadji! Howadji! Badra! Badra!—Mustapha caught us frantically by the coat-tails, and wept aloud, while he pointed toward the jail, and cried, Badra! Badra!

We met Demetrie in the saloon. His fine face was clouded with trouble. "Have you heard the news?" said he, "Ba dra's in jail! Yusef Badra's in jail. O, Howadji! can't you get him out! He's a good fellow! He drinks; but he's a good fellow! O Howadji! Howadji! Badra! Badra!"

We went straightway down to the office of the American consul. At the door we met Eleas, the servant of the English captain, who was weeping bitterly. "Badra's in jail," he cried, "poor Yusef Badra! They put him in jail for nothing at all—they'll punish him for nothing at all—only beating a miserable Turk on the road! O, Howadji! Howadji! save him! Save poor Yusef, your friend and dragoman!"

It was even as Eleas told us. The withered little man, whom we had met on the road, was the victim of Yusef's misguided courage; and had laid his complaint before the Turkish authorities that morning. Yusef was accordingly seized, as already stated, and put in jail.

The American consul, in compliance with our request, sent for Yusef; who was accompanied to the office by a guard of Turkish soldiers. There was much talk on all sides; but the authorities were immovable. Nothing could be done. The case was an aggravated one, and must go before the Sultan. It was for the Grand Seignor to decide what was to be done with a man so inspired with courage that he could not pass a decrepit old Turk on the road without attempting to kill him. The consul did all in his power; we said and did all we could; the friends of Yusef wept all they could. It was to no purpose; the laws of the land must take their course. Poor Yusef! No more was he Yusef the Brave! Yusef the Destroyer of Robbers! Throughout Beirut he was now, "Poor Yusef!"—nothing but "Poor Yusef!"

We went to his prison. There he sat behind the bars, surrounded by thieves and vagrants, and stared at by the idle rabble outside, crushed down in body and soul. The big tears rolled down his cheeks. When he saw us he covered his face and groaned: "My niece did it, gentlemen; she made me drunk. All my misfortunes have come from devils in the form of angels. Take warning, O Howadji, and never put faith in woman!" We told him how sorry we were that we could do nothing for him; that he was a very pitiable object to be sure, but he could only blame himself for it; that it would be greatly to his advantage in the end, perhaps, to spend some time in prison, inasmuch as it would enable him to refrain from visiting his nieces, and save him from the mortification of being made drunk on arrack; that confinement has its pleasures as well as its pains; and should he be kept in jail six months it would doubtless be a continual source of satisfaction to him to reflect upon the blood of the six Bedouins he had slain, and anticipate the pleasure of killing six more as soon as he was set at liberty; in short, that although he would present a most pitiful and heart-rending sight behind the bars, to all his pretty nieces who might chance to pass that way, and was a fit subject of commiseration for all the muleteers whom he had beaten on the road, yet that, considering the thing in its proper light, there was every reason to congratulate himself, inasmuch as he would be comfortably provided for in the way of bread and water, and not suffered to spend his money extravagantly, for it would all be taken care of, and properly appropriated to the use of the Turkish authorities, and that of the old man whom he had beaten on the road.

Having thus afforded all the consolation in our power to the unfortunate Yusef, we bade him a kindly farewell, never more, perhaps, to see his familiar face again. The steamer for Alexandria, was already getting up steam.

We returned to Demetrie's, with a crowd of Arabs after us, who still cried out to us, as if they thought the Howadji all-powerful, "O save poor Yusef Badra! O Howadji! Howadji! take pity upon poor Yusef Badra! the friend of our heart! the joy and pride of Beirut!"

As we sat down to our last dinner at the hotel, Doctor Mendoza and the Madam entered. They had arrived the day before us. They were delighted at the happy termination of the voyage through Syria; Doctor Mendoza said that the Madam was a little indispose, in consequence of the horse-fight at Tantura, which had disordered his (the Madam's) nerves; but he would be well directly.

Doctor Mendoza had, with his customary kindness of heart, evinced the most profound concern for the fate of our drago-man from the moment he had heard of his arrest by the Turkish soldiers. He went to the Portuguese consul's that afternoon, before the steamer sailed, and stated the whole case in the hope of obtaining Yusef's release. On his return he popped his head in at the door of our room, where we sat smoking our chiboucks, and lamenting the unhappy fate of the Destroyer of Robbers. With a clouded brow and desponding voice, he told us of the interview:

"I have speak my consul for your dragoman. No-ting can be done. She are necess to remain in jail, because she can not get out. No more she shall voyage at present. 'Tis imposs.. It will be necess for her to remain tranquil. Very bad hotel in jail, because it are without the convenience for eat and sleep. Consequent she shall die. Dis is all. No more at present she shall get out. I am very sorry, but— 'tis imposs!"

THE END OF YUSEF.

www.ingramcontent.com/pod-product-compliance
Lightning Source LLC
Chambersburg PA
CBHW030550300426
44111CB00009B/930